COUNTRY/CITY: A YEAR AT THE RIVER

ALSO BY BOB ARNOLD:

STEELHEAD WATER (1993)

STEELHEAD AND THE FLOATING LINE (1995)

BOB ARNOLD

Country/City:
A Year At The River

KINGFISHER PRESS 1998

©1998 by Bob Arnold. All rights reserved. No part of this book may be reproduced without consent of the author and publisher, except for brief excerpts in critical reviews or articles. No electronic reproduction without permission.

Published by Kingfisher Press, 8208 317th Place Northwest, Stanwood, Washington 98292, phone (360) 629-9074. E-mail rcarnold@greatnorthern.net.

Printed by Gorham Printing, 334 Harris Road, Rochester, Washington 98579

ISBN: Hard Cover Limited Edition 0-9663489-0-7
      Paperback Edition   0-9663489-1-5
Library of Congress Catalog Card Number: 98-65542

Printed and bound in the United States of America.

First Edition
A

Preface

Trivia may well mark the outer edge of the recognizable world. You have to experience it to believe it. Then you've deep plunged into inner space, and become lost in a void of your own creation. Is this all there is, you ask—as many have asked before you? You decide to try to force some sort of form on the chaos of daily life. You start writing it all down, what happened to you, selecting out of the fracas, the fray, the most discernible parts. You begin to believe the effort is worthwhile and the trip may lead in some meaningful direction.

I was in an enviable situation. I'd left my job as editor in engineering at the University of Washington, and taken on a series of free-lance assignments that paid, well, poorly is the kindest word for it. My wife and I had enough money on hand to last for a year. My writer's soul yearned for a big project. I was tired of piddling little articles for magazines nobody read. What I faced was the opposite of writer's block. And I had the requisite amount of time, which I determined was to be one year.

The idea of a journal about the events that daily happen to a man who loves a river appealed to me; could something of value be knit out of such mundane yarn? Could it be kept interesting? The act of writing itself is drab and dull. When a writer has his "At Work" sign up, he is no longer living life but reflecting on it. Instead of gathering new experiences, he is trying to pin down old ones. Meanwhile, life churns on; it may be passing him by, he thinks, for the writer lives but on the edge of the active world. He believes he is missing all the fun.

I decided to try something different. My new book would involve traveling back and forth to the river that I loved; this journey happened every few days. It was the end of June, and I was laid up with a knee injury, which put me deep in a lounge chair for most of the day, my right leg elevated like some old duffer with the gout. Forced inactivity made me irascible. I wanted to be out in the world. Most of all, I wanted to be wading my favorite river, the North Fork of the Stillaguamish River in Washington State. In summer it is flyfishing only. This is my great love.

But I had hurt myself in the aftermath of a couple of days crisscrossing the river in search of fish, then leaping out of my car to buy a loaf of bread for dinner. (See section 28 for the awful details.) This put me at home, idle, for a couple of weeks. Surgery was decided against. My doctor sent me to the Group Health Physical Therapy Department, where I was started on some gentle leg lifts. For these I used a pillowcase full of sand and balanced it precariously on my bad ankle.

The idea was to increase the weight in the bag, week by week. I started out with two pounds and advanced to about ten. And while I doubted that it would get better this way, it slowly did. Or else I just healed, which would have happened without the leg lifts. My knee remained badly swollen and handicapped my movements throughout the following year. From time to time I tried running. The swelling came and went most mysteriously, perhaps driven by the same forces that move the tides. I don't think the running or the fishing harmed it.

When you are injured, the rest of your body remains just fine, thank you. It comes as a great surprise. As a boy I had been rarely injured. It is different from being sick. You have no fever, don't feel queasy, and your appetite remains good. Your injured part doesn't hurt much unless you twist it or in some other way abuse it. Anyway, this is how it is at first.

So you read and wait for your body to heal. It takes longer than you expect. Even for somebody who loves to read, there are daily limits. Reading too long burns out your eye sockets and leaves you rubbing at the holes in your head. Tired eyes lead to an afternoon doze. A doze keeps you from sleeping well at night. The process is circular. You lie awake for hours, then plunge into a zombie-like trance near dawn. Awaking from it is like coming out of ether. In short, my knee injury was messing up my head.

In writing lay my salvation. For one thing nobody falls asleep while writing—at least nobody that I've ever heard of. Writing keeps you alert and active. You are never more alive. I told myself I would make daily entries, no matter how busy or distracted I was. Of course I didn't do this. I'd miss a day and vow to catch up on it later. I always did.

Yet most days I wrote something. Occasionally I wrote at length. That felt good, in spite of my vow to write short. Some things require greater length in order to be said, or said correctly. Most of my entries were short. But they began to pile up. Eventually I had a longhand manuscript of more than 700 pages.

Time is a tunnel and looking back too hard, too long, gives a man tunnel vision, which is not good. He begins to miss what is going on around him. I didn't want this to happen and it didn't. So this is a book very much about the present—though that present is now long past. The book starts with my catching a hatchery-reared steelhead and killing it for a family barbecue on the Fourth of July. This is a normal event. It could have happened any year, and usually does. My knee had improved in a month's time enough so I could stand in the shallows and cast out to the middle of an easy pool. I had a place I could retreat to when the weather got bad or when the knee began to bother me again, for we had bought a riverfront lot a few years back and installed a sixteen-foot travel trailer on it. Soon we added the lot to the East to our property. Now we had 150-feet along a wild section of canyon.

How lucky I was to have it and how much I appreciated it. I've written about this in my book, **Steelhead Water**, so I won't repeat it here, but a man's enjoyment of a river greatly exceeds his fishing of it. He learns to love the land, the river valley, and the moving water as a special entity. It keeps drawing him back. During that year, and the ones to follow, I visited the river every chance I got. I shuttled back and forth between the country and my city, Seattle, much like a metronome.

At the time the journal begins, I had no water or electricity. This was the year I acquired both. It involved a lot of hard, physical work, plus some political maneuvering. It was fun as well, and in no way interfered with my perception of what was going on around me. In fact it probably enhanced my vision of the natural world.

I discovered that I needed both places in my life, country and city. (The use of a diagonal slash brings the two even closer together than the word "and" does.) But the river and the land adjacent is more important in my life. The river weaves in and out of it, always a little different, sometimes greatly different. Occasionally the river floods. The sight is horrible, as the river leaves its banks and consumes the countryside. This particular year the river experienced a prolonged drought. A drought is more awful than a flood, for a river can recover quickly from a flood; a drought's effects may last for years. Fish and wildlife die. Two drought years in a row is pretty bad. Three is deadly. This was the second.

As I wrote, I tried to make sense out of what was going on around me—that seemingly endless parade of days and events that will end soon. I was determined to follow wherever they led and write down what happened. Each year is typical, while at the same time different in its amassed particulars. Looking back on this one, it seems extraordinary. But I have a hunch that every year, so examined, will prove to be exceptional in several ways.

Therein lies the mystery and the joy.

This book is for my wife, Norma, who has always been there for me, for more than forty years.

Special thanks to my editor, Tracy Mediema and my friend, Loren Smith, illustrator of this and my previous two books.

COUNTRY/CITY:
A Year At The River

1

In the city, the Japanese maple in our backyard is at it prettiest, its shapely leaves a balanced mixture of bright green and scarlet. Where the two colors come together is most striking. Nearby, our fish pool reveals a pair of huge white water lilies. If you bend low over the water to smell them, (better grab your glasses), they'll overwhelm you with their fragrance. The smell is sweet and mild, but hardly worth the risk of dropping your glasses into stagnant water for.

It is warm, but not hot, with no measurable rain in weeks. Wednesday's high of 88 degrees F. ended with wind and clouds scudding in from the West, as the temperature dropped into the mid-60s. Slowly it returned to the low 70s, where it's holding. I'm glad, for hot weather wipes me out. In many parts of the country, the 80s would be considered idyllic.

2

The drive to the river takes about an hour and a quarter from my home in Northeast Seattle. Oh, I can pare five or eight minutes off of that if I encounter advantageous conditions. These consist of dry pavement and light traffic; more often it is the opposite.

The drive used to take twice as long, when I was a boy. The route was up Highway 99, a slow commercial avenue peppered with traffic lights. Then it was through the South end of Everett, a small city, across the Snohomish river and a couple of sloughs, into Marysville, along a winding road named Smokey Point into Arlington, a town of a couple of thousand. The twelve-mile drive on to Oso was pretty, twisting, and bucolic. Also it was slow.

No more. The trip is along the federal highway, I-5. It is posted at sixty-five miles an hour, in some places seventy. So it is fast, though usually congested, the traffic heavy until Everett, then gradually thinning out. I leave the interstate at what is sweetly called the Island Crossing; it is a bunch of gasoline stations staring contemptuously at one another, along with three or four restaurants, only one of them good.

The road to Oso and beyond is State Highway 530. Follow it long enough, far enough, and it will lead you across the North Cascades Pass into the Okanogan. The road has been straightened out some, over the years, and no longer jogs sharply at each property-line boundary. It is posted fifty-five, but most people drive it ten miles faster. Even more, when the country folks are drunk.

Then often there is havoc to pay, with a crumpled metal corpse lying on its back in the roadside ditch, its belly exposed, its wheels grabbing air. The drive to the river is through dairy country, with placid cows staring dumbly off on both sides of the road, along with Black Angus beef herds, a llama or two, and some penned-up ostriches looking sad and out of place.

I used to stop at the hamlet of Oso, where I rented a cabin for thirty years, but now continue on another three miles, leaving the state highway at its junction with the county's Whitman Road. (Named after some long-gone farmer, and not Walt.) It is a deadend. A mile down the road is a cluster of mailboxes to the right. One has my name on it. A private road drops down the hill off and winds a short distance to parallel the river. Mine is the place right at the bottom, where the road forks.

You'll be welcome, but please phone first. The number is unlisted. Oh, there is a phone? Yes, but it's been disconnected. So please excuse me.

3

This year I discovered salmonberries. They're new only to me. My wife, Norma, and my son, Garth, gorge on them every spring. The berries come in two colors, burgundy and orange. The flavors differ slightly. The burgundy ones make me think of raspberries and half-rotten strawberries. I preferred these, but my wife said the orange ones are best. I finally tried one, and she's right. They are sweeter and more flavorful. I'm sure they've fallen in the river and, because of their brilliant color, steelhead mistake them for spawn and eat them.

The locals prefer the Himalayan blackberries, which grow wild and are worse than a weed. Quickly, they spread their sharp tendrils and form an impenetrable brier hedge. Their fruit comes on much later. They are tart, watery, and make you appreciate the salmonberries, which are then long gone. You have to be careful and not eat too many at once or you'll get the trots.

Many of our berries are wasted and fall to the ground, where they become part of the rich mulch. And birds eat them, dropping the seeds. By July there are a few sad specimens drooping on the bough in the shade where they are protected from the sun. They are sour. To ripen sweetly, flavorfully, they have to have direct sunlight. And rain turns them to mush.

On our property, canes rise to ten feet. I threaten to cut them back because of all the space they take up, but I usually don't get around to it. It's Norma who goes after them, with a vengeance and an ax. My job is to get rid of the woody corpses she leaves in heaps on the ground. I use a machete and, sometimes, an ax. Soon I have blisters. The wood is spongy, resilient, with an orange pulpy center. Roots growing in soft soil can be pulled up, but with great effort. If you don't get them all, they'll be back next year, thicker than ever, to haunt you. If you bend the stalks to the ground, they won't break off; they'll shatter, forming pongee sticks. Watch out where you walk, soldier.

But I'm sure I left enough for next year's crop.

4

Lately I've been reading nature books. Like peanuts, one leads to another, and soon I'm devouring more than is good for me. Presently I'm working my way through Edwin Way Teale; I learned about him from reading Annie Dillard. She values him highly, and I can understand why. I see his strong influence on her wonderful *Pilgrim At Tinker Creek*. He is a close observer, with a pleasing style. He cares a lot about the natural world and preserving it. His heart and his mind are in all the right places.

5

Because I caught a fish on Thursday—a bright nine-pound hatchery steelhead from the Monte Hole—we are going to have a family cookout on the second of July. We'll hold it up at the river, and there will be everything imaginable to eat. I picture the picnic table laden with potato salad, ham, fresh baked steelhead, various breads and rolls, tossed salad, beans in a crockpot, coffee, soft drinks, beer.

Sunday is a much better time for everybody, for the Fourth falls on a Tuesday, which is terrible. Besides, it always rains on the Fourth of July. That's a good reason for having this cookout two days early.

Norma's side of the family is large, while mine is small. With both sides present, the picnic is apt to be a mob scene. Most family occasions are. But if they weren't, some essential element would be missing.

6

It began to rain about five A.M. on the second. I heard it and awoke briefly. Should we call the picnic off and have everybody over to our house in town, where we could remain indoors and stay dry? There were elderly people coming, and we had little shelter to offer them. We tried a telephone consensus. Everybody wanted to come to the river. So we decided to plunge ahead. Later we learned that it had poured all night in town. So much for trying to trick the rain gods. They are the gods precisely because they can't be fooled.

We cooked the fish out of doors, over the coals. This meant leaving town earlier than we'd planned. We knew we had better bring dry firewood, for everything up at the river would be sopping. And it would take an extra hour to build up the coals until they were hot enough to bake the fish.

The steelhead was wrapped in heavy-duty aluminum foil, and we placed it on a grate which we had fitted inside our fireplace, which is made with river stones. The fire proved hotter than expected and tenting the fish with sheet metal proved unnecessary. The fish was done in an hour and a half. Norma, who is fussy about fish, thought it slightly overdone. Everybody ate a lot. That's gratifying.

My aged parents are not comfortable in the woods. We have an outhouse, for one thing. So they arrived intentionally late and left early. That's okay. The rains of early morning stopped by noon, leaving us with only a clouded sky for the remainder of the day. The temperature soared to a pleasant 60 degrees.

The river rose six inches overnight and was full of clay from the slide upstream. This will remain a problem throughout the summer.

7

A few days ago, I observed a pile of foreign matter down by the high-water mark. It looked like bear droppings. Bears here are rare. Occasionally one is killed nearby and hauled to the Oso General Store for everybody to gawk at. Most people hate bears and are glad to know there is one less.

During the picnic I told my brother-in-law, Barry Morrison, about the droppings. "Let's have a look," he said. He had grown up in the interior of British Columbia, where bears are common. I had not seen droppings since my years in the Army, some spent in Alaska. We walked down the trail in the direction of the river.

"These look like cherry pits to me," he said, after a moment's study.

I looked again. Yes, they did look a little like cherry pits, all balled together. But a few days ago, they had had a different appearance. They looked like bear droppings then. Now they had mushed up considerably.

Barry and I reasoned out what had happened: Our tree of bitter cherries (inedible to humans) had dropped its fruit when it became too ripe; the individual cherries distributed themselves over a wide area of land that was marshy. It slowly drained, as the watertable lowered. The individual cherries were buoyant and floated, and gravity brought them all together into a heap. When I first saw the pile, they were decaying and looked as though they had passed through the digestive system of a bear. Meanwhile, the cherries rotted further. Eventually, all that was left of them were the stones. They resembled tiny wooden beads strung on a necklace of the type sold at country fairs. I was greatly disappointed. I much preferred the bear theory.

8

Our little fish pool in town draws visitors. It is probably the big orange gold fish that brings them. First come the neighborhood cats, among them our aged Siamese. He loves to sit staring into the pool's black center, thinking his feline thoughts. An occasional Lab or spaniel sneaks into the yard for a quick dip, which causes great havoc. They churn up the water and discolor it for days. The goldfish dive under the lily pads and won't come up until tomorrow.

9

Fat, sassy, and rather nasty are the gray squirrels that live in our city neighborhood and proliferate, probably because of the bounty provided by my neighbor's big black walnut tree. He has have never harvested a nut, nor I one of the peaches that grow on our two dwarf trees, because the squirrels always beat us to them. Each year the trees blossom, leaf, and start to put out nuts and fruits, and each year the squirrels strip them clean long before the fruit ripens. Human concerns count for little in their minds.

Squirrels are rodents, ones not much superior to the rat, in my opinion. They are wasteful, as if the nuts and fruits are toys. It is a never-ending game with them, this industrious play. They do not eat what they steal, nor do they save it for winter. They cache it some place and do not return.

The squirrels come to the side of the fish pool to drink and wash their hands after they have eaten something. Probably the goldfish can't tell a squirrel from a cat and do not realize that with squirrels they are safe. These rats in gray overcoats run an irregular course, never for more than a moment holding to a straight line. It must be to evade enemies, of which they have a legion. They make a difficult target. In the city they have never been shot at because they are protected by law. So why do they twitch so?

The squirrels have thoroughly intimidated our aged cat, looking neither to the right nor to the left as they flash by him. But our neighbor's young Siamese chases every one. He is a natural hunter, a killer. He stalks squirrels and birds, all day long. But these squirrels are tough guys. Their manner says they have cats for breakfast.

Nor are they frightened of me. Whenever I stomp my foot at one, instead of retreating, it charges. It whirls and comes straight at me, as if to bite my ankle. I back off. For such a small creature, it is surprisingly fierce. I think such behavior is ingrained. Yet when the young Siamese pursues them, they go up the nearest tree or telephone pole. Then the cat stops at the bottom, and turns away without bothering to look up. Suddenly the cat is bored.

10

The crows and Stellar's jays make a discordant racket, starting at dawn. It's worse early, then dies down to a din by mid-morning. They contest dominion with the squirrels. The jays are pretty. What a deep, intense blue. It is the color of an Icelandic salmon fly hackle.

My neighbor to the East, Lynn, complains that she cannot sleep because of the noise. I have gotten used to it and can sleep right through the din, well, almost. I wake and doze until it is time to get out of bed. The crows and the jays have overlapping territories, and regularly issue challenges to each other. The jay's are resident, but the crow invaders are big and fierce, and, like the squirrels, fearless. Both are scavengers, but I'd like to think the jays are fussier about what they'll eat. I may be wrong.

Children from down the street come into the yard when we are not home and strive to catch our goldfish family with dipnets. Once they were successful, and cleaned us out of our dimestore darlings, and I had to replenish the stock with tiny strangers that cost a quarter each. One side of my mind congratulated the kids on their success as fellow fishers. But the property owner in me was outraged. I came running outside, shouting, trying to frighten them away. I came close to catching them in the act. They ran away just in time, but left their pails and nets behind. I confiscated them, of course.

Once a year we try to rid the pool of accumulated debris and leaves. We first reduce the volume of water by bailing. This is an awful job and seems to take hours, though if three of us pitch in we can do it in just over one. Capturing the Big Guy is a challenge, though trapping the little fish is more difficult, for they are quicker and elusive. Soon they quiet down in their temporary home, a tub of clear water, and when we return them to the sparkling pool later, they poke around its corners, investigating the niches for the rest of the day. The world is a frightening place to them. Best hide in the lily pads until dark.

Then—the pool clean and fresh water trickling in from the hose—I relax in my knowledge that we won't have to go through the trapping process for another year.

11

All of America is under siege today, the Fourth of July. From afar comes the deep thuds of fireworks pretending to be mortars and bombs. It is either the tagend or the beginning of somebody's blitz. Much nearer is sporadic small arms fire—the pop of pistols and rifles fired in the manual mode. Every once in a while comes the startling, irregular burst of semi-automatic weapon fire; in reality it is a string of firecrackers, being set off Chinese style. A Whistling Pete portends a great explosion, like a shrieking fiend, but dies out disappointingly. The odd sharp report of a single firecracker suggests a sniper.

In the morning, curb and city street are lined with the residue of the celebration, with the cardboard tubes and holders that contained the gunpowder, burnt and blasted, and the tattered red, white, and blue wrappers from the Whistling Petes. A boy of ten stands poking through the graveyard of the Fourth, hoping to find a few that haven't exploded.

12

A man buys a piece of property and constructs a fence around it. He wants to enhance his right to own property and keep others off. Up at the river, what people do is post their land. Usually they don't fence it. Perhaps this is because of the high cost of steel or cedar fencing. Wherever you go, there are these red and black signs, "No Trespassing." "Absolutely No Trespassing." "Violators Will be Prosecuted." "This Means You." They look like the owners mean business. I remember a sign at the end of the Fortson Mill Road. It said, "Keet Out." Wonderful.

Sometimes people post a "Beware of The Dog" sign— and the people don't have a dog. They are depending on you not wanting to be bitten. The people who bought the white house at the end of the Whitman Road, up at the river, promptly posted it. About the only person who might want to go through there is the occasional fisherman, someone like myself, whose sole intent is to reach the water's edge, where he will start wading downstream. He isn't going to steal your livestock or rape your daughter.

Whether or not the beach has common rights is unclear in my state. An old ruling holds that owner's rights extend only to the high-water mark, not to the center of the river, but this may apply solely to navigable rivers, and what is navigable has not been clearly defined. The ruling may pertain to boats or powerboats of a certain size, but probably not to inflatable rafts or canoes.

On many rivers, such as the Kalama and East Fork of the Lewis in Southwest Washington, landowners come out on their porches and shout boaters off their stretch of the river. They believe they own to the far side. Even when the boater is slowly drifting down the center of the stream, intent on making his casts, he is considered to be trespassing and treated accordingly, whether this is legal or not. The boats all move along with the speed of the current. Where's the harm, I say?

Trespassing to reach the river probably constitutes a civil violation. Pure of heart, I take my chances. You'll have to catch me first. A landowner does not have the right to use violence to enforce what he believes to favor him, under the law. Only the law can use force. In the country, the locals don't know this, or much care. They have some strange ideas about the law. They presume, because they make mortgage payments, The Constitution permits them to shoot you if they see you on their land, whatever your reason. This is a gross misconception. (If you are shot dead, however, it matters little if you were legally in the right.) Soon some ignorant, self-righteous bumpkin will kill somebody, perhaps a wading fisherman, and then everybody will learn that you can prosecute a trespasser, but not shoot him.

The above reflections are triggered by my discovering— on the night of the Fourth—that somebody has cut down one of my vine maples. This is a special tree to me. The crime was committed by a person from the cabin next door. Perhaps it was a guest, not my neighbor.

From year to year, I have carefully cultivated these small trees along the high-water line because they are beautiful and their complex root structure holds in the bank. They are slow to grow. The culprit took it down with one deft swipe of a chainsaw, wielded at waist-level. I tripped over the corpse at dark, and thought it was a limb brought down by last week's windstorm. But when I studied the ground in the last light of day, I could see the even marks of the saw's teeth on the bough and the white sawdust piled at the base.

On the downstream property line, slightly to my neighbor's side, a second, smaller vine maple has been cut. It is not mine. The culprits sawed the tree into one-foot lengths and stacked them neatly on the Owens's front porch. A guest's small contribution to his host's generosity, perhaps. Wood as green as this won't be burnable for at least a year.

My tree was left right where it had fallen—straight across the common river trail and blocking it. I was furious. Returning to Seattle, I looked up the Owens's phone number and called them. I tried to remain calm. A year ago, their son and his friends had broken into Schlotman's cabin and stolen only some kindling. I reflected that, although we breathe the same air, we are very different in our values, and what is important to us. Why this great thing about firewood? The Owens don't have a wood-burning stove. Their sole source of warmth is electric baseboard heaters.

Over the phone, Mrs. Owens sweetly explained that they had lent the cabin to "some good friends." As if there were any other. The friends had promised to "clean up the place"—brush it out, too—in return for the use of the cabin. I remembered seeing one of them. He had a mean, sour, slightly stupid look, with dull eyes.

There must be some half-digested backwoods spirit lingering in the minds of certain people, who believe the woods are there for their convenience, whether they own them or not, and these people are free to ravage anything and everything. Man is the master of nature, and it had better obey, or else.

How terrible it must be to have such ignorant thoughts and try to live your life by them.

13

"Loveliest of trees, the vine maple now. . . ." The Owens have promised to remove the corpse from my property. What? It is my wood, not their garbage. Okay: Let them try to chop or saw it into stove lengths; it is like iron pipe. Boy Scouts used to be encouraged to make their pot holders and fire sticks out of vine maple, for it won't burn up. (Today Scouts are instructed to cut no green wood and to carry little alcohol stoves, instead.)

Well-aged vine maple makes a wonderful fire, though. It is hot as a blast furnace and burns clean, leaving a tiny white ash in its wake. Roderick Haig-Brown said it was his favorite firewood, for it burns like anthracite. He knew his timber.

Vine maple is found in two forms, the first a small, upright, bushy tree growing in clearings (we have one such tree, up front, by the road) and the other, more often encountered, a snaky version that lives along the riverbank, with twisted roots and limbs that grow like vines, all in a tangle. When the river floods, these strong threads keep the bank from collapsing. I encourage vine maple to grow freely on my property.

The leaves are small, deep green, and shaped like the broadleaf, but much reduced and more striated. The tree produces spinners, which are reddish, veined, and nearly transparent along their edges. During a mild autumn, with no nighttime frosts, the tree is apt not to change spectacularly, as the leaves slowly pale to apple green, then yellow, and finally mottled brown. But with crisp nights, the tree produces instantaneous brilliant colors.

Overnight the leaves will turn bright orange or scarlet. The green leaf caught in its turning reveals many intermediary colors in marvelous contrast and intensity. The tree is related to the Japanese maple, which we have in our backyard in the city. But it behaves differently. That tree is presently in transition from spring green to deep scarlet, or wine, for purposes that I am unable to discern. The tree goes through this odd change annually in spring or summer, when everything else is holding its green. Then in fall, its new burgundy-color leaves cling until the start of true winter, when all at once it drops them. Often this is at Christmas time.

14

My reading is eclectic. And I have trouble remembering what I have read. It surprises me how Thoreau kept all that Greek, Latin, and German alive in his head, up at suburban Walden Pond. Surrounded by trees, he remained deeply emersed in the rich intellectual life of the city. What a wonder he was, in so many ways.

Edwin Way Teale—who writes much better than anybody gives him credit for, except maybe Annie Dillard—was a fine stylist, both in his writing and in the shape of his daily life. He rose before dawn and walked a mile for the morning papers. On Long Island Sound, these must have been of *The New York Times* and *The Herald-Tribune*. Perhaps he bought some of the local weeklies, as well. A man in the country must have his books, magazines, and newspapers. Otherwise, his mind will perish. I know this for a fact.

When he was not out in the field, observing, he was ensconced in his study, either reading or writing. There was always the daily work to get done. Did he eagerly await the arrival of the mail, as I do? Roderick Haig-Brown did, I know. Many writers maintain an extensive correspondence with other writers, and with family and friends from whom they are separated by a distance greater than miles. When they're not writing, writers are reading; they read practically non-stop. This is no secret. Besides books and newspapers, they read scholarly journals, popular magazines, short fiction collections, old histories, technical reports, novels. They'll even read matchbook advertising and the stuff with coupons to clip. They are in love with the written word.

Dillard—who may be the quintessential writer—confesses to reading constantly. She also smokes heavily and drinks endless cups of coffee which, as I recall when I did it, are often finished cold. She teaches. She chides her students at Western Washington University for their unwillingness to "give up everything" to be writers. But she could not give up cigarets and coffee, I suspect. Well who says she has to?

It may not be requisite, or prerequisite, to give up everything in order to write, only to sacrifice a lot. A writer spends his life—in Stanislavski's term—preparing. He is getting ready for the main event, his next bout with words. Seldom does he rest, and when he does he feels miserable, guilty.

John Irving, in *The World According to Garp*, states, "Writers don't read for fun." I understood this at once. They read out of dire necessity, a rigorous compulsion. A writer shapes his life so that he may write fully "out of it," out of what he has become, largely from reading. To say this sounds pretentious and is embarrassing. It is more a fact of life. His sad life.

It is Saturday when I write this, and the evening paper now comes in the morning. I guess it gives the journalists a longer weekend rest. This upsets my schedule because it overloads my morning hours and then leaves a gap toward evening. I suppose I could hold the evening paper, that is, the one that comes on Saturday morning, until evening, but I can't wait for the additional crumbs of knowledge it may bring. So I hurry through it, probably missing much, then cast it aside, with a sense of relief.

The mail is vital to me, but today's load proves inconsequential. Yesterday's brought both *The Village Voice* and *Esquire*, which overwhelmed me. It also brought *The Argus*, the local weekly for which I write. In this issue is the first half of my article on Susan Sontag, which has been languishing for two months in their editorial offices. Their idea was to run it when the managing editor went off on vacation. Neat. That is a clue to what they think of my efforts to write about anything that does not directly concern this insecure city. I live in my head, not in Seattle.

This week's article was on her book, *On Photography*, with a wonderful photo by Al Sundstrom to accompany it. With luck next week, part two should appear. It is on her book *Illness as Metaphor*. It is a good one, and I worked hard on the essay. Sontag has cancer. Her book deals with it and TB, the two great diseases that manifest themselves in societal (great word) and literary terms. So a small check will be coming in the mail.

Late in the day, I read Naipaul, a favorite, and speed through 76 pages before snapping off the light at one. I immediately plunge into a dreamless sleep. Or one that seems like that, for in the morning I can remember nothing of the night.

15

There are, this Sunday, the usual two heavy newspapers waiting to be read, following a traditional big breakfast. And there is the question of how much of each paper I will get through, since to read both in their entirety would eat up most of the day. But it is a pewter morning, dark and dank, and I shan't hurry. Norma and I have decided against going up to the river, where it is probably raining hard. Perhaps I'll go up by myself tomorrow, solely for the fishing.

The Seattle Post-Intelligencer is the more interesting of the two papers. I give it the most attention. Today in the *Brunch* section, there is a horror story about publishing. A woman with 30 years experience as an editor says she no longer enjoys it. All the people in the business "have hard eyes," she says. I've had a little experience with that look myself. There is also a discussion of a book by Authors' Agent Donald MacCampbell, entitled *"The Writing Business."* He recounts many nefarious activities of publishers, editors, agents, etc., in regards to cheating, false promises, publishing intentionally for the book-remainder market (art books, especially), duping authors out of royalties, etc. It is sad and discouraging to read about. It must be worse to experience.

Publishing, says MacCampbell, is a quick-buck scheme, and Archie Sattterfield, the editor of *Brunch*, suggests that "the gentlemanly profession" now resembles the world's oldest one, that is, the performance of whatever it takes to turn a trick or make a buck. It reminds me a little, on the local level, of John Murray's efforts in publishing *View Northwest*, after it went into receivership.

He made it into a slick magazine full of ads and no editorial principles at all. And then he folded it.

16

Another day the color of lead, with rain falling all through the night. You call this July? The rain will fill the river with clay for more than a day before it will start to clear again. Generally, by this time of the year the bulk of the summer-run steelhead are already in the river. The next ten days mark the high point of the fishing.

My spirit is lifted by the ritual act of getting the car loaded and driving off. The funny clothes we wear fishing—waders, vests, little billed caps—are all part of the process of transforming ourselves. We don't care what into, so long as it is different from our quotidian city selves.

Fishing is my excuse for going to the country. It renews me. I return, my batteries charged. I can face another bout with civilization.

17

My neighbors, the Owens, have not bucked up or removed the vine maple their friends felled on our property, as they promised to do a week ago. It lies where it was dropped, all fifteen feet of it, its delicate green leaves wilted and beginning to curl. What a sad sight. "Good fences do make good neighbors"—provided they are ten feet tall and made of steel. We have a little stone one that is easily stepped over. It is more psychological than physical. But there are many irresponsible people in the world, people who will promise anything to be rid of you. All the while, they know they don't intend to do what they say. Thus, the person's word is worthless.

All along I've known it will be I who cut up the tree and dispose of it. The voice of conventional wisdom says to drop the matter. Animosity among neighbors is to be avoided. Up at the river, there has always been hostility among landowners. It is as though people buy land in the country in order to get in touch with their primal selves and to exercise a viciousness that they can't get away with in the crowded city. Here they eagerly shed their civility and their veneer of being civilized. Why, they can't wait to fight.

18

We are each of us many different people, but only one of our separate selves is allowed to come forward and exert itself at any given time. This is bad because it sadly limits us and our potential; but it is good because it protects us from our lesser selves. There is no worse enemy.

19

The river has dropped noticeably since the rain, and it is now possible to wade nearly out to the center in low boots, without having the current to fight. Norma is frightened by the push of the water against her legs and retreats. I take it for granted and have accommodated myself to it, long ago. Garth is so self-confident that he will not back away from the strongest current. If he is faced with crossing a difficult stretch to get to where he wants, he will risk going down and getting wet to the chin, or worse. It happens eventually to everybody who too boldly wades a river. I've had many an unwanted dip, but find each year I am willing to run fewer risks.

For the first time this year I find I can easily walk around and poke the bottom of the river with a stick, observing the changes in the substrate from last year. Islands of golden gravel rise out of the shallows where there used to be pockets. Some will grow in size as the river drops. The first big boulder has a deep gouge carved round it; it will never form dry riverbed, this year. Last year it was a large mound rising out of a flat field of gravel and we used it for a backrest when we sunned ourselves and, later, when we had our evening beach fires.

Fires had to be built in the middle of the river because, overhead, there were tree limbs, wherever you looked. In August, this led us to the farthest promontory of our gravel beach, nearly a third of the way across the river. The upper portion of that beach, where I used to pitch my tarp and mattress, is gone now, washed away. It appears the lower beach will be sizable again. It is not, however, so nice or isolated a place as it was.

Since we have acquired the additional seventy-five feet of riverfront upstream from us, we have found fresh attractions, such as a high sandy beach on which I can park my box springs and mattress until November, if we don't have too much rain. And there is an assortment of boulders poking up out of the river where, I hope, all summer long there will be cool pools and eddies where the fry will congregate to feed on minute food particles brought them by the gentle current. These will be good places to take a dip when it gets unbearably hot, for the river is deeply shaded here.

I can feel that time rushing on.

20

The warm weather is back and the wetness is gone. Grass cutting is no chore, either in the city or up at the river, for the sun has burned it dry and it is green only where it has received watering. In town, my neighbor to the West has never sprinkled and his lawn looks like most of Eastern Washington does, parched and withered. We sprinkle the lawn zealously, and the water runs right off and goes streaming down the street. This is not good practice in a drought year.

Meanwhile, up at the river, after furious growth all May and June, the wild grasses have kindly slowed their advance. Norma scythe-cut an area around our travel trailer, the picnic table, and the stone fireplace weeks ago, then weeded the azalea and rhododendron beds, and chopped out paths to the outhouse and to where I sometimes sleep. Then, on the second of the month, we gave the whole place a light cutting, almost as an old-fashioned barber would. Two weeks later, it has not grown an inch. The need to whack it back is not any petite bourgeois conditioning, but simply to avoid having feet and ankles wet in the morning from the dew. Following clear nights it is heaviest.

The blackberry continues to grow, as they say, by leaps and bounds, even while it is blooming. Practically overnight the canes inch out. They are clustered with tiny white flowers, each with a pale yellow center. Soon the blackberries will produce fruit that is watery and nearly tasteless.

My trees put out twiglets and new leaves. I previously thought all this growth business of trees got accomplished early in spring and by summer trees were steady-state. Not so; nothing in nature is without continuing change. These new leaves will be the last to go, the last to change color and shrivel up, when the summer ends.

Even a dying plant or tree will continue to put out fresh greenery while the major part of it is succumbing. How strange it is to see the living and the dying conjoined in the same specimen. And how beautiful the colors often are.

21

I thought I had identified three distinct varieties of blackberry, but learned today there are only two. The one that is currently in bloom is called Evergreen, but we had always called it Himalayan. (*Rubus lactinatus*.) I wonder how many other things that I've long believed in are wrong? As a kid, I collected buckets of the big tart watery berries for pies a girl I knew liked to bake. I helped her eat them, providing the vanilla ice cream that goes on top.

Today the blackberry is for me a noxious weed devoid of sentiment or affection. It takes over vast unoccupied areas along dikes and riverbanks, and makes access impossible. It forms a natural fence and may be what Frost had in mind when he said the result was good neighbors. Maybe I should introduce them along the line between myself and Owens.

The berry was brought to the Pacific Northwest for domestic purposes, but soon escaped and established itself widely. It spread like a virus. Whole areas have to be eradicated. But some people love it. A woman wrote to the newspapers in its praise, suggesting that it be planted along the medians of freeways. There the blooms

A Year At The River

and the berries would improve the scenery, she argued. A highway department spokesman shot back, "The runners of the evergreen blackberry are capable of extending themselves fifteen feet during a season; under your plan, the freeway lanes will soon be invaded by its tentacles and it will halt traffic."

Where I have cut back the vines to ground level, they are quickly reestablishing themselves. They are getting their length and thickness back. When the shoots are green, they quickly snap off when I try to uproot them by tugging them upward; next spring the dead shoots are dark brown and tough, and if the soil is loose or loamy they can sometimes be pulled up with a great deal of effort. Having wet ground helps some. Whatever time of the year, the thorns are wicked, with a backward curl to their tips that make them scimitars. Or rattlesnake fangs. They can both puncture and slash.

Not so the smaller, more highly prized (at least by me) trailing blackberry *R. vitefoleris*, which bears a pretty little leaf, soft and green and shaped like a triangular heart. The leaf is different from the shaggy, sharp-looking leaf of the Evergreen variety. The creeper sometimes appears to be from two separate plants, for one will have male flowers about one and one-half inches across, quite noticeable, while the female plant has flowers measuring but 3/4 of an inch across and obscure; hence my thinking they are different varieties or species. Petals of all three plants reveal the plants' generic relationship to the salmonberry.

The trailing-type blackberry creeps along the ground at modest height and produces very few berries. But how sweet they are. Many of ours ripen and drop to the ground unnoticed, where they are lost. A few bloom in the shade and remain wet; they mold on the vine and turn blue, then white. Others are wizened and their berries become hard brown shards, which are inedible.

According to Norma, the red huckleberries are now ripe. Distrustful, I taste one, expecting my mouth to flood with tartness. But they are sweet—as sweet as they will ever get. We picked a pint for huckleberry pancakes tomorrow.

We are grateful to have them, for many people have to drive a hundred miles into the mountains and come back with only a few handfuls. We have them because of an old cedar stump. The tree was either cut down, decades ago, or hit by lightening and burned. The stump nurtured the huckleberries, along with some tiny hemlocks which we have since transplanted to better location. This is the usual forest progression. A rotting cedar stump is a clue to where you may find huckleberries. Burnt, logged-over land is best.

Says Norma, "Now if we could find some wild *blue*berries," as she licks the pink juice from her fingertips.

22

Hard rain last night and through this morning. The river will soon rise and fill with mud and clay. The huckleberry pancakes this morning were great, and enough were left over that we refrigerated them and will have them for snacks. Buttered and rolled up into tubes, they are delicious. This crop of berries will not last for long, not with so much rain, which hastens rot.

Best enjoy them while we can.

23

This year's young steelhead are an inch and a quarter long and shy. They are about six weeks out of the gravel, the progeny of fish that spawned in March and April. They seek the current and gravel bottoms which will blend them in with the stones that make them nearly invisible.

It is great fun to look deep into the water and finally locate some. They are almost transparent. Their color is that of the river bottom, the grayish-brown yellow of tiny stones colored with algae and sediment. The tiny fish are quick to dart away when they feel vibrations from footsteps approaching or see an unfamiliar shape looming on their horizon. Yet they quickly return to their former stations and resume whatever it is they do all day long—look for food, mostly—when things quiet back down.

Other fry in the river—offspring of various salmon and scrap fish—are nowhere near so shy, nor do they seek fast water and stones. In fact, on a micro-scale, the baby steelhead behave just like mature ones. They are easily identified in the water by their skittishness and how quickly they will vanish, when disturbed.

Caddis creepers are also found in the shallows along the river bottom, the larvae bound up in self-constructed prisons of twigs and coarse gravel out of which they will be delivered soon. They have two methods of locomotion. One is to inch along the bottom or across the face of some submerged rock; this they can do surprisingly fast. I've seen them move several inches in a minute. The other way is to decide to abandon their foothold and allow the river take them wherever it wants. This must be the most excitement experienced in the life of a caddis creeper.

"Decide" is a poor word to describe the randomness of the environment they permit themselves to be moved about in. And "allowed" is an equally bad word, drawn as it is from the vocabulary of human behavior. In nature, most of what happens has a randomness that is breathtaking. The caddis creepers are suddenly set adrift in what corresponds to the cosmos or an ocean. It is the vagaries of the current that determine their destination. This voyage is conducted in a thimble of a world. In nature they are no more than inert twigs or curled-up leaves. In spite of their perfect disguises, the young fish know better and gobble them up by the thousands.

Mature steelhead eat them, too, though this is not widely known. Steelhead have stomachs that have atrophied because of their approaching spawning; that is the only reason they have taken this long, uphill river journey. But they grow bored and resume feeding on creatures that give them no sustenance. It may be largely habit.

One summer, several of us fishers began to find bits of gravel and bark in the gullets of fish we killed. This led us to examine more closely the entrails of fish whenever we cleaned one. Soon we found recognizable caddis cases, often with the larvae still inside. Occasionally the larvae would be alive. We kept rough count; fishers are inherently competitive. Who would find the most would be declared the winner. If I got a Friday night fish, I kept the guts intact for Bob Taylor to examine the next day. He was a Canadian who would arrive in camp on Saturday. He had a marrow spoon, which was good for making an accurate count. Also, he was a keen amateur biologist.

We achieved counts up to about sixteen. This was routine. Then Bill Stinson caught a steelhead with 34 discernible separate caddis cases in it. He won. Bob concluded, at season's end: "Steelhead don't feed, but they take food." This was not quibbling, or an overly nice differentiation between words, but an acute assessment of the situation.

Often we found a lot of brown slime in the guts of our fish. If the fish couldn't digest food, something similar was going on, in the fish's gullet. What was it? Enough was left of the stomach juices to dissolve the cases of the caddis and reduce the insect inside to mush, even though the fish could not profit from the process. Or were the biologists wrong? We couldn't tell by looking. Surely the waste was expelled through the fish's vent. The process was so much like ordinary digestion we couldn't understand why the fish didn't obtain nourishment from it. We decided that they did, but it wasn't much because of the small size of the fodder.

Some of the spawned-out fish—kelts, they are called—begin to feed as soon as their spawning is over, but there is little food in a spring river and they remain ravenous. They are easily taken on flies. I remember seeing spawned-out fish caught past the Fourth of July. Some had recovered nicely, turning silver again and regaining part of their strength, while others remained dark and wasted. The females recovered best, in spite of the rigors of nest-building. The males—who do little more than dart in and release their milt—are more depleted by spawning and most of them die afterwards. It is not uncommon to find the corpse of a male steelhead on the beach, late in the winter.

The result of this complicated and time-consuming process of reproduction? Why, these inch-plus progeny found quivering and darting about in the current by the thousands in mid-summer. Their bodies are clear as cellophane, mostly eyes and tail. Yet they are completely at home here, near shore, in some rivulet side channel, a microcosm of the great river.

24

Every steelhead and salmon that ascends the river must swim past my property. Think of it. However briefly, they are mine. Hundreds and thousands of adult steelhead and salmon, all in a season. I speak poetically, of course. They belong to no one.

Along the far bank is a narrow channel, with the necessary depth, and most of them pass through there because of the shallow water everywhere else; they move mostly at night, and under the protection provided by darkness they may use the shallows as well. Salmon will stream upriver at night, utilizing the whole channel. In difficult stretches, their backs will be out of water and they will have to wriggle to get across stretches that are but inches deep. Once at mid-morning I saw an adult steelhead move across the stones out from my beach in six inches of water. He was traveling leisurely but determinedly upstream towards deeper, heavier water. Such behavior is the exception.

25

A few nights ago I set up a collapsible cot on a narrow gravel bar, just off the walk leading down to my beach. This was a yard or two away from where the steelhead fry congregate in the bright sunlight. At dusk the river was still and visibility beneath the surface clouded. The surface, however, was full of activity. First, the water striders were dancing about. Small flying insects were busy, as were the bats and barn swallows that were after them. The black flies were absent, but mosquitoes were everywhere, as they are on these warm, clouded evenings.

The river had a cool edge to it; I could feel it on my forearms. I lay for a long while, my arms locked behind my head, thinking, waiting for sleep to overcome me. The river had gathered up what was left of the light and was dispensing it to the edges of the darkness. All around me the river crackled with the surface activity of juveniles feeding on insects in the dark.

It never grew exactly dark. All around me glowed a soft ambient light. As time passed, I found I could see well. It was familiar territory, of course. I was at home here. But I couldn't sleep. There was too much activity around me—nature calling out on every side. Finally, I poked my head beneath the covers and in my private darkness was swallowed by tardy sleep.

26

Sounds. How rarely do we truly listen. Yesterday, back in town, I read in the 80 degree heat, but quickly yielded in to the sun, closed my eyes, tilted back my head, and gave into to the heavy yellow oppression. Immediately my ears became attuned to the busy world of the city, a world that—eyes open—I could ignore. It was as though my eyes had shut out my ears.

Mid-afternoon, the birds were still for once. I could hear occasional noises from next door. My neighbor to the East is named Ryan. He and his wife are going through a separation, and most likely a divorce is in imminent. He is a drummer by profession, and I hear he is building a set of timpani in another location. He sleeps most of the day, with the windows open, and leaves the porch light on all day. When his phone rings, I, who have a hearing loss in one ear, can hear it better than my own, and leap to my feet to dash inside to answer mine. My son finds this hilarious. Nothing a son enjoys more than signs that his father's mind is going. Sorry, it is only my ears.

When the phone rings on television, I often rise to answer it. Phone calls are important to me because I work at home and don't see people often. Some days a phone call represents my sole human contact during the daytime and is to be cherished. But to rush to answer a phone that has never rung, well, that is the height of foolishness. I suspect Norma gets a big laugh out of it, but is too prudent to let me know.

Lying semi-comatose in the backyard on a chaise in the sun I can hear Mrs. Thomas's air-conditioner's muted roar. She is an elderly widow who lives to the North. Her husband was a jeweler whose hobby was raising chrysanthemums. To replace him, she has several cocker spaniels; I hear their various barks and whines throughout the day. Now I detect Ann Downs's Pinto starting up; she lives across the street and up a couple of houses. It has a hole in its muffler. She is constantly apologizing for the noise, saying she doesn't have the money to get it fixed. She doesn't believe buying motor oil is necessary for her engine, either; gasoline, yes, for the Pinto won't move forward without it. The Pinto is on its last legs, and each time it starts up may be terminal.

There are a few propeller-driven aircraft still around. These hum like flies trapped in a bottle, strong coming on, faint when going away, and I can detect, with my eyes closed, when they are directly overhead. Jets remain farther off and come and go in my consciousness less obtrusively. A police car today within the city limits uses a whirling device affixed to its top, instead of a piercing siren, yet this can be clearly heard a mile away. Am I the only one who thinks its noise is. . . sinister?

Packs of wild young girls (a phrase I greatly enjoyed writing, by the way) shriek from passing cars, down at the corner, and other shrill female voices of indeterminate age are heard throughout the afternoon. I spark slightly. Sexuality begins much earlier than I thought it does. The girls are probably already sexually active. By being my age, I am undoubtedly missing out on something not so readily available to me as a boy.

In our backyard, the big goldfish—he must be a Sumo goldfish, he is so gross—is the only one of the five heavy enough to make a plop when he comes to the surface to eat something, or simply to investigate the world of air. He dives with a little curl of his tail, and makes a softer sound. I hear his splash repeatedly, as I lie with closed eyes, feigning sleep.

A power mower starts. The man who runs it lives half a dozen houses to the West, and across the street, and doesn't really need one, for everybody's lawn down there is postage-stamp sized and can be cut with a hand mower in minutes. The man is retired and drives a Cadillac, which is badly out of place in this modest neighborhood. I see it as an affectation. I have a manual model mower. I would wish everybody had one. I like the idea of pushing hard to cut grass—even with a sizable lawn. Exercise is involved. It provides just the right amount of workout for a warm day.

The sound of the mower dies out; Mr. Cadillac's lawn is done, though he'll be back at it in about three days. The new-found silence doesn't last for long. The squirrels begin quarreling again. By God, they're worse than people. They live in an egocentric universe and believe we maintain the pool as their drinking fountain.

Coming from a source indistinct is a strain of rock and roll. My taste is every bit as good as the next guy's, probably superior. And I pride myself on my diversity. So why is it that the music played on a radio down the street is always offensive, even if it is what I normally would listen to? Because somebody else's music constitutes an invasion of my privacy, that's why.

Lying in my self-imposed darkness, I hear cars continually squeal around corners. Isn't that what corners are for? Drivers gun their motors and grind their gearboxes to achieve top locomotion fast. They race up and down hills, of which there are plenty. The heat increases my sensitivity to sound, I think. Doesn't sound travel faster in warm weather? I am fairly broiling. Time to move the hot bod into the shade before I become bacon.

If a breeze comes up, I don't want to miss it. Before you can feel a breeze, you can hear it coming, rustling the leaves. Your pores open expectantly. Your nerves wait, trembling. You listen, and sometimes a gust of cooler air actually hits you.

27

For the past two hours, the temperature has nudged 96 degrees. It is most unusual for the Pacific Northwest, and we natives are beginning to melt into our shoes. Yesterday the mercury hit 93 degrees, which was a record for that day of the month. A cooling trend is forecast. Clouds are supposed to roll in this afternoon. I don't see any. The breeze remains warm and light, the sky a solid blue.

Last night it did not cool off in town and at ten it was 80 degrees. This evening, Norma and I joined half of Seattle in taking a walk around Green Lake. Absolutely flat, it is an easy stroll. It was a bit cooler by the waterside and most of the people I suspect were apartment dwellers who live nearby. As usual, there were the showoff joggers.

Most "joggers" are really runners and have developed a comfortable, reach-out stride that suits them. Literal joggers go up and down, while remaining nearly in one place. They cover very little ground. Am I being petulant, in all this heat? Perhaps.

28

A true runner is lean to the point of gauntness. He eats the right foods. Oddly, many distance runners are prodigious drinkers. Usually it is beer. They burn up their calories in a wink. Many people who cannot control their eating try to run off their excess weight. This is a mistake. You can't eat a lot, then run off the calories. And one's metabolism has a lot to do with it. Some people metabolize at a high rate. Others, often women, seem to metabolize hardly at all. It is difficult for them to lose weight and exercise doesn't help. Running in heat like this is bad business. People get heat prostration, maybe strokes and heart attacks.

I've run enough to have had a taste of the pride and satisfaction it can bring. A runner enjoys achieving his great distances and gets high from what he has accomplished, though there is often pain associated with it. I am in fairly good health and in medium good shape. I know the joy that comes from lengthening out one's stride and watching the distances disappear. I've experienced shortness of breath overcome and the great feeling that comes as one's regular breathing returns and he gets his second, then third and fourth, winds. I've never "hit the wall," as they call it; I've never run that far. But I am respectful of those who enter marathons. I can taste what they taste, on the back of my tongue.

The truth, now: The sight of runners makes me sad. A bad knee injury around the first of June has made walking difficult and jogging impossible. It happened like this. A week into the new season, I was fishing daily, walking long distances, crossing riffles easily—becoming as they say lean and mean. I felt great. One evening after fishing hard I stopped off at the Whitehorse Mercantile to buy some groceries for dinner. Getting out of the car, I pushed off with my right leg and turned my knee as I stepped to the ground with my left foot. I felt a sharp pain of unbearable magnitude. I stood balanced on my good leg, hanging on to the roof of the car, and waiting for the pain to abate. It didn't. If anything, it became worse. Tears streamed down my cheeks.

After ten minutes, I climbed back in the car. It was next to impossible to extend my right leg to reach the gas pedal, but I did. To move that foot from the gas to the brake was excruciating, so I didn't. I drove back to Oso with my foot on the gas and braking with the clutch and gearshift, which required exertion only of the left leg. At the cabin, I found I couldn't get out of the car, for it necessitated bending my knee. I sat for a few minutes, then decided to exit the only way I knew how—by rolling out of the car and onto the ground. Then—leg extended behind me as in doing a pushup—I lifted myself to my feet with my good leg. There I moved along by hopping until I reached a door or a wall, which I clung to.

On one leg, I cooked dinner. Nothing was wrong with my appetite, I found, only my knee. I heated water and washed my dishes. Then I headed for home. Again the pain getting into the car was terrible. Once driving, the car in fourth gear, I was next to okay. I drove cautiously, defensively, slowly. At home, I shouted for Norma and Garth to come out and help me. When they didn't I fell out of the car, onto the city street, where they found me and helped to my feet, or rather foot. My arms around their shoulders, I hobbled up the front steps. The next day, my knee thick with swelling, Norma took me to Group Health and the family doctor. X-rays indicated no damage to the bone, nothing that surgery could help me with. Said Dr. Steven Smith, my physician, "In cases like yours, when we've tried surgery, we found it made matters worse. I recommend plenty of rest and, immediately, physical therapy."

Nearly two months later, I am barely able to run a dozen steps, and know I had better not try for more, or else I will pay the price afterwards with pain and resumed swelling. This has kept me from fishing my river until the past week, when I caught the steelhead for the Fourth of July celebration.

Tentatively venturing out since then, I've learned that wading is the wrong kind of therapy for a knee injury. So, this year, instead of fishing at the height of the season, I've started this book. After a couple of weeks of walking successfully, I tried a tentative run. Quickly, the muscles in my leg cramped. I stopped and waited for them to relax and loosen, as they always had in the past. They didn't. I went back to the doctor. He returned me to physical therapy. During these sessions, one is given no sympathy for having endured pain. It is to be expected. A physical therapist refuses to discuss pain. That's *your* problem. I now know it will take a long, long time before I am finally over this injury. In the meanwhile, I watch the joggers and runners with envy. And write.

29

John Burroughs describes the coming on of a snowstorm like nobody else in the world, and gently takes Emerson to task for his poem that begins, "Announced by all the trumpets of the sky, / Arrives the snow." Burroughs says that, to the contrary, the beginnings of a snowstorm "are, as a rule, gentle and quiet: a marked hush pervades both the earth and sky." He goes on to render one of the most precise and closely observed descriptions of the storm imaginable. That night, during the height of the blizzard, he goes for a two-mile walk.

We would describe his Uncle Nathan today, as "something else." He was a self-professed "outdoors man." He shot over 200 moose in his day, most of them at night, many of them while they were standing still or, I suspect, lying down. He tracked a bear and, when she wasn't at home, shot her cubs. Then he waited in the clearing for the old girl to come home. When she did, he blew her away. Great guy.

Burroughs himself shot for no good reason and killed whatever came his way. The myth of the limitless frontier was still strong in people's minds. Generation after generation has believed in the continuous availability of most everything—natural resources, fish, game. We have inherited the waste and resource depletion resulting from the popular myth. Burroughs contributed his share to the destruction. Yet he was a naturalist and in many ways exemplary.

Burroughs and Uncle Nathan, the ultimate woodsman and hunter, caught many brook trout in remote Maine locations, held them in a submerged wicker picnic hamper for a day or two, then released them, in hopes they would double their weight before being caught again. This corresponds to our modern catch-and-release practices. Their fish were caught on flies, by the way. Very sporting of them. But all game that came their way was slaughtered quickly and skillfully, usually by Uncle Nathan. Burroughs shot and killed birds from boyhood on. He called them specimens.

Once he shot a loon and mounted it for his study. He disliked how loons were usually presented, standing flatfooted, like a chicken. His was mounted flat, its nearly useless feet tucked well back, as though swimming, giving this diving fisher the sleek, efficient look it has in real life, yet we rarely observe.

30

I took the Deer Creek surface temperature in the sun around five PM and it was 72 degrees F. The next day, cloudy, the thermometer registered only 62 degrees at the same hour. That indicates the degree of daily solar loading. Weekly, there is less water to cover the fish and offer them protection from predators (including fishermen).

I am beginning to fish again the easy pools, ones that do not require long walks to reach or call for difficult wading among big rocks, once I get there. Tonight at the Monte Hole I surprised a family of common mergansers down at the tail of the pool, quite a ways off. I'm pretty sure they were the common type and not the hooded ones, which are scarce. The birds were shy, and at such a distance I couldn't make them out too well. Perhaps their shyness comes from the fact that they now have a brood to protect, and the ducklings are without defenses.

I'm not certain whether little birds of this size can be called fledglings, because already they are quite large. Can they fly yet? It may be unimportant, for they scoot along the surface of the river at surprising speed and thus evade creatures that feed on ducklings. Besides their ability to swim fast, their mother is always near to protect them. Often their father is with them, as well. He remains off to the side, observing the wet world, very laid-back and casual. Yet he is very much part of the ducky procession.

They certainly can move fast, even when headed upstream, swimming against the current. There is very little water displacement. Generally they stick to the cutbank side of the river, where the brush hangs low and forms a canopy over the backwater eddies that provide them with cover. When a real or imagined threat appears, they race upstream on the surface, creating a great flutter and splashing. They each appear to be a ball of brown fuzz and can cover a surprising distance in a few seconds. It is impossible to ignore their presence because of the noise from all those wings flapping, however tiny some of them are.

Never is there a problem with mistaking them for tame birds. They remain remote, aloof. They have such disdain for human company that they will not share a large pool with a fisherman but move on, to settle off to the edge of his vision, where they are only dots. Their activity, and the tightness with which they are packed, identify them as mergansers at any distance.

It is usually a pair of common mergansers that come whirring upstream, low in the sky, like jet aircraft, their heads pointed forward, like arrowheads, their bodies pressed flat to enable rapid flight. They move so fast that almost as soon as they arrive they are gone. They have sleek, slick heads, with long, narrow, down-turned bills that have a serrated edge that serves as teeth. Male and female have white throats, and she has a rusty crest (but not so pronounced a one as the female red-breasted merganser). Males have dark, green-black heads, a little like a mallard's.

Because the parents of young ducks keep such close watch on them, I speculate over what predators pose a threat. Would a hawk or an owl go after them? No doubt. Mink and weasels are a danger, too, for they are ever on the prowl along the stream's edge.

Fishermen inadvertently trap and kill birds when they leave monofilament lines and leaders behind, which trail in the water or get lodged in wads in the brush. Plastic six-pack carriers are another culprit. Ducks become entrapped in the mesh and cannot extricate themselves. Their death is slow and ugly.

It is a sad fact that the young of all species undergo attrition. I watch broods of mallards and mergansers being diminished, one by one, throughout the season. It is like the game of Ten Little Indians. Soon only half the original number is left. Those who survive grow big and strong and, by autumn, have developed the flight feathers necessary for their upcoming migration. In July, it is not all that far off.

The principle of gross reduction is necessary for the species' abundance. It's hard to understand. Burroughs says at one time he went to great length to save nests, eggs, parent birds, chicks, fledglings, etc., but most got destroyed anyway by natural processes already well underway when he came upon the birds. So he decided it was best to leave things as he had found them and not interfere.

Also observed today at the Monte Pool were two belted kingfishers. They were "having at each other," as the English say. I'm not sure what causes this antagonistic behavior, once the mating season is over. To further complicate matters, I can't tell the males from the females. Who is after whom? Is it two territorial males, engaged in a dogfight over a territory? Or is something else at work here, a different motivation?

These bright, blue-gray guys are marvelous pilots. They are fish-eaters, in spite of having the appearance of living on insects, and are able to hang in the air, hovering over the river, until they are able to spot their meal of fry below. Then they ball up and plummet to the water like a lead weight and penetrate it like a knife blade. They pursue their quarry under the surface with the speed and agility of a fish. This I must picture for myself, for I am of the terrestrial world.

They are veritable arrows of pursuit, watery ghosts of Confederate hue. Yet I've never seen one emerge with a fish in its beak. Do they swallow fry, while under water? In the air, the kingfisher is truly king. Some times he is a helicopter, other times a fighter plane. Their maneuverability is incredible. You know they are present before you see them, for their cry is unmistakable. It is a high-pitched rattle. Inside the trailer, I hear them screaming at each other and know they are playing their game of hot pursuit. It is their basic form of communication, but it sounds like a fearsome quarrel, with a serious misunderstanding at the heart of it.

31

Only the Elbow Hole holds sizable fish now, and these may be salmon. One fish I saw rose head-and-tail and looked very much like a small pink salmon, though they are not due until next year. A few show up only in even-numbered years.

Most likely the leaping fish was a steelhead. A week ago, three steelhead showed near dark, and they seemed to be all different fish. I got excited and fished hard until full dark, but touched nothing. This year's run of summer steelhead was small and disappointing. Now is the time for the first summer Chinook to arrive, but their numbers are greatly diminished, also. In mid-July, the river ought to be full of fish. Maybe this is the byproduct of a drought year.

Back in the city, our foolish goldfish have become tame. Perhaps they are stupid from heat; I know I am. One day I saw Norma lean over the pool and they swam up to her. She says she doesn't feed them now, but they act like she does. The Big Guy came over and sucked on her fingertips. Can they remember back to winter, when she took pity and threw them some powdered fish food? I decided to try to charm them.

Feeling like Emperor Hirohito must with his royal carp, I leaned over the pool and dangled my fingers in the water. Sure enough, the big goldfish swam up to me to be fed—or petted, or whatever. But he would not let me touch him. He kept drifting away, just out of reach. Evidently—as a fisher—I am a person not to be trusted. I must send out the wrong vibrations. How I wish I could close the distance. Feeling envious, I told Norma about my problem.

"I feed them from the other side of the pool," she explained. She meant winters.

"But shouldn't they come to me, all the same, if I wiggle my fingers? They can't be that hidebound to a traditional feeding station."

She said nothing. I invited her out to the pool to watch me and tell me what I was doing wrong. She was reluctant to join me. I dangled my fingers in the water and they advanced their usual short distance and stopped, treading water. I looked to her expectantly.

"They're used to receiving their food from over here."

"I don't believe it."

She went to the other side and drooped her hand in the water. Immediately the school swam up to her and nibbled her fingers.

32

At ten A.M. it is as dark as twilight. There is a peculiar smell in the air—dank, musty—that means rain is on its way. Distant thunder, too. The air is deathly still, and the spooky effect is enhanced by the sky's deep gray. It has been much this way all yesterday and last night. Change is in the air. Yesterday's high was 88 degrees, and overnight it dropped to 74.

Early this morning, the sun was concealed by massive clouds. They smothered everything. Now the thermometer is stuck at 80 degrees. Though we have all the doors and windows open, and have had since last night, it continues to be miserable and close. Not a breath stirring. Because of the open doors, the house is full of moths, thankfully inert in the thin light of day. They hang on windows and walls like faded flowers.

Thunder and lightning move closer. The lights just blinked. The dry smell—like mold—increases; the air contains so much static electricity it might explode. (Is that smell ozone?) The first rain drops arrive and fall in a large splatter. They are huge individuals. The temperature plunges from 74 to 69 degrees in a wink. The sudden shot of coolness brings no relief. We are experiencing a hard shower. The air hums, the ozone smell increases. Water pours off the roof in torrents, worse where the rain gutters are broken. The garage roof, which is flat and lower than the house, develops puddles on its tarpaper, and they gather and take on the look of a small pond.

A few gusts of warm wind arrive. The rain slackens to a pitter-pat, causing great circles to form and widen in the standing puddles on the garage roof. They fascinate me. They evoke thoughts of primordial events. And the noise they make is a symphony bursting with watery life. Raindrops mimic the disturbances produced by water striders, tadpoles, tiny frogs, dragonflies, etc.

The rain stops and a muggy sky presses down. If the sun pokes through its hole, the temperature will zoom into the 80s. Tomorrow the prognosis is for a high of 72 degrees. Good: I'm planning a drive to the Kalama River, in the Southwest part of the state. I need to fish a different river, perhaps only to appreciate more my own.

33

On a cloudy day, with the daytime temperature less than 70 degrees, I am on the Kalama, about 150 miles from home. Only, nothing works out as I planned it. I have endured (1) a jammed camera, (2) an engine that won't restart, when briefly stopped at the start of the Kalama River Road, (3) a pair of reading glasses that got lost, without which I am unable to tie on flies and leaders tippets, not to mention read anything other than a road sign.

When I first noticed the glasses missing from my vest pocket, I retraced my steps of the previous hour, which were numerous. This ate up much valuable time, during which I could have been fishing. Finally, as I was poking among some rocks by the edge of the river, a young man came up to me and asked if I had lost something? Perhaps some glasses? Indeed I had, I said. He proceeded to describe a man he had been told had lost them. Oddly, that man resembled me, as I had looked some time ago. Then I had a dark beard (now shaved off), Orvis hat (with Mickey Mouse ears), sunglasses, Tackl'pac fishing vest, Hodgman bootfoot waders, and so on. On the Stilly, this would be unmistakably me, but it was a me as I used to be. My beard is quite gray and I have grown paunchy.

This man he had heard thus described had crossed to the other side of the Kalama—no mean feat, at this water height—and had hooked two steelhead, landing one. No such luck for me. Later, he was identified as a trout fisherman from Pullman. No, but the glasses were mine. That part was right. I welcomed them back into my pocket and made sure they were securely zipped up in my vest. I could see up close again, and so the day held promise.

As for the stalled car, the wire between the solenoid and battery had broken. The wire was loose inside its sheath of plastic insulation. Sometimes it made contact, other times not. After a man and his wife kindly stopped alongside my car, its hood open, and gave me a piece of wire with which to jumper around the break, I restarted the engine. What a joy, when it roared into life. This meant I could drive again, but had better not turn off the engine.

Now for the camera. Its shutter advance was jammed, the camera useless, until I got home and unloaded the film inside a changing bag that restricted light entry. A sprocket hole had torn and got caught in the advance ratchet. It was nothing serious, and easily fixed, but it prevented me from taking any pictures of the day's events. These were largely forgettable.

I watched a man catch a nice steelhead, however, and learned something in the process about waking flies and how to fish them. Often you can salvage something from a day that is a failure in every other way.

34

My knee is acting up again, so I've decided not to fish. I'm back on the bucolic Stilly, where everything remains green, is spite of the drought. It is plenty hot. Norma and I sit outside on aluminum lawn chairs, our feet in the river, reading or trying to. She is concentrating on her book, a novel, while I keep interrupting her with a barrage of comments and silly observations. My attention keeps returning to the steelhead fry in the swift shallows at my feet. The bottom is golden brown, with algae thinly coating the stones, and the fry blend in perfectly with it. First I see their shadows, slender wispy forms, then above them the ghostly fish themselves, very tiny; an invisible thread seems to connect them.

The fry vary from 3/4 to 1-3/4 inches long and compete vigorously for food items I cannot see. They are darting out to seize

A Year At The River

bits of plankton, midges, larvae of small insects. If I look hard (and have on the right glasses), I can make out tiny parr marks along their flanks. Norma says she can't see the marks, so maybe I only *think* I can. But I know they're there. Their tails I can see clearly, though; the fry are so transparent they seem to be tailless. I see them because the rear of the fry is continually throbbing.

It is by their shadows that we get to know fish. Every fin on each small fish is perfectly formed, and their tails are slightly forked, coming to definite points at the tips. The fry lie near but not on the bottom. They are found either schooled up or else eager to participate in group formations. They are wary of a shadow, and when I pass my hand over the water, they flee. They don't return to their old stations for several minutes. Perhaps the smart ones go somewhere else.

Are they the ones destined to be survivors? Will they be left, when the less shy ones are gobbled up by some predator?

35

Several rafts and innertubes containing young persons, or adventuresome middle-aged ones, come drifting down the river during early afternoon. We wave to them and greet them with some light-hearted remark, mine usually with a sarcastic edge to it. I ask them if they know about the waterfall half a mile downstream? It contains a vertical drop of sixty feet, I tell them. They think I'm kidding, of course—but maybe I'm not. I've planted a doubt in their minds. Good.

There approaches a small yellow liferaft so over loaded with large boys that they keep spilling out and climbing back in, even though there isn't room enough for all, in the first place. It's a game, and fun to watch. They come to a stop by the big rock at the head of my property and pile out. Then they begin to dive into a pool about the size of a pickup truck and only five feet deep. It's all they can do to stay submerged.

Suddenly they begin to throw stones at each other—or is it beer cans they've brought along, stashed in the bottom of the raft? I can't tell. They have grown nasty. Some large fish is disturbed from its lie and bolts for cover through the shallows. It is a salmon. Then, as if hearing a signal, the boys pile back in their raft and paddle off downstream, their conflict evidently forgotten. We exchange hale pleasantries of departure. They sound a little drunk. Soon they round the downstream bend and pass out of sight, out of mind. I hear their noise fade into the roar of the next riffle.

Twenty minutes later two empty beer cans come floating down the river behind them. They are silvery, Hamms. The next day we find several unopened cans sunk in our shallows. They are silvery, too. These are the "stones" they threw at each other. At twilight,

Norma and I open them, lifting them tall in a toast to the rafters's thoughtless generosity.

36

I smell autumn in the air. I always detect it earlier than most people, perhaps because I look forward to it so. There is a faint haze that makes me think of burning leaves and football games. The temperature holds to the low 70s, which is to my liking.

Of course I am jumping the gun. All of August lies ahead. It will remain plenty hot. The soft haze is from a "controlled burn," used to dispose of logging waste wood. The smell is the smoke from smoldering slash, far off. At this time of the year there are forest-fires inadvertently set by careless campers or by lightning. In the deep woods "Hoot Owl Regulations" are in effect, which means they can cut timber only during the cool part of the day. Work takes place early in the morning, the fire threat is so extreme. By noon the loggers have all returned to the valley and are swilling beer in front of the Oso General Store.

37

What is there to do on a hot day like this, but sit on the beach in lawn chairs and conduct the Annual Caddis Creeper Race and Bet-a-thon? How is it played? Glad you asked. I'll be happy to explain, since I invented the rules.

The game is simplicity itself. Each player is issued a folding chair. It doesn't have to be aluminum, but aluminum doesn't rust, so you can leave it in the river, in the sun, in all kinds of weather, and never have to worry about it turning brown on you. Right away, you are handed a can of pop or beer, for it is necessary to keep bathing your tonsils. Players generally wear bathing suits, but rolled up jeans or cutoffs will do. Women may go topless, according to my rules. None ever have, a fact that continues to disappoint me.

Key qualities discovered among past winners include the ability to remain motionless while seated in the river for long periods of time. Sun-seekers station their chairs in the direct rays, while others are free to move into the shade, when the heat becomes oppressive. There is a big maple on the beach expressly for this purpose.

The honor system is essential, for are we not all friends, families, lovers? It is important to study the field well, the caddis creepers right out in front of you, before choosing a favorite. Be slow in committing yourself. Caddis build small houses of twigs, bark, and pebbles. With only their heads and forward set of pincers showing, they drag their heavy abodes behind them as they explore the watery world. Some individuals, I've noticed, are more vigorous than others and make better progress. I have no clues as why this is, since caddis creepers look pretty much alike.

Behavior patterns are vital. Look for individuals with daring and verve. Before choosing a contestant and placing a bet, study the bright side of sunken boulders, where the caddis show up well and are apt to move along fast. After everybody has made his choice, bets are placed. You may cheer your favorite on to victory, if you wish, though you should remember that the creatures have no ears, and don't hear you. However, your enthusiasm may be communicated to them through vibrations in the air and water, so your cheers probably help some. You are not allowed to kick your feet in the water to spur them on, however. This is considered cheating.

Caddis—like many of us—move in fits and starts. Poor candidates tend to budge not at all. A few caddis appear self-conscious and will not move while being watched. If you pick one of these, it is best to keep your eyes averted. Some individuals move only at night. There is no way of telling ahead of time and, if you should choose one of these, I pity you, for you lose.

Participants in the game name their own starting and quitting times for a given race. I've found that some people have more enthusiasm than others. While a race is in progress, you may sit quietly or make noise, according to your temperament and how much beer you've drunk. Winners usually announce their victories loudly, and it is common for players to dispute results.

Races often are close, with the apparent winner being declared emphatically, such as: "Did you see that? My Charlie moved six inches. Pay up." But no money ever changes hands. This comes as a big disappointment to some contestants who have placed serious bets. Seriousness in such endeavors is always a mistake.

Losers console each other and victors gloat. Toasting takes place. The end of one race often signifies the start of the next. Contestants search the pool for fresh competitors that exhibit lively signs. He whose entry went the shortest distance is sent for more beer.

38

The robber fly is dead, after several insincere attempts to make us believe it had happened earlier. He would lie there, pretending to be a corpse, but we knew better. Some tiny sign always gave him away. The slightest twitch of the tip of his antenna did it. No more.

A week ago, we trapped him under an inverted glass, using a piece of cardboard slid across the glass's mouth to keep him there, while we transferred him from the window pane to the top of the table. There we watched him daily, waiting for his demise. He lived much longer than we expected. The days dragged on, and he walked around in circles. He buzzed angrily at times. At the end, the buzzes grew feeble, but I thought he was faking them. Now he is dead and I half miss him.

At first, I imagined him studying the walls of his prison, planning an escape. He'd fling himself here, he'd fling himself there, but in each direction was the encompassing glass. The only course open to him was to play possum. He lay pathetically on his side, his many legs curled tight, trying to look brittle. When that didn't work, he became manic again. Sometimes he'd stand squat, looking out at the world beyond the thin glass. His look was contemptuous. Then he'd repeat the antic phase. Thus the days passed. Often he lay stock still.

Once I moved the glass around the table, until one prison wall touched his leg. He betrayed himself with an involuntary twitch. Instantly he knew the deception was over. Furiously buzzing, he battered himself against the glass, careening off his walls. What a warrior. Soon he tried the dead-fly routine again. I had to admire his aplomb.

I touched his leg again with the glass and he didn't budge. He was learning, fast. What a spunky lad. Insects, like larger creatures, are capable of benefiting from their experience. That is, they learn. Their mistakes, though, usually doom them and are not oft repeated.

During his awake moments, the robber fly looked to be adjusting well. He'd go for walks necessarily short and poke into his round corners. His nervousness vanished by degrees. I shouldn't have, but I gave him fresh air each day by cautiously tipping up the edge of his prison. Then, one day, he lay still. No faking now. The sight filled me with sadness. I threw him the garbage. Perhaps he deserved a better funeral. I should have buried him at sea, by flushing him down the toilet.

According to Barron and White's *A Field Guide to Insects*, the robber fly is of the class *Diptera*, family *asilidaw*, and his face is usually bearded, as are many of us today. The authors state: "Some are robust and hairy, and resemble bumblebees." Ours was clean-shaven, though I detected the hint of a mustache. "They are predaceous, often attacking insects larger than themselves." We saw none of this, though we gave him no chance, *in vitro*. Baron and White say he could have bit us painfully. We did not offer him any food, which was against our principles. The book says he would like the larvae of other insects. He would eat his own kind, of course. His soul was a cannibal's. When he truly died, it was probably from starvation; suffocation was unlikely, under the bell jar to which I secretly admitted air. Or perhaps our police-state methods crushed his spirit, and he died of a broken fly heart.

Our choice of ultimate disposal was wrong, I now see. Neither the garbage nor the toilet was suitable. What we should have done is feed him to the big goldfish.

39

We are putting up galvanized rain gutters on our house in the city, in 80-degree heat. Why now? Well, Norma found a good buy. And they should be put up in dry weather. It is that, all right.

Bone tired and aching in every joint. Arms sore from so much overhead lifting. Bad knee aches from climbing up and down on tall, aluminum ladder. Weariness prohibits use of direct articles, also forming complete sentences. Write short, sleep soon.

The three of us—Norma, Garth, and I—are able to work together only when it is absolutely necessary, but there is much squabbling and vying to see who is boss. Nobody will let me be. My wife and I can work together pretty well, after more than twenty years of marriage, I suppose because each has learned to give in, under varying circumstances. Stir in a son of sixteen, mix well, and you have an impossible situation.

Norma is the chief planner and hardest worker. Women outwork men, almost always. And Garth is very strong. He is also argumentative, resentful of authority, quick to become bored, ridden with power ambitions, easily martyred, readily distracted: in short, all the things normal for a boy of his age. It is necessary for Norma to keep reassuring me of this. The situation gets pretty testy. Yes, I was this way myself, at his age, I recall. Yet somehow we get the work done, and everybody is happy, proud of his accomplishment.

Rest, drink beer in deep chair, go to bed early.

40

I am to wear bifocals. The Group Health optometrist, a gentle, somewhat effeminate man named Dr. Lamb, tells me this. They will solve my problem, he says, which is not seeing very well up close. Nor too great even at a distance.

While giving me the glaucoma test, he leaned close and said, "Has anybody ever told you have such long eyelashes?" A look of panic flitted cross my face. (Answer: Yes, but not recently, and then always by some flirty girl.)

I have the feeling I will be happy with my new glasses. In fact, I can hardly wait for them to be done. To see is a joy. It will take two weeks for them to make up the glasses for me. Then I can see small print again and read a book with my elbows bent. And I shall be rid of the nuisance of taking two pairs of glasses with me always, unless I'm willing to forfeit either near or far vision, by carrying with me only the one.

41

There are cars parked in the usual slots along the river road, but they are not the familiar vehicles of fishermen. They belong to innertubers. They seek the same easy access points that we do. At our place, sitting in my lawn chair by the river's edge, I watch them drift by in gregarious clusters, some on repeat trips. They have an upstream shuttle. The more experienced ones have truck-tire tubes, which are big, adult-sized, probably more than is needed on this tamed river. The river is so shallow now that the tubes grind to a halt on gravel bars an inch or so under the surface and the tuber has to effect a short portage. It's walk and ride, walk and ride, throughout the day. They'd do better to forget the tubes and stroll down the river's edge in tennis shoes. But it's not the same thing as a float trip, however interrupted.

There is an upstream breeze, but it is faint and quickly dies out, leaving me wondering if I imagined it. Long, wispy tendrils slide across the sky from the South. There may be thunder showers tonight.

42

When reading Edwin Way Teale, we do not encounter some woodsy sprite, but a practical man of the world who tries to spend as much time as possible out-of-doors. Teale rose invariably early "to observe the sunrise," which arrives with appropriate bird chorus. People who get out of bed early deserve such a bonus. He went for an early walk to get "the papers," he wrote. After completing his morning routines, his reading and writing, eating a meal or two, late in the day he went for another walk and came back with the day's mail.

My point is that Teale was, first of all, a literary man. Though he lived in the country, it was important for him to keep in touch with the broad world. I almost called it the "real" world, which is wrong, for it implies that the country— the world of trees, narrow roads, cows, and chickens—is not real. It assuredly is.

His choice of a rural life—one however with the "necessaries" built into it—made him a lot like Thoreau. Both have a somewhat urban life-style, though they live in the country. That is, they do not pitch hay or milk twice a day.

Thoreau was financially independent, Teale was not. A writer in the country will probably be engaged in some form of commerce. Maybe he will be a naturalist-writer-scholar. If he doesn't write books, he does articles and expects to be paid for them.

The family pencil factory was vital to Thoreau's survival. It permitted him to live the life that he did, free to exist frugally without regular employment and to observe and write the journals that we now recognize as his life's work. They were much more important than anything else he is known for. To complete them, he needed to write day after day, year after year. It was important for what he called his "economy" to provide him with what he thought of as his "necessaries." This need brought him into the company of people. He gave lectures and performed odd tasks, and in return the Emersonian world gave him his bread and butter, plus his freedom. But he did not meet with any degree of literary success in his lifetime.

Teale has been able to support himself from his books. Annie Dillard, who writes books and articles for *Harpers*, saw Teale's value early and cribbed considerably from him, generally through a brand of paraphrase at which she excels. There is much learning from others in her writings. She would be the last to deny it.

Dillard is a teacher, besides. She is a totally dedicated literary person. An inveterate reader and a tortured, compulsive writer, she asks her students if "they are willing to give up everything" in order to write. I can picture them fleeing in panic. A few will remain. These are the ones she wants, the ones she is after, the ones who will not a waste her time. They will "give up everything," poor souls. You could say the choice made them, not they the choice. Dillard is giving them their first opportunity to come out of the closet.

Such dedication is tragic. Such a life misses out on so much that is normal and pleasant. By asking so much, Dillard is putting them in monasteries and nunneries. It is a decision that will effect the remainder of their lives. That is a long time, for these are young people.

Dillard understands this; she is lonely herself, but knows what they cannot know yet, namely, that writers offer each other slim consolation. They are locked into loneliness. It is not the loneliness romanticized by the image of the long-distance runner. It is more like the cup of cheer offered each other by the prisoners awaiting the executioner. And many will be making the sacrifice for naught. They will fail. I recognize these elements in myself.

Dillard is a sophisticated woman who writes out of anguish and moral dedication. I admire her. She measures out her life in cigarets snubbed out and in cups of coffee turned cold at the side of her typewriter. She produces only a few taut pages per day. Consequently, she is jealous of time taken away from her work and doesn't want to waste it on students who are uncommitted.

She maintains that she "hates" the act of writing. Surely she can't hate it, in the sense a poor student dreads the composition due the morning after the weekend of avoiding it. Or the factory job, or today one on the electronic assembly line. Maybe she means she is the masochist who feels so good when she stops writing for the day. One relaxes into the ordinary sloth. There is a private reward that comes from having written well and knowing it. It is the daily effort of the journeyman that moves him along. It is what carried Thoreau along, from journal entry to journal entry. Only he knew that what he wrote was of the utmost seriousness and importance.

43

Dillard tells her young audience that she did not go into the wilderness to write *Pilgrim*, but only to the hill country of West Virginia. Her Tinker Creek flows through the "suburbs," she explains. She knows the difference between country and wildness, rural and suburban. Surely she is being ironical.

But maybe Tinker Creek is truly suburban. She makes it seem genuine country. That is her accomplishment. It is a form of artistry, without a doubt. It puts her in the company of those naturalists who are involved in what Thoreau calls "wildness." Maybe the wild part is all in our heads. What we have left of it today is the tagend of wildness. It is that unsatisfactory thing, rural living, life in the country. Nobody can live in the true wilds. It is bleak, inhospitable, barren, unsustaining. It will do only for an idea or a place to visit. Then quickly scoot on home to shelter and warmth. Heat is very important to someone who is out in the woods all the time.

What is a naturalist, anyway? One who observes the natural world and passes along what he's noticed. For instance: Human shit smells worse than animal. If you agree, you're a naturalist. But if you vehemently disagree, you are a humanist, or whatever.

I go to the country for relief. It may very well be relief from my city self. The country changes me, I believe for the better. My need for the country is frequent and severe. Once I am renewed, I am eager for the city again. It's paradoxical, but true. I wish I loved the country more; I only have my uses for it. But isn't it supposed to work this way?

The city is more real because it is where most good things happen. For instance, while I write this, the mailman drives up to my house in a little blue Jeep and hands me a box from Marlborough House. It is a firm that advertises remaindered books with a tabloid sent through the mail; they send out millions of them. In the box are seven books I ordered some time ago. The books will open wide the world outside my door.

I could have sent away for books in the country. I would have had to drive or walk to the post office, like Teale and Thoreau did, and lug my new books home with me. No doubt this effort would have improved my character. A three-mile walk eats up a lot of time that could be spent more profitably. "Profitably" is a New England word, with a host of utilitarian associations. A walk may be good for the spirit, but it usurps time. I like the idea of a mailman who comes up my steps and to the door with a box.

I need the city, need it badly. But without the country to escape to, upon my desperate occasions, the city would be drear and deadly. It is a paradox, not finally to be resolved until death. Life here, life there, both are to be reexamined continually. It is the process that is important and meaningful. This is the point of my book, and I must communicate it many times, in many different ways.

I must make it interesting, too. And I must give it some variety. If not, I have failed. Each day the writer must overcome boredom and inertia. This is his starting point.

44

Being landed is to be saddled with custodial responsibilities. One cannot truly "own" land. Your land owns you, you soon find out. If you cut down a tree, you'd better have a damn good reason for it, too. It can't simply be "in the way," or you have a need for firewood. Won't do, sorry. Someday you will have to answer for your bad deeds, including those committed with chainsaw and ax.

You are accountable for what you do with your land. Do you hear me, Weyerhaeuser, Scott, Georgia Pacific, Simpson Timber? You are going to be confined to a remote circle of Hell for what you've done. That is where the fire burns the hottest. It is a forest fire.

I hope to go Environmental Heaven, but am not certain I'll make the grade. I've cut down trees, sure, but only alders. And I've replanted them in other places. It is an act of atonement.

If you cut down a tree, some say you murder it; you open up a wound and it dies. The tree's spirit escapes into the ether. It joins the other lost tree souls. I don't know whether this is an Indian idea or not. It sounds a little like one, but doesn't quite ring true. It sounds, as a matter of fact, like I just made it up. All the same, I believe it, this new notion.

Some tribes believe that living trees contain the spirits of their ancestors. They aren't really dead, only living inside of trees. If you cut down one of their trees, you send the spirit of Grampa Ned, let us say, into tree purgatory. Most Indians don't really believe this, or else they wouldn't have agreed to the wholesale clearcutting of their reservations. They would be dooming their ancestors to perdition for a few bucks.

Most of us in the Pacific Northwest are economically dependent on the cutting of trees, however indirectly. I worked for ten years at the University of Washington as an editor. We print on paper, made from pulp, made from the death of trees. I am doubly guilty, for the University's capital building fund and the other public schools in this state are funded from the sale of timber off of state lands. Still, I deeply resent the cutting of even the lush second-growth firs, which have replaced the original forests. It seems only right for them to continue to grow to cover up the original mistakes.

Back when the first trees were cut, no replanting was required, so the new forests have risen through an understory of broadleaf maple and alder, which have delayed their maturity. But eventually all these trees come into harvest cycle. Today they are being cut again, cut for the second time. Am I responsible for the rape of the hills? I would like to think not. The Stillaguamish valley is one of many logging communities. Practically everybody is logging-dependent. Most trees I see being trucked away are going to be shipped whole to Japan. This brings top dollar, and top dollar is what logging is all about.

The Japanese don't want our finished lumber. It is milled to a different standard and to do it to their specifications would require building new mills or completely retooling existing ones. The cost is too high for such an uncertain business. So I watch the trees disappearing, with sadness. There is nothing I can do about it. The economics are international and complex, way beyond the influence of any individual. All I can do is try to be responsible for my own small piece of land and tend it in a thoughtful manner.

45

Behind our property up at the river lies the broad swathe of an ancient clearcut formerly owned by Pope and Talbott. They are gone, absorbed by Georgia Pacific. The land was first cut at the turn of the century and the scar is what remains from the second cut. G-P has divested itself of its land holdings, which are owned by Hancock Insurance. The lower portion was sold to Scott Paper. Now small conifers are growing up nicely among the neglected slash. I can't tell whether the young trees are the result of planting seedlings or are from natural regeneration. The latter would indicate biological neglect and "letting nature take its course."

First the deciduous trees grow back—alders and broadleaf maples—and then tiny conifers start up in the shadows but do not achieve good growth until the alders die of old age (after twenty years or so) and the sunlight can reach them. Modern forestry disdains this method and now plants seedlings and periodically sprays and kills the hardwoods. Some fifteen years later, they will be thinned to produce a vigorous stand.

Down by our place, Pope and Talbott sold off the riverfront to a developer, who short-platted it. This can't be done today because of legislation requiring a minimum lot size of five acres along the river. It is called a green belt. We were fortunate in finding this small lot, since we couldn't afford anything larger. Once this acreage belonged to a man who fenced it; it was probably used for pasture, for it is still grassy, in among the alders. A meadow for grazing would be a pleasant place, and the river would keep the cows in without an additional fence being built. I would have liked it then. If you poke around with the tip of a shovel, you can find rusty barbed wire and rotten cedar fence posts under the year's mulch.

When we come across a buried fence post, we resurrect it, dry it in the sun, then chop or break it up into pieces of fireplace size. Often we have to saw them up with our bucksaw and they fracture in long, rotten shards. We burn them here in the open fire ring we use for outdoor cookery. The barbed wire that remains in the fire we gather up carefully, and put aside for the next trip to the garbage dump.

46

Last Sunday, my family and I, plus a visiting couple from the city, hiked into what we call The Outback, which is the reforested area off the Whitman Road behind our property. It is a favorite, easy uphill trek, and can be accomplished in short time, before or after a meal. We wanted to experience the vast territorial view from on high, and examine the fresh clearcut on the steep slopes of Mt. Higgins that doesn't show from the state highway. We also wanted to check on the new deciduous growth.

Instead, along the old logging road, we found dented beer cans, broken glass, shotgun shells, and assorted garbage cast aside from motorbikes and drivers of four-wheel vehicles. They are about the only people who come here regularly, besides ourselves. Some of the litter may be from Scott pickup trucks, which regularly patrol the area and spray the shoulders with pesticides. Besides the alder and broadleaf maples, which compete for space and light with firs and hemlocks, and must be killed, all the berry bushes get poisoned. Already this summer, the salmonberry and thimbleberry are death-brown for twenty-five feet back from the logging road. This bothers Norma greatly. After all, it is her land—she lay claim to it on first sight, as did Balboa the Pacific. She considers it her private preserve.

Much of it remains dense and green, however. The new trees are coming back nicely. Only last year we looked out over gullies choked with rubble; now they are thinly veiled in fresh foliage. Alders and cottonwoods block off our view in many places where they didn't before, and Douglas firs, noble firs, hemlocks, and cedars rise over them. All are vigorous and healthy.

The road increased in steepness and began to switch back sharply on itself. I took the lead. This I like to do because I'm not a particularly strong hiker and can better control the pace. It is entirely to my benefit and highly selfish. Oddly, I find that my easy pace leaves others trailing, puffing. Their pace would do the same thing to me. Hikers tend to stretch out their ranks so everybody finds his own stride. It is important to be comfortable in the woods. After all, hiking is not a competition. It is a means to get from one place to another.

At last we reached the point where the old logging road ended. It petered out abruptly and became what appeared to be a game trail. These can be deceptive; they look like ordinary trails, but soon develop a low canopy of arching brush that makes it clear that only four-legged creatures use them. Norma said to forge ahead, so we did. It was slow going, all bent over like a deer.

Overhead an eagle circled. It was pointed toward the Skagit River and was small and appeared as a silhouette, so nobody knew if it had a white head and tail feathers, which are the signs of a mature bird. There were no deer spotted today. New deciduous growth blocked our vision and our path. Last year we saw fresh clearcuts to the South.

Our trail quickly disappeared and we were pushing through thickets of willow and thimbleberry. The stuff parted easily. Soon the terrain grew rugged and steep, and we began climbing over rockpiles and reaching out for handholds. Then we came out in a vast flat area; later I learned this was called the Whitman Bench. The trees were thick and tall, and of a uniform height. It was an immense tree farm. We wound in among the firs, with no trail to guide us. I soon became confused as to where exactly we were. Norma said not to worry. She has a canny sense of direction.

We pressed on. Clearcuts ran across the tops of most hills. At first they were difficult to recognize as such, because of the deep shadows caused by the landform and the way the shadows fitted the land. Then there appeared a little clearing. We looked down on rounded hilltops and valleys obscured in dark brown dreck. All was newly cut and raw, without any evidence of this year's green beginnings. The low sun told us it was time to head for home. It was not a good place to spend the night.

Norma took the lead and I was glad. She guided us unerringly back through the portion of the woods that had no trail. The light was fading fast. Soon we struck the logging road. From here on it was a simple matter of placing one foot in front of the other and not stumbling. We reached our river place in less than half the time it took us to ascend.

Light lingered along the river, a streak of tangerine above the alders that was captured by the riffles, turning them the color of sky. It was very pretty, but an August night usually is.

47

I am reading David G. Measures's book, *Bright Wings of Summer*. It is about butterflies. He is an Englishman, a naturalist, a teacher, and an illustrator; in short, a Renaissance man. Like so many Englishmen, he is a fine stylist—are they born with this skill, or do they pick it up at their superior schools? Why should it be easier for them than for us?

I've never thought of salmonids having anything in common with butterflies. It comes as a surprise to learn the males of both genera are called cocks, the females hens. Both have scales, and both lose them through tribulation. But they are very different, otherwise. One creature's world is water, the other's air. The two don't mix. George Kelson believed that Atlantic salmon *ate* butterflies. Perhaps they do, but not many of them and not often. It would be a rare treat. And the nourishment they provide would be slim.

Often the fish I catch (like Measures' butterflies) are much the worse for wear. They show line cuts and abrasion from nets. (A butterfly can be damaged by the net used to trap him, too.) Sometimes there is an open wound on my steelhead caused by a sea lion's bite. Like butterflies, they show scrapes and patches of scales that have been torn away.

Butterflies start out life unmarked. Soon they give up scales to the rigors—they give up their feet and legs, too. Their wings get frayed along the edges, much like salmonids rub off scales. Butterflies do battle and—klutzes that they are—bump into things. They are not awfully hardy, to start with. Birds feed on butterflies and pose a constant threat. When a butterfly comes out of his cocoon, he is helpless for the first half-hour, until his wings dry and he is able to fly. Until then, he must remain perfectly still in the sun, for the slightest movement will attract his enemies. In a gulp, he is gone, the dinner of some fat robin.

Though he avoids movement at this critical moment, later movement will be imperative. It is how he mates and exerts his territorial imperative. A male butterfly drives off his contenders with aggression. He wants both to be seen and unseen. The underside of a butterfly's wings is camouflaged and, when glimpsed from beneath, his slim wings folded above him make him blend in with the twigs on which he knowingly alights. (O wise, provident butterfly.)

The wings of many butterflies, when seen from above, are bright and beautiful, clearly meant to attract. The huge eye-like patterns on the wings of some species resemble the eyes of hawks, making attacking small birds think they are being stalked by their arch-enemy. They veer off, frightened, and the butterfly escapes. Color, motion, and pattern (or shape) combine for protective purposes. All the same, the attrition is tremendous.

48

I can see again. In spite of constant, increasing eye strain, the image before me is sharper. Yes, I have to admit it. But my eyes burn and my forehead aches.

The new bi-focals are here, and they will take some getting used to. The close-up patch, the bi-focal lens, is tiny and positioned to the lower right of center, and my eyes have to search it out and be careful not to move off of it in order for me to read. Probably I needed them years ago, but neglected being measured until discrepancies at both the near and far ranges made seeing difficult.

Will I ever get used to them? I continue to experience a swimming sensation and a slight dizziness.

Now, with the new glasses, the upper half of this page is blurry. To make it sharp, which is very sharp, I have to tilt my head back and look at it, as it were, along my nose axis. If this gives me a snooty look, I'm sorry. But it is wonderful, too. Suddenly I can see whatever is in front of me. It's like coming out of the darkness. My previous life was the world seen through a smoked glass, as in a Ingmar Bergman movie.

My cuticle, for instance. I haven't seen the edges of my fingernails for years. Now I study them as do those reported to be high on mind-expanding drugs. The tips of my fingers are pretty ugly, as a matter of fact. I've chewed my fingernails, off and on, for years. There is no nourishment in that bony growth, and I've decided to quit, as of this moment.

The nails on my little fingers are what I'm concentrating on. They're gnawed to the quick. As you proceed toward the thumbs they look a little better, that is, they resemble those of a normal human being, though cut into pretty deeply.

I can see clearly now the whorl of my fingerprints. These tiny circles blend into each other, very much like the rings on a tree; they are what make me who I am, at least to the FBI, which keeps records of such things. A mosquito lands on the back of my hand and I kill it with one quick swing of the other hand. I observe the whole process. The glasses are nifty. I study the corpse. The little guy has spotted wings. I don't suppose most people notice such things.

Suddenly I am Superman, at least micro-visually. The body of Mr. Mosquito is rather smashed up. Four of his legs remain—is that all he had, or did I vanquish some? Each is a slender bit of monofilament, slightly angled, thread-like, quite distinct. I don't need a magnifying glass to know what I have just discovered, namely, that the world of the smallest of the animal kingdom is infinitely revealing. And interesting. I think I will spend the remainder of the day exploring the microcosm at hand.

But my eyes continue to ache miserably. If I had a choice, I think I'd pick my former world, the realm of dim sight and a head that does not hurt. Perhaps my bi-focal patches are too strong. I can't go backwards, though. I must live in this world of brave new sight.

Meanwhile, I discover that my fishing flies have been tied by a method akin to Braille; worst are their heads, the tapered finish of silk or nylon that completes a fly's appearance and holds it firmly together. Mine are ragged, uneven. I am ashamed. I not only vow to do better, I begin tying immediately, and, in spite of painful vision, achieve decent, tapered heads I'm proud of.

What else do I learn? I can look at the point of the hook of a fly and have a pretty good idea of whether it is sharp or not. Most aren't, and require a stroke or two of a fine file. And my leader tippets gleam like strands of copper wire, though they mic at .008 and test out at eight pounds. I can see abrasions and, worse, nicks along their length. I think I should go fishing and give my eyes a rest by looking at things from a goodly distance.

49

Alder leaves are falling in the breeze. Isn't it a bit early, or do they descend, unnoticed, throughout the summer? My family and I are back at the river. It is where we notice things.

The air is tense. For some reason, we are all hyper, super-keen to sights and sounds. My son asks, "What is that?" A soft noise occurs in the vicinity of the roof of our trailer. It is only a leaf, Son, but to us it sounds like the footstep of someone approaching. Leaves have been falling all summer long, but I never noticed them before. Nature is full of such untimely surprises.

A great parasitic force is at work in. . . . Oh, go ahead and say the word; in fact, capitalize it: NATURE. There you go. Easy, wasn't it? The force that exerts itself in Nature sets out systematically to destroy every leaf it's produced since first it came out of the bud. My super-keen vision searches for a perfect leaf, one untouched by blight, bite, bird, fungus, or insect, but cannot find one. What comes closest is some small specimen newly emerged. In time it too will grow marked.

Did Plato search for the perfect leaf, the leaf that epitomized Leafiness, signifying it had reached the state of . . . Leafdom? What a silly pre-occupation, but what else to do but think one's private thoughts? They are secret because only a fool, or a writer, would reveal them.

The function of the leaf is not precisely known, even to scientists, who repeat each other's descriptions of photosynthesis and make vague speculations on how a leaf "works." The leaf's relationship to the parent tree is mysterious. Teale writes of how a leaf's stem pivots the moisture and light-gathering expanse of its surface in the necessary direction to capture what is offered by the sky. He describes how the leaf is "instructed" to fall, how the nerve center of the stem has three sets of cellular structures and how they are signaled separately to shut down, permitting the nutrient flow to the leaf proper to terminate, etc., so that soon the neck of the leaf narrows and the leaf is released, with a little ping—and perhaps a sigh. This is not awfully different from how seed pods are told to "go," and are exploded or propelled forward, sometimes for great distances.

Scientists don't understand the processes well enough to communicate them to lay persons. Instead, they revert to commonly agreed upon terms that describe these processes but don't explain them. Content am I to watch the leaves fall and, when it rains, watch them speeded along by the impact of drops. The field grass, which I've kept mown all summer like a good burger, is lightly littered with leaves of the alder—the Western red alder is its full name. Blades of grass poke out from between leaves and remain dominant in the landform. Some of these leaves are yellow-brown. The broadleaf maples are following the alder's progression, but very faintly, almost invisibly, so you must attune your eyes carefully to see any color change.

This year, a warm one, unbroken by cool nights, the vine maples pale unspectacularly. This is disappointing, for it is my favorite tree, and I expect a great show from it annually. Where are my crimsons and brilliant oranges? I am a shutter-bug, and many of us are waiting for an opportunity to capture this year's bright colors. My son looks up, as another wind-driven leaf scuds noisily across the roof of our aluminum travel trailer, sounding like a small, scurrying animal. His eyes, Norma's, and mine trace its route. Then we look at each other and laugh.

50

Unobserved, the wild grasses have all died back. They used to be two feet or more in height, dripping dew on clear mornings. Sometimes the sun didn't reach them all day. When it rained, they streamed water and that water accumulated in vast puddles that reflected back sky, bare treetops, and tiny circles that looked like a million trout rising. Now they lie brown and pummeled flat.

The 11 Douglas fir seedlings we obtained, free, from Ernst Hardware Nursery this spring were completely buried by the tall grasses. These are sedges, I understand. To keep the seedlings from getting accidentally whacked by my manic mowing, we stuck in the ground alongside each a dead alder branch, with a red flag, but eventually these got buried too by the advancing growth. Now the grasses are in full retreat. We can clearly see the red flags again, and below and beneath them, the seedlings, some of which have turned yellow.

There is going to be high mortality among the seedlings. It was expected, and the unusually hot summer will add to the toll. It is sad to see how so many have lost their needles already, or have needles turning pale. They can survive a small amount of needle-loss. The wild grasses at their feet helped greatly, keeping them wet and shaded.

Douglas firs need sun, once the seedlings are established. It is a truism of forestry that these are the "sunshine trees." Hemlocks and cedars enjoy shade and grow well under it. Doug firs (as the loggers call them) are best planted out in the open. If a rising alder canopy doesn't kill them outright, it will retard them. (Nothing worse than a retarded Doug fir, believe me.)

The soil we planted them in ranged from terrible to barely adequate. It was a beggar's choice of deep gravel or a mixture of loam, sand, and clay. We put some in each, and took our chances. You learn as you go along, and pay the price. Those that received full shade, perished. And others did because they were stuck in poorly drained soil where their delicate roots were puddled. There is also the unknown factor, X, which we will call blind luck. It isn't the-luck-of-the-draw, but it comes close.

Some seedlings drown, some are burred brown by the sun, some are set back a year in their growth, and some miraculously prosper. Destruction is a large part of nature (say, 90 percent) and one must not pine for what falls by the wayside. Norma and I do our fair share of destruction. As they say in the veldt, if you don't destroy nature, it will destroy you.

Our little cedars, transplanted last winter, are doing well. They are nice and green. Norma has a special touch with plants and few of hers die. Last winter we transplanted some alders, which is unheard of in the country. We would be a joke, if anybody knew. I remember them as having practically no root system, yet about half have survived, the hardy cusses, and this spring put out small widely-spaced leaves, none of which are changing color yet, probably because they are seasonably set back. Whatever the sun strikes is the first to undergo autumnal change.

Autumn was important to John Cheever, that sad man with talent to burn, who fried it to a crisp. Autumn is to me, too. I go down along the beach walk and study what's becoming of the old broadleaf maple. Its leaves are yellowing prettily, and are riddled with brown, as if somebody had slapped a paintbrush at them from a distance of a yard. All its leaves are hanging by a thread. They are individually so big that soon they will accumulate on the exposed gravel bars of the beach and obliterate the stones. They'll bury the beach to a depth of several inches, much as snow does.

Snow is coming. What, in August? The thimbleberry proclaims it. The salmonberry adds its two-cents worth of leaves to the ground, leaves that are splattered and specked with burnt umber. The bracken fern, or fiddlehead, has turned a peculiar shade of violet-green, which means it has begun the process of shrinking back to its roots. It will live in its roots, all winter long. Yet winter is at a distance beyond imagining.

51

At Cicero, the great blue heron recognizes me, I'm sure. When I come to fish, he moves off a ways, but not to his old safe distance. When I start to cast at the Pipe Pool, he stands down at the bottom of the run, by the railroad trestle, doing his herony thing, which is to perch on one foot, with the other tucked up under him, trying to look as much like the numeral "4" as possible. What he is really after is fry and fingerlings innocently swimming in the shallows. If he is quiet enough (and who on the river is quieter?), they will swim right by his single scaly leg and provide him with a snatched dinner.

I stand still too, still as a flyfisher can, rhythmically rocking back and forth as I lengthen out my casts before I release line for what is called the shoot. Then I become as heron-like as I can, while my cast fishes out. That is the time when the fish is going to strike, if ever it does. Generally it doesn't, and the rocking, lengthening, shooting, and waiting is repeated, as I try again and again, in a slightly different downstream location. The heron—who like God sees all—keeps me in the corner of his vision, and so long as I don't hurry in his direction we remain in peaceful, remote juxtaposition.

Wild animals, including birds, never grow tame, of course, only less wary. Many people come to visit the river in summer, for the hole under the railroad bridge is the deepest for diving and swimming of any around. Deer and herons get used to seeing people. They keep their distance but grow unalarmed. As I inch downstream, fishing through the drift, the heron pretends to ignore me. I note that his fishing is no more successful today than mine. But when I close the distance by an amount I am unable to prejudge precisely, he lifts his great wings, beats them slowly and thunderously, and lifts off into the air, with a squawk of contempt. Often he will shat the ground. Hey, Bird—I thought we were better friends than that?

52

Already hunters are readying themselves. The season for birds is not far off. I hear occasional pops from target practice. The deep bangs are shotguns, presumably aimed at clay pigeons. A real pigeon is a dove, but not all doves are pigeons. The local doves, off in the hills, are related to the purple pigeons we see in town, pecking in the streets. They are mourning doves. They help keep the city clean, in one way, but dirty it, in another. It is a trade off. In the woods and down by the river, I never see the doves men go hunting for.

Last night at the Monte Hole, around a bend or two, I saw some fishermen carry out the litter stupidly left by the people before them. On my river, fishermen often do this. This hole happens to be one where people can drive down on the beach, which makes it a favorite of picnickers. They frequently leave their garbage behind. I hailed these fishermen and took a quick look at their collection in passing. Besides the usual aluminum cans and potatochip wrappers were bright yellow shotgun shells. Later, on the beach, I found the gray shards of clay pigeons.

I thought about the family of common mergansers I spotted here, earlier in the month. I tried to imagine myself a hunter, who shoots at clay pigeons to sharpen his eye. Would I be able to pass up a shot at the odd merganser, either in the air or on the water? I doubt it. Any fisher/hunter would know mergansers are fish-eating ducks that devour countless salmonid fry and parr. He might well think he was doing the natural world a big favor by blasting away a merganser and his family.

What about helping the fish by shooting the great blue heron? It would logically follow. He is a voluminous fish-eater and presents a big target. It would be hard to miss him. No wonder he keeps his distance. Shyness is directly related to size and the need to present a small target. The bigger the bird, the farther he must stay away from people. Nature obeys this dictum, which when looked at closely seems only reasonable.

53

Perhaps it is the new glasses, and their incredible close-up capability, but I have just uncovered the beauty of leaves from the black cottonwood tree. Some are huge and their range of colors is almost infinite. It is not my favorite tree, what with its puffy white seedpods caught by plants and bushes down below, all season long, which look streamy and unlike snow. The wood is soft and highly susceptible to disease. If disease doesn't kill the entire tree, various limbs succumb throughout its lifetime and break off during storms, and can be found lying around crookedly on the ground in the storm's wake. They make poor firewood. Even to burn it up for waste requires combustible wood from other trees, such as alder, which could be put to better use. But the fact that its giant leaves are beautiful in autumn wholly redeems the tree to me.

The tree's lower leaves are small to normal sized; only those at the top of the larger individuals seem to grow into elephant ears. They are huge, heart-shaped, with a short stem twisting off to one side, like a cherry, and are single veined, looking as though they have been folded once, lengthwise, then carefully unfolded, retaining the crease. The cleavage at the heart is minimal; the leaf tends toward the round, with a nicely pointed bottom. Forgive the florid anatomy, which is verging toward the erotic. What the cottonwood leaf mostly has going for it is its marvelous colors.

Leaves that get knocked off the tree, such as the ones disturbed by the auger sent in to erect our power pole, are unspectacularly green and undistinguished. They are huge and olive, unworthy of notation. But leaves that have naturally fallen to the ground run a gamut of colors. They may be brown or yellow or orange, pale gold, or green flecked with rust, usually a combination of these, some looking as though they have been airbrushed by a person of talent. They are reminiscent of abstract expressionist canvases or else paintings based on the microphotography of materials seen through a scanning electron microscope. No two are the same.

Down by the river's edge, on the broad exposed shingle, an assortment of leaves accumulates. The alders are dull, unexceptional, gnawed, and brown. There are very few fallen maple leaves so far, either from the big broadleafs or the smaller, more sensational vine maples. I find smaller leaves from the black cottonwood, slick and rounded. Why don't I remember them from past years? Weren't they spectacular then? The fact that I notice them now is what matters. I wonder how much else I've failed to observe in the past? I'm sure it isn't entirely the new glasses.

I pluck three large leaves that particularly strike me from off the gravel of the beach and carry them up to the car, intending to give them to Norma so maybe she will find them suitable as a centerpiece for the dining room table. But I forget to bring them in the house and, the next morning, they are mummies of leaves, curled tight into the shape of cigars. Their colors have faded into buff nothingness. If I give them to her now, she'll think it a sick joke.

54

We shall call this the Saga of the Lost Goldfish and, I warn you, it is not pretty. I've mentioned my small pleasure of watching the goldfish in my backyard pool, and how the solitary one—the Big Guy—often plops on the surface, like a feeding brown trout. Say I am writing out-of-doors—the sound is startling, but I enjoy it and the diversion it provides. Subconsciously I look forward to it as part of the subtle punctuation of the day. I recall Proust's essay on reading, and all the distractions a reader has to put up with, while he strives to concentrate on his text. Well, a writer has even more problems.

One day no plop greeted me. When there should have been one, my ears were met with silence. I went to the pool and searched its murky depth. No big fish. This called for some detective work.

I pieced together the following: While I was up at the river, three pubescent neighborhood girls stole into the yard, took up my five-foot spade, and attempted to catch the Goldfish Children with it. Now, a shovel won't do the job. They stirred up the bottom of the pool badly, whacking off some water lilies and spidery weeds. Norma and Garth saw the girls leaving the yard, identified them, and pursued them, as they cleverly took off in different directions.

Norma went to the homes of two of them, but their parents weren't there, only the girls, who knew trouble was afoot and wouldn't answer the door. When I returned home, she told me about it. I went into my usual immoderate rage.

One of the girls was Tia, daughter of the Johnstones, next door. I told her mother and she was appropriately irate. She called the mothers of the other two girls. Tia said she was sorry, she was innocent, she only "watched" and did not wield the shovel. I thought this might be the truth. I studied the pool for clues, finding none. It was roiled, but I spotted two small goldfish. The Big Guy was nowhere to be seen. The loss seemed just short of tragic.

Now Walter from down the street came to the our door. He had his daughter, Kerrie, in tow. Walter is black, his ex-wife white, and their daughter dark but with her mother's red hair. It makes for an interesting color combination. The girl admitted to wielding the shovel. She denied killing or stealing any of the goldfish, however. She asked what she could do to make amends. What was fair? I told her to go to the neighborhood pet store and buy us a goldfish replacement. A cheap one would do fine. Her father looked on approvingly.

A few minutes later Kerrie was back at the door, in tears. In her hands was a basin. In it fluttered a big orange swallowtail goldfish. It wasn't ours, but one very much like it. Big. It was hers.

She wanted us to have it. Instantly I was filled with remorse. She explained how she had raised the goldfish ever since it was a fry, or whatever it started out as. I protested that a single small goldfish from the store would be sufficient. Such a fish should cost about a quarter, I reasoned out loud. She bit her lip.

No, it would be her swallowtail. A fair exchange. She had talked it over with her dad and he was in agreement. She would willingly sacrifice it on the altar of my wrath. I was just as determined not to let her. It would be unthinkable to deprive a girl of her pet goldfish. What kind of a monster was I?

Ceremoniously, she walked round the side of our house and dumped her fish into our pool. He immediately began to swim around in the murk as if he owned the place. He was a feisty and unusual fish, I saw at once. He immediately dominated the small goldfish, as one by one they emerged from under the lily pads and queued up for his inspection. There were more than I had realized. Had they been hiding earlier? They followed the new big guy around the pool. He was a natural leader. One, two, three, four, five. So many?

"My God," I said aloud, "where did they all come from?"

"I thought you said they were dead?" the little girl hissed.

"I thought they were," I said, abashed. "But my Big Guy is still missing." She glared at me. Had I misrepresented the situation to her?

"They sure take to your big guy," I said cheerfully. "And he seems to feel right at home with them."

She nodded sadly.

"Feel free," I said, magnanimously, "to come visit your fish, anytime."

Tear-streaked and smiling, she left. I felt terrible. Was it because I had triumphed over a child?

An hour later, I went into the backyard to see how all were doing. The water remained clouded, but I could make out an orange shape every once in a while. There was the new Big Guy. The school of tiny fish followed him around the pool in tight formation. How they loved him. They looked like tiny submarines, cruising on the surface. I spotted a second big goldfish. What was this? It was *our* Big Guy. Where had he hidden himself, these past five days? Help.

The swallowtail(ST) had spotted the big guy and was pursuing him. It looked innocent enough, but comprised an actual attack. The ST was pecking at the tail of our Big Guy(BG). Always the ST was off to the side or just behind him, nibbling away, giving him no rest. It was a bad sign. It meant the death-by-a-thousand-nibbles in a trout hatchery. It constituted a form of psychological dominance.

I decided I had better net out the ST; the BG's life was at stake. I got the big strainer we used to clean out the pool and began to swing it around in the water. The fish quickly disappeared into the muck. All I did was strain the slime. The goldfish were badly spooked. Whenever I approached the pool, with or without my net, they dove to its depths. It was no use.

In morning, the ST was still pursuing the BG, making his life a watery hell. Norma and Garth and I chased him around in circles, but had no luck at capture. We tried using pails of various sizes. Then we went for my old trout net, but it had rotted full of holes and we had to patch it first.

The net caught the slime but not the goldfish. We lowered the water level and made the pond smaller, more manageable. We bailed and bailed, dumping the water on the lawn. In half an hour, the level dropped an inch or two. The goldfish continued to evade us.

I had a bright idea. Why not sink the net, wait for the goldfish to swim over it, then lift the net? It's what we did in a boat to land big steelhead. Norma and Garth exchanged looks of doubt. So I took up the net and began waiting, lurking. My family soon got bored and went inside. After twenty minutes the ST passed over the net. I lunged and lifted.

"Gotcha," I shouted triumphantly. I transferred him to a pail and took it into the house. "Look what I captured," I told them.

"Theirs or ours?" Norma asked.

"Theirs. Take a look."

"You got the swallowtail?"

I smiled modestly.

She looked. "That's the Big Guy you got."

"What?"

"Look at his tail."

I had not looked. It was long and streamy, but not divided, like a bird's. She was right. Oh, God. Couldn't I tell one kind of fish from another? Back to the yard I went, pail in hand, like a child going to the beach. I dumped the bucket's contents gently into the pool. The BG sunk back to his depths.

I stood by the pool's edge, my child's net in my hand, feeling like a fool, as a medium rain began to fall. I studied the inky water. Nothing of interest was there. Many minutes passed. The rain fell harder. I saw the BG pass by once. A wispy pinkish-orange shape finally appeared in the murk, looking like a ghost of a fish, not the fish himself, and I swung at him. I nailed him—I wasn't a fisher for nothing. Unceremoniously I dumped the ST into the pail, then added some water from another pail, for it wouldn't do to have him expire on his way back home.

The ST swam around mightily. I hated his assuredness. He behaved much like a Samurai warrior would, if he were a fish. His scales were much larger than our Big Guy's and he weighed half again as much. He would have murdered our fish in another day. I could see that they looked nothing alike.

I carried the pail to Walter's house. He was working on the engine of his old VW; he always was. I told him my long story. He smiled with that sympathy of one father to another.

Finally I asked, "Is Kerrie home?" It was as though I wanted her to come out to play. He nodded slowly, as though he thought it was a matter grown men should be able to solve without a child's involvement.

Kerrie came to the door. How old was she—twelve, thirteen? Only a child. I am too old to be able to tell the ages of children accurately. Her German shepherd, Thor, walked over to me to have his head scratched. I obliged. He looked into the pail and saw that it contained nothing to eat or drink. I told Kerrie about my fish adventures. It took longer than when I told it to Walter. And I had trouble keeping my chronology straight. Guilty? Yes.

"It's okay," she said. "You can keep him."

"But we have all of our goldfish now," I protested. "This one is yours."

"Keep him. We were going to get rid of him, anyway."

"Get rid of him?"

"He's too big. He picks on the smaller fish. He eats more than all the rest."

I said, "Thanks, but no. He keeps attacking our Big Guy. He'll kill him, if you don't take him back."

She shrugged indifference. "Oh, all right." Unsmiling, she reached into my pail and plucked him out with her bare hand. He remained docile. As they say, he "stood for it." Evidently, all some people have to do is hold out their hand and a goldfish submits. I am not one of these. She carried her fish into the house. I was left with my pail of dirty water in my hand.

55

Hard rains gonna fall, says Bob Dylan, and they did. The new rain gutters work well, except for a bit of minor leaking at the joints.

This can be fixed with caulking. Two-thirds of an inch of rain arrived today, all within a few hours, and the volume of water coming from the downspouts and their extenders (which carry the water away from the cement foundation and prevent our basement from flooding) issued forth in a steady stream, all afternoon.

Outside my bedroom window (Norma has one window, I another, and they are in the same room), water from a drain spout ran silently into the flowerbed filled with the newly transplanted azaleas and rhododendrons. The silence of the water was disappointing; I am used to the roar from a leaking raingutter, which sounds like a river in freshet and lulls me happily to sleep. In the city I had an auditory river of my own. It is gone, and I miss it.

My very own industry deprived me of easy sleep. Now when the rain falls and runs off the roof, I no longer know it for a fact and am robbed of its lulling effect. I lie abed and wonder what is not happening outside. Does that make any sense? No? My own disappointment keeps me awake.

If I were to loosen the drainspout a little, so that it leaked again during only the hardest rain, and if I were to place a bed of stones right below the leak, next to the azalea bed, I might have my pleasing sound back again. My city river. And I would sleep, the happiest of men.

56

Think twice before you plant potatoes in your vegetable garden. It is I, the amateur gardener, who tells you this. If you plant them once, you will have potato vines to contend with all your life. And you will be sorry.

In our Western side yard, in town, each spring we are greeted with fresh sprouts from a single bygone potato planting. It produced a veritable jungle of vines. They are red spuds, and not very good ones—huge, watery, tasteless, inclined towards black rot. Each autumn we go out with spade and pitchfork in a vain effort to harvest what is edible and to destroy the rest. Each year we fail.

While we were putting up raingutters, the three of us lugged around tall aluminum ladders. Our feet, or the feet of the ladders, kept getting tangled up in the vines and, as we ripped ourselves free, we tore up the vines. When we were done with the gutters, there were few vines left. Destroyed are they? I doubt it. Underground, tiny potato seed eyes are gestating. Next spring there will be more potato vines. I know this as surely as I know God makes little green apples.

Nature's assessment seems to be, "The individual doesn't count. Life, *en masse*, goes on." Once we threw some half-rotten potatoes into the compost pile. Don't do this ever! It was just what they wanted. By spring, we had a healthy crop of vines. The considerable heat generated by the compost pile was perfect for them. Tomatoes are like this, too.

Compost from an earlier year was mixed into the soil of one of Norma's mixed flower-and-vegetable gardens. What's that I see growing over in the corner? It's not the Andromeda Strain, but more potatoes. Luther Burbank's curse remains with us. We will never be rid of it.

57

Last night I slept down by the river on my cot again. I wanted to try out a new sleeping bag, a summer-weight one. Near dawn, I had to cover myself with the extra blanket, it grew so cold. In the dawn's early light I looked up through slitted eyes and saw clusters of pinkish-orange vine maple leaves at the end of their boughs. The color wasn't there yesterday, I'm sure. I conclude the change of color will take place eventually, independent of cold nights. Being long struck by the sun's rays will do it.

It is generally agreed among scientists that the leaves on the branchlet change all together and by a similar degree. It's no secret that the leaves are dying. The tree "sends a message" down the branch, telling the stem to "shut off" the flow of nutrients so that the life-sustaining cells of the individual leaf are deactivated or shut down. Thus, the beautiful colors of fall. They are the hues of death, of course.

Daily the leaf deepens in its particular shade of russet, scarlet, or orange, the new colors overcoming the green of spring and summer. When green and orange are in balance, leaf and tree are their prettiest. On some leaves, the pinkish orange coloration spreads inward from the edges. On others, the color change is so gradual that the tips of the leaf change last, or do not change at all.

The winged seedpods grow at the ends of the branches. Spinners, they are popularly called. The seedpods have little wings that on a great puff of wind travel long distances. They are literally exploded off the twig they grow on. They travel much like dragon flies, and even look like them. Previous to this year, I thought vine maples extended their territories by sending out snakelike roots in various directions. The seedpods indicate that they have this additional means of expansion.

58

The art of sitting still is not well developed in America. It is an Eastern idea, and often seems one developed expressly to punish children. T. S. Eliot wrote, "Teach us to sit still." Ah, but how difficult it is. Stillness in sitting is an art, which all naturalists and outdoor people strive to develop.

I say strive because I am a long ways from being able to do it myself. I twitch and fidget. My nose itches—shall I scratch it? Better not, or say goodbye to all wildlife in the area. I make numerous small movements which I tell myself are essential to comfort and which, I state, will do little harm, but I notice that birds don't come any closer. In fact, they stay at about the same skittish distance as when I move around in my normal manner.

In his book, *Bright Wings of Summer*, David G. Measures speaks of remaining so still in a field while searching for butterflies that he is mistaken for a scarecrow. How wonderful. He is proud of his impersonation. I don't blame him any.

It is impossible to be truly motionless for more than a moment. It is a like trying to maintain a blank mind; you can squeeze out worrisome thoughts, fantasies, tomorrow's schedule, today's miseries, etc., but not for long. One can try to superimpose some new thought pattern on the old stuff, and fight off buzzing thoughts of a negative nature, but it won't work for long. To make one's mind a blank for more than a minute requires a type of concentration not encouraged and rarely found in daily America.

For this we need the East. Eastern philosophy and religion aren't available in the supermarket. It's a pity. Westerners are a long way from being self-reliant, though long ago Thoreau and Emerson wished us so. We didn't get the message.

If I could clear my mind, I would be better at sitting still. But I am a restless American, eager to get ahead with things, anxious to move along, and any form of stillness is evasive. I can achieve it only in bits and pieces, which is not good enough. If I were better at it, mosquitoes could land on me and I wouldn't notice them, or have to brush them away. Like a stone, they could come to light on me. Birds would make me their roost—*if* I were different.

Even if I could give up my tendency to move about, that is, lose my restlessness, I doubt if I could give up my awareness. There is so much to see and—in seeing it—think about. Nor should I wish to give it up. If I did, I would stop noticing things. I would sleep my life away, and then what would I have? Nothing. The examined life, though often painful, is the only one worth pursuing.

59

Saturday morning and the great American hardware store has me in its grip. Or does it really exist? Is it not an icon of a vanished past, a relic of the dream of a certain kind of man who loves doing practical things, things with his hands? Such a store exists, but it is getting hard to find. They are being replaced by another kind of store, where everything comes prepackaged, done up in bubble wrap.

Such an institution is worthy of preservation. I'd hate to see it disappear into the mist. The American male rises early on Saturday, the day which belongs expressly to him, after goosing himself out of bed for the past five days for the benefit of others, namely his wife, children, boss. Today he belongs to himself; he is his own master. He will probably work harder this day than he has all week, for he has a series of projects outlined in his head. They belong entirely to him. He is their author.

My project is electrical. I've decided to put in the electrical service for my lot up at the river. I am not skilled in this particular direction but am determined. I can read, can't I? Well, then I ought to be able to do it. I have become the archetypal Mr. Fixit, only, in this case, I must do it from the start. The telephone pole is already in the ground. I must now buy what Thoreau called "the necessaries." In my case, it is more than food and shelter. It is the very source of light. It is electrical power. And I have become the typical Saturday husband, with a project in mind. What I do today is what each of us must do, if he wants to be able to live with himself.

He breakfasts out in order not to disturb "the wife," who is in the habit of sleeping in, since their kids are grown and moved away to start families of their own. Leaving home on an empty stomach is one good way to start. He drives to the nearest restaurant, pulls himself up to the counter, uncrinkles the morning paper left on the stool next to him by its previous tenant, and orders the house special—cakes, eggs, and bacon, with lots of butter pats and a squeeze bottle of imitation maple syrup. The coffee is served in a bottomless cup of stained china. When he's done mopping up the last of the eggyoke, he's ready for Hardware Store Saturday Morning. It's a psychic necessity, in his awakened state.

In his pocket is a list of what he needs to buy; he's been refining it since Sunday past. Once he's made his purchases, he will hightail it home, or else drive hurriedly to the country, for he has a place like mine up on a river or else on a lake.

Up at the river, one of our neighbors, Ann Schlotman, maintains that her husband, George, can't drive past a hardware store. Its magnetic force pulls him in, every time. I'll admit, the appeal is new to me. All those bins full of nuts and screws, washers and bolts, and nails—so many different kinds of nails; they have a seductive appeal. Nails have special, complex uses. I'm just beginning to discover some of them. Boxed or lying jammed together in great galvanized bins, you buy them by the pound, clawing them out with a pronged implement like a garden tool and bagging them up in tough plastic you hope they won't poke through. Careful, or they'll draw blood.

I've never been much of one for repairing things, let alone building something new. After trips to three different hardware stores, I've found all the parts needed to install the electrical service on my new power pole. With a little time and effort, I will soon have light and heat, up at the river. This will be a considerable improvement over the Coleman lantern and cookstove.

It is painful to have to learn something new, and the older you are, the tougher it gets. One floats along happily in his epic ignorance. If a man is ever going to appear stupid in public, it is in a hardware store, on a Saturday morning, when many people are about. Men and women who work in hardware stores are generally kind, helpful. They have to be. If you make a mistake in buying something that won't do the job, the purchase can usually be made right, sometimes by exchange, or else by keeping the item for some dim future use, and buying something new. Oh, joy. This permits you to go to the store again to make another purchase.

The plumbing and electrical departments of a full-service hardware store are even more interesting than the nail bins. Their wares are complex and varied. There is a something for every purpose, and each thing is unique. Take meter and fuse boxes, for instance. It's easy to buy the wrong item. There is no roadmap to lead you to the right shelf. Look at all the connectors, outlets, plugs, wire gauges, and switches. With a vague goal in mind, a man can pick and choose and dream and shop his heart out, going through multiple options, putting together the pieces of his puzzle.

Of course he may be wrong in what he decides to buy, and in his idea of how the pieces will work together, once he starts the job. Then he will find himself in a race back to the store to get there before it closes to buy what he should have known enough to buy in the first place.

The hardware clerk reigns over the store as demi-god, his host of knowledge available to you and your pocketbook, if you approach him right. Often he is busy or elusive. He is a little like a physician in his remoteness and calm superiority. You are at his mercy, when he gets around to you.

On Saturday morning, a clerk is asked a hundred wide-ranging questions by the uninformed and uninitiated, people like myself, and he nearly has life-or-death power over whether a person is going to succeed, or fail dismally, in his self-assigned task. And there are clerks who don't know much more than you do, but won't admit it. You will get led astray if you aren't careful.

Generally, a clerk wants to be helpful. He has a stake in seeing you get your work done most efficiently. He knows the shortcuts. He can lead you to the right tool or the wrong one. A hammer is not a screwdriver, for instance. This may seem elementary. All the same, the difference is important. A screwdriver can do many things—pry lids, stir paint—but its intention is to turn the head of a screw. Do not pound things with its handle.

It is normal to make mistakes and find yourself with the wrong implement in hand. When you do, often you are many miles from the store, and it is late in the day, unable to correct your mistake before the store closes. You discover the next day a basic truth: Most hardware stores are not open on Sunday.

I know a few that are, however. Most are attached to discount department stores and have a small hardware department in which everything comes sealed in a bubble pack. You don't learn that it is the wrong part until you buy it and tear the plastic off. Inside is unfamiliarity and confusion. You find that the threads, for instance, are the wrong size. You rage in frustration, as the problem looms insoluble. You soon learn to open the bubble packs with your pocketknife, deftly, neatly, from the back, while you are still in the store. You peek inside. You do not purchase the item until you are sure. It's somewhat unethical, agreed, but so are the people who thought up bubble packs.

Okay, so I had a problem and I didn't solve it. All of the above is my oblique way of coming to grips with it. I hem and haw, and jaw around it, but the problem continues to await solution a week later, while I remain in town. So today, another Saturday, I'm off to a different hardware store, in search of solutions. I have great hopes of finding a clerk with a sympathetic ear, one who will take my case in hand. I'll describe my situation to him and he'll listen attentively. Nobody will interrupt us with a question and the phone won't ring. He'll know just what I need and lead me straight to it. The cost will be less than I expected. I'll bat my eyes in happy disbelief.

Back at my lot on the river, the pieces will fit together the way they were meant to do. The result will be, in this instance, a happy electrical connection. Soon the juice will be flowing in the dark in the form of bright lights.

60

The word, research, literally means to search again. Not a bad idea. Most things would benefit from being looked at a little closer. It doesn't take much time and won't hurt much. What you see might be important.

The little vine maple's "spinner" that I mentioned earlier— well, I was wrong about it. It works differently from how I thought. I had the idea the seed was enclosed in a hard sack that extends between two wing-like supports. A less hurried examination would have disclosed but a single wing; if two are present, there is also a second seed sack. This makes the vine maple seedpod a monoplane. One wing it has to carry the seed the necessary distance. But one wing is incapable of true flight. Instead, it produces a downward, skittering gyration, carrying the pod back and forth in the air, and maybe on a skewed course. But a wind comes along, and it goes farther. You might say the pod is dependent on a breeze for its locomotion.

Often two seedpods are found loosely attached and traveling together, like old maid schoolteachers. Then they achieve a true aerodynamic effect. And sometimes a third spinner is joined with them, and all three are bonded at the center. What you have here is a three-bladed propeller. The tri-bladed spinner functions best in the horizontal mode, I've noticed. Much like a helicopter, the blades revolve and lower the seed pod gently to the ground. Often the softest of breezes impresses it from behind, causing it to act like a rotor blade. I don't know what the need is for all this gentleness. If the seed descends harder, it may speed up the time necessary for it to burst and get on with its germination.

How efficient the little spinner is, how well designed for its job. In its own right, it is a pretty thing. Very little in nature can be improved upon. The so-called wing is beautiful, intricate. Paired, they behave much like the veined flight of damsel and dragon flies. The same architect is at work. Nice job, I say.

Only a few of these seeds will ever produce a tree. It is the process of natural selection. Often these are the same ones that have traveled the greatest distance. The wind and aerodynamic design permit them to extend their range. Far away, they settle to the ground, heat, swell, burst, begin life. The unsuccessful provide food for birds and critters that eat seeds; the rest mulch into the soil and add to its nutrients.

There are spinners, too, on the Japanese maple in the backyard of our home in town. The tree's final act of the season is to produce and distribute these. Right now its leaves are undergoing metamorphosis from green to wine-brown. They will cling heartily to their boughs long after the other trees are bare. Only the unfamiliar oaks hold them as long. Both shed in mid-winter. The spinners remain until January or February, long past the last leaves. Then, with spring rushing on, the days lengthening out once more, the spinners are released and start their random long journeys.

We are overdue for a cold winter. The past few years have been mild. I remember seeing snow along the bough of the Japanese maple and the spinners firm and intact. Scientists claim that many things—insects, seeds, even small animals—are hardiest following a cold winter. This may be so, but I suspect there is much attrition and it is the survivors we notice. The others return to the soil, forgotten, unobserved.

61

Old hardware store's got me in its grip again. I spent about $16 yesterday, purchasing the last of the electrical equipment for my power-pole service and enjoyed it greatly, since now I know more about this stuff than most clerks. I'm not bragging, for the ones I've encountered understand very little, or else they are keeping it to themselves.

At each store, there is a pecking order, and the clerks show deference to one—it is almost always a he, but I know of one or two shes. At Ernst Hardware in University Village there is an old man who appears to know more than the others all put together. Let's call him Sam. Sam has a professional aura. He moves slowly because of age, but accomplishes a great deal in a few deft strokes. In most stores, Sam is the manager.

Today I seek out this particular store's Sam. In the back of his mind is a lifetime's accumulation of data, especially electrical; I want to tap it. What Sam doesn't know isn't worth knowing. He doesn't volunteer a whole lot, however. Most times you have to drag the information out of him. If he likes you, it comes forth more readily. If he doesn't, it's tough luck, Jack. Sam likes people kissing up to him, so long as it isn't done wantonly. Like a good student, you have to strike just the right degree of obsequiousness.

The store's Sam is always busy. I have to wait my turn. No matter; it's fun scurrying round the store like a squirrel, sorting through bins of screws and nuts and washers, trying to find the ones that will do the job. If I learn something, it's time well spent. Sometimes I find the answer for myself and don't need Sam.

Yesterday I came across an odd little item in the package that was included with my trailer electrical service, and thought it was a grounding rod clamp. I already had something much like it. It turned out that the other was the true grounding rod clamp, for it had a slot with a screw fastener for the solid copper wire (very bright and pretty) that runs down the pole and fastens to the ground. I knew it was the right item because nothing else would fit into the slot, where there were galvanized teeth to bite down and hold the thick wire in place.

What, then, was this similar thing? Why give a man two objects that will do the job, if only one is required? If not a grounding rod clamp, what could it be? There is a kind of desperate logic that can be called on, when things get most black. It never deserts us, though it sometimes gets obscured with details and trivia. I decided to try to contact it. I sat down in my aluminum lawn chair, as the rain sifted down, and listened to my battery-powered radio play (I kid you not) Handle's *Water Music*. I meditated on the possible uses of this clamp-like thing. Finally, it dawned on me. It was threaded like the plugs on my electrical receptacle box. These permit various cables to be run in and out of the box, and the connections to remain dry, out of the weather. But there was a difference. In the difference might be a clue to its intended use.

Suddenly I understood. It was for the *top* of the conduit box. The clamp was intended to encircle a flat cable and hold it down smoothly, making a water-tight connection. But I used round conduit, which was already enclosed in cable. I didn't need such a connector. I could safely discard it. It was included in the assembly package, just in case somebody needed it. One doesn't expect to find such thoughtfulness in the realm of electrical manufacturing.

How marvelous everything is, once you see the picture and envision how the parts go together. It is an ordered world, after all. I remembered that I had still to fasten the flat, gray, underground cable to the power pole, then to the four-by-four post set in the ground behind the trailer. So I stopped off at Arlington, where there is the oldest and largest hardware store in the world. If they don't have something, there probably isn't one. When its elderly owner dies, one of the big chains may buy it and hang its walls with bubble packs.

Arlington Hardware has oiled wooden floors. Looking down from the walls are heads of caribou, elk, sheep, goats, and moose shot by the owner when he was young. Today he is frail and infirm, hunchbacked with illness and age, capable of shooting nothing. He is this store's Sam, clearly. Though supposedly retired, he can't keep away from the store he founded, where he has spent the bulk of his life. And he is surrounded by satellite Sams. You must already know a lot to clerk under his tutelage.

I catch his eye. He stops and waits for me to walk over to him, which is easier than for him to move. It is a small price to pay for tapping into what he knows. I ask about some staples—actually, tough metal cleats with which to fasten my flat cable to pole and post. He leads me to the bin where they are stored, in cardboard boxes, not plastic. I'd have spent fifteen minutes trying to find them.

"Six be enough?" he asks, when I specify the number I am seeking. "Have to break open a box." But he says this as though it is no great matter that he breaks open boxes routinely for uncertain people like me. The staples are large. In fact, I've never seen such big ones. What else can they be used for, I wonder, besides fastening cable or wire to poles? In the city, you either buy an entire box or you go without. You end up with 94 leftover staples so big you'll never find another use for them in your lifetime.

"I'll take ten," I say impulsively.

"Ten," he says, and counts them out on the counter top. One, two, three. . . . It takes a minute to complete the count. "Fifteen cents," he announces.

I hadn't realized that fifteen cents would buy anything today.

I continue on to the river. Finishing the wiring easily, with the right fasteners, I find a light rain is falling. The alders are catching the drops and slowing their descent; above them, it is raining harder. I have yet to bury the cable, before the job is done. This will be hard work, for I haven't dug the trench yet. The ground is rocky and laced with alder roots which rise to just under the surface.

The cable is supposed to be buried eighteen inches beneath the surface, but who's counting? The state requires an inspection, but I don't expect the inspector to dig down to measure the depth. The reasons is to protect the cable from later digging accidents. But it is tough stuff, heavily shielded with plastic. You'd have to swing an ax hard, several times, to sever it intentionally. So I cheat a little in its depth, here and there, because of the alder roots. I chop some of them away and, in other instances, worm the cable between them. Over all, the trench is about a foot to fifteen inches deep. Good enough.

The rain drips through the alders and dampens my shirt. My hands and arms ache from shovel and ax. I have a deep need to straighten my back and never bend over ever again. I want to fish, but am too weary. I doubt whether I can lift my arms high enough to cast. So I head for home through a gathering dusk.

Twilight is when the last visible brightness takes a hike. I reflect on what a marvel electricity is. I've always taken it for granted. Here—if I'm fortunate—I will soon have lights to banish the dark.

62

Steady hard rains running along the new raingutters in town and down the spouts. They began yesterday, but did not descend in earnest until midnight, at which time a steady downpour arrived. It is now mid-afternoon and still raining steadily. The river will rise, discolor rapidly, and go out, for just how long it is impossible to say.

These hard rains are welcome, the happy sign of autumn fast approaching, and we Pacific Northwesterners look forward to them each year, for they bring a peculiar feeling of renewal. Autumn is not entirely a time for dying, and in the seeds and spores abundant now, along with the arrival of the salmon, are signs of rebirth. That time is admittedly a long while off, but the prolonged winter's hibernation and period of gestation are essential to it.

If the seasons and cycles continue, it is less significant that we, as individuals, are no longer around to view and respond to them. The fact that they operate quite independent of us—with all our delusions of self-importance—ought to be humbling and bring us down a peg. One's own death in due course ought not be too chilling a fact—once one gets used to the idea of no longer being around to see what is going on.

63

Consider the dogwood. It is one of my favorite trees, yet I know little about it. I decide to consult a reference book. It tells me that the "dog" in it has nothing to do with canines (not even its "bark"), but is a corruption of the word "dag," from dagger, signifying a sort of spike, which was fashioned from the meaty center of a limb lopped off in an irregular angle, as with an ax's glancing blow. Be this as it may, the tree has a singular beauty, especially in spring, when it puts out many flowers, green at first, then whitening as its season comes on. The flower has a seedy core, with many tiny facets, like the lenses on the eye of a house fly. These generally go unobserved because attention is riveted by the attractiveness of the white bracts, which number four to six per flower.

Some dogwoods (*Cornus nuttallii*, the Pacific dogwood, usually found as a tree, but will form itself as a shrub under certain conditions) bloom twice a year, a real surprise. There is one up the street in town which does so each year; it is presently in full bloom again. Those trees that do not provide an autumnal surprise remain deep green, but at the core of the old bloom from last April appears now its fruit. Bright scarlet peppercorns of varying size form on the surface of the old core and are a slender acorn shape, with an upper black center. The cluster consists of a center spot with a number of inward turning folds. The folds eventually open up, expanding outward, to let whatever is inside out.

I pried open an immature fruit, but could find inside only a waxy yellow substance. If there were any seeds, I did not locate them. I've read that about the only way new dogwoods get started is by birds eating the hard seeds, which are "cracked" by their digestive system. Then the broken seed is germinated in the dung wherever the birds congregate; thus preparation for the new growth is achieved.

The solitary dogwood we have up at the river Norma gave me as a present a couple of years ago and was bought at a nursery. It has made excellent growth this year, after an original period of accommodation during which nothing much happened and we thought the tree was dying. It was just busily establishing its root system.

64

One would think there is lots of time for rumination, while digging a ditch, but in actual practice there isn't much, one is so busy plotting and fuming against the constant frustration. Perhaps this is why few great thoughts have been attributed to ditch-diggers, in spite of Milton's theory about great minds at work in England's coal mines. But it was Hamlet, not the grave digger, that brooded on Yorick's skull. The guy with the shovel (my brother) was too busy removing the buried rocks.

My ditch for the underground wiring must be at least eighteen inches deep, according to the State electrical code. Earlier, I had scraped out a line a foot or so deep, and thought it would do, since who would know but me? The State electrical inspector informed me over the phone this morning that I must deepen it, the bastard. And so, armed with five-foot spade and ax (for the alder roots), I set out to dig it again. It must be right before the inspector will sign my permit and the power be turned on by Snohomish Country PUD. I only fooled myself.

On a cool day, one hour into the job, I had dug a trench six feet long. I felt fresh, strong. A bit later I was wringing wet and sweat dripped from my brow into my eyes and stung them. I was too hot to stop and eat, too tired to continue what seemed to be an endless task. And I was hand-sore and blistered. The big problem was the alder roots. A few inches down into the earth, my shovel refused to budge. I used the point of the shovel to scrape away hardpan until I could view the obstruction. At first I tried chopping away the root with the shovel's point. This worked fine for the tiny roots, but most were thick. It took the ax for those, and many times the blade struck a stone and produced a brilliant spark.

The low level at which the work was conducted bent me over and tired me quickly. This is called "stoop labor." Frequently I had to straighten up and mop off my face. My back ached. It hurt while I was bent over, but it was worse when I stood up straight.

Suddenly I was through the roots and into some easy dirt. It was loam or sand. The work sped along, with few and only hairlike roots to impede my progress. The gravel thinned to no more than three inches deep and I was soon knifing into brown soil that in another few inches took on a clayish characteristic, while still retaining its brown color. It did not crumble but chipped away nicely, so that the sides did not slough in and I could shape the ditch.

I worked hard and the ditch moved rapidly ahead. At the halfway point I stopped and took a quick walk around the perimeter of my property in order to cool down and catch whatever breeze I could find. Then I ate lunch. The remaining digging distance no longer seemed oppressive, and I was anxious to conquer it, though I could see problems toward the end of the line. This proved true when I neared the trailer and the alders roots became considerable again.

The ditch took me three hours to dig. I strung the cable along the bottom and, stepping low into the ditch, trod on it hard. How I longed to fill it back up, and be done with it. I refrained. If I closed it up, and the inspector didn't like my work, he would require me to dig it up again.

As a reward, I let myself go fishing for the last four hours of the day. I'd like to report that my reward was a steelhead. But all I caught was a large whitefish, which got snagged in the side and came in spinning like a herring bait cut for salmon. I kept it for the cat.

65

It was a little hard getting out of bed, this morning, because of stiffness, especially in my upper arms. Also, my knee is worse from pushing on the shovel. Two blisters on my left hand, a small one on my right, comprise the total damage.

Twenty-five years ago I did pole-line construction for the Army Signal Corps in Alaska, and during my first few days on the new job I thought I was going to die. Instead, I thrived. I started going to bed about ten o'clock at night and eating enormous meals. Not only did I survive but I prospered. Could I do it again, at 47? Probably, if I needed to badly enough. But thankfully I don't. Such thoughts comfort me this morning, as I lie in a hot tub, soaking away the miseries and letting my muscles ease back to normal.

66

My hardware store mania continues, though slightly abated. The privately owned hardware store is becoming an anachronism. The big chains have taken over, and the smaller independent stores are allying to meet the formidable competition. Even so, many will fail. When one does, often an ethnic restaurant moves into the vacancy.

One independent chain of self-owned stores is True Value, which pools its advertising and promotions, and much of its buying. There is one at the edge of my extended neighborhood in the Wedgewood District of Seattle. It is about two miles away from my house and is notable for having a highly personalized touch, with the owner behind the counter taking a long time with each customer—as much as the customer thinks he needs.

In the window of this store sits an old-fashioned water pump—the kind you prime with a ladle from a bucket, then draw down hard on the handle, before it will pop and gurgle and belch forth the first cup of water, with a heavy sigh. When you do it right, you can hear the water coming, a long ways off. I remember such a pump from my childhood, when we visited my maternal grandmother in Tecumseh, Michigan. The act of drawing water was mysterious and awesome.

The price of the black enameled cast-iron water pump at True-Value was unreadable from outside. It is how they lure you in. I bit and went through the door, circling the cashier counter and heading for the window, where the price tag could be read. Is $26.99 a lot of money? I have no way of telling. If it will fetch you water, it is worth plenty.

"We sell a lot of these," said the saleswoman behind the counter. Oh? Who buys water pumps today? What are they used for? Surely not to pump water? Maybe they are conversation pieces. Or they could serve as small planters. Here in the city everybody has piped water. It is chlorinated and fluoridated. For such a pump I would need pipe to bring the water up from the river. It would not be potable, of course, but I could boil it for dishwater and also water the shrubs and flowers.

I waited my turn to ask the manager about the pump and its prospective uses. He was stocking a shelf and seemed glad to stop.

He took me over to the wall and showed me a coil of black plastic pipe. It costs 20 cents a foot. To pump river water 100 feet would cost me an additional $20. He could let me have it for $16, he told me. Either price was worth it. Or I could use garden hose, he said. Really? What would 100 feet of garden hose cost? About $7.50, he said, though it comes in 50-foot sections, and would have to be joined at the center with a coupler. The coupler doesn't cost much.

The pump and the hose are not really needed. We bring our drinking water from town in a jug. Chlorinated, it keeps. Our wash water we lug in a pail from the river. Although it is heavy, fetching water in a pail—as Jack and Jill did—is an enjoyable act, except when it is raining. So we will probably pass on the pump. Would our life be any richer owning one? I doubt it. All the same, my heart cries out to have one. Something that pretty does not have to be useful.

67

The landscape has opened up some. I find myself able to see for long distances, a discovery that arrives as a surprise and may at first be mistaken for sharpened vision. Also, the air is bright. The carpet of leaves is being steadily added to by all the trees of the woods.

A week or more of rain, with the afternoon temperatures nudging up to 70 degrees, then backing off to the mid-60s. This is precisely the weather that Pacific Northwesterners are known to love.

The rains have turned my new dirt road into a mucky sea. We do not drive on it and use the old, heavily graveled exit from the old lot, which has regenerated with soft grasses and buttercups and false Solomon seal. If I drive it too often, though, it will turn to mush.

I saw Burger (pronounced Ber-jer) Bryson standing in front of his house on my way up to fish Fortson and hit the brakes. I promptly reversed the car and headed back, but he had gone inside. I found him at his kitchen table, eating lunch. He is the man who did my backhoeing for me in the past. I asked him how much a load of gravel might cost.

"That depends," he replied laconically—his usual way. "I've got two trucks. One is twenty, the other thirty."

"Is that cubic yards?" I asked.

"Twenty dollars and thirty dollars," he explained.

It seemed reasonable enough and we agreed to get together to look over the site and see how much I needed, after he returned from a week's vacation and the land has dried out enough to bear the truck's weight.

Summer and Indian summer can't be past, so soon? I don't want to believe it. The weatherman on FM says a series of bad weather fronts is on its way. Thus the drought is over. The end of the series of storms is nowhere in sight.

68

I must have my morning paper, be it country or city. In the Pacific Northwest, it is the *Seattle Post-Intelligencer*, a good newspaper, though I prefer the *San Francisco Chronicle* or, especially on Sunday, the *Los Angeles Times*. The *Seattle P-I* is a good read, and I miss it when I don't have it, even though it takes a big bite out of my morning.

Now, the other Seattle paper, *The Times*, is thick and dull, and I can easily dispense with huge sections of it—perhaps the whole thing—and not feel I have missed much. It is Norma's paper, and she insists on it, though I've noticed that she never reads it as thoroughly as I. (Often I give her an infuriating test on how much she's read of it, before suggesting we cancel our subscription.) I resent its bulky tyranny and the added cost.

Sometimes I think a perfect day would be to awaken, eat breakfast, have my coffee, and have no newspaper to read. But I don't really mean it. In fact, up at the river, I drive three miles (Teale and Thoreau would have walked) to the Oso General Store and buy the *P-I*. And there is hell to pay, if they are sold out.

69

The National Electrical Code is an obscure document whose mysteries are known to only a few; still, its provisions affect our lives in many ways, especially when one attempts to do one's own wiring. Then he is quickly initiated into its mysteries. I am beginning to learn a smidgen of its contents out of necessity. I learn most things at half the speed as others, and with great difficulty and pain.

Apropos of this: I returned to the river to find a note saying that my wiring had failed on four counts. Not only must these be immediately corrected, but I can't fill in the damn ditch until they are.

70

So it's off to the neighborhood hardware store again, Rocinante, on another mad tilt at windmills; namely, passing my electrical test.

How gullible I am. I will believe anything anybody in a position of authority tells me I need, and—what is worse— buy it. Today I purchased (1) ten feet of rigid PVC conduit; (2) five feet of armored cable for my grounding wire, for I've learned I may use flexible insulated #10 wire in place of the thick copper bar some nefarious clerk sold me earlier, provided I first put it in conduit, (3) a host of small assorted parts, such as S-fuses and their adapters, for once again I was misinformed, and sold the wrong things, it being illegal (according to the Code) to have installed anything else for the past 15 years.

A hardware store dolt blithely sold me old-fashioned 30 amp fuses—when 15 amp S-type ones were required by Code, for safety's sake. Did he know? Was it a joke on me? Did he want me to fail or, worse, burn myself up? Now, now, no point in getting paranoid.

This stuff cost plenty. And the old stuff was not returnable.

71

The wiring nightmare goes on, leaving little time to write. After much frustration yesterday, and the day before, I decided I needed to go fishing badly, and drove to Fortson, in deep despair. The river rewarded me with an 11-pound acrobatic steelhead, which I released gratefully.

I am such a klutz. While doing my wiring job, and then redoing it, I dropped two machine screws into the loose dirt of the ditch. One was off a duplex electrical outlet—no great loss. My screw-box screw fit it but did not cinch down tightly, making the weatherproof receptacle box prone to leak. My sense of craftsmanship, highly imperfect, sent me to the store to search for the proper screw. I found it. No big deal.

The second lost screw was important. It was the special bonding screw for my neutral strap. (Notice how I bandy these new words about, fresh from the guidebook, just the way a licensed electrical contractor would.) But the replacement screw for the strap doesn't fit, so I must return to town tomorrow and buy another one and make yet one more trip back to the river.

Besides being a natural goofup, I have a close-up vision problem, and bifocals is not the answer. Until I can see at mid-distance, I will keep dropping and losing screws, and other such tiny implements necessary for life on this planet.

72

A good book on the subject of electrical installation is H. P. Tichter's *Wiring Simplified, New 30th Edition,* published a long while back for $1.00. Much of it holds true. Practically a throw-away price. It appears to be an annual publication of Park Publishing in Minneapolis, for what it's worth. It is worth a lot.

I found a replacement screw for locking down the strap at the store that sold me the service box. It cost 25 cents. Okay, so that was a bit high, but I don't mind, at this point in my journey. I would have paid $5 to be rid of the problem for good. I did not drop the screw in the ditch this time, I am happy to report, and it fit perfectly. I am properly connected to ground. Now I can notify the

State Inspector and wait on pins and needles for him to make his second, and I hope final, visit to my site.

Assuming that I pass his inspection—and there is no good reason to think I will, even after all this time and fixing these glitches—the Snohomish County PUD will be notified by phone by the State and their man will come out to my property, climb the pole, make a connection, and the juice will begin to flow. Lo, there will be light. O God, I hope so.

73

There are fish in the river now, after a dearth of them during spring and summer. What an odd year it has been. The steelhead are almost entirely in the upper river, in the Fortson area, and are big, strong fish that run 8-12 pounds. Nine or ten pounds is a good average. The males are highly colored, almost as dark as October and November fish, with a wide rainbow stripe down their sides, green backs, lots of spots, and muddy-colored flanks with creamy bellies. But they are vigorous fish, and the good ones (like the one I got Monday night) will jump, time after time, leaving the water frothed each time.

Meanwhile, the first dead spawned-out Chinooks are showing up along the edge of the beaches. I saw my first one at Boulder Creek yesterday. A trout fisherman was dancing around in the long diagonal riffle we cross to reach a narrow undistinguished run which sometimes yields a fish; I think he was chasing the huge fish around on their spawning beds. Afterwards, he began casting to them, attempting to snag them. If he ever was successful, they would break him off quickly. I suspect he was out for searun cutthroat and became fascinated by the big fish on their redds and wanted to come into contact with one, whatever way necessary.

74

Wonder of wonders, I passed my electrical inspection, on the second try. This calls for a drink. I feel as if it were my Ph.D. exams. Inspector Jack Smith (who, by the way, cannot spell a variety of simple words used in his trade, such as "neutral" and "rise"), said I did "a good job." Elation and great satisfaction. I feel like a little dog, patted on the head. There shall be a party tonight, albeit a small one, since I am up at the river alone.

75

How still the woods are on a mild autumn afternoon, with low valley fog hanging in the pockets formed between the hills. The leaves are all pale green and gold, with some scarlet vine maples sprinkled in among them, and the broadleaf maples dark brown and crumpled looking. The few last leaves cling to the alders, and when I observe them in rows against the dark evergreens hillside along Eby Hill, at Cicero, they look surprisingly like they did when newly emergent in spring.

At home the grass is growing fiercely. And the slugs have returned and are attacking the tomatoes that have sagged to the ground because of their weight. Rain causes the skin of the tomatoes to split, and we have lost many of them already. It is a field day for slugs.

76

What a splendid day for going to the country! The temperature this morning is about five degrees cooler than usual, putting it in the mid-50s. All the way to the river there was cold sunshine and, off in the hills to the East, a tumultuous gray cloud mass.

The Oso Fair began at ten o'clock. We joined the event-in-progress after lunch. It turned out to be a flea-market, full of people's castoffs—a halfway house to the garbage dump. We found nothing to buy, having a basement at home jammed with much the same kind of stuff.

At such community bazaars such as this one, there is a strong suspicion that all the good stuff was snapped up by, or perhaps swapped with, the people in charge of the fair. Ah, but there was hot, fresh corn on the cob, 25 cents an ear, with nothing more for all the salt, pepper, and butter you want. Brownies. Macaroni salad galore. Cookies and cakes.

As I waited for Norma to arrive, I pawed through the $1.29, take-your-pick tool bin. The stuff was mostly from Taiwan, sealed in a tough plastic wrap. There were three attachments for a 1/4-inch drill that enables you to polish, grind, and sharpen, which greatly appealed to me, but my drill is 3/8-inch. Plastic insulated handles that you must soak first in hot water to soften enough to slide on your pliers for a custom fit; then they will stay on forever. Two-way calipers, which are cheap locking pliers, with teeth like a dog salmon; a huge C-clamp; a U-clamp, also large; a nifty screw driver with a light in the handle to test electrical circuits (handy, now that I am a journeyman electrician) good up to 500 volts, which ought to be enough for anybody; it can also be used as an ordinary screwdriver. A set of open-ended wrenches. A plastic handle that claims to fit "all" files, so you can bear down on it and not chew your fingers to the bone. A sandpaper bar, with replaceable sanding strips, both fine and coarse. And a rasp. That's about it.

Norma and I returned to the lot, each armed with a five-foot spade, and together filled up the ditch containing the underground cable. It didn't take long, but was heavy work. It's the kind of thing she does so well. Then we tamped down the soil until the ghost of the ditch disappeared into what appeared to be a fresh path.

A hard rain moved in at the completion of the day. We holed up inside the little trailer, while Norma bent over the three-burner propane stove, and pretty soon I was being called to an excellent spaghetti dinner.

Ah, roughing it.

77

These cool gray days return me to my passion, photography. Bright sun is the antithesis of black-and-white photos, through color photographers do their best work during the first two, and last two, hours of a sunny day, when the rays are at a warm slant.

Last night there was a huge late-rising autumn moon. It began as golden orange, paling and shrinking as it rose and was absorbed into a darkening sky. It made me long for a color camera, tripod, and the cable release needed to get the long exposure that would capture it, but the car was moving and the traffic was heavy. There's always some alibi.

This month I guest edited *Northwest Photography*, a small local tabloid, with a circulation of about two thousand. I wrote the lead article on Charles Harbutt and previewed 37 of his prints at the Yuen Lui Gallery. A phone call today told me the "flats" are ready to be viewed, after which the publication will be run on a Webb Press. The act of laying it out in dummy form last Thursday was enjoyable and reminded me of my happy days editing *Trend* magazine.

Four times a year I laid it out, and chose and cropped all the photos for the issue and sized them. Again I found myself happily whistling away, and chuckling to myself, as I measured column lengths with a pica "pole," selected type for heads, and snipped galleys with the special long scissors used solely for this.

78

It has long been my belief that Henry Miller should have been given the Nobel Prize for Literature long before that young upstart, Saul Bellow. This apropos to my being given a copy of the Penguin edition of *The Colossus of Maroussi*. It is marked "not to be sold in Canada or the USA."

I thought I had read most of Miller, but had never heard of this joyous book.

79

For reasons that escape me, I sleep fitfully my first night back at the river. I wake up often, but go back to sleep quickly, and end up well rested, after a normal length of time abed. Perhaps it is a way of transitioning from one life style to another, one so different.

After that first night in the country, I sleep just fine. I am snug in the place where I feel I belong, comfortable in the sack, the woodsy side of my personality taking over.

Sleeping down by the river, as I have this year, provides broken sleep. Do I listen for threats approaching? And placing my mattresses and ancient springs a few yards from the river may not be the best place. Until dawn my sleep is light. The river's purl is hushed because of extreme low water. If a dry leaf falls to the stones, I know it. I recognize it as non-threatening, on a primitive level, and dismiss it.

I awake at two, at three, at five, then generally pass through the early morning hours in a trance until eight or nine, when I wake in a stupor, and have to fight my way out of my bag, hot and sweaty. I gather up the "necessaries" that have seen me through the night and stumble up the steep trail to the trailer, where I drink my juice and fry my eggs and make my toast on the toaster Norma manufactured for me out of a tin can and love. It browns the bread just right.

80

Today I write with a pen for a change, taking care how I form the words so that I won't have to scratch them out a moment later, since one can't erase pen strokes. This journal entry may take an hour, it may take two.

Afterwards, I am thinking of hiking into Boulder Creek and traversing the long riffle that leads downstream to uncharted territory, at least for me. The crossing changes annually, and I have not attempted it yet this summer. Of course I will take a fishing rod along.

81

The phrase "to pay attention" interests me. It is used idiomatically, often in a thoughtless way. In another language, one might say "to make or to do" attention. Or it could be reflexive. "To make or do one's self to pay attention."

The idea of paying attention connotes a debt of obligation, on the one hand, and, on the other, a giving out of something one holds dear, as in paying out money. Does one lessen one's (financial) resources by paying (out) one's attention? Perhaps. In other cases, paying attention will bring in money, as with the stock market. Yet in most cases paying attention distracts one from the work at hand and brings in neither bread or money. Hence, to pay attention may belong to the nonproductive part of life, the portion of the world assigned to art.

One must pay attention to art, or else. Or else it'll slip by, happening in its own context, and no one will notice it. That would be a shame. Music will turn into background noise, or a way of averting silence. (Silence may distract us simply because it is the absence of sound, when we are used to having our ears filled with constant commotion.) Painting and photography will become part of the visual blur that crosses our vision. And so forth.

To pay attention is hard work, tough dues to pay. It is, in Emerson's words, "man thinking." Now, thinking isn't easy. (If it is *easy* you want, turn on the tube.) To pay attention requires a supreme act of will to vanquish competitive sensory impressions and takes more self-discipline, more outright pain, than most of us can muster, at least for long. Such moments are rare, unless they are cultivated like a garden.

To look and not to see; to listen and not to hear. These axioms hint at what we do instead of paying (the debt of) attention, which we "owe." To whom? We owe it to life. Most of the time I do not truly see. As much as I love photography, I rarely am able to spend the time necessary—put out the attention required—to get within a picture and travel around inside it long enough to learn what is going on there: the details, the richness. A pity, for I miss what is important. Instead, I hurry along, anxious for the next distraction to take me off in some new tired direction.

82

The river is as near to flood as I've ever seen it in September and is full of frothy brown water. One and two-thirds inches of rain fell yesterday—a record for this time of year, in such a short period. It is still descending in buckets full. The freeway was awash and the heavy Friday afternoon traffic forced to inch along with its headlights on. The river is in danger of minor flooding. This means water will get into the trees, undulate the flood plain, raise the water table to surface level at our enclave, but do no serious damage. It will not break over dikes and bury in water any land that is not already well used to it.

I am worried about a certain ancient alder of ours that overhangs the river on the new property. We've been watching it closely for several years because what happens upstream directly effects what happens down. During one of the early winter floods in a recent year, the river took away a chunk of our riverbank. It was just above where I sleep on the beach in low water.

The corner of bank simply disappeared after a high water, and the alder began to list disturbingly out over the water. Since then it has increased its angle. The more I study it, the worse the angle appears to have grown.

The tree is old, huge, gnarled, and probably rotten at the center, which means it is slowly dying. Aside from these things, it is perfectly healthy. A tree often dies by degrees, one element at a time. The collapse of the root system may have something to do with its death, for the increased angle of repose breaks off some roots and deprives the others of nutrients. My old tree may be starving to death, too.

Once we had a vine maple that hung too low over the river trail, so we were always walking through its branches and leaves or else bumping our heads on one bough or another. Its limbs spread low and wide, and the route along the river was narrow and hard to transverse, so I tied back its main trunk with some old burlap sacking. It helped clear the path. But after a couple of years, the tree died. It died in protest for my not letting it follow its natural course. This taught me a lesson. It surprised me, that a tree would die because it was treated badly. I won't make the same mistake again.

Auxiliary limbs of alders die all the time and fall to the ground. It makes room for new growth on higher branches. We find the deadfalls on the ground, after each winter storm, and have to remove them before we can drive across our road. They supply us with much of our annual firewood.

Some of our biggest alders have healthy limbs all the way up their trunks, which are thick, while other trees, quite slender, have lost their branches, clear to the top. Suddenly a tree—one growing straight and tall and healthy, uncrowded—will up and die on me. Why? What is the rule that governs this behavior? We do not notice the tree withering until spring of the next year, when we discover that it has not put out leaves like its neighbors. Such a tree is usually two to three inches in diameter, and indistinguishable from the rest.

The ancient overhanging alder by the river is going to topple over soon, I suspect. We will lose it, plus another chunk of bank. There is not much we can do about it. If I intercede and fell it with a rented chainsaw, four-fifths of its length will fall in the river, and we will lose it.

Instead, I shall watch it and learn something about natural processes. If the flood doesn't claim the tree, this winter, it will live on, fighting gravity and hydraulic forces from the river. I shall cheer for it from the sidelines. A brush pile directly upstream, which I've neglected all summer, may shelter it from the current, and its huge exposed root system may have enough tensile strength to bind it to the bank. There are signs that a new brush pile may be forming at the base of the tree itself, which would help to protect it further.

To wish things to remain in a steady state is romantic and unrealistic. Besides, they won't.

83

The Snohomish County PUD has hooked up my electricity, and I am blessed with light. They climbed to the top of my power pole and made the connection with the wires I provided for them. I've had the deep satisfaction of plugging in the external plug to the trailer and seeing my lights come on for the first time. Was the experience extraordinary, or ordinary? I can't say that the lights burned any brighter as the result of my labors and the frustrations overcome. Still it was satisfying. Any special brightness I thought I saw might simply be the contrast produced by the dark and stormy day.

84

Today the old watch died and I replaced it immediately with one from the nearest drugstore. Timex again. The old one had lasted about five years, which is par for a watch costing less than $20. That's four bucks per year to know something close to the correct time.

The watch is self-winding, the motion of my arm (however sedentary) being enough to keep it going. It is a little like a perpetual motion machine, or else I am. The watch tells me the month and the day of the week, which is nice to know, for I often forget them. And now I have a friendly reminder, not to say a nag.

It occurs to me that a short, narrow, and probably quite boring history could be written from the standpoint of all the watches a man has owned in his lifetime. To write about it is risky. The big danger is of losing your audience. Hello, goodbye.

My new watch shows me the days of the month by number and the names of the day of the week. At the end of certain short months, I must advance the number of the day. The start of February is the worst time, for there is the danger of advancing the date too far. If you advance the date one number too many, you must push it ahead, day by day, for the full month, for there is no backing up with a watch like mine. And to turn the hands around sixty revolutions is a nightmare.

The end of daylight-savings time is coming, which I dread, for then watch and I will have to return to normal time. The effort is so great, it hardly seems worth it.

85

I awake deep in a litter of leaves to a pale pink dawn, the river purling beside me. The sky portends a warm, pleasant day, with clouds moving in by mid-day and rain probably by nightfall. This is autumn.

Spiders have been busy all night long. Fall hurries them. Their webs festoon the paths, dripping dew in the low-angled morning light whenever a vibration shakes the ground. Full of fried eggs, toast, and coffee, I sit listening to a Bartok string quartet, then one by Mozart played on my tape machine. The Mozart is very sad and dissonant for his time, but lovely. Meanwhile, the spiders rebuild the webs I damaged earlier by going to the outhouse.

86

Each year about this time come the fall and winter catalogs from the fishing and hunting stores, announcing that Christmas is not far off. The catalogs provide much enjoyable reading. The same companies issue spring and summer catalogs, which are fun, too. They indicate that the trout season stretches ahead. The fall catalogs are slanted towards hunting, which is not for me. Shotguns, bows and arrows, hunting rifles and scopes cause me to fan the pages. The sections that deal with clothing and novelties for the holiday seasons are more interesting, and my eyes linger there.

Catalogs are designed for browsing and to dream over. You need not buy anything. They should not be taken seriously. Their relationship to real life is like pictures of movie stars. Better clothe yourself in a dream, or in a poem, than expect catalog ware to keep you warm and dry—which is what is needed, these days.

87

Outside our house in the city stand three tall birch trees. They are not indigenous to the Pacific Northwest. We planted them as pups. They are now are about twenty-five feet tall and measure five or six inches in diameter at breast height, which is how you measure trees. They are mature, at last, for their bark is scaling, which is a sure sign. Sometimes large, thin, curled pieces of parchment appear on the lawn, with telltale horizontal striations.

They are the type of tree that Indians in the American East made canoes out of. The bark is heavier and thicker than I would expect; a canoe made out of it would not be light in weight, but why I should expect it to be? An Indian's canoe is at the mercy of the wind and waves. A storm would dash a light one to pieces. Out here in the West, Indians build them out of cedar. They are indestructible to everything but fire.

What interests me about my birches is how rapidly they are dropping their leaves. It seems early. I decide to describe the color of the leaves, but can't, precisely. I would say they were a pale golden yellow, with a touch of brown stirred in, to create a patina, or else a transparent undercoat, very hard to detect, over which the warm yellow is thinly applied. Now you try.

A carpet of leaves appears at the base of the birches, which will grow until it is several inches deep. All the leaves will be gone by Halloween. This is a full month away. The de-leafing process is barely started. I look forward to having them gone. Until then, I must rake them once or twice a week, depending on how fastidious I want to be, or to be known as being.

We don't burn leaves at the curb, here in the Pacific Northwest. That is a Mid-West practice, or used to be, until smog became too much. I like the old-fashioned burning smell, at least in small doses. Here, they go into plastic garbage bags and await the truck pickup on Thursday morning, for which you must pay extra. Or else—as we often do—mulch them into flowerbeds.

The raking up of the birch leaves is hard work. The leaves are made sodden with rain, and the tines of the rake skate over them, or else get trapped in the mass, each time I make a pass at them. But their golden sight on the lawn is cheerful on a leaden day. When they are finally gone, the last bit of color will have been subtracted from the day, the season, the year.

88

Women have either bleached or dyed their hair darker for centuries, and nobody has paid it much heed. Now that they have had their revolution and won many worthy gains in the areas of personal choice, employment, salary, etc., what are we poor males to do but emulate them? All of which is preamble and apology for the following: Today I dyed my hair and beard, which had grown pretty gray. Blame it on the women's movement, not on my particular vanity. Oh yeah.

Cleopatra did not put up with graying hair, you can bet, nor did Elizabeth Taylor, who played her in the movie. Not unless either of them believed gray hair fashionable and actively sought it. Nor will other women. So why should we aging, graying males tolerate gray on our head or chin? Why do I feel defensive, then? Because the world expects women to dye and men not to. It is how we were reared. Residual guilt ensues. But I can still treat it as a joke.

And the result? A much darker beard, but one in which some of the gray remains, albeit thinly disguised. Not bad. The balance between light and dark is about right, I'd say, for a vain-glorious man nearing his fiftieth birthday. One side of my mind says that it was the right thing to do, under the conditions. The other side says it is a shameful activity for any man or woman to engage in. Whatever kidding I receive—especially from my son—I deserve. I fear his ruthless gaze.

Looked at another way, I have struck a huge blow for men's liberation. If there ever evolves such an atrocity, I will be in its front ranks. A leader.

89

As counterpoint is the cornerstone of musical composition, so duality of vision inherent in all writing intended to be other than sheer reportage, or exposition, forms another important cornerstone, the one of pleasing balance. Thus in this journal, the movement between country and city is intended to serve as counterpoint, or as a classic pattern, the two elements providing a binocular vision and happy sound. I had not thought of it in precisely these terms until today, when it dawned on me. A form of dynamic tension will result, if I do it right, one not unlike that expressed in music, or in a dramatic dialogue with two voices played off against each other contrapuntally.

Artistically I have split my personality into halves, my city self and the countryman that I pretend to be, or also am, or am trying to be. Maybe that second self is more a "dude" or "gent." But I cannot imagine myself living comfortably with either persona long suppressed. Both are necessary to my physical and mental health. This attitude is slightly schizophrenic, I am aware. I'll admit it. At the same time, I recognize it as being healthy.

90

Yesterday, in the scant hour before dark, Norma and I took a stroll around our old neighborhood. We walked as though we were in the country, with a quick pace designed to cover rough ground.

It was a beautiful day. We walked North for two blocks to study from the street a brick house that was for sale and to speculate on its asking price. It was nicer than usual, for our old but well-maintained neighborhood. I asked Norma, "What do you think they want for it?" She said, "Oh, maybe a hundred and thirty thousand." I said I thought it might fetch five or ten thousand more. Real-estate prices have been increasing insanely for the past four years or so, all over the West; up until lately, they had been increasing only *neurotically*, one might say.

Out in front, the house still wore its For Sale sign. The yard was small, we agreed, but nicely maintained; the two-car garage was not of matching brick, but that's a small point, admittedly. In the front window was a pot of gold chrysanthemums from when the house first came on the market.

The neighborhood has undergone much change in the twelve years we have lived here. Originally there were numerous retired couples whose mortgages had been paid off. Gradually these people were dying off and their houses sold. In time, the houses of the elderly are purchased by young couples who have babies. These kids have a way of growing up fast. Pretty soon they are in high school. Our son will soon be starting college.

Many of the homes are single-storey, built in a style called "Seattle bungalow," with a half-daylight basement and no second level. They are usually constructed of cedar shake, which gives them a falsely modern look, but then again they are modern, for they are designed for living all on one floor, as are the majority of new homes. They date from the late teens and twenties of this century.

When we bought our house, one reason was so I could walk a mile to work, instead of driving and finding a parking problem. But I walked to the University infrequently, as it turned out.

Seattle remains a small town, in many ways, and if you live here, you can expect to find ties to some of your neighbors. You don't have to reach very far. People claim the city came of age during the 1962 Worlds Fair. That's not true; it simple grew bigger, but kept its easy manner which, though folksy, is not without charm.

People in our neighborhood are always talking about how little they paid for their houses—ten, fifteen, and even twenty years ago—and speculating about what the houses must be worth today. It is a friendly competition, and so is the continual chatter about it. Rumor says a "reasonably priced house" in our neighborhood will sell within three days of being put on the market. The prices we denizens paid for our homes were $10, 13, 16, and 19 thousand, respectively, some twenty-five years ago. The difference mainly is how many bedrooms and baths they have. It has been only in the past six years that prices have skyrocketed.

This is a modest area. It is not run down, and we take pride in our fresh paint and neat yards. A few Seattle neighborhoods of our vintage have deteriorated badly. Most have not. Their price keeps escalating. There is a saying, "You can't afford to buy the house you live in." True, true.

A day later we learn the asking price of the house up the street. It is not $130,000, which was Norma's guess. Nor is it $150,000 or $160,000. It is $184,000. And it was sold the day before yesterday, for just that amount.

91

The Cicero heron is not mute. Yesterday he gave me a royal bawling out. I was fishing the run above the railroad bridge, trying hard to be my usual quiet self, but my presence was enough to arouse in him a great squawk of indignation. He had been occupying himself inland, where I know of no standing water to intrigue him, when all of a sudden he took to the air, flying low overhead from stage right to left, all the while emitting the most horrendous noise, a sound halfway between a duck's loud quack and a hoarse, froglike croak, which rattled around deep in his voluminous gourd before issuing forth through that spear he calls a beak.

The heron never fails to impress me. I called him a he, but it might be female, for all I know. He swept away from my presence with a long, slow flap across the horizon, headed South, from whence he disappeared behind a massive screen of willows along a stretch of river so desolate and inaccessible that my eyes could not follow him. I looked downstream with longing. Often when departing, the heron leaves behind on the stones copious excrement, as if he dropped a small white bomb. Not today, however. His exit was discrete; he vanished over the trees as neatly as an airplane would.

92

My knee continues to bother me. However, there is never any immediate danger of it buckling and dunking me in mid-channel, as bad knees are known to do. I feel safe on it, in water and out. I guess I will have to learn to live with the swelling and pain that follows hard use. The swelling thickens the joint and reduces the agony. I come to depend on the swelling.

By lifting weights—I am up to ten pounds, raised 60 times on a rigid leg—the knee has grown very strong. But it seems peculiar to have it both strong and injured.

93

Cries far off of crow, kingfisher, woodpecker, and— at greater distance—a plaintive bird I can never get close enough to identify. Perhaps it is a loon, bittern, or the great blue heron, its voice muffled. But I suspect it is merely the ordinary crow, which has a variety of voices. Crows have greatly proliferated, in both country and city.

They are bold, predacious birds, and very smart. Usually I hear them screaming harsh alarms, but sometimes when they communicate among themselves, they speak more softly, with a wide range of sounds, each of which must mean something different, if you are a crow. I am not, so it remains a terrible din.

94

While I stand cutting up firewood, birdsong fills the air. It is a beautiful afternoon, the sun out, the temperature in the low 70s. Did Thoreau saw up wood and split it, then pick up his pencil and write about what he did? I can hardly picture him writing in ink, when pencils must have been to him free. His mind probably remained on higher matters, all the while he was engaged in obtaining the mundane necessities. "Necessaries," he called them, meaning shelter, fuel, clothing, and food.

Today I finished sawing up the remainder of the large fir log Garth and Norma uncovered, and which he began to cut up with our large bow saw. It is an ancient implement, and Thoreau must have used one much like it. I decided I had better get at it, because the rains are coming and these beautiful days soon will be over.

The saw bites best into green wood; an ax does, too. This tree has been down for a couple of years, but it is still solid and good enough for fuel, though by spring it will be beginning to rot. It is a knotty, straight-grained, dense kind of wood, and when I split it with a wedge and sledge it resists, then rips as the wedge forces it to divide in a direction it doesn't want to go. As much as I dislike this kind of hard work, I know it is good for me.

So I saw up the fir log and split it and lay it in a big, uneven pile, but do not finally stack it because I don't know where it belongs. I want it near the outdoor fireplace, but in such a location that I can cover it with a tarp and keep it dry, all winter long. There are also considerable deadfalls from last spring and two small green alders we had to take down to make room for the power line. So I am sawing up a lot of wood today. It is fairly easy to do, and I have found a way to do it at waist level by inverting one picnic bench on top of another, thereby improvising a kind of log holder.

It is hot, tiring work, so I saw away, then read a bit. My text is Andrew Saris and Eliot Fremont-Smith, in *The Village Voice*. Then I write in this journal. It makes for a pleasant change of pace, the one thing balancing out the other. Back and forth I go, through the long afternoon.

Three hours of hard work have taken place since the last sentence. I sawed up the last of the deadfalls, many of which were in various stages of decay. I am hot, sticky. But the woodpile has grown impressively.

To fetch a pail of water with which to wash and cool my sweaty face, I went stumbling down the path to the river and startled four birds. All flew away, but not very far. I recognized most of them as old friends. But there were two I didn't know and have no idea what they were. I must dig out my Roger Tory Peterson and learn the significant differences between certain types of familiar shorebirds and ducks.

95

While reading Peterson's *The Field Guide to Western Birds*, I come across a description of the Canada goose and become arrested there. They are common birds, but I've never singled them out for examination. White-fronted geese look much like them. Now swans are pure white.

There are ten races of Canada geese (*Branta canadensis*), six of which winter in the West, along with variations of each of the different races, and something called "clinal blend," which I take to mean individual variations of identifying marks, rather than blending from mating across racial lines. I might be wrong.

Canada geese vary widely in size. Some are huge, some as small as mallards. Mine from yesterday was notably larger than his mallard companions and dwarfed them. As for sex, male and female Canadas look exactly alike. To a goose, I suppose there are differences, and during the mating season they become significant.

Canadas wear a black "stocking" over their heads and a short distance down their moderately long necks. They also display a white cheek patch. I've heard this jokingly called a chin strap. What I noticed most yesterday was a patch of black and white barred feathers under the folded wing.

Peterson says Canadas are inclined to graze on land and forage on grasses, seeds, and aquatic plants. (Brants prefer eelgrass, while the emperor goose dines on shellfish.) The Canada is "gregarious most of the year." (I am, too, though in hot weather I tend to be cross. From this behavior pattern I may be told from others of my species.)

Various geese emit different sounds, but it is impossible for the untrained ear to tell the races apart. Bird lovers and writers love to try to capture in language the crazy sounds birds make. Often this is ludicrous. Here are attempts from a bird book to characterize the various sounds of Canada geese:

ka-ronk or *ha-lunk, ha, lunk* (slurred up)
lo-ank, lo-ank, a-lank, a-lank
yelk, yelk, a-lick, alick, or *lick, lick, lick*

My good sense tells me just to go, *honk,* and let it go at that.

Canadas make a plaintive sound, a bit like when one blows across the neck of an empty bottle of some volume. Words fail me here. I'll never be a bird writer until I train myself to pay closer attention to bird sounds and their human equivalents.

Canadas nest in the tundra in summer; also on lakes, bays, marshes, prairies, and grainfields. They set up residence in muskrat houses, old trees, cliffs, tree platforms, or in the abandoned nest of some large bird of prey. Eggs number four to six and are white.

Reading further in Peterson, I learn the Black Brant has a throaty call: *r-r-r-rnk* it goes, or else *krr-onk, krrr-onk*.

I rather like a bird that makes such a sound. It's the same noise I would make, if I were a bird—especially a small dark goose.

96

Often there is fog in the morning now, which hangs on till noon. On some days the fog is heavy and dense; others wispy and light. The sun comes bursting through by early afternoon, producing a blue sky, crisp colors, deep shadows in the lee of things. And when the sun sinks low in the sky, a decided coolness descends. Often the sunset is spectacular, the sky a flaming tomato.

It is produced by what is called "an atmospheric inversion." I'd call it a perversion instead, however pretty.

Last Friday night, Norma and I gobbled Big Macs and dashed off to Meany Auditorium to hear the Philadelphia String Quartet in their first series for the year. The Bartok Quartet No. 2 was disappointing, though I'm not sure why. Perhaps a lack of enthusiasm on the players. The Haydn piece that followed was in a minor key and somberly pleasant, familiarly structured throughout, and requiring some extended virtuosity by First Violinist Stanley Richey, which he provided. After the intermission, the group performed Dvorak's Fourth Quartet, which is lyrically beautiful. I really like Dvorak.

There is a singular absence of Beethoven in each program. It is intentional. Last year they performed all sixteen quartets. Next season, they will repeat the cycle. How wonderful.

October in the city is an exciting time, even if you don't have any Beethoven. There is a time when life in the city definitely wins out over the country. In the country, I'd have to fall back on my audio tapes. They are mostly Beethoven. To hear him I have to go to the country. How odd.

97

The bird hunting comes first—doves, pheasants, grouse. Then it is the season for game animals. Once again dead deer will be seen riding on the fenders of pickup trucks. Recently there has developed a gruesome variation: a buck is decapitated and his head displayed on the front of a vehicle, like a hood ornament. Or like the figure on the bow of a Viking ship. Boy, talk about your ugly.

Bear are rarely seen by most of us, all season long, but there is a year-round open season on them, and many get shot now because of all the hunters ranging the woods with large-bore rifles. A few bear will be bagged in the Oso-Darrington area and proudly displayed in front of various general stores. Am I the only one sickened by such a sight? I suspect there are many of us.

Up at the river, deer are returning. I thought dogs kept them away, but I'm not so sure. I think the real reason may be the river's presence and because of the surrounding terrain. Deer get boxed in and frightened. They'd soon get their backs up against a steep bank from which there is no escape. So they stay away. The place is not healthy for them. They keep to meadows and open fields. There their legs will rescue them.

We do have many small animals and birds. Raccoons are numerous, but rarely seen, since they are nocturnal. Sunday, out for a walk on our property, we flushed a ruffled grouse. They explode startlingly from tight cover. It is good to know we have some.

They are pretty stupid, and make a chicken seem smart in comparison. Today our neighbor to the East was shooting skeet

A Year At The River

with a friend, a couple of hundred feet away. The shotguns made a big boom. Meanwhile our grouse "hid" in plain sight with nearby thick cover. It did not flush but held, with each gun blast. It flushed only when we nearly trod upon it.

Each year men and dogs take to the woods in concerted effort they call sport. The woods are lovely, dark, and mysterious now, filled with dappled light, golden leaves, and a bright river nearby. And what is the purpose afield of man and dog? Why, to shoot and kill small woodsy creatures that are simply going about their daily business. This is called sport. I call it a travesty.

98

As I drove away from the river yesterday, at dusk, an enormous broadleaf maple leaf squatted menacingly in the middle of the Whitman Road. I drove around it, thinking it was some live thing. It appeared to be hunched on all fours. I swerved sharply. I think it moved a little from the breeze created by my passing car. It looked about the size and color of a basketball. Only when I was well past it did I look back in the rear vision mirror and see it for what it was. Only a leaf. But huge.

99

I went to sleep under the stars, a new crescent moon overhead, an early dew down on the grass. I slept deeply. A few big drops fell near morning but, snug under my tarp, I did not hear them. When I awoke small puddles had bagged the tarp.

An occasional strong wind brings the rustle of leaves. Clouds are low and tumultuous, but no rain falls, and the wind dies away for long periods of stillness. But a storm is on the way, make no mistake about it.

Now the deluge starts. An October storm is a splendid thing, provided you are prepared for it. And you have to love storms. A good raincoat is important. It takes the country to make me enjoy a storm. The right conditions I find only in the country, by a river. In the city, I am as much a sissy as anybody. I stay indoors.

100

In Darrington today, there are two kinds of men. Those who got their deer and those who didn't. In the cafe where Norma and I drink coffee, a millworker (suspenders, plaid shirt, billed cap, corked boots) says lamely to his friend, when asked if he got his buck, "Naw, but I seen two does." He is trying to save himself from ignominy. What a sad creature.

Outside, draped across the trunk of a sedan, we can make out the haunches of a buck and, through the car's rear window, its pointed ears and tiny spikes. Its owner hangs around the cafe, drinking coffee, telling his hero story, over and over, and accepting congratulations from each newcomer. We gulp our coffee and get out of there.

Hunters are everywhere today, Saturday, because of the opening of the general season on bucks. Cold and snow bring deer down from the high country and into the lower areas that are more accessible by hunters and where they can be easily shot. Last night was clear and cold, but not cold enough to motivate many deer, I think. This means fewer killed on the opener. I hope so. Monday morning's newspapers will tell me if I am right.

Later, near dusk, while stretching our legs off in the woods, we heard occasional distant gunshots. It sounded like quail and grouse loads—but what do I know about it? I didn't think it was somebody shooting near us, but it was possible, and they might be close. When we heard voices in the brush, across a ravine choked with logging slash and nearly impassable, I started whistling and chattering loudly to Norma. She looked at me strangely. Then she understood and appeared a little frightened.

True, we didn't look much like deer, but who wants to take a chance, with the woods now full of fools and guns.

101

Chrome river flowing beneath an moon that is fat as a pig and equally brilliant. Ripples and waves gleaming with highlights, mysteriously, luminous. All is muted in tones of silver, lovely.

I've slept for the past two nights down by the river on my bed of rusty bedsprings, with an old foam mattress thrown on top. Overhead is stretched my pale orange tarp. Inside I can see the moonlight shinning dimly through the fabric. Outside it is nearly as bright as day.

About a third of the leaves are left on the alders, making the sky open and spacious. Light carries a long way now; so does the eye. It promises to be cool tonight. Norma and I build a great fire in the large outdoor fireplace. Just before dark we scrounge up some deadfall alder and lug the pieces into camp. They break up easily into sticks with which to feed the fire. A few are too long and tough to break with our hands, so we burn them the way the Indians did, pushing them into the fire as the ends are combusted. The fire grows hot and we keep pushing our chairs farther back. Finally, we are eight feet away from it.

At bedtime, I knock the fire apart and rescue a big fir slab, turning it up on end while still burning and kicking away the fierce coals. In the morning I will find about a third of left and will save it for the fire next time.

The virtue of alder is that it is plentiful, fast-growing, and easy to cut and split. Demand has driven the price way up. It is $110 a cord in town, green; $125, dry. A year ago it was about a third these prices.

102

Yesterday we went searching for some transplantable trees to reforest the new property. We found ten small alders growing on the shoulder of the communal road. We took half of them. In a couple of years they will provide a screen between us and the cars headed down the road. In the years to come, they will give us firewood.

Last spring Norma thought she had found two small dogwood trees (one *Cornus nuttallii*—the Pacific dogwood), the other bunchberry, (*Cornus canadensis*, the tangle-rooted shrub), but upon a closer look the former turned out to be willow, and the latter, the *canadensis*, proved so sprawling and spreading that we couldn't dig it up without killing it. So we left it alone.

Canadensis has small-to-medium leaves that display, at this time of the year, a dazzling variety of colors. They range from green-black and sooty (as if it would come off on your hand) to gray-green to yellowish to pinkish-yellow to orange-red to deep scarlet. The scarlet contains blue-black tones—so different from the scarlet-orange of the vine maples that I can tell them apart at 200 feet. It would be colorful to have both bunchberry and vine maple, down at the water's edge.

All along the beach now are clusters of red-violet rose hips. Single-blossomed roses grow wild everywhere. And there are opaque white waxberries.

103

I spot many more frogs along the still water of the beach than before, including little green tree frogs. These call out at odd times of the day, in a variety of voices. You have to listen hard to separate them from all the other river sounds. Frogs are a favorite food of raccoons. Perhaps their increase is related to the rise in the number of raccoons. Whatever, the raccoons must be grateful for the abundance.

Grouse live in the thick tangles of salmonberry, and after the first surprise, each time Norma and I take the trail down to the river we can almost depend upon flushing one. Sometimes we play a game. We approach the copse from opposite sides. She flushes towards me, and I flush towards her, but the grouse never flies exactly where we want it to, for its course is diversionary.

It can be diagrammed thus:

```
C
 \
  \
   \
A→B→
```

"A" flushes to "B," who flushes the grouse back toward "A," but the grouse heads in a 45 to 90 degree angle away from "B." This direction is represented by the dotted line "C," which is not a person but a destination.

Grouse are really stupid. Often they do not make that intense whirling sound when surprised, but stand in plain sight stock-still, as if invisible. I have no idea why they sometimes burst, other times remain motionless, and other times scamper. You'd have to be a grouse to know. I wouldn't wish that fate on anybody.

The fall is a wonderful time for going out in the woods and crashing through the dry leaves. If you are not a hunter, what does it matter if you scare some birds and animals? It is an opportunity to experience nature with visibility less obscured than earlier in the year. In a way I envy hunters. Of course I can always go fishing to see what is going on. And I do.

Nights when the moon is full, as now, provide additional outdoor viewing opportunities.

104

Those characteristics and mannerisms in a person which endear him or her to us, and which we look upon so fondly, are precisely those which annoy us greatly when we are not predisposed to like, love, or trust a given person. Then, instead of an affectionate response, those characteristic quirks of behavior provoke annoyance, a pained look, or a venomous response, depending on conditions. So love and like are different shades of the same color. Love and hate are the emotional points on a wild compass ride, often sent whirling by a quick change in the magnetic field. We don't know which way it will turn us until it is too late to change course. The loss is permanent.

105

Autumn is a time for reflection, but often it is better simply to look and not think too much about what you see. Take the wild bamboo that grows down by the river. Its leaves are a rich reddish brown. A few weeks ago they were yellow. They resemble tobacco, though smaller. What would it be like to smoke dried bamboo? An ex-smoker, I don't much care to find out. They would taste bad, I suspect. I'm sure people have tried it. If curious, you could shred up a bamboo leaf and roll it into a joint the size of a cigar.

In the spring a tassel like corn silk blooms on the tall stalk. What would it be like to stuff that dried stuff into a pipe and inhale it? I have no personal interest, you understand. I only speculate.

I have been reflecting on the nature of food—what is edible, what is not, and how we find out. The process of discovery must be painful. During the long history of people on the planet, they must have tried to eat everything. Some have died as a result of their curiosity. Call it bad science. It is how we learn some things are poisonous. Just imagine who first ate snails, oysters on the halfshell, tomatoes, all those ugly bottom fish in the ocean, the small scampering animals that live in the ground. Mice, rats, slugs. Try to imagine the mindset of the pioneering people.

Man carries into adulthood the same oral curiosity he had as a child, the baby who crawls along the carpet ingesting everything in his path like a human vacuum cleaner. Bits of fuzz are not to be excluded. Whatever it is, down the hatch. Sometimes it stays down, but often it comes right back up. It is how we live and learn.

As a civilization, it is a wonder that man has endured. But he is a hardy old soul and has survived many hard knocks. Much of the earth is edible. Untutored vegetarians once maintained that man can live on grass, like a horse or cow. Not true. Those who tried it got deathly ill. Man cannot digest things a placid cow can. Some grasses produce a grain that is not edible until it is baked. The food chain is fixed and inviolable.

Vegetarians eat meat dishes with a resigned futility, as if to say, "What am I to do, living in such a society? If I don't try to eat, I will starve."

I once knew a man who ate only brown rice for two years. He began his day with 100 pushups. He avoided the sun. Once he told me the smell of my bologna sandwich nauseated him. I guess I was supposed to throw it away and eat brown rice with him. Sorry. He was weird in other ways and used experimental drugs; each night he locked himself up in the basement, got high alone, and listened to music through his headphones. I don't wish to emulate him in any way. Brown rice seems the least of it.

106

Where have all the flies and mosquitoes gone? Far, far away. They were a terror, in advancing spring. They have expired, evidently. They are short-lived creatures. How long have they been gone? Since the end of August, anyway.

There is an occasional malingerer, true, but it is a groggy individual. It seems lonely, lost. I saw a green-winged horsefly yesterday, a sort of slow character that just managed to elude the hammer I swung at it, with an unsure motion myself. I was knocking apart an old, slanted table I found buried in the sand at the edge of the river. Long ago people ate meals here, down by the water, as I do, and now they are gone. There must be a story here, but I don't want to hear it.

From the table I got some wood for the fireplace, a few heavy timbers for which I have no immediate use, and about two pounds of ancient nails, long, worthless, and badly bent. The horsefly had spectacular emerald wings, shaped like a delta, golden at their base. I thought the fly attractive, until I remembered that one had bitten me and the wound was big and slow to heal. It left a scar at its center that I can still see. Such a fly must have a role in the overall scheme, and contribute to the ecosystem, but nobody has explained it to me what or how. So I will continue to kill them.

Flies pollinate only a few flowers, but do not carry away the filth they track in on their feet. They merely spread it around. They are a bane to horses and cows, who have no hands with which to shoo them away or flatten them, and humankind does not have hands with palms fast enough to nail them often. So they proliferate.

Flies are swift in taking wing. Their body weight is so great in proportion to the lift of their wings. That it is a wonder they get airborne, let alone quickly. Knowing this, I manage to miss three out of four I swing at.

107

How peaceful and calm the woods are at this moment. The earth is momentarily still. It is not always so. There are the hunters to contend with. Bang. Pop, pop. They did not fare well on opening day, according to the papers. I am glad.

There is a disconcerting story on the front page. A 35-year-old man and his 14-year-old son were found dead at 9:30 A.M. The man's weapon had not been fired. The boy's was. Police speculate that the boy accidentally shot his father, then turned the rifle on himself, in agony and remorse. The shot to the boy's head was self-inflicted, judging by the intensity of the powder burns.

Take a boy hunting. Teach him the joys of autumn in the woods. Go out together and kill something, if you must. But not each other.

108

This morning I saw a solitary raccoon footprint on the sand. The creature had walked through the water, but stepped out at one point, leaving the lone print. Without it, I would never had known the raccoon existed.

They feed on all sorts of things and are not finicky—grubs in rotting trees on the ground and tree frogs or bullfrogs, take your pick. They'll eat whatever they find on their nocturnal prowls. It would be a mistake to brush out our land near the river and take away all the rotting deadfalls. These provide cover and sustenance to the animal population.

My neighbor, George Schlotman, one lot away, has tidied up his land, and now has flowerbeds and a lawn to mow weekly. He has limbed most of his trees to improve his view. But what view could be better than green boughs? He has left no habitat for any wild creature on his land, which is probably how he wants it.

He is not one for sharing.

109

Last night I tried running again. After a trial trot of two blocks the previous night, I decided to give it another effort. I more than doubled the distance, with little pain or swelling. This marks a great advance. My injury was three and a half months ago. The healing process has taken its own sweet time, one quite independent of my wishes. The leg lifts have helped some, I am convinced.

In mid-August, I could not run across the street to escape if a car was headed for me in a crosswalk. A month later, I could run a few feet, though painfully, and my knee would swell and stiffen for a week afterwards. Now I can run slowly two blocks. That's something.

The memory of the injury is strong, and so is the fear of re-injury. Running is a terrific shock to the system—to the joints and tendons and muscles; one hard jolt follows another, step after step, with hundreds of foot-pounds of pressure coming down on each square inch of foot surface as it strikes the pavement. Yet last night I enjoyed the feel of my calf muscles tightening, and the dryness in my mouth and lungs which comes from mildly aerobic running. Nothing special, but another step forward, and it felt good, the knee solid.

110

Today, while a beef stew of mine simmered in the oven, I circled Green Lake (2.7 miles) on foot, running it in five segments, interspersed with brief walking periods to restore an even breathing and to reduce sweats and leg cramps. The cramps were not bad. Betty Greene, a neighbor in town who runs often, informs me that leg cramps are to be expected and are perfectly normal. I shouldn't worry about them.

None of my books mention them, however. Nor hoarse breathing and heavy sweats. They mention being able to sustain a normal conversation while running. I'm a long ways off from that. Perhaps, given enough time and practice. The old knee continues to feel good.

Clothes are important to people, especially runners. You must always look right. People are terrible snobs. As I churned around the lake at my plodding pace, two young women passed me, headed in the opposite direction. One of them glanced down at my brand of footwear.

It is what mattered most to her. Well, she wasn't noticing my terribly slow pace. I laughed aloud.

III

On Tuesday, after nearly twenty years of home-style haircuts from Norma, I decided I required a more up-to-date look. I walked into a "salon" and made an appointment to have my hair cut and styled. It required a forty minute wait.

Long ago, a man walked into a storefront barbershop, took his turn, was beckoned to the chair, and got shorn of much of his hair. He climbed out of the chair with white, see-through sideburns and a bare neck. He plunked down $1.25 and maybe a fifteen-cent tip, and exited the premises. Every two or three weeks, he returned and had it done again. When time gave him a son, and that son was about three years of age, his father wrenched him away from his Mama's side and introduced him to the masculine world in the form of haircuts. He screamed when his locks were first shorn. This had its earlier counterpart in circumcision.

Today things are different. One covets a natural, airblown head of hair that is specially shaped or "crafted" to one's unique skull. Sideburns that you can see through are *déclassé*. Also a visible back of the neck. All the barbers of old have either adapted or are gone. Nobody wants an old-fashioned haircut anymore. The salon reigns. It is a twenty-year-old institution that shows no signs of going away.

"Raleigh's" is named for Sir Walter Raleigh, an excellent sixteenth-century man who sported long wavy locks, wrote poetry, explored new continents, and served his queen, Elizabeth. He brought back the leaves of the tobacco plant to the New World, leaves which, when dried and smoked in a pipe, were mildly intoxicating. Raleigh was "a fun guy," you would say today.

Raleigh in my neighborhood is a hair salon with stereo, potted ferns, wicker chairs, off-beat magazines to read while you wait, and a laid-back ambiance. Two male barbers assist the owner, who cuts both men and women's hair by appointment. And his name isn't Raleigh.

For a man, the initial cut and styling includes a shampoo, conditioning, cutting, shaping, second cut, blow dry, and advice on how to wear your hair in a number of new styles, all of which are soft and natural.

My Raleigh was named Jerry. He was my barber—er, Stylist. He began by examining the shape of my head and its irregularities.

He walked around my chair, stroking his chin, studying me. It made me more than a little nervous. A true professional, he did not laugh at what he saw.

I had a lot of extra hair, or "bulk," he announced, which he intended to cut away. I agreed. After all, I had come here for a haircut. The bulk prevented me from having hair that looked normal, like other people's. I badly wanted hair that looked like other people's, I told him. He was pleased.

"The way I am going to cut your hair," he said, "you will be able to part and wear it in a variety of styles."

"Even parted down the middle?" I asked. My father and my son were able to part their hair in the middle, but me, never. My head bears a ridge.

"Of course."

This was precisely what I wanted to hear. In my esteem, he now ranked somewhere between my doctor and my stock broker. He held out the promise of great things for my head. I decided to put my faith in him totally.

First came the shampoo. (You could hardly expect him to work on dirty hair.) He leaned me back, back, back, to about dental level. He took away my glasses, so they wouldn't get "splashed." Then he wet my hair with a hose attachment, added some shampoo out of an unlabeled bottle—some "commercial stuff," he told me—and began to lather my head briskly. After a while, he hosed me down and rubbed in some different glop. It was thicker and he didn't wash it off.

"Conditioner," he explained. "You have to lie there for a few minutes for it to do its work."

I closed my eyes. Perhaps I dozed. The room was abnormally warm.

Soon I felt him hosing me off again. Then he toweled me lightly and brought the chair back to attention, first warning me and my stomach, "We're going up now." It was good to be back in the vertical mode.

It was scissors time. Whack, whack; away went my "bulk." It soon littered the floor. I began to feel light headed. It was a happy, positive sensation, all that hair coming off. The circle of wet, dark snippets grew around my chair. Could he be cutting off too much?

I thought he must be about done, but, no, he had switched to small scissors, and was snipping away still, taking off smidgens of my short, wet hair. I tried to catch glimpses of myself in his mist-blurred mirror, but failed. What was there left on my head to cut? I decided to ask him what he was doing.

"I'm just truing up the cut," he explained, his eyes in the wet mirror telling me I wasn't supposed to look. I was being contrary. It was all right about the truing. Who would want to leave with a haircut that hadn't been "trued up"? Not this cowboy.

Jerry was about thirty, with mustache and wavy hair which he had assured me used to look very much like my own wild mane. He had tamed it. Oh? That it no longer looked like mine, and was sleek and slick, was tribute to his skill and taste, I was led to believe.

How did he get into this interesting line of work, I asked? Well, he started by cutting his brother's hair, just once, and discovering that he was good at it. Everybody said so. And he enjoyed it. Why not do it professionally, he asked himself?

He was now shaping my crown with a huge blowgun. He held it deftly in one hand. With the other he wielded a small brush with rounded bristles.

"Won't the heat cause my hair to wave?" I asked, concerned. I had an excess of wave in my hair and hated it.

"Where did you hear that? It is heat that takes the wave *out* of hair."

"It is?"

"Trust me."

He had brush-dried my hair into a huge pompadour. It was weird, ugly. He handed me a mirror with which to admire myself. How gray my hair was, almost silver. Through the blurred vision produced by missing glasses, I thought I looked like Lon Chaney confirming—in a similar mirror—that he was indeed the Wolfman. The look on both our faces was plaintive and puzzled, curious, not yet angry. It was the look that precedes the howl of protest.

Jerry remembered my question about a center part. He combed my hair forward as far as it would go, then deftly parted it. It was as though he was wielding a scalpel, not a comb. The part ran jaggedly down my scalp, not the way it was supposed to go. Then he changed his mind, whisking my hair off in a different direction and parting it on the left side, as I usually did, only much higher, alarmingly high, and at a crazy angle, starting low on my forehead and zooming up to the top of my skull. I wanted my own comb in my hand, to right this great aesthetic wrong.

A zany wave rose in front, as I had dreaded. It was the product of short hair and too much heat. Seeing the alarm in my gaze in the mirror, Jerry waved his wand and made the wave disappear. How did he do that?

"Water," he told me, "is what produces waves, not heat. But a wave is nice. Ladies like waves. And you should backbrush your hair. See?"

"Backbrush?" I asked.

He showed me what he meant. "You had trouble before because your hair was improperly cut. Now it's cut correctly. You will have no trouble in the future. If you do, simply backbrush it and the wave goes away." I thought he was going to say, "*Voila*," but he didn't.

My hair was now smooth in front, without a wave. My watch told me, as he set me free from the chair, that an hour had passed. I rose stiffly, as a prisoner might after interrogation. I didn't know the protocol, it had been so long since I'd had a professional cut. I decided to ask. "Tell me, Jerry, is a tip in order?"

"It isn't *necessary*," he began.

I understood at once. I stuffed three dollars in his hand and went over to the cashregister, where he joined me and took my $25. The tip was probably less than it should have been, but it was all I had free in my wallet.

My glasses back on, I looked at myself sharply in the big mirror on the wall. I smiled at the glass.

A suave stranger smiled back.

112

Thursday was sunny and in the low 60s. Friday, rainy and in the low 50s, for the first time this year. Thursday was a day fit for softies; today is for the hardliners. I ran at Green Lake between showers. I was met by a profusion of college sweatshirts, including ones from nearby UW, and by a complex of men billboarding their devotion to Adidas.

A few wore T-shirts in school colors with tiny shields emblazoned over the heart, whose names I couldn't make out, at least not without great impertinence. And I remember well from today a woman in a bright yellow T-shirt whose unshackled breasts bounced every which way.

One half the track is given over to bicycles, half to pedestrians. Walkers and runners must share and do so politely, most of the time. The bicyclists are bullies. Skirmishes with them are minimal, for they have a big mechanized advantage. Walkers leap aside whenever a cyclist draws near. Bikes are supposed to yield, but not one has yet. For us to jump aside seems the more prudent course.

The wind was up enough to keep the sweat down. Ducks, geese, and swans were out in record force, for it is October and the resident population of birds is overwhelmed by visitors. I ran long and moderately hard, then walked a ways. There is a temptation to run too hard at first, for it shortens the long end of the run.

Some of the people I pass are marvelously fit. One man runs the full circuit, hard. There are many people out in pairs—two men, two women, occasionally a mixed couple. One old lady was all wrapped up in plastic, against the rain which had not yet fallen. From her face, I would guess she was 80.

And there was an elderly gentleman, slender, with white hair and tanned face, who had already circled the lake once and was on his second lap. As I neared the end of my run, walking now and breathing heavily, I passed the girl in the bright yellow T-shirt. She was walking, too. Her breasts were more or less at rest.

"Somebody else walks, I see," I said to her, for I am not one to avoid addressing strangers.

She gave me a sweet smile of commiseration. "I try," she said, "but I just can't make it all the way around without stopping."
I know just how she feels.

113
My body is tired and I should not have run today. It was the sixth consecutive day, which is foolish, by everybody's standard. But it was a splendid morning, and I had to get out. That is the trouble with living in cities. The running felt good. Nonetheless, I shall lay off for the next two days, and listen to the messages from my body before starting out again.

114
Each year in mid-October I must drain the water-holding tank on the trailer, or risk a freeze and a rupture. The rupture would be very bad, because the tank is integral and would be difficult and expensive to replace. I've drawn down the tank expectantly, over the past month, so that the danger is lessened.

Norma and I bought a small dogwood at half-price at Malmo Nursery, and will plant it, next trip up to the river. Its leaves are scarlet and emerald, very pretty now, but I think it is the result of nursery conditions and, up at the river, it may behave differently. Its colors will be muted, like all the others, at least they are this year. All over town domestic dogwoods are a uniform burgundy color—pretty, but not sensational. Dogwoods can be exceptional.

I asked the knowledgeable lady at the nursery if she ever had bunchberry for sale, since it is hard to transplant from the woods because of its intricate root system. She smiled and said, no, it was one of her favorites, too, but it was never available. Then she launched into an attack on bulldozers, which she said were destroying bunchberry and all else that grows wild and naturally.

115
Yesterday I got a taste—just a taste, mind you—of what it must be like to be a good runner and have the distances tick away under my feet, as I churn along with a measured gait. And yet I ran no farther than in the past. It was just that kind of day. Things went well, physically speaking.

116
I awake an hour later than usual because I stayed up late last night trying to finish a Doris Lessing novel, *A Proper Marriage*. (The title is ironic, of course). But I gave up, fifty pages from the end, because I kept drifting off to sleep.

This is the second volume of her sequence, *Children of Violence*, which is comprised of four or five volumes. The first was *Martha Quest*. (The symbolism of all these names and titles is heavy, but after a while you learn to live with it.) Written in the Fifties and taking place during the late Thirties and early wartime Forties in Rhodesia, it follows the early years of a woman much like Lessing in her search for independence from a terror of a mother and from a dull secretarial job. She married a "sundowner" in the civil service, as had Martha Quest, and walked out on him, with a child to raise alone. Then she became involved with another weak man and the Communist Party.

Her books are good, though dated, and each is very long.

117

It is a very different thing, running in the country. There are the hills, for one thing. In town, Green Lake has only a couple of gentle rises. A country road runs up and downhill continually, but with a constant change of scenery to redeem it. I find myself looking forward to such a run.

I began at the top of the gravel road, where our private road meets the Whitman Road. I first passed the algae-covered bogs, where last summer legions of bullfrogs sent out a greeting, until I scared them silent; the bogs are silent now, their surface wearing a coat of skim ice across the green scum. I ran to the white house on the right and past it. The air was cool, crisp, inviting, different from the city. Though it was approaching noon, I ran through a deeply shaded countryside that felt like early morning.

The season is unreal. Noon is like seven A.M., while three P.M. resembles noon. Night comes so early now that it overcomes you, startlingly. When there are clouds, it is dark by six. But on a clear day, the visible world is bright until six-thirty. Winter remains at a distance.

I ran to the second telephone pole past the white house before slowing down for my first walk, a little weary and starting to get winded. The course, so far, was mostly level or slightly downhill. It was important not to get tired too soon. The route back would be mostly uphill, which is exhausting, coming at the end of a run. The prospect was demoralizing. The run so far had been easier than expected.

I walked along in the shadows, blowing hard, until I came to the bright sun at Carl Bates's mailbox. Ahead I saw the green latticework of the Whitman Bridge and the black asphalt road winding towards it in a pretty curve, looking like a calendar illustration. To my right and to my left stretched green fields with cows. A hunter's pickup rumbled by, two heavily clad men inside, guns visible in the rear-window rack. I began to run again.

I saw myself as a dynamic figure in an essentially static landscape. My shadow told me I did not lift my feet very high, or lean forward in my run with much style and grace. Well, so be it. I am not out to impress anybody. At a measured gait I ran until I came to the bridge, and reached out and touched the metal, slapping it hard with a ringing sound: One goal reached.

Breathing hard, I walked back and froth across the wooden planks of the bridge, sucking air and enjoying the sight of the river below. Upstream, I could see as far as Montague Creek; downstream, I watched the river disappear gently around a bend below the Solie Farm.

I had run half my assigned distance. The route back was gradually uphill. My knee began to bother me. The trip back was becoming a grind. I ran to Carl Bates's mailbox before slowing to a stop, trying to catch my breath. Now I walked, tired to the bone and lightly sweated, along road that was drained of sunlight and whose shade grew progressively deeper. The sweat dried on my skin and the air bit at the bottom of my lungs each time I drew it in. I felt good.

I began to run again, even before I told myself I would, and soon reached the white house, and passed it at a good clip, beginning now to climb the steepest grade, which I had descended so easily at the start of my run. It was a killer, and I soon realized I would probably not reach my target—the row of mailboxes where our private road begins—before I had to slow for another walk. This was permissible, though unwanted.

I had lost the race with myself. I halted, puffing. My watch told me I had been on the road for only twenty minutes. At the trailer I pulled on a sweatshirt against the prospect of a chill. I felt the sweat start to dry on my upper arms and chest. In spite of a throbbing knee, I felt excellent. The knee is a problem I am going to have to live with.

118

The birches out in front of our house in the city have dropped many of their leaves, and it is just a matter of days before rain and the next strong wind dispose of the few that cling. Then the lawn will get its final raking, the leaves their bagging, and the grass a cutting. Meanwhile, the squirrels are burying everything they can get their paws on.

I bought a box of old, spotted Jonathan apples from the green grocer at Albertsons for $2, and left them out on the front porch, where they would be cool and handy for lunches. The squirrels raided them and started carting them off a short distance, where they would take a bite or two and run off to attend to some more important errand. We tried covering the box with cardboard, but they pushed it aside.

We left some ruined apples out on the porch rail, hoping the squirrels would accept them, but they preferred the untouched ones. They have destroyed our corn, unripe peaches and Delicious apples—even the green tomatoes on the vine. One trial bite and the fruit is cast aside and not returned to. I experience no pleasure in watching their antics, consequently. All day long they dart around the yard, stealing my fruit, sitting back on their little hind legs, spaniel-like, to take the initial and the final bite, which is the same one.

Once one got in our house. This was just after we moved in. Not knowing about their basic character defects, Norma had given them some food. She put out some nuts on a window ledge. One of the squirrels fell off the ledge and landed in the kitchen. (This is probably the first recorded instance of a squirrel falling.) Frightened, it ran first this way, then that, urinating on the linoleum. (Note: Squirrel urine is no sweeter than any other.) It dashed into the dining room, then the living room, where it finally found the front door we had opened for it. This marked the end of our affection for squirrels and feeding them.

119

The raccoons up at the river have grown industrious, though much more subtle and mysterious than the city squirrels. We have raccoons in the city, too, and many are said to be tame, going into people's backyards and begging for scraps. They are probably as obnoxious as squirrels, and downright dangerous, if they don't get what they want.

Our soft sandy beach is covered with fresh raccoon tracks each morning. And though I sleep a few feet away from the water, I never hear the raccoons moving around, even though there are enough dry leaves now to produce a clatter. My presence must keep them at a distance.

Where do they live, our raccoons? Up in a tree, or down on the ground? Perhaps they have a den inside the big dead alder, or under the bowed hemlock, where there is a little cave. Or else they utilize the base of logjams, crowns of trees, hollow stumps, and deadfall alders, which abound on my property.

Do they hibernate in winter? I suspect so. We seldom glimpse them in the daylight. But once Russ Miller and I walked into Boulder Creek, and he halted me with a hand on the arm. He pointed up in a tree, off to the side. Ten feet up, a raccoon hung sleepily from a limb, regarding us. Hushed, we moved away on tiptoe.

Often at night I will see them along the highway, their beady eyes gleaming in the headlights. And sometimes on the shoulder lies the lump of a dead one. More likely I get a whiff of skunk, instead. But I remember a special raccoon, trapped in the glare of my headlights, peering back at me over his shoulder, reduced to a rump, his bandit face looking like a cartoon criminal caught in the act.

If they hibernate, they must be presently gathering up food supplies for winter. If it is to be a cold one, as it is rumored, there will be high mortality among all hibernating creatures. The raccoons will freeze in their dens—an awful fate, though I can imagine worse. But maybe some raccoons only half-hibernate, like squirrels do, and slumber until there is a warm spell—a thaw or a Chinook wind. Then they stir in their burrows, venture out, poke around in the dry leaves, and grub for grubs.

Last night, following my country run, my leg ached all night and I had trouble sleeping. This morning I find myself gimpy. Back in town the knee is better, but it is doubtful whether I will run again for several days.

Incidentally, the distance from the trailer to the Whitman Bridge and back is 2.2 miles. I measured it with the car's odometer. This makes it half a mile shorter than the circuit of Green Lake, but much more difficult and taxing. It is good to have such a challenge so near at hand.

120

A week from today, a Saturday, Norma, Garth, and I are going to watch a live football game. No more of that close-up stuff TV provides. We are going to sit in the stands and observe twenty-two dots move along a green field about the size of a hand towel.

There will be no instant replay, either. We will have to see what is there without recourse to a second and third reexamination in slow motion. Like life itself, we must get it right the first time, or suffer the consequences.

The night before, we are going to walk through Greek Row and view the Homecoming signs at the fraternities and sororities. Such festivities are back in vogue, after a decade's eclipse because the war in Viet Nam made them seem superficial and superfluous. My old college fraternity is serving a brunch at 11 A.M., which Norma and I are going to, at my insistence.

121

We have gained an hour during the past twenty-four. What a bonus—to have gotten something for nothing, instead of giving something up. Where did the hour come from? Do workers on the midnight shift get paid for nine hours? They had better, or else get to go home an hour early. The extra hour is the one we lost last spring. I regretted it then, though it made for a long, golden twilight. Now losing it seems a cruel trick, an amputation of the arm of time. By five o'clock it will be dark tonight. Moving the hands back marks the start of a long, dreary period. From a practical standpoint, it is winter.

122

Yesterday evening, Garth cried out, "Dad. Come quick. The front porch." I hurried, but not quick enough to see two raccoons. Norma beat me there and got a peek. Then they were gone, vanished into the nighttime neighborhood, and no amount of searching would uncover them. Something wonderful had happened and I missed it.

Garth had been alerted to their presence by the throaty alarm of our old Siamese cat. Suspecting another cat's intrusion, Garth flipped on the porch light and beheld two masked creatures. Norma hurried over. What a disappointment for me, who is the family outdoorsman. I have seen few animals in the wild, if the truth is to be known and spoken. While prowling around in the woods, all I ever find is tracks. I am ever the country bridesmaid. Wild animals are more wonderful and mysterious to me than to those who see them regularly. The romance is mostly in my head, I am aware. But isn't that where everything starts?

So country and city are not such different worlds and sometimes get mixed up. They overlap. No longer can I separate the various elements and different lifestyles.

The frontier remains, sometimes pressing close. Skyscrapers and super-highways merely rise out of the wildness, without dispensing or dispersing it.

123

It was probably the box of rotting apples on the front porch that attracted the raccoons, as it had the squirrels before them. Unintentionally, we had provided the bait.

Garth said they were much bigger than the family cat. Though our old Siamese growled, and hissed, deep in his throat, he is cowardly, no match for a raccoon, and he knows it. A raccoon is wild, tough, predatory.

We kept discussing the raccoons, throughout the evening. Weight was an important topic. Norma guessed twenty pounds, Garth a few pounds more. He was the hero—the knowledgeable one. He had spotted them and got the best look. He had the last word, accordingly.

Me, I didn't have anything to say, for once.

124

Up at the river, the first light snow of the year fell last night, airbrushing the tops of the nearby hills. It left them coated with a thin white veneer. It did not touch Mt. Whitney, but Mt. Higgins was painted white along its several diagonal slopes, and the stuff has lowered the snow line on the glaciers of Mt. Whitehorse. The first snow always melts away; this one will, too. And then the river will flood.

Because November is pressing, I must dismantle my streamside camp before the river rises from the inevitable meltoff and I lose everything. At first I thought I might move it to just above the floodline, but there are no trees there to lash it to, and the autumn wind must be taken into consideration. So I took it down and stowed it. For the winter I will sleep inside. With a strengthened flow, I shall be able to hear the river just as well, even though it is farther off.

Today at mid-afternoon, the temperature stood at 54 degrees. Presently, an hour before dark, it is ten degrees cooler, and promises a solid freeze by tonight. There was scummy skim ice on the roadside bogs this morning; the surface was too smooth and still for ordinary water.

125

Afternoon sun engenders brief renewed activity for some flying insects. The bees are sleeping, and the mosquitoes. The spiders have grown big and immobile with egg masses. In spring the pale balls of eggs will open up and spill billions of baby spiders into the world. My trailer contains two spider balls. I will attend and wait and watch them through the winter.

What eats the baby spiders? Surely something must. Birds, no doubt. And beetles. Spiders give some people the creeps. The fear of spiders is called arachnophobia. I don't have it, and Norma positively likes the little critters. She'll go out of her way to save a spider's life.

I go back outside. The air is still, and along the tops of the ridges, through the thinned trees, an orange October sun sinks slowly into the dip at the top of Mt. Ditney.

126

The logging activity in Darrington is frantic now. The prospect of snow is hurrying the loggers on, and the trucks rumble down from the hills at a rate of one every two minutes. They come in clusters of two and three. Then there is a halt. All are up loading or else at the mill. In an hour they will appear again.

Meanwhile the Burlington Northern Railroad is running two trains daily to Darrington. I see their boxcars stretch across my river view, laden with lumber and deep bins of sawdust for Presto-logs and fiberboard.

Along the hillside opposite can be seen the long diagonal scars of logging roads. In summer they were screened by leaves; now, outlined by fresh snow, they resemble fingernails angrily scratched through a heap of spilled sugar. Clearly you can make out the twin tire tracks inching off at a steep angle. They disappear about a quarter of the way from the tops of the hills and ridges, twisting around behind them. Much is recent work. The logging companies are cutting with a fury, for the market price is good. They will continue work until the snow bogs down the trucks, and the booms and towers are sucked into deep muck.

When the work stops in the woods, the loggers and truck drivers are transformed into steelhead fishermen. They fish with bait and draw unemployment compensation. They have been looking forward to this time and the daily fishing a layoff provides. As with me, fishing is an important part of their life. This is about all we have in common, however. The pay for not working they believe is their due for the hard work they did last summer. Maybe they are right, but I doubt it.

It is piercing cold at night. Fresh showers over the weekend brought the river up a couple of inches, but left it low and muddy—the worst possible conditions. Cold nights are clearing it fast, and soon it will be back in fishing shape. Only a week ago we set our clocks back an hour, and commented on how dark it got, so early. Now it is dark by five o'clock. It seems incredible. It is a terrible hour to have to quit doing what you love to do outside.

The last day of the month, it is Halloween. Tonight urchins in costume will clomp up on our front porch in town, and we will distribute rations of candy bars. They will go away, assuaged, and in the morning it will be November.

127

November first is the day I expect the first bright dog, or chum, salmon to return to the river, usually in the vicinity of Blue Slough. But not this year, because of the low water. It will take a good freshet to bring them in and up, though I suspect there are some dogs already in the lower main river, say, in the vicinity of Silvana.

Dog salmon are powerful fish and take more readily than other salmon in freshwater. At first it is great fun to hook and try to land the big salmon, but soon the fun wears off and it becomes hard, back-breaking work. In saltwater they are almost always caught with gillnets.

The first ones are pretty fish, almost silver and with only a slight pale green coloration to coat their flanks. They have mean-looking heads, with cruel mouths, especially the males. I suppose the early dog salmon would be good eating, for they are still bright;

later, they will be fit only for smoking and, after then, for nothing at all. They are thick flanked, with plenty of meat on their bones. But the law won't permitting keeping them in this river. So I will never know.

I look forward to the seasonal respite they provide with their arrival. November's high water will usually do it. On a year like this one, my calendar is thrown off. So I find a gap in my expectations.

128

Hawk sailing across a November sky, the clouds a pearly quilt, layered, very bright, but crazily reversed in their pattern. It is as though I am trapped under a down comforter. Is there some special quality to the light this month? It would seem so, on a good day such as this one, with the strato cirrus clouds streaming by, ever so very high.

The sky is a far cry from yesterday's; gone is that high bright layer which did not bring rain by nightfall. The sky lied. The light is flat, uninteresting, and the quantity is low. We may have a shower before dark.

129

George Schlotman, my neighbor up at the river, underwent hernia surgery yesterday and was feeling a lot of pain when I went up to see him today. He was under sedation, that is, drugs, which made him practically unconscious. I brought him a potted mum to cheer him up, but he slept on.

In a note I left with the flowers I offered to split his firewood, since he is anticipating a long period of recuperation up at the river and won't be able to do any work. His wife Ann said he is "not even to tie his shoelaces" for six weeks. My father had several hernia operations and none produced this much discomfort. Most men don't handle pain well. We must be destined for something less taxing. I wonder what it is?

130

Rain—hard November rain—at last. About time, too. September, normally a dry month, was a record wet one. And October, when it ordinarily rains more than half the month, brought us practically none. All those clouds I saw drifting by, so high and innocent, marked the advance column of a Pacific Ocean storm that made its seasonal debut today. A doozie.

Last night Solly, our Siamese cat, did not go right to his garage hideaway where he sleeps, when I put him out about midnight; instead, he circled the apple box, which was covered with cardboard, acting very alert and curious. I joined him in his search. First, I removed the cardboard cover and peered inside, but could not see into the interior because of the slanting angle of light from the porch. Observing nothing, I replaced the cover.

Solly was not satisfied. He continued to circle the box, looking it up and down, sniffing, his ears perked, his tail bushy—if a cat's tail can be said to be bushy. So I pulled the cardboard aside again and moved the box of apples to a better angle. A large mouse jumped out and ran off the porch. Solly followed, but not as fast. The mouse disappeared into some bushes.

I do not know the outcome but think it was in the mouse's favor. If Solly had caught it, he would have eaten it. He had a good appetite, the next morning, however. He is a poor mouser. Oh, he's eager enough to make pursuit, but lacks any special interest in the kill. He is a Hamlet-type cat, I fear, and delays taking action too long. His resolve escapes him like a vapor. He is too deliberate, too intellectual, for success in this kill-mouse world.

He is aware of all the ramifications of capturing a mouse: "Is it the right thing to do?" he asks himself. "What are the moral consequences of my act? Are there political aspects? Social? Psychological? What is the current state of the mouse population in these parts? Need that population be protected for future propagation of the species? What will be the consequences of eradicating this mouse from the rodent-based ecosystem, etc.?" All this passes through his mind, while the mouse is escaping.

The box now contains one gnarled apple, many mouse droppings (what do mice do, shit while they eat?), and many intact apples. How different mice are from squirrels and the havoc they produce. A squirrel would take one bite out of each apple, eating no more. The mouse fastidiously sticks with his first choice. He gnaws away until he and it are done.

There is something economical in how the mouse goes about his business—something understandable and complementary to the human mind. The mouse is highly efficient. I understand the mouse and respect him. As for squirrels—well, I could spend the rest of my days without ever seeing one again, and never miss him.

131

What is interesting, what is not? This is a matter of vital concern to writers and their readers. Life is not often exciting, thank goodness, for we couldn't maintain the pace. Life would be like a cross-country race. Instead, it is made up of largely pedestrian matters and mundane concerns. As a nation we have become so factionalized in the past decade that each ethnic, professional, socioeconomic, or political group is interested only in hearing about itself and its advancement. It is concerned with no news from any other sector. This is a big loss in terms of human sympathy and understanding. It is a national tragedy.

Domestic essays such as those that comprise this book may not interest many people. I report no murders, advocate no wars be fought. Here you will find few pyrotechnic displays. Instead, there is the gentle change of seasons, the flow of the river (and the various fishy visitors to its riffles and pools), the wind, rain, sun, and probably soon now, snow. These are the dramatic characters. The discovery of a mouse in the apple box, a raccoon track in the soft sand left by a dropping river, some new plant or tree appearing, is a major event in the interior life of some of us, but perhaps we ought to keep it to ourselves.

A writer is a person who decides to bring his private life out into the open and put it on display: His dirty linen, his secret thoughts. The trick is to find significant form and a suitable persona. It has to be done interestingly, informatively, and in a literary fashion. Well, we try.

I write: "These hard rains will bring in the dog salmon in large numbers as surely as . . . ." I search for an image that is not already trite. What will do the job? What is fresh? . . . As surely as anything is sure are the dog salmon each fall. No, that won't do.

God makes little green apples exactly the same way as he manufactures salmonids. The big question is, How many apples and salmon, this year? Will there be just a few salmon, or will there be wave after wave of them, coming up the river and spilling into the spawning riffles, clotting them? The dog salmon and the humpies are the only species left that arrives copiously anymore. We have undergone a huge loss in Chinooks and silvers. So their arrival looms even more portentous than in the past.

132

A great Pacific storm has rolled in from the southwest, bringing winds up to 40 knots and a hard, steady rain. The river began to rise—how high it will go is anybody's guess. It will provide enough water to issue in the dog salmon, however many or few of them there are. And some late summer steelhead will arrive, too.

In town, the full brunt of the storm struck about noon. The temperature rose to 58 degrees, then plunged within twenty minutes to the low 40s. The storm continued into the night, dumping more than an inch and a half of rain on the city in a few hours. Numerous car accidents took place, including one fatality on the West Seattle Bridge. Beneath Aurora Avenue, at the Mercer Island Viaduct, three feet of water flooded traffic and caused it to back up. In Seattle's North End, many homes in valleys had their basements flooded with storm-water runoff.

The rains raged through the night, the wind howling. When we awakened in the morning, it was to fresh blue skies and brilliant low-angled sunlight that hurt my eyes.

133

At its worst, this book of short essays resembles the type of letter one writes to an aunt condemned to a life in a nursing home, powerless to find anything better to read in the archives of the institution.

This element must be guarded against on my part and must be put down with a slam. Yet the surface of everybody's life is comprised of repeated dull occurrences; it is the interior life that matters and must be nurtured. It contains our hard kernel of truth. The kernel holds whatever meaning and purpose we are able to find in life. It holds our individuality, as well. The nature and quality of our inner life is what is important to us. It is up to each of us to work on it and nurture it as an art form. If we do, we will manufacture art, or something that comes pretty close.

134

When men meet, they very quickly ask, "What do you *do?*" They mean: *What* are you? Who are you *with*—what company? It is best to have an answer ready. You want to put them at ease and stop the questioning. Fast.

If you say, "I am a writer" (one not presently employed by a company or newspaper), you make people uncomfortable, not to mention yourself. People want to pigeon-hole you so they can forget you, or this aspect of their query. They want a label for you. Best give them one. Once you are able to see the query for what it is, it is ultimately forgivable.

Often I get defensive instead. I should invent some plausible false ID, not so much to impress people with, or mislead them, as to put them at their ease. And make myself more comfortable, in the process. These reflections are provoked by the simple prospect of going to a post-football game celebration at my old fraternity house, with my family in tow, and being asked, "Bob, what are you doing now?" Which means, "What *are* you? Who are you with?"

I wish I had a good answer for them. I can't very well carry this long manuscript with me and haul it out, three inches thick now, all in crabbed longhand, and push it under their noses, exclaiming, "See? *This* is what I do. Isn't this something? Just feel the bulk, the heft."

Boy, talk about defensiveness.

135

Nobody asked, "What do you *do*, Bob?" Nobody said much of anything, as a matter of fact. This is why:

We decided against brunch because Garth couldn't attend; he had to take the Scholastic Aptitude Test that morning. Instead, we three agreed to stop by the frat house for the post-game celebration. We won, beating Arizona by ten points.

The victory celebration was a disaster. No, it was not really that, for it would have to have happened to be that, and it never came off. It was canceled, only nobody was informed, except the people who went to the brunch. The others, like us (who had received an invitation in the mail), kept drifting in, looking round, and abjectly departing.

I decided to take Garth on a tour of building, where I had spent nearly three years of my confused youth. Much to his chagrin, I led him into rooms, bathrooms, dayrooms, etc., where boys' books, clothing, sports equipment lay around in homey disorder. Secretly I think he liked what he saw. (Secretly is the only way he'd admit to liking anything at his age.)

The dining room, which is in the new wing, with many windows, held the remains of the brunch. Garth and I tried to puzzle it out. Little flat squares remained in great baking trays—what were these? A dry, yellowish substance resembled pizza (for *brunch?*), but might have been baked scrambled eggs, or more likely a quiche. Some fatty residue in another pan hinted at ham. Drinks had been served, we gathered from all the abandoned highball glasses. We didn't drink in the house when I was there. The University outlawed it and we dutifully obeyed.

I met the current alumni chairman. (I was he, twenty-six years ago.) He said they had decided against "cracking open another bottle" for the post-game celebration. Nobody seemed much interested in it around noon. So it was called off. It seemed unimportant to them.

All looked a shambles. The first floor was ill-lit and funereal. Well, it was so when I was a boy, too. The upstairs study and sleeping rooms were small and jammed together. I remembered them as much larger. Everything was filthy, cluttered. What surprised me were all the houseplants. Guys with plants? Jesus. Most were ordinary plants, though a few looked suspiciously like marijuana. They were growing under special lights, anyhow.

Several young men strolled around the halls with glassy looks, beer bottles in their hands. How strange. In my day, we had to drive or walk a mile for a beer. Usually walk. Boy, did it taste good, after you had earned it. But marijuana was practically unheard of.

I saw only one familiar face. It belonged to John Slater, now a lawyer. He looked much as he had then, but with much less hair. I thought how I must look very different from my school days—my beard gray, horn-rimmed glasses on my face, a golf cap atop my head. He peered long into my face, as though he was an eye doctor, but was not able to recognize me, not even after I said my name. He disbelieved I was who I said I was. "No—not really?" I assured him I was I.

There was no resemblance from our days living in this house. I didn't look like who I said I was. Ah, but then there are days when I scarcely recognize myself.

136

The graceful Japanese maple in the backyard has lost its leaves on the Southwest side, but has thick clusters of brown spinners everywhere else. These are the seedpods and I have no idea what happens to them, or what useful purpose they serve, since I've never seen any young trees starting up from them anywhere in the neighborhood.

What takes place, then? The tree puts out thousands of seeds and they exert their winged means of travel. The winds scatter them to no useful issue or purpose. Why all this labor for . . . nothing?

The leaves of the—I want to say "little," but its no longer small—Japanese maple are slender, delicate, and scarlet. Russet might be a better name for the color of some leaves. If properly scarlet, there is a lot of pink and brown mixed in it. A month ago the leaves were burgundy. They have paled some. At the foot of the tree leaves lie fallen in a wide circle, as though artfully arranged by gnomes. As long as they remain moist, they will lie flat and colorful. When I bring a few inside, they quickly dry, curl, and fade. I have to throw them out. It is impossible to make an indoor arrangement out of them.

137

The Goldfish Children, including the Big Guy, have grown all summer, but still will not be able to tolerate a hard freeze. In bad winters past, Norma collected them and brought them inside, keeping them in the basement in an old galvanized bathtub from Sears that I bought to use up at the river. Now, dipping my hand repeatedly in the water while retrieving needles, I wonder how the goldfish are handling the transition from summer to winter? They must be hardy creatures to endure a thirty- degree temperature drop in so short a period.

The weather people say the chances for a mild winter are three-to-two. But, what do they know? And where do they get their information? From the stars? The tides? Do they measure the depth of fur on the backs of squirrels? If so, judging by what I've observed, this will be the fourth mild winter in a row.

138

How does it happen that we meet and marry the women that we do? A lot of pious blather has been written *around* the subject, but rarely is the truth spoken, and then it is disguised as romance, which is far from the truth. Romantic love plays a very small role in what happens.

People of a domestic bent marry—or at least they used to; today many of them simply live together—which is not so simple. Idyllic at first, it often develops its own weirdness and complicity. But married-type people are only comfortable as a permanent twosome.

My fishing friend Heinz, a naturalized German, lost his wife to cancer a year ago, and ever since then has been hard at work finding a new one. His wife was an old-fashioned *hausfrau*, so Heinz can't cook, clean, sew on a button, etc., or do much of anything else around the house. He is lost, miserable, helpless. He will remain this way until he finds another woman and marries her. It may not be long, for he is closely tied to the German-American community, and there are women who want a German husband.

Heinz's son is scornful and contemptuous of his father's search. The boy cherishes the memory of his mother and doesn't want to see her replaced. Since I am exactly Heinz's age, I tend to speak paternally to the boy, whose name is Ron. I do this partly because the son speaks insultingly to his father in front of others, while we are all fishing in some crowded fishing hole like Fortson. I don't think he should be allowed to get away with it. I think the son wants to be told to shut up. Heinz doesn't do it, so I oblige.

Once I explained to the boy that Heinz was "a totally married man." By this I meant he was miserable without a woman to share his life and give form to it. It wasn't his fault, only the way life pushed him. I knew the boy's mother slightly and liked her. I told the kid Heinz's search for a new wife was no sign of disrespect to his mother. In a way, it was a compliment, for if the first marriage hadn't been satisfying, Heinz wouldn't be so eager to repeat the experience. The boy stood and listened. I told him I could understand his father's plight, for I was a long-married man myself. I do not know what I'd do without my wife. Could I function?

Not often does a son understand and respect his father, and the man's needs. There are powerful forces that work against such empathy. The son remains outraged, furious. The risk of intruding seemed the lesser sin. I felt I could get the message across and it was important to him. To his sanity and his relationship with his father. I doubt whether anybody else would have bothered.

My topic is finding wives, not placating sons, which usually comes much later in the scheme. Before marriage, it is good to live alone and not be too unhappy in the process. Marriage won't solve any problems a person brings to it as surplus baggage, except perhaps a peculiar type of loneliness. Another kind of loneliness always remains.

Marriage solves one kind of boredom, but replaces it with another. The concept of romantic love denies the prospect of boredom, and that is why marriage always is the antithesis of romantic love, at least in its expression in the ballads from Provence and in the convention of courtly love.

Why men and women select each other remains a mystery. Why this person and not that? The people we choose are often a big surprise to our friends. Bodies call out to each other, and are responded to on a deep biological level. It is deeper than reason. One can only wonder at it.

A middle-aged man is a ridiculous object. It is a husband I am talking about. More and more a man finds he can't locate much in the world of commerce to hold his interest or to give him satisfying work. In time women will feel this way, too. Give them time. At best today they are reconciled to how things are because they feel they have no choice.

And how does this relate to my friend, Heinz? Only in an oblique way. How do we marry those we do and not some others? It is a matter of coincidence and a matter of fate. Plus need; need is an important factor. Will Heinz find a replacement wife? He will; this I know in my bones. And I wish him good luck.

139

The mutability of seasons, especially when they are in transition, is my subject. Yesterday while I was writing, a din began to mount in my ears. It was hail striking the aluminum roof of the trailer. Instantly I knew what it was. I ground away with my pencil, as the tapping grew to a crescendo. Then it faded. I looked out my window to see if the ground was covered. There was only a thin scattering of ice pellets on the bed of brown alder leaves. They melted even as I watched them. They were the size of baby peas. A few minutes later the sun was shining.

The river is in near flood from a peculiar storm that missed Seattle entirely, except for some strong winds, but dumped a couple of inches of rain in the Oso-Darrington corridor. It was a warm torrent, a Chinook storm. By the time I arrived, the storm had blown itself out and a cool front had moved in behind it. Fresh snow hung in the old-growth silver firs on Mt. Higgins.

The mood of the day was one of quick change. One storm followed another. There is a local saying that, "if you don't like the weather, wait a moment." The implication is that something much more to your liking will arrive soon.

Later, driving home, I encountered a wide brilliant slant of light. The sun bathed the highway in gold. It hurt my eyes to look at it. The sun had broken out from behind some dark storm clouds and was beaming in my face from behind Eby Hill. Meanwhile, a downpour fell like a curtain between me and the sun; it is what was causing the brown-orange light. I'd never seen anything like it. Off to the sides, mist hung in pockets between the hills, and the sunlight bent around the hills and crept out from the pockets. Such light is the photographer's dream.

Soon another rainstorm struck. The sky opened up like a clam shovel and the highway was soon awash; water ran as though chased. The car slowed of its own accord, as it encountered a huge standing puddle. Then I was back on dry pavement. As I crossed the South Fork Bridge just outside of Arlington, I saw wet tire tracks in a substance that looked like melting asphalt. Gradually two narrow gauges formed in it. They vanished into ordinary wet pavement at a point ahead. The lane pointing in the opposite direction—towards Darrington and to the East—was bone dry.

Suddenly I understood. The storm lay behind me. Ahead waited only good weather. The water was mostly slush and had been carried in on the cars and tires, then had spilled off. The skies had cleared, but the water had no time to evaporate, and the slush kept it thick.

At home in the city the temperature dropped all evening long, as a new storm rolled in. This one was depositing fresh snow in the foothills. I sleep well under winter-storm conditions. The wind is down and the rain is softly falling and gurgling in the new gutters. I will be snug tonight under the covers and happy in my knowledge that the river will drop and clear fast because of the cold.

140

Full moon, clear skies, and frost bathing my parked car by early evening; in the morning, a heavy condensation coats the highway under the bridge underpasses, and a black-ice condition is created. Cars hit these slicks while accelerating and shoot across the road and into the ditch. Norma saw a couple of accidents being cleared away by wreckers from the express lanes of the freeway this morning on her way to work, and a fresh accident in the shadows of the 45th Street Bridge.

In the country, on the lee side of Eby Hill, hoarfrost lies heavy in the shade, all day long. The weak rays of the sun do not strike it until just before sundown and won't melt it. Cicero is always the coldest spot around. It receives the most snow and the thickest frost; ice holds the longest. Fortunately the grade is level, but the road has curves, with deep drainage ditches off to the sides. Often a car or a truck can be spotted, nose down, off the shoulder. It takes a cable and a winch to right the vehicle, and usually it has to be towed twelve miles into Arlington to be worked on.

A Year At The River

I have learned to drive slowly and steadily along this stretch on wintry days and avoid acceleration or fast braking. I use the gearbox and touch the brake gingerly.

141

Berger Bryson is a Tarheel. That means he came from North Carolina. I'm not sure whether the term is derogatory. To me it is simply descriptive, and that is how I use it. It tells you where a man comes from and evokes many special cultural values.

Bryson is one of the few absolutely honest and trustworthy men of my acquaintance. Though I know him only slightly, I am as sure of this as I am of the morning sun. I would trust him with a large sum of money (had I this) and sleep well the following night. How do I know it for a fact? Well, I don't. It is largely a matter of faith. A thing is no less real or true for being based on faith, is it?

For instance, electricity is never seen, only its manifestations, the work that it does. But it exists, indisputably. I mention electricity because Bryson believes in magnetism. He says, "Anything that can cause a needle to swing at so great a distance from its source impresses me." It's a valid point. Like a great many things I don't entirely trust, I can't disprove it.

I mentioned to Bryson a character in the comic strip, Dick Tracy, a certain Diet Smith, an inventor of spurious objects, such as the wrist radio, with TV attachment. (It is now a fact, of course.) Diet Smith was the first man to reach the moon, remember; he did it by means of magnetism, but expressly how, Chester Gould, the comic-strip creator, didn't explain. Perhaps it was in the "space coupe," which was powered by magnetism. A little box at the bottom of the comic strip's final panel (where "Crime Stoppers Notebook" appears) reads: "The nation that controls magnetism controls the universe." How true!

I have never forgotten this important political message. Today, when I quoted it to Burger Bryson, he looked at me as though I were mad. I think this is what I was after—a strong reaction, countering one mad notion with another. Did he think I—a city person—was ridiculing him? I hope not. I was drawing a crude parallel, and making a joke in passing. I dropped the analogy, since it didn't seem to be working well. He doesn't read the funnies, evidently. Not serious enough for him?

He continued to expound on the power of electro-magnetism and motors, while I drove him the six miles to my riverfront lot, where he looked over my situation and agreed to spread a load of coarse gravel 100 feet along my mushy drive. We had already agreed on the price.

Bryson fears a great recession. The word depression was barely mentioned, for the word still holds grim memories for him. He was a young man at the start if the Great Depression, and like everybody who does manual labor was hard hit by it. I found it hard to understand, though I was a child then. Too much has changed.

He told me that there were only two presidents who had done a decent job. He paused, meaning I was supposed to guess who. I began to sort through my mind. FDR and John Kennedy? Truman and either Hoover or Nixon? Or maybe Nixon and, his cohort, Gerald Ford?

"Eisenhower and Johnson," Bryson announced, with a wise smile. To me, it sounded like an odd running team.

Rather than zero in on these two men—what particular qualities they had to elevate them so—I let him involve me in a general discussion about presidents, including those who didn't make the short list. For a busy man, Bryson seemed to have all the time in the world to shoot the bull. I asked about FDR. Surely he wasn't an indifferent president? People either hated him or loved him. When he remained silent, I pressed on.

I said it was possible to go into many neighborhood taverns in Seattle and find a framed picture of FDR behind the counter, with a tiny American flag flying alongside. Roosevelt, Bryson said, did some questionable things. They were illegal, according to the Constitution. Many Tarheels are strict Constitutionalists, I recalled. Roosevelt packed the Supreme Court with people who would do his bidding. Was this the crime Bryson had in mind? Or was it forcing through Congress things like the NRA? I asked him.

He nodded grimly, remembering. All of these and more was the message of the nod. These gross indiscretions automatically ruled FDR out of the running for greatness.

I persisted. Wasn't Lyndon Johnson a man very much like FDR—a disciple, in fact? Only in some ways, Bryson replied, with a look that told me not to pursue the matter farther. As for Ike, we never got around discussing his qualifications, other than that it was he who led the nation to victory in World War II. Perhaps to Bryson that was accomplishment enough to be a top-ranked president.

The conversation jumped around. It was dynamic and had a life of its own. Somehow we got on the subject of the war in Viet Nam, and agreed that it was a terrible waste of men and resources. Soldiers returned home ruined and drug-dependent to an ungrateful America, who would just as soon forget them. They wanted the veterans and the war to simply disappear. It had not existed, from a certain point of view. This was a popular opinion, but not one I might have expected from Burger Bryson. I wondered what he thought of the war, back when the fighting was the heaviest? Was his opinion the same or different from now?

Bryson owns 250 acres of good bottom land just upstream from the mouth of Boulder Creek, the second biggest tributary to the North Fork. (Deer Creek is first.) To the North, the river is boundary to his land, and on the South, Highway 530, which stitches Arlington to Darrington. Just off the highway is his shingle mill. Somehow it has avoided the usual fate of turning into a torch. Berger Bryson would not burn down his shake mill for the insurance money. A rare man among many who are not.

He must be six feet two or three and slender to the point of gauntness. He is as strong as two oxen. Once I saw him pick up a cedar bolt and carry it ten or twelve feet to where the splitter was. The bolt weighed over 200 pounds. He lifted it easily and carried it with minimum effort. I stood astonished, impressed. It was no matter to him. It's what he has been doing so most of his life. I doubt whether I could have so much as rocked it from side to side.

Bryson has been troubled by his back lately. I don't wonder why. It is all those cedar bolts. He is in his middle sixties, judging by appearances. The mill is part-time. His main business is installing septic systems. He also does custom backhoeing. In fact, he can do practically anything that needs doing in the country, which makes him valuable—to me, and to others less skilled. It isn't a bad arrangement. The country people do the hard work and the city people pay them for it. Both groups benefit.

Bryson once owned a large white German Shepherd. The dog was very good at frightening away trespassers. The dog would wander down to the great fishing hole that lay above a small island where Boulder Creek emptied into the North Fork. I enjoyed wonderful fishing there, most winters. The dog was dignified and not overly friendly. Wolflike, the dog regarded me from a far. He didn't bark, he didn't growl. Imperial was the look. He might accept a quick pat on the head from me in passing, but no more. He seemed embarrassed by the human contact, at the same time he sought it. Yes, he was Bryson's dog, and like him.

What he enjoyed most about me was I went for walks in the woods. Soon he'd join me, every time I went down to fish. He'd trot along, his tongue lolling. It looked as though he were laughing. It was only his way of ventilating, though And when I caught a fish—as I often did—he was uninterested. In fact, he seemed to look the other way. But he knew what was going on. You could say we had a relationship going. Then I bought a German Shepherd of my own. The two males did not get along, even when mine was a pup. They fought, each chance they got. It was awful. This saddened me and I went to extra efforts to keep them apart, for nothing is more awful than a dog fight between two dogs you like. Yet I had to go fishing there.

The white dog no longer walked down to the river with me, now that I had my own dog. I missed him. And what happened now, once I got there, was very different. My dog, Hans, went crazy whenever I hooked a steelhead and it began to jump. He broke command and went into the water after the fish, when it was time to land it—something the white dog would not condone. The white dog was too mature for such behavior. Yet the two kept encountering each other. Perhaps both enjoyed the tiff.

I hated the fights, and rushed boldly in, kicking, trying to separate them before either got damaged, especially my own dog. Once Bryson watched me with amusement. He explained his attitude. "In the animal kingdom," he said, "creatures never fight to the death." What? "No," he added, "only man does that."

I was impressed at this bit of country wisdom. Later I wondered if it was true? I'd heard about dogs killing each other, but had not heard it often. Animals fought for dominion and to claim territory. I had probably added to the antagonism by leaping into the fray and upsetting the natural course. Bryson was no doubt right: The dogs would have fought until one had yielded. Then there would be peace. Probably my dog would be beaten, because he was smaller, younger, less sure of himself. But how badly would he have been hurt? I didn't want to know.

In time Bryson's dog grew old and infirm. One winter he died. I shed half a tear. Bryson has a new dog. It is the way with dogs. Again it was a German Shepherd. But it was young and friendly, so far, glad to see visitors. Young dogs almost always are. In a few years my own dog died. He died early. It was a sad event. Bryson and I, in passing, occasionally allude to the fact that we both lost dogs. There is the hint of a bond here. But only a hint.

Owning so much rocky stump land and, and loving it so, tax increases in recent years have hit Bryson inordinately hard, but he doesn't want to sell it. Zoning laws are made in far-off Everett, the county seat, and the bureaucrats and elected officials are hated by the country people, but by nobody more than the Tarheel population. They want the Eastern half of Snohomish County to secede and to form its own "more perfect union." Two names have been put forward: Tarheel County and Whitehorse County. Each has its advocates. Nothing is apt to happen.

To alleviate the tax bite and still hold his acreage together, Bryson sold one small tract and leased some of the others, most along the highway and fronting it. In the past half dozen years a number of cabins and mobile homes have sprung up. They comprise a motley community and some would say they are an eyesore. Places acquire names and ask to be up on a map. For instance, Oso is a hamlet, and one not much bigger. It is named only on large maps of the state. This settlement ought to be named Bryson.

Near the highway Bryson's wife, Faye, has opened an antique store. You will find it where the dirt road leaves the highway and leads off to the fisherman's public access. Their children are grown and she has only Bryson to cook for and worry about now. The store gives her a daily activity and, perhaps, some egg money. There is a wagonwheel by the entrance, chained and locked into place to thwart thievery, with many rural artifacts in the window. Weekends, the Brysons scour the countryside looking for bargains at rummage and estate sales. Frankly, it seems out of character for him, but wives have a way of getting husbands to do what wives want. I suspect he drives the truck and waits in the cab while she negotiates her acquisitions.

One of their children lives in a double wide on Boulder Creek, by the highway, only a few hundred yards away from his parents. Bryson owned sixty acres over here, but sold it. He regrets doing so. Land is about all that counts, in his opinion.

I first met Bryson some twelve years ago, when I drove down his private road, past the small shingle mill, and came to a narrow grassy road leading down to the river. I found it blocked by an iron gate. My plan was to walk down to the river—a good distance—along this road and the path it turned into until I came to the willow-choked floodplain channel. But this was trespassing. Often I risked it here. As I was deliberating, an old flatbed truck pulled up alongside my car. The driver stared evenly at me for a long moment, reluctant to speak. He had a sharp face, a shock of white hair. "This is a private road," he finally muttered. The message was clear enough. He sounded as though he regretted having to speak even one word to me.

Then he kindly directed me to an area far off to the East, where he had bulldozed an area for the public to park. Two trails led off at right angles to separate fishing holes. Neither was very good, however, and neither led to where I wanted to go. The best fishing hole lay directly behind Bryson's gate. His efforts at accommodation had backfired. Fishermen still tried to reach the river by the old route. I was one of them. I've always figured fishers weren't trespassers, only people looking for a quick way in to a fishing hole. On my own property I've never turned a fisher away, though others I look askance at.

The gate was new and marked a big change. Fishermen don't like being run off land they are used to walking through to reach the river. True, the landowner had property rights. All the same, to exercise such rights in effect cut off another mile of access to the river. And this was an exceptional hole. I fumed. I drove a short distance away and parked on the shoulder. Then I circled back on foot. Bryson was gone. I hurried around the gate and through his property, as fast as my little feet would carry me. In the future I continued to do this, whenever he wasn't around. And I caught lots of fish, even though I had to smuggle them out to my car at dark.

I'm sure Bryson recognized my car, parked so often on his shoulder, just down the road. But I managed to evade him. A busy man, he usually was off doing something. And I have to admit, the trespassing element added excitement to my day. Even smuggling my fish out at dark was secret fun.

The years passed. When I bought my land, the country put a work requirement on my septic-tank permit that made it possible for me to construct a privy. First I had to ditch 150 feet of right-of-way to divert what the land wept. I needed someone who had a backhoe and knew how to use it. Naturally I thought of Berger Bryson. Was he friend or foe, I wondered? A little of each, I decided. He lived only four miles away, which put him nearest; I didn't want to pay a lot for travel time. So I went to his door and knocked. He recognized me, I think. (One is never sure, with Bryson.) We hunkered down and talked some business. He agreed to put in my drainage ditch for me. Would he also, at the same time, backhoe a hole for my privy? Sure, he said. How much? The price he quoted was $70. I thought it reasonable.

The job turned out to be more difficult than he anticipated. It took him a full day, not the half he planned on. I arrived at my property to find the work neatly accomplished. I didn't know the particulars. I promptly drove to his house to pay him. He came to the door, wearing the only garments I've ever seen him in—slate gray work pants, with matching shirt. It probably was bought through the mail from Sears. I suspected that he had six such outfits and started out each day with a clean one. By dark it would be filthy and quickly go in the wash. On Sunday he probably donned a dress suit of gray worsted wool, the same one he had worn for twenty years, and went to church. Afterwards, he took off the suit, hung it up, and put on a clean work uniform.

I speculated more about him, drawing on my little evidence. That great thatch of white hair, for instance. Each morning he would wet it down with water, especially the front part, which tended to loom. It tried to dry into place in a cowlick and conform to the natural contours of his head. The shock in front wanted to rise and pitch forward, as though about to ask a question. His was a beak of a nose and his eyes small, dark, and alert. They didn't miss much. They told the world that nobody took advantage of him; he was prepared for them. Such a look comes from having been cheated once. Yet he remained cautiously trusting. He smiled rarely and the few times he did I thought it a great occasion. Then I saw that his teeth were badly stained. He smoked Pall Malls, the deadly, unfiltered kind.

I had never thought him a smoker. The first time I saw him light up, I expressed surprise. He smiled, keeping his teeth hidden. "I've only been smoking a short time," he informed me. "About forty years." This was Tarheel humor.

I told him I was prepared to pay more for the backhoeing, seeing how difficult it turned out to be. But I hoped to myself it wouldn't be too much more.

"No, I said seventy dollars." he said. "That's the price. We'll chalk the rest up to experience."

What did he mean by that, I asked?

"I learned something, didn't I? Don't you always learn something from experience?"

I learned something, too, that day. I suspect many people before me had learned the same thing. Berger Bryson would get my future business. If he could do the work—and he could do practically anything—I would call on him, every time—not because he worked cheap, but because he was intrinsically dependable, and this was a rare quality.

142

Last night on the news at eleven, Channel 5 showed dog salmon being caught by commercial white fishermen in Puget Sound, near Olympia, which is at the bottom of the big enclosed bay. They were very dark and appeared to be in spawning condition. Areas near Hood Canal are now open late in the season because the Indians have reached their quotas and there are more fish left over than are needed for escapement. But the fish are so dark, so ripe, to be near worthless on the market. They're even in worse shape than we find them high in our rivers. I've been putting back better fish than that.

A dark, dreary day, with clouds thickening all afternoon and closing down solidly early, which brought on dark by four-thirty. Is this not winter? Not yet. Light rain fell. I watched Mt. Wheeler get swallowed up by a galloping cloud mass; it was wearing white on its clearcut saddle. This marks the first snow that has clung so high, so early. Wheeler is a low, insignificant mountain—a big hill, really—though a local landmark, and pretty with fresh snow on it. It is about 2500 feet high, with a rounded crest.

Tonight the temperature is rising, and I suspect that soft snow is falling again at the higher altitudes. Thus Wheeler is receiving a fresh coat of paint. But by tomorrow the air will have warmed, and the snow—both old and new—will be melting and causing the rivers to rise anew.

143

It is three P.M. on one of those November afternoons when it looks like the end of the world will arrive in about ten minutes. Or else the simple hand of night will press down early on the earth, flatten it, and we will live in mole-like obscurity for the rest of our days. A dark, rainy afternoon in the Pacific Northwest makes even longtime residents hasten inside and turn on all the lights. The temperature hangs at 52 degrees. In college we all knew this season was no time to study Shakespeare's tragedies. The alcoholism and suicide rates soar.

Winter another month away? There is something wrong with how we measure the seasons. If you look up at the skies, you will get your face wet. And the season for catching colds is upon us. Garth has been home for ten days with an "upper respiratory infection," which is a fancy name for a bad cold. But he won't call his newspaper-delivery substitute. He is presently out delivering his papers in a downpour. But he is too sick to go to school. It doesn't make sense to me, either.

This rain, if it persists long enough to raise the river, will bring in the first winter steelhead into the rivers. They will arrive in the Skykomish and Snoqualmie first. My river comes next.

144

On a rainy Saturday like this one, with the river running full of mud, it is not unpleasant to sit at my desk in town and tie a dozen or more flies for when the river clears. Soon it must.

I have been a flytyer—let me see—since the age of sixteen. I am not especially good at it, and in the smaller sizes of flies am absolutely terrible. I cannot consistently spin a good dubbing body nor pair up wings for a dry fly that will cock perfectly on the surface of a table, let alone still water. But I get by. There are tricks to compensate for these failings.

If I had to pay going rates for all the flies I lose, I would be destitute. Some hang up on the bottom, a few break off on the rocks behind me, others fall off the lambswool pad on my fishing vest. They cost a couple of dollars or more each in the stores. By tying my own, I bring down the unit cost to five or ten cents. A vast savings.

This makes me reflect that all the Atlantic salmon patterns—vastly complicated creations of the Victorian Period—were dreamed up in Irish and Scottish winters, when there was no fishing to be had. It is how it is with me today. Lots of time in which to do nothing. Fly tying is the next best thing to going fishing. And it is vaguely worthwhile. A fly tied in winter may produce a fine fish in spring.

Rain streaks my window. I sip coffee, gaze out at the wet evergreens, and insert a fresh hook in the vise. Five completed flies lie on my desk, their head cement drying. I will need more—least a dozen—before venturing out again. This should take me another hour.

145

White, clingy snow lies everywhere. An intense white world calls outside my study window, a realm transformed overnight. It is so bright that the glare makes me momentarily blind and I must look away, even though the sun isn't shining. What a difference a few degrees of temperature makes. It might have been a sloppy rainstorm, the gutters running with water. Instead we have this sudden white world. I like it, the change.

Reports trickled in as early as yesterday morning of snow flurries in Everett. I had the feeling the country roads could be tricky, receiving snow all day long, which might not be so bad for travel, except at dark the mushy cartracks become solid ice and dangerous. Plus there are all the hills and curves, with no shoulders alongside and deep drainage ditches a few feet away. Many times I've driven the Arlington-Darrington highway under these express conditions and found the experience (shall we say?) adventuresome.

So I stayed in town. Some second sense warned me not to make the trip to the country. By early evening a thin steady snow was falling; it left a film on the lawn, beneath which you could see the grass. It stuck on parked cars, but left the streets clear except for an inch of slush. The slush seemed innocuous enough, but felt slick under foot where it had been compressed by car wheels or pedestrian traffic. No real problem loomed, unless the temperature dropped below the 36-38 degree range at which it was holding.

By midnight it was snowing hard—and sticking everywhere. Norma's dinner party for her fellow librarians had broken up and they were all safely home. Norma kept taking glimpses out the window at what still seemed a benign situation. We soon turned in. At five A.M. Garth left for his paper route, it being the weekend. I glanced out. The world was white and snow was deepening hourly. But the buses kept running, though they skidded around a bit, and were behind schedule, or so my son told me later.

It took Garth an hour longer than usual to deliver his papers, for he had to pull his cart through snow both level and drifted. When Norma and I shuffled out of bed about nine, the wet stuff hung heavily the trees, bowing them prettily, and four inches stood on the ground. The neighborhood children were out in droves, with sleds and plastic discs that resemble giant Frisbees. The snow was too soft, wet, and without the necessary substratum to support the sled runners, and we could hear the runners grinding on the pavement, giving off sparks. The children persisted. They are a determined lot, when it comes to snow.

The cold is expected to last. In mid-afternoon the snow still holds in the trees. This is unusual. Will the snow and cold push into winter? Or will the stuff soon be washed away? One has to wait to know.

146

Yesterday I reported that the snow clung all day in the trees. This morning, after a clear night, the sun came out. The world was blinding. About half the snow in the branches loosened and fell to the ground; it also melted off the rooftops. Now, at eleven, more high gray clouds have moseyed in from the South and the melting has halted. It could mean more snow. Seattle schools were declared closed today. This means nothing. Every time there is a hint of snow the superintendent shuts them down for a day. I think he is in cahoots with the kids. He probably likes to sled on the hills himself. But they are due to be disappointed—there is not enough snow to coat the ground and make sledding and sliding possible.

147

I drive to the country and find the following:

The pond at Hazel is covered with ice on both sides of the road, and has been like this for more than a week, but no snow has fallen. How different from in town, where the remains from our four-inch snowfall linger along the edges of the streets and on lawns. It melts a bit during sunny afternoons, but refreezes each night to become patches of icy slush and glare ice. Along the Whitman Road the ice on the bogs has expanded out of its constraints, shattered, and fallen back on itself, where it lies stacked in uneven columns. Great panes of glass appear to have been broken and lie crashed among the deadfall slash.

There are waves of dog salmon ascending the middle river now. I encounter them quietly finning in the fast shallow water of the Monte Hole, as I close out this short day fishing briefly in a persimmon haze left over from a sun that set before four-thirty. But because the sky is clear and cold, the light held, golden-orange, until shortly before five. I drive home under a faded moon, which lies pathetically tipped on its side, like a hospital patient.

148

Although the late-morning temperature hangs at 41 degrees F. in town, an eighth of an inch of ice completely covers the fish pool in our backyard, where reside the Goldfish Children. (God, what a mawkish name I've given them, the slimy darlings.) I can just make them out beneath what is left of the lily pads and water weeds. The Big Guy is buried deep, out of sight. On the skim of ice are embedded thousands of needles from our mock-cedar—the *Deodora*. It looks and feels like a giant spruce, but it's not.

I press my forefinger down on the ice until the sheet tilts, cracks, and a piece breaks off; this sends warning vibrations up and down the length and breadth of the pool. Two of the smaller goldfish stir. So they are alive? Beneath a ceiling of cold glass, their life goes on, though at a reduced rate. Since we never feed them, they must lie dormant, all winter long.

I am tempted to buy them some goldfish food, but don't, out of innate cheapness and a respect for the integrity of their life-support system. If they can survive without me, I must not tamper. Inherent in man is a need to meddle in the physical world. He just can't leave it alone. The tampering forms the basis for biological engineering. In all his messing around with the environment, man has shown great technical skill but little wisdom. And he has caused much harm.

149

Thanksgiving. I tend to underplay holidays, much as a golfer intentionally underplays a hole because he is afraid he will overshoot it. But you can undershoot Thanksgiving, as well, and that may be a mistake. The commercialization of holidays in America meets with resistance in some of us, along with a sense of annoyance and a fear of being exploited.

We now give gifts of flowers and candy on Easter; soon we will be exchanging Thanksgiving presents, I fear. Of course we celebrate by eating too much. We "pork out," as the kids say. When much of the world is hungry, if not actually starving, we announce to the world that we produce an abundance and can gorge on it. And a lot of it gets thrown away as garbage afterwards. This is shameful. It is obscene.

Once I had a terrible job. Consequently, I have never cared much for eating turkey. In the summer of my nineteenth year I worked at the end of an assembly line, packing freshly eviscerated turkeys in a box for freezing. It took five turkeys, turned head to tail, to fill a box. Then I added up the weights and wrote the total on the box. It was a hot, steamy room we worked in, and it started at seven in the morning. Behind me and my assistant, women on an assembly line gutted the plump pink carcasses and tucked the viscera back inside. I soon trumped up an occasion to quit and found another job.

More happily I remember another Thanksgiving. I was in the Army, briefly stationed in Anchorage, Alaska. A serviceman's dinner was provided by the YMCA. We had everything imaginable on the long banquet table. Local sportsmen donated a variety of game. I piled on my plate pieces of moose, bear, caribou, deer, elk, ptarmigan, grouse, duck, etc. It was a cross section of Alaska's bounty. Now ready to eat, I couldn't identify anything on my plate. So I guessed. The bear—if it was bear—was dark, tough, and greasy. What I liked best I think was moose, which was tender and tasty, much like pot roast.

This year Norma bought a 16-pound Butterball turkey. My parents helped us eat it. It was a pleasant occasion, but I went light on the bird. Those days on the turkey line are not entirely past. And I'm not sorry the holiday is over.

150

Next door behind us in town, and to the West, the nephews or grandchildren of our neighbor have built a pair of snowmen; I can see the statues from my study window, which opens up on their backyard. Only the vestiges of Sunday's snow remains. It is warm out and lightly raining. The snowmen have tipped slightly and are leaning against each other like a couple of drunks. One is a third again bigger than his buddy; he is the one who leans the hardest.

The little guy tries to shore him up. It's a losing battle. Hour by hour, the angle to the ground becomes more pronounced. By nightfall they will be joined in a gray rubble.

Fascinated by the process of disintegration, I check on them hourly. Are they still standing? At last glance they were barely vertical. Both have their backs turned to me, so I am unable to see their faces. This may be for the best. Their faces must have mushed horribly. They are unisex creatures, two mere humps of snow. The big guy is atop the little guy now. Imbedded in the backs of each are tiny leaves rolled up in the initial ball. I recognize them as being from my Japanese maple.

The ice is gone from the fish pond, and even from forty feet away, out my Northern study window, I can make out the Big Guy finning near the surface. He is an orange blur. The temperature hangs in the mid-forties, with the sun beaming all day, so perhaps insect life has been awakened and my goldfish are feeding. They like to come up on top, whenever the neighbors's cats are away.

151

I would rather flyfish than eat ice cream. And—remember—I am the guy who goes to the refrigerator, every night of his life, to build himself a vanilla cone to complete his dinner and his day.

This afternoon, Norma and I took in two photography shows in downtown Seattle. One was by Wynn Bullock of Carmel, California. He was the commercial photographer for the Army at Fort Ord when I took my basic training. So once I was his model, so to speak, along with 400 other soldiers in my infantry-training company. Nearly everybody bought a print but me. Another missed opportunity for me, because Bullock is now famous. The show was at Silver Image Gallery.

Down the street a block is Equivalents Gallery. It has a show of photos by Andre Kertesz, who is simply magnificent, one of the world's finest photographers. Before he died, confined to his apartment above New York City's Washington Square Park, he snapped numerous pictures from his window with his Leica rangefinder or his Canon SLR. Often the park was dipped in snow. How beautiful his shots are, with their wide aerial perspective.

152

Next door, the Johnstones's huge dogwood, *Cornus nuttallii*, extends well into our side yard, and we can see it from our dining room window. It is a year-round delight. I love that tree. I think of it as mine. I suppose the part that overhangs our property *is* mine, legally speaking. But I consider it—like the Johnstones themselves, Marshall and Karen—good neighbors and friends of a sort.

The dogwood is presently holding its leaves, which are undergoing their annual metamorphosis. I broke off a small branch—a big twig—and brought it inside the house to study it. The low humidity is causing the leaves to curl and dry fast, almost as I watch, and I am sorry I did it. By nightfall I will have to throw it out.

One leaf—not so large as my hand but bigger than my palm—forms a wide oval that comes to a point at the end opposite the stem. I see on the withered branch some smaller leaves, with a bract from last spring's bloom at it terminus; this is the same mottled nub that was surrounded by scarlet pinheads a couple of months ago. What a lot of activity takes place in a single tree, from season to season. And so much of it passes unobserved, unappreciated.

The Johnstones's tree is pretty in a subtle way. It is very low keyed in its appeal, which might be easy to miss. One has to look closely to see the beauty, and be satisfied with muted shades of purple, green, gold, and brown.

Meanwhile, up at the river, the white Cherokee dogwood has wrinkled its leaves, and they are an ugly gray-green, pale on the underside. And our *Cornus florida*, which we bought and planted this fall, still holds its foliage of brilliant scarlet and wine, after having dropped about a third of its leaves when we transplanted it. However, the color is starting to fade badly. Next year, because of chemicals in the soil, or the lack of them, I suspect the *florida*'s leaves will be as dull and colorless as the Cherokee's.

153

Today I am forty-eight. 'Nuf said.

154

The world is aswim in wan gray light. The macadam is the same dull color, but shiny. Everywhere I look, in this flat light, I see the same color, or lack of color, extending in every direction, just like water. The interstate is awash from heavy rain, and I cannot judge the depth of the water until my car slows alarmingly and shudders from side to side. It makes me feel like I've lost control and will crash.

The hard rains continue. Isn't this what I asked of the skies, a month ago? It is, indeed. The rivers are steadily rising and turning to mud, as they gain height. But this will bring in the fresh winter steelhead.

155

The water ouzel is a curious bird, small and discreet. My dictionary lists him as a "blackbird," but surely he is not, or else the name is used descriptively, not generically. The ouzel is a diver and should belong to that genus, though he really looks nothing like those birds, either. He slightly resembles a coot or a scoter, or perhaps a murre. I'd have to check "none of the above," though. The illustration in Roger Tory Peterson's *Field Guides to Western Birds* places him among the nondescript birds. Right.

The ouzle feeds on weeds and, when available, insects, but finds much of his food at the bottom of the river. This is why he is always diving. He will eat salmon and steelhead eggs, one at a time; I know this for a fact, because I've seen him do it when salmon were spawning in the shallows.

The ouzel is—if not the fisherman's friend, certainly his frequent companion. He is not especially shy. Today I saw one come bopping up to my feet while I waded. When he ducked under, I could see him flatten out triangularly and swim along the bottom smoothly, like a fish, as he went after a small single egg from a fisherman's discarded bait. He did this a number of times, coming to the surface with a pink dot clamped in his small beak.

Apparently no water can ever be too cold for an ouzel to submerge himself in. Me, I'd be walking around the edge of the ice on my birdy tiptoes, and never, never go under. Here there is ice on shore, but the ouzel is happily splashing around in the shallows. He must have a high body temperature and rapid heartbeat, as so many small birds do, to survive the cold. It is a commendable bird, though not pretty, dun colored and unmarked. In appearance, the harlequin duck puts the ouzel to shame, as does the kingfisher. And while the belted kingfisher is an acrobat, the ouzel can fly circles around him.

156

Overnight the vacant lots in the city have grown Christmas trees. Most are of a uniform size—about seven feet. Since yesterday trees are appearing everywhere. Most lots have rows of colored lights strung across their fronts, drawing the attention of passing cars. Often a battered travel trailer is parked along the edge of the lot. Its purpose is to give shelter from the rain to the man selling trees. He remains overnight to prevent people from stealing trees.

Who would steal a Christmas tree? Many people, I suspect. The man who runs the lot usually has a dog that bites. All in all, a lot is not a friendly place. It is a place of opportunism.

It annoys me to be reminded of Christmas so early. I am not mentally prepared for the season. If I bought a tree when they first go on sale, such as now, it would be brown by Christmas Day. Its needles would be all over the livingroom carpet and the tree would resemble a coatrack. It would be a skeleton of a tree.

Some years ago, when we were terribly poor, Norma and I didn't buy our tree until Christmas Eve, when the lots were well picked over and what was left comprised a buyer's market. The next two years we erected a synthetic tree we inherited from my parents, after they decided they had enough of it and went back to the real thing. Wife, son, and I *assembled* our tree in kit form by putting notched limbs into holes already drilled for them. It was a little like playing with Tinker Toys. At one point in the assembly process, the tree resembled a cross, which reminded me of Christ's ending, instead of his beginning.

The fake tree was a mistake and soon we returned to a real one. The artificial tree remains stored under the house. It is the real McCoy for us again, a green tree. Another way to get one is to go to the country, pay for a permit, and cut it yourself. You can drive to a tree farm. Or drive to a corner lot and buy one that has been dead a long time from a man with a cigar butt clenched in his jaw. Whatever way, the time is soon upon us.

Here's how it goes: I drive us to the lot and Norma inspects tree after tree. She rejects many that I would buy. No matter which one we purchase, it requires modification, once we get it home. Under close supervision, I get out the brush saw and am instructed to take an inch or two from the bottom, so that the top doesn't press against the livingroom ceiling. Then we crank the tree into the special stand and tighten down the four thumb screws that hold it in place. We add water to the bowl in the stand and cover the base over with a fluffy white cloth that is supposed to be snow.

It is way too early to play this game. Each year I put it off as long as possible. But finally its time comes. Going out and buying the tree is not exactly dreaded. It is more a thing to be put off and off. I hope for three weeks more of avoiding the task. When the tree is purchased, it means Christmas time is upon us.

157

This is the time of the year when 80 percent of the perfume is sold, and probably 90 percent of the lingerie. The Christmas catalogs have been mailed out three months ago to charge-account customers and the ads in the newspapers are clamoring, "Buy me." On TV the perfume ads promise a very specific bliss for men who put out sufficient coin to please their ladies. Can it be true that women perform sexual favors for men who shell out for perfume and lingerie? Or is this just advertising?

Do women in real life wear these flimsy nighties? Or do they sleep in snug flannel, like my wife does? Her long nightgown indicates little of what lies underneath and seems designed to prevent carnal access. Most adult women have a drawer full of sexy underwear and nightgowns given them by their men, over time, and shun donning it. Does it make them feel wanton? Should it? What they want at nighttime is to be warm and have a comfortable sleep. Each year at this time I am tempted to buy Norma some lingerie, but stop myself in time. But men must buy women *something*—what? The lingerie business is thriving. Men keep rising to the lure—or is it allure? Without lingerie, women shall sleep in old sacks, which none of them would mind doing, I suspect.

All of the above is preamble to the fact that I have to go Christmas shopping and buy gifts for people I know well and those I don't. I can't put it off much longer. Is it just me, or does everybody hate Christmas shopping—everybody but the retailer, that is? Christmas is a traumatic time and puts great stress on families. Husband and wife, father and mother, children and parents—all quarrel and often never resolve the rift. The suicide rate increases. Sometimes divorce is the kindest way out of an impossible situation.

Christmas is a time for children. Yet they are inevitably disappointed, their expectations beyond reasonable fulfillment. Christmas is a time that was never meant to be. Yet it can't be avoided.

I run to do my shopping late. I do it in a fevered rush. I dash from one department store to another, not knowing what I'm after. I've reached the point where I will buy nearly anything put in front of me. This is typical.

It is always raining around Christmas. Besides having cold feet, I find they are wet, also.

158

Now forty-eight, I am properly "an old fart." Or improperly. Young boys and girls look at me with derision. The gray in my hair and beard is dominant. I may soon be obliged to do something awful to live up to people's expectations of me.

I don't hear any too well in my right ear. It has been this way for some time. Often I have to ask people—Norma, mostly—to repeat what they've just said. The loss goes back to my Army basic training, when for days we fired rifles at the range to qualify, while wearing steel pots on our heads; a procedure called coaching is what did the major damage. It was the guy's rifle next to me, while I lay beside him at right angles. My ears rang for days afterwards. Over the years my hearing loss has grown worse. Perhaps my mind strays, as well.

I have but 23 teeth in my mouth, six of those caps, and some caps with a root canal underneath them. When I fish in winter, my hands get colder than they used to do. The tips of the fingers on my left hand are the worst. And my joints creak and groan, particularly mornings after a hard day's use.

Christmas season is a time of assessment and evaluation. Often it hurts. I have accomplished less than I expected or intended. I've published little and not earned much. Nonetheless, much can be found on the asset-side of the ledger. I have a wife and son whom I love and who love me, or else they are clever enough to trick me into believing this, and I am no fool. We are loved, not as we expect to be, but as we deserve to be, and it is earned, so we had better learn to recognize it before it is too late. The recognition that one is loved comes as an astonishment and a delight. In itself it comprises a minor triumph.

The land we own on this beautiful river, the North Fork, is about as choice and beautiful and wild as tamed land ever gets. My enjoyment of it never ceases. The way I live and work—my life style, that is—is modest but satisfying. My writing says what I want it to say. I hope someday others will enjoy what I have to say as much as I have had, saying it. It strikes me as meaningful and unique. At the same time it is ordinary. To many it would seem a mundane life.

I fish often. Good music and literature fill my idle moments. The money is holding out. In this time of winter celebration and the rebirth of the land, I find much to be thankful for. Let us then praise what civilizations loosely and multifariously call God. And this time, as with nature, capitalize it in reverence.

159

Two years ago, with money from an article I sold to *View Northwest Magazine*, I bought a Pioneer stereo system and a BIC phonograph. At the same time, I purchased a Pioneer tape deck and two huge speakers (12 inch) from Radio Shack. With the tape deck, I've pilfered off the public airwaves much good music. Beethoven and his string quartets comprise much of my collection.

The magazine paid me $450 for the article, which was probably a record payout for them. But a lot of hard work went into the article. It was very solid and included a host of color transparencies, plus numerous black and white prints. I made the prints myself and paid a custom lab for processing the color slides. I charged them $590. They howled in protest but ultimately paid it.

I watch the newspaper listings for programs on the FM stations and mark on my calendar when something special is going to be played—a Beethoven quartet, for instance. But my taste isn't strictly classical. I taped a Grateful Dead concert, just the other day, and some albums by Joni Mitchell and Linda Ronstadt.

It is Beethoven—with all his variety and profundity—that I keep coming back to, however. Many must feel about him as I do. What a range of moods his music reflects. Foremost are his string quartets. Everybody recognizes his symphonies, of course. But I am getting to know his piano concertos and sonatas. And his violin-piano sonatas are wonderful. I have much music by Mozart and Haydn, as well. Only Beethoven makes me write in superlatives, however.

Someone once wrote, "He who knows Beethoven can never experience complete despair." I hope this is true.

160

The Cicero heron comes in for a rude landing behind me, as I stand up to my hips in the Grant Creek Drift, fishing. What an gangly bird. He doesn't see me, or else mistakes me for a stump, I am so still. But not nearly so treelike as he, once he is rooted in the water.

He settles down on a mound of silt about 100 yards away, under the shade of a huge cedar that rises from the edge of the beach. The act is a little like folding up an umbrella in a phonebooth. Immediately he becomes invisible. His blue-gray color blends in with the winter world—the leafless alders, the wet beach itself, the raw earth of an undercut bank, the yards and yards of blackberry thicket. His eye catches mine and he realizes that what he is looking at is human. I have encroached on his territory and pose a threat. He cocks his head—or is it merely his eye? Head tucked into his chest, his long beak jutting downward, his slender stork legs delicately supporting his lumbering body, he is difficult for me to extract from the scenery, there on the beach, even though I know exactly where he landed. I took my eyes off him for a moment, which was a mistake. Now I can't relocate him. He *has* to be there, somewhere. If he'd flown off, wouldn't I have seen his huge shadow cross the beach?

Ah, there he is, still on the ground, next to some brush in the shadows, disguised as a piece of driftwood. He is like the mountain in the Zen poem. First you see him, then you don't, for he is the same color as the fog-enveloped landscape.

I am much impressed—perhaps awed and mystified are the right words—by herons. Once threatened, they never quite achieved "endangered" status. They have become fairly common recently and, thus, are less mysterious. But I will never become oblivious to them or take them for granted.

My vigorous casting suddenly disturbs the bird and he takes to the air in a precautionary maneuver, doing so quickly, quietly. The first thing I know he is mid-air and his shadow is passing along the beach. Then he drifts in for another landing, two-hundred and fifty yards down the beach.

Goodbye, Heron, I think; see you another day.

Suddenly two dark shapes pass overhead, their shadows lagging. What, two more herons? It is so. They light far down the strand. They are very different from the earlier one. One is young, with no black on its crest. The other is bigger, fatter, older. He wears a black skull cap, trimmed in white. I can learn a lot about herons and their respective maturity by studying this pair. The trouble is, they won't let me get close enough for a good look.

Is there a way to tell a male from a female heron? My bird books don't mention this aspect. Perhaps these are a mated pair, one young, the other not. Do herons mate for life—like bald eagles and, I hear, ospreys? Again my bird books are silent on the subject. Ospreys go to Chile every winter, I hear. They won't return until spring and the time for nesting. They raise their young in special trees that are protected by regulation. They are called roosts.

Herons have reasons for hanging around all winter. They are homebodies. Thus they are more my kind of bird. They do not venture far, but get to know their small territory well. I commend such behavior.

161

A certain willow tree has leaves that resemble the secondary flight feathers of ducks and geese. Whenever I see these fallen on the ground I think of diving ducks. The leaf also looks a little like a dagger, or a letter opener, especially when its underside is turned up, revealing a silvery sheen along the belly. The resemblance is so strong I'm sometimes moved to pick one up by the tip of the blade.

At the Lime Plant Road the river snuggles up to the inside bend on a long beach of smooth cobbles. Here I find leaves from the willow. The trees are bereft of any still hanging. I search the bare boughs, trying to find the parent tree. I fail. Naked, they all look alike.

These willow leaves are different from others I've seen lately. Those were fatter, rounder, with no general resemblance to anything recognizable to make them memorable.

162

The logged-off land up behind our river property we call "The Outback," though that name properly comes from Australia and describes land that is arid and has few trees growing on it. This land is dedicated to growing trees and they are young and dense.

I once thought Pope and Talbot owned The Outback. I wrote this down, because I believed it. Well, I was wrong. I got the idea because Pope and Talbot short-platted the land at Stillaguamish Meadows. Scott Paper owns The Outback. All logging companies are pretty much alike, in terms of what they do. But Scott cuts its trees primarily for pulp, out of which is made paper, often toilet paper. A tree doesn't have to be very old for them to saw it down.

Because it was cold and dry, and Norma was taking a week's vacation, we went up to the river to perform our regular bout of landscaping. We are trying to return our land to its natural configuration and flora. We transplanted about 25 alders, all of them small but one which was about ten or twelve feet tall. The tall one was a tree we had transplanted five years ago, but now required moving, for it was blocking our driveway and the car was regularly bunging it. It had grown nicely. Moving it probably saved its life from repeated car nudgings.

Most of the alders came from The Outback. They were alder saplings, with large soggy root masses and very heavy. They grew along the right-of-way on the logging road that slowly rose toward the Whitman Bench in a series of switchbacks. We brought along a couple of pressed-fiber buckets and a five-foot spade. We were looking for some small conifers, besides.

We inched up the hill along a road whose flanks were choked with ancient logging slash, making them dense and impassable. The Outback is an ecosystem comprised of young second-growth hemlock and Douglas fir. The alders were not wanted and would soon be destroyed with a pesticide.

An old broadleaf maple, three-quarters dead, had fallen across the old logging road, just where it commences its steepest climb. This had happened since we were there last, a couple of weeks ago. Somebody had cut a path through its thick trunk with a chainsaw, then moved the huge sections off to the shoulder. The tree was nearly dead already. Much of the wood was punky brown and flaky.

A large sign warned people not to salvage any of the dead maple. Or did it? It read, "Cut No Trees!" We decided that it did not mean us, for we only intended to dig some up. Alders to Scott were a weed. Undeterred, we pressed on. The road became steeper. I wondered if anybody could drive it in anything less than a logging truck? Surely not in the family car.

After a bit, we became aware of the purr of a well-tuned pickup truck behind us. Slowly, almost soundlessly, it was tracking us. I motioned Norma into an old draw ahead. The truck eased by and passed where we stood hidden behind a screen of small red cedars. I listened for the truck and decided it was gone.

We continued up the road. A couple of hundred feet ahead we came to another turnout. It contained just what we were looking for. In addition to the alders it held numerous tiny hemlocks. We could use some of those, too.

A young hemlock is a weepy, spindly thing. Its tiptop droops to one side and its tiny needles are lace-like, delicate and pretty, much like the fonds of a maidenhair fern. When you transplant a hemlock, it weeps for months. Then, if you are lucky, it adjusts to the trauma of being uprooted, and puts out tentative new growth. These needles are pale green. The earlier growth is dark. In time the new growth thickens and becomes old and the tree's trunk increases in diameter. Eventually the tree develops the sturdiness and sweeping grace that makes it the favorite of many.

Cramming a couple into our fiber pots, we looked up and saw the pickup truck glide past, almost silent. We saw only the top of the ghost truck, and we weren't certain whether we had ourselves been seen. The sound of its motor died away—*too* quickly, I thought.

"Let's get out of here," I told Norma. We picked up our pots and began hurrying down the road. Each of us carried a potted hemlock, plus some tiny alders with near naked roots. I spotted the pale blue of the truck up ahead. Uh-oh. Cautiously we closed the distance. The driver-side door was wide open, but nobody was at home.

"Let's ditch the trees in the woods and come back for them later," I urged Norma. We did this, walking quickly past the empty truck and down the grade leading back to the Whitman Road. When we were a short distance ahead, I heard the truck idling softly behind us, moving at exactly our rate of speed.

We split off to opposite sides of the road, which was narrow at this point, so that the truck had room to pass between us. This put only one of us on the driver-side window. I hoped it would be Norma, but it was me.

The driver stopped. He addressed me in a mild, not unpleasant manner. "When I saw you with those pots and shovel, I thought something was up, but I figured you wouldn't be doing much harm. If you live around here, we don't mind you taking a Christmas tree for your personal use. Or even two of them. What we worry about is people who come in with trucks and carry away trees that are maturing and worth money. There we lose."

Boldly I asked, "So you don't mind if we walk off with a couple of four-foot hemlocks?"

He smiled. "Well, I'm not supposed to let anybody take anything. But personally I don't care. Scott doesn't mind if you want to cut yourself a tree for Christmas. But you, you're digging them up. You must want to *grow* a tree. Do you folks live near by? We're neighborly."

He pointed to a tree that was twenty-five feet high. "See that one?" he asked. "It's worth twenty dollars to us, right now. It's obvious that you aren't about to cut and haul away a tree of that size. Not on foot, anyway, with only a shovel. In a few years, that tree is going to be worth plenty on the market. It's a loss like that we're concerned with."

Since he seemed so friendly, and because we had already been caught in the act, so to speak, I asked him a few questions about trees. He seemed happy to have somebody to talk to. He told me the slash area had been hand-planted with three-year-old trees about fifteen years ago. Most of them were grand firs (*Abies grandis*), but there were some Douglas firs mixed in. My small hemlocks and cedars were not planted; they were the results of natural regeneration, as had been the "weed" trees—the alders and broadleafed maples.

He said Scott regularly sprayed the area with pesticides, one year going after the alders, the next the maples. A big broadleaf maple can "shade an acre," he told me. Doug firs grew poorly in the shade. I had thought this a rationalization for clearcutting but now realized it was also a fact. Douglas firs were properly called "the sunshine tree."

The grand firs he indicated with a broad sweep of his hand. They were about fifteen years old, as I had guessed earlier. I hadn't realized they were hand-planted, though. Already the firs had outdistanced the few alders and maples Scott had left standing by error. The firs were getting plenty of sunshine.

If tree rustling was a problem, I asked, why doesn't Scott put up a gate?

"Company policy," he explained. "Scott doesn't believe in locked gates."

How odd, I thought. Here they were worried about tree loss. At the same time, the obvious remedy of a locked gate was not their response.

I had more questions, but there wasn't time. The pickup truck drove off. We headed back for our cache of alders and potted baby hemlocks. And the work of getting them into the ground before dark.

163

Of the eleven free Douglas fir seedlings I planted in the spring, seven are doing splendidly and should put on good growth next year. They are fully acclimated to the front of our property. Two seedlings quickly died, and two more pulled back to a overall rust color, but still contain a bit of green and may survive, though badly set back. It will take them several years to recover to the point the others have. But they probably won't make it.

Consistent with what the man from Scott told us, the Douglas fir seedlings planted in full sunlight are doing best. The two that died, and the two that are doing poorly, were stuck into boggy soil in deep shade. My mistake. But we haven't room enough to accommodate 11 full-sized Douglas firs on our property, so the natural selection is all for the best, even though it is sad to see the trees you've planted die.

These are trees that will enter their prime long after I am dead. It is a chilling thought, but helps explains the immortality involved in gardening—and in landscaping, in particular.

164

Norma says the man from Scott must have said "seed," not shade, an acre. The seedlings from the maple's spinners would compete for nutrients with the commercial softwoods. Evergreens are softwoods, though their wood seems plenty hard to me when I must cut it. They are called it because they are conifers, and retain their needles year-round. It has nothing to do with the relative hardness of their wood. Conversely, hardwoods are leafed trees, which drop their leaves in winter.

I read a book once where the author had it backwards all throughout the book, but at least he, the editor, copy editor, and proofreader were consistent. There was not one instance of it being right. The book had been reprinted by a big New York publisher, who has a reputation for good editing, and nobody bothered to correct it. Perhaps nobody pointed it out to them.

Foresters maintain that a single mature Douglas fir can seed twenty acres from its lofty stand. Hence the maxim that forests can be cut in twenty-acre clearcuts without the need for replanting. What folly this was, and what greed. We are paying the price for it now, in terms of slow regeneration of early-cut forests.

165

To live by the season, not by the clock! What a noble goal! Yet how difficult it is to accomplish, in today's society, when life is tightly scheduled and people no longer "meet" but "interface."

What a sane man must do today is pick and choose wisely from both worlds—the world of nature, where all has its moderately slow, inevitable cycles, replete with beauty and death, and from the world of technology, where all our livelihoods, our creature comforts, our necessities, derive.

Archie Satterfield, in his book *After the Gold Rush*, alludes to this dichotomy. Only some of the people in the Klondike were able to achieve a successful life in the bush. Many could not and perished. "You cannot expect to live off the land," he writes, which is the lesson the Counterculture failed to learn. Whatever made them think they could? If they thought this was what Thoreau was telling them, they seriously misread him.

The simple life *is* possible today, but not many people will opt for it. Most people spend up to and past their incomes. They don't want a life of simplicity. They want to posses most of what the modern world offers. They will not say "no" to themselves and their impulses. In a way I don't blame them. They want what they have been conditioned to want, and they want it now.

I once wrote that Thoreau might approve of my sixteen-foot travel trailer—its efficiency, its utility, its economy. He might even agree with the amount of labor I had to exchange for my tiny "house on wheels." It was a good purchase, by his standards.

As for how land is used today, he might view land as a commodity to be used wisely—but used, nonetheless. He might not be in favor of locking up land in parks, say. Or he might—it is hard to tell, for he writes from multiple perspectives. The land belongs to man, is his credo. It is man's choice how he uses it.

He would probably be for the benevolent use of land and the exercise of privilege. I think of Scott Paper and its policy on locked gates. Most disagreements about land arise from conflicting ideas on how it is to be used. I like the unlocked gate concept.

Nothing should be taken from the land that cannot be replaced within a reasonable period of time. "Reasonable" is the key word and is disputable. This period might be defined as within one's lifetime, or less. Cutting, or sustainable use of, say, alder for firewood, is replaceable well within this time frame. Redwoods and Douglas firs are not. Nor are the climax stages of the Western hemlock and the mountain hemlock that grows slowly at high altitude. Or the Western red cedar. Other trees are roughly renewable, that is, within one's life span.

In any case, one must discern the truth of competing claims. Few public figures represent interests other than those who pay them through campaign contributions and by promising to provide voting blocs. The claim that "trees are a renewable resource" is true, but only over a very long time span, which doesn't count for much. A three-hundred year old tree—old growth—cannot be replaced in any less than five lifetimes. There is no honest way of claiming otherwise.

Saying a thing over and over, and presenting it as a fact, does not make it true. Yet the point sinks in through repetition. If not a lie, it is not the whole truth. Weyerhaeuser advertises itself to be "The tree-growing company." But they have to plant trees only because they keep cutting them down.

I am mainly worried about old growth—trees that are hundreds of years old. The U.S. Forest Service owns much of such land. The private companies have cut the last of their old growth fast. Because it is gone, many timber companies and mills are dependent on the Forest Service for their source of trees. And many mills are calibrated to cut only old growth. The demand is for this kind of timber. Too much was cut too soon. The timber companies simply can't wait for their seedlings to grow to harvestable size. It is too long a wait, without any profits coming in.

Today much timber is shipped to Japan. The argument against doing this is balanced against our unfavorable balance of trade with that country. We import more than we can sell them, and are not willing to do without their cars and electronics. The sale of our old trees is about all we have with which to counter their industrial superiority. And that is not a manufactured product but a consumable natural resource which—despite advertising claims to the contrary—is not renewable within a reasonable period of time.

Selfishly, I use my own remaining life span as a yardstick. It is not long. It is not long enough.

166

It takes more than a one-day spate to bring fresh fish up the river. I keep forgetting this, and venture out optimistically, and am met with fresh disappointment. This year the Stillaguamish Indians are netting the river five days a week. The tribe has no reservation, no landed claim, no treaty with the U.S. government. Yet it is recognized, along with the Tulalip Tribes, as a political entity. Both tribes have indisputable fishing rights, under the Boldt Decision.

Storms have been appearing in cycles, one right after another, heralded by strong winds and rapidly changing skies—cloud masses advancing in towering columns, for instance, then breaking apart to permit glimpses of patchy blue sky. Hours later the wind abates, but by then the rains have arrived in force and the sky is a close, depressing gray. The rain lessens to showers, heavy and abrupt for a while, then stops. Skies clear, the cold moves in, and a heavy frost descends. In the morning the frost is thick as snow. The sun bursts forth and a glorious day dawns promisingly. A few hours later, the winds pick up and the cycle commences again. So goes December.

Some years such cycles have produced extraordinary fishing, the rivers rapidly rising half a foot, or so, and dropping and clearing fast, with fresh fish ascending daily. But not this year, at least not yet.

167

My father learned today that he has a prostate problem and must undergo surgical examination Monday morning. He has had a physical exam, which was inconclusive and incomplete because of the pain he experienced in having a catheter stuck up his penis—well, pushed up as far as it would go, anyway. It must have been awful.

The fear is of cancer, of course. My heart goes out to him—in fact, my whole body does. A son feels biologically close to his father, no matter how much they may differ or disagree on many matters. Blood is blood; body, body. There is also the terrible feeling that, "There go I, in two or three more decades."

Often it is the case.

168

Beethoven's birthday today. He was born in 1770. The modern composer, Kodaly, was born on the same day—but who cares? Beethoven is without peer. The day should be an international holiday, with everybody lying back on his couch and listening to nothing but symphonies and string quartets on stereo headphones.

We might carry it further, to the point of hyperbole. On this day, each of us should strive to be heroic, pastoral, choral, etc. But I suspect we would only manage to be pathetic. Pathetique, I mean.

169

A day of unceasing hard winds, but little rain. This has been the pattern, with the rains holding off. It is a drought year, I keep forgetting. Most winter storms have failed to materialize. The sky darkens, as if threatening with a raised fist. Then a small rain falls. With the daytime temperatures in the mid-40s, snow is accumulating in the mountain passes. Moisture from the Pacific passes overhead and descends when it condenses over the Cascades. Thus our badly needed rain falls far to the East as snow.

The winds were so strong this A.M. that they carried the foot mat away from the front door and blew the Sunday paper into a wad against the corner of the house. I had to bring it in as loose pages and reassemble it. This was a big job, for it was a big paper. And I never got all of the pages and sections straight.

Norma and I bought our Christmas tree this afternoon—our first live one in several years. We are genuine again. This year's tree will remain outside, where it is cool, until we bring it inside later this week and trim it with feeling. We rationalized cutting down a tree by telling ourselves that they are grown specifically for this market, and we are not killing one that would have grown to maturity. I don't know whether this is true or not. The smell of a tree in the house will be a pleasant change from recent plastic Christmases.

In the Pacific Northwest it never really feels like Christmas. This is the land of rain. Rain is what makes the land so green, the rivers swift. But it is depressing and robs Christmas of much of its charm. So far we have managed to avoid the Christmas Specials on TV. It is not entirely self-control. Our big color Zenith is in the shop. This makes us morally pure. Instead of watching pap, we listen to good music. You know who.

Our shopping for Christmas is almost finished, except for some specialty food items. Probably we'll be done by Friday. Christmas falls on a Monday, which will play havoc with people's work schedules, since they are entitled to two days off, and the second one can be spaced anywhere in the week following. Different combinations have been worked out by different people, according to their special needs.

I am feeling a bit more Christmasy than usual, but will try to hold off good feelings for a day or so longer and remain my old curmudgeony self. It shouldn't be difficult. I've had lots of practice.

170

"Your father has cancer," says the doctor, following surgery early this morning, and the family blood chills in my veins. The news, despite the frequency of the event in fiction and in drama, is poignant. It is a heightened occasion. How many children have dreaded hearing the bad news, then had to listen to it? Nearly everybody, in his time.

The doctor *might* be wrong, but he doesn't think so. He's seen a lot of malignancies. I tell myself, doctors have been wrong before. It is why biopsies are performed—to provide a second opinion, the option for the microscope to confirm, or deny, what the practiced eye *almost* knows to be a fact. The lab report will come back on Thursday and the doctor will tell my father the results.

If the diagnosis is correct, Dr. Miller, an urologist and surgeon, says Dad will have 3-10 years to live. This is about normal for a man of 74 today, who has already outlived his expectancy by about five years. But we all want more from life, and I want more for my father.

Cancer at his age grows very slowly. The doctor thinks it is more likely to spread to his bones than to any major organ. He will treat it conservatively with hormone therapy, not with chemotherapy, which is painful and unpleasant. During surgery the doctor removed only that part of the gland that was enlarged and pressing against my father's bladder. This caused him to rise several times in the middle of the night to try to empty a bladder that wasn't full. It is a telltale symptom.

An illness in the family is upsetting. It brings up unpleasant matters. As soon as we are born, we start to die. It takes each of us different lengths of time to reach the same place. For this great gift—life—we must pay the price, the great debt, which is a death. It is the human situation.

And cancer is the humanist of situations. The Big C—as it's callously called—is waiting in the wings. It hits its target like a bull's eye. Poor Dad. I love him so. What a great guy.

171

To get my mind off matters of my father's illness, and as relief for all the trips back and forth to the hospital, I have been reading John D. McDonald. He writes mysteries about a beach-bum sleuth named Travis McGee, who stands for fierce individualism in a supermarket world. For spare change, he rescues sexy damsels in distress. Most of the dames have come into large sums of money, one way or another. McGee's fee is half of whatever they have, but is no more than what any lawyer charges, he points out. Also a lot of sexual gratification gets thrown in.

It is much silly fun. Each novel is about 200 pages long, which must not take him long to write. At least it wouldn't take *me* long, if I could write them. Each book has a color in its title, McDonald says, so he can tell them apart. He has written over 60 colorful novels.

His books seem filling, but have little nourishment. One quickly develops a taste for more. But they are a little pricey, so I borrow them from the library. Like other carbohydrates, they should be served with a light white wine or, better yet, a lager.

172

Our big Zenith is home again, after being in the shop for repairs, and I am the poorer for it. The Christmas Specials now can come at us, like kamikaze pilots bent on the destruction of our common sanity. This has been going on for weeks now, ever since the Thanksgiving Specials ended with the Macy's Thanksgiving Day Parade. The parade is the official kick-off for the Christmas season and is broadcast nationwide. The football games that follow it are much alike and anti-climatical.

The Friday after Thanksgiving accounts for more income to the retail stores than any other day of the year. It is then they generally know whether or not they are going to make a big profit. The stores remain open at night until the day before Christmas, when the buying frenzy ends in a mad rush.

Similarly, TV specials are a bonanza for actors, for they pick up residuals. One network pits its special against the others and strives for the highest rating. Their advertising rates are dependent on success. On a given night, we hungry watchers must choose from among them the one that is most appealing, that is, the coyest and most fetching. This is what Christmas has come down to. And we, having been deprived of our stupid TV, watch hungrily.

173

The shortest day of the year, and a dark and dreary one, too. The precise time of the sunset has held steady for a number of days. The slight lengthening out has all been on the other end of the clock.

Sunset is at 4:15 p.m. today. So early? It has to do with the sun's relative position to the earth. In my medieval heart I remain a Ptolemyist who believes the earth tilts on its axis because all the bad folks have gathered in one place and have thrown it off kilter. It is they who have stolen daylight and won't give it back. We must perform incantations and obscure rites to bring back the sun to his throne.

One way is to take a tree indoors and erect it. You plaster it with candles or light bulbs, and bedeck it with tinsel and ornaments that reflect the lights. You must hang long stockings by the chimney with care. The row must be exact. Recite a litany about reindeer and rooftops. Done right, Christmas will follow.

This is the festival of light. We pray for the sun and spring. Do not leave us forever in the Land of Perpetual Dark. I believe mightily in the renewal process. For instance, buds loom on bush and bough. On the rhododendron—if you look closely—you can tell which will be a leaf bud, which will be the bloom. Under the patchy snow, the grass is pale green, ready to burst forth. Birds that do not migrate surround us: Hawks, eagles, crows, herons, sandpipers, not to mention chickadees, sparrows, and Oregon juncos. What is there for them to eat? It doesn't really matter, not unless you are a bird, and have a hunger problem. Most around here don't. The land is too lush.

174

It has been confirmed. My father has prostatic cancer. Last night I visited him in the hospital. I already knew the basic facts. My brother-the-minister wormed the advanced information out of the doctor, then phoned me. Goddamn him. "I told you so," was the nature of his message. He and the doctor share in what is hidden from others. It forms a kind of conspiracy.

My father will be told this morning by the doctor what I have known unwillingly all night. I am ashamed of my knowledge. It is not as though he is feeble minded, or something. The doctor will solemnly relate his sad tale. My brother-the-minister will be present, perhaps perched on one corner of the bedstead, like a vulture on a limb. I will not be there for the unveiling. I would rather have my father tell me, once the horror has been assimilated, in his own sweet time. After all, it is his health, his prostate gland, that is at stake here.

What a terrible blow to him and his family. He looks so healthy, so vigorous, so sound of mind. He has a few minor signs of age, including a tendency to dwell in the past, and to tell the same stories over and over, and not listen to other people's statements. But minor, I say. Nothing wrong with his mind, nothing that needs such babying.

The doctor committed a gross breach of medical ethics in not telling his patient first. It is the patient, after all, who pays the doctor, and in this case, pays him quite well. Where is his allegiance, his integrity? Is the intimidating influence of ministers so great that all precepts of decency are overridden? Does he yield to another authority, one whose specialty is grief? Is the physician eager to defer on the subject of communicating bad news? (Or am I just sore because I can't bear to hear it?)

I can only sadly speculate on the course of events. What a travesty. What an insult. Not to me but to my father. Forgive me, but this has been a bad two weeks.

175

The prostrate gland is a partly muscular, partly glandular "body," located at the base of the urethra. It provides an alkaline fluid involved in climactic ejaculation. Hence it is an entirely masculine gland, the source of trouble or discomfort for five out of ten men as they age. It is prone to enlargement, infection, and of course cancer.

The prostate may be reached with a greased middle finger, in the form of the classical male insult. This examination determines whether the prostate is large or stiff—not a good sign. It may be operated on rectally (a surgically "dirty" job), by abdominal incision, or in the following manner, which allows for examination, sampling of tissue for biopsy, and removal of a portion through surgery accomplished at the same time.

First a catheter is forced up the penis and into the urethra, or chamber, where the surgery takes place, for this is what it is—call it what you will. If performed under local anesthetic, it is most unpleasant. Few can bear it, yet it is routinely attempted, I hear. My strong father begged for it to stop, and finally the urologist heard his words. Absolutely no information was gained this way, and the doctor had to repeat the process, this time under hospital conditions, with the patient mercifully unconscious.

A catheter is a tube. A wonder of slender instruments, made possible through the invention of microcircuitry and fiber optics, are utilized in the procedure. They may be inserted through the tube and perform inspection and surgery. The enlarged portion of the prostate pressing on the bladder and causing the annoying symptom of frequent urination (perhaps hourly) of only small, hesitant quantities can be removed this way, which produces quick relief. It doesn't always last for long, however. A biopsy can be made this way, and taken to the tumor clinic, where results are produced in two or three days by technicians with a heavy backlog. The report is then reviewed by several oncologists. The decision is reached by committee. This is or is not cancer. It takes time.

Meanwhile, the patient is sent to the recovery room and then—when he is feeling better—to a two-person room. The catheter is left in place and through it a flushing solution is steadily fed into the urethra, while the bloody residue of the operation is flushed out. Blood that hasn't mixed with air yet is a beautiful ruby red, without a trace of blue. It is the color of fresh strawberries. As the flushing and healing processes continue, the bag beside the prisoner's bed turns from red to orange. As he improves, it becomes golden amber, the color of inexpensive sauterne.

After three days, the drained solution has returned to a near lemony color, and the catheter is removed. It is a painless procedure, I'm told. Quite a contrast to the other time. The prisoner of the tube becomes a person again, and is grateful to the medical world for being permitted to perform once more the small daily functions, such as taking a pee unassisted.

The patient reports not feeling too badly, except for worrying about what the biopsy will reveal. He is allowed to eat food with a fork, but not to go to the bathroom or leave his bed. In the morning the doctor and minister/son break the news to the patient/prisoner. He accepts it courageously, fatalistically, the way he accepts everything that comes his way. ("God's will be done.") The doctor explains the patient's limited options; the minister/son translates them into psychobabble.

To control the cancer, there are two possible treatments. One is a large dose of female hormone, estrogen, which may cause a hormone war in his body and some distressing female side effects, such as male breast enlargement, etc. Or else the testes can be removed. This is a relatively simple operation. It is called castration. A 74-year-old man is not expected to have strong feelings about his masculinity, sexuality, etc. The doctor is ten years younger.

Castration is recommended because doctors *think* male hormones *may* cause cancer cells to grow faster. They aren't sure, but in mice. . . . Mice? My father is not a mouse, though it might be said he is slightly mouse-like in agreeing to do what his doctor suggests. He will give up his balls to the disease. Castration is performed by the same surgeon on Friday morning, four days after the original inspection and biopsy. The surgeon's bill is thus more than doubled. One has the feeling this scenario has been repeated many times. The older son sighs heavily but holds his tongue. Gone are the gonads that sired him. He feels his own scrotum tighten, in empathy. Gone, gone. (A "gone" for each testicle.)

The patient is told he can go home the following day, a Saturday. Christmas is Monday. My father is feeling enormous relief to be home for the holidays. Christmas means the world to him, and not just because he is a retailer. It always has. He is a sentimental cuss. The doctor tells him he will be well enough to leave for an extended California vacation by January 11, but must not play golf until after February first, nor should he lift heavy objects. It is a small enough price to pay for having left death a distance behind.

Prognosis is for three to ten years of what might be termed ordinary life, from this day onward. You live one day at a time, like a former drunk. Chances are, it will be something else that will "carry him away."

The patient looks and says he feels no different from in the past. I'd say he has always looked about fifteen years younger than his chronological age. He is bright-eyed, lightly tanned, lithe, active. What is going on in his mind, I can only guess at, but I can guess pretty close, being his son. The experience was horrible. It is no less terrible for being discretely conducted, in sanitary surroundings.

Outwardly he is calm, tranquil, accepting. He is grateful to be alive. He is eager to resume his life of routine, unchallenging events. Who wouldn't be?

[Note: My father died two and a half years later of heart failure, not cancer. This was predictable. But the strain on his heart was produced, without doubt, by the advancing cancer, which had metastasized to the lymph glands in his abdomen and legs. It kept dragging him down, and it finally nailed him at his large heart.]

176

You can't always get a steelhead when you want one, but sometimes you'll find you get one you need. (Apologies to the Rolling Stones.)

After a pretty dismal week—let's see, seven trips to see my father in nine days, and five to the hospital, with the sixth one this morning, to bring him back home—I drove to the Sky for a couple of hours fishing, late in the day. The Channel 5 television crew was filming a feature, but nobody had caught a fish and the crew was about ready to leave. I found myself in the middle of the action and began chatting with the cameraman. A steady rain fell. A few moments later I hooked a fish—a soft take, with a logy fish on the end of my rod. I looked up for the cameraman, but he was gone. The steelhead continued to fight poorly. Several people were anxious to exercise their nets, but I shooed them away and slid the fish up on a small sand spit. It was a beautiful nine-pound male. No other fish were caught by the crowd for the remainder or the day.

I appeared twice on the local news, but without my fish. Once, hooded and casting away, the second time, with my hood down, talking to a man I know only as Stan. Fishing intimates will recognize me. The fish we will eat for Christmas dinner at my parents's house. There will be turkey, too, knowing my mother and how much she likes it.

177

When I took my father home from the hospital this A.M., he was running a low (101 degrees) fever. He is being dosed with sulfa drugs, and should throw off the infection. When I left him, he had changed into pajamas and bathrobe, and was preparing to nap in his favorite chair, TV on in front of him. He greatly enjoys the array of football games at this time of the year. They are the perfect complement to people like him, who must remain sedentary for a reason.

Christmas Eve Day, with a Chinook wind rolling in from the Southeast, bringing balmy temperatures. Fifty-five degrees, it remains cool in the shade. These clear skies mean a light freeze by midnight. Besides benefiting Santa—making his sleigh run more smoothly—it will help to clear the rivers for fishing.

At dusk we drove to Lynnwood for the routine madhouse Christmas Eve celebration at Norma's mother's, where eight grandchildren vied for attention. What a clamor. But we would not be happy if it were any quieter or more orderly.

178

Saying grace over Christmas dinner, my father was so glad to be home from the hospital and functioning halfway normally, he broke down. Tears flooded his cheeks and he was made speechless by the fact of simply being where he belongs and alive. The presence of his two sons, their wives, his two grandchildren, plus his own wife of the years, comforted him greatly. His vulnerability was evident; oddly, I loved him no less for this sudden show of weakness.

He used to be an austere and formidable figure—to me, to everyone. He wanted to be respected for what he was, a business man who had gone out into the marketplace and carved out a good living for himself and his brood. He was the same kind of person he respected most. And he got respect from my brother and me. But respect often precludes love or affection. Now, weakened, brought down by illness, he got both. He had to fall in order to rise, at least in my esteem. There was a time when I would have despised him for not being strong. Today, I loved him more. How ironical.

After dinner, while crossing the livingroom on the deep pile carpet, my mother stumbled. My father lunged forward to catch her. He missed by a country mile. I told him, "Dad, if she ever fell, you'd never be able to get there in time. Nobody could." He nodded, grimly.

Later, he told me, in an aside, "If anything happens to your mother, I don't know what I'd do. I couldn't get along by myself. I live in dread of that day." And he is the one with cancer.

She is older than he by several years and, since the cancer discovery and hospital stay, she seems so much stronger, in spite of her many complaints and legitimate health problems. For instance, she has been a chainsmoker for more than fifty years and drinks enough coffee daily to float a rubber ducky. They are mutually devoted and dependent to a degree that might be called pathological by those with a clinical bent. Symbiotic is a kinder word for this relationship. They would be at a terminal loss without each other.

According to the actuaries, my father will precede my mother to the grave by many years. That is for the best, for she could survive alone better than he could. He admitted as much to me earlier tonight. So I hope he goes first, since one of them has to. It is actuarial. What a sad Christmas, all in all. This best you could say is it is bitter-sweet.

Today I know but this: A swift death is the only one worth having.

179

On Christmas Day, Norma and I walked around Green Lake, while Garth delivered his newspapers, late in the afternoon. I should have run the distance, but running is anti-social. Great mobs of wildfowl were in evidence. Canada geese (large), domestic ones (smaller), many paired and communal mallards, grebes (or are they scaups?), and a couple of odd-looking characters that I am totally unfamiliar with. One of the males had a pale green head, with white Pompadour-like stripes, and another bird has similar markings, but with a bronze (called rufous, in the bird book) head. I know not their names.

Returning home I consulted Roger Tory Peterson—the book, not the person. The birds were (1) the American widgeon, (2) the European widgeon, sometimes called Asian. That explains the similarities. Also the differences.

What an interesting find. Ordinarily we spot only mallards and mergansers, so I was unprepared for a new species and baffled by appearances. If pressed for their identity, knowing so little, I might have guessed blue-winged teal, for that species is reported to be a pretty bird and a surface-feeding duck. I wonder how many other things I am wrong about? Or don't know for a fact?

Also spotted was a duck floating with its head under water, its body bobbing lightly on the wavelets. When it didn't right itself, after a bit, I realized that it was not sleeping but was dead. Well, birds die; they have to die some place. A water bird should die in the water.

Green Lake is an urban park where I used to catch a lot of trout. It is crowded on nice days, when people don't have to work, such as on Christmas, when a walk is known to aid digestion. The lake is jammed with bicycles, joggers, and people like ourselves, out for a walk. The lake has many moods. One of my best photographs is of the fog lifting, with sunlight filtering through the trees. I took it one October. The special light lasted for seconds and I caught it.

Many locations at the lake provide Seraut-like formal settings and I am tempted to try to grab some with the small camera. They are ever shifting and reforming, never exactly to be repeated.

180

Our lives are ruled by statistics. Relative numbers tell us the extent of our successes and inform us of how badly we have failed, when we do. We also use numbers shamelessly to advance our causes. When the numbers work against us, we pretend they are different or don't really mean what they say.

Viz. In the past three afternoons of fishing, I have caught three steelhead, releasing two of them. Okay? I fished about four hours each afternoon. Right? Therefore, I averaged a fish every four hours. None of these data is to be trusted. It is a false sample, as the scientists say. Usually it takes me much longer to get a fish. But I forget about those instances.

The truth keeps intruding, keeping us honest, or less dishonest, as the case might be. My friend Bill Peterson tells me, "Fishing keeps us humble." He means, we usually don't catch any fish. Having been defeated repeatedly early this month makes a fish now all the sweeter. These times arrive as a bountiful blessing, a bonus.

181

The Whitman Road is covered with black ice and crusted snow, making driving in and out of the river place difficult and choked with excitement that I don't need or want. But our steep community drive was bare and the ground frozen solid, which made driving easy. I found the door to the trailer iced shut, and I could not warm it sufficiently with my hands to open it. The thermometer read 22 degrees. An angler was wading down the river on the far side. I knew exactly how the cold and icing were effecting him and his fishing, for I've been there.

Snow hung in the cedars and on the old hemlock, and bent the rhododendrons nearly to the ground. The original dogwood has given up all its leaves but two, which flap resolutely in the breeze but refuse to fall. The stones along the edge of the river are frozen into their beds of sand and will not budge to the toe. Skim ice on the edge of the stream fractures prettily into smithereens when I step on it. The mud puddles are solid ice, and if I jump on them hard enough they shatter into thick shards.

This is the usual stuff of December. Tonight it takes me hours to get warm in the city, after my hours out-of-doors in the country. Even then I can't forget the cold. My study warms to 62 degrees, after several hours of gas heat blasting through the vent. I remember that it was 58 degrees when I started out.

I will not return to the river until the thaw. That may not be until next year. It's only a few days off.

182

Cold, colder, coldest. That's how you decline this weather. But what beautiful bright days we are having. Not a cloud in the sky, and at sunset a pink glow spreads across the horizon to the South and West.

I can just make out the outlines of the goldfish— including the bulge of the Big Guy—through their ice ceiling. It is about an inch thick and wavy from repeated thawing and refreezing. Occasionally one of the fish moves an inch. All are near the surface, probably because that is where the dissolved oxygen is. What is their body temperature, I wonder? A few degrees above the freezing point. They must have antifreeze in their veins.

Some years we lose our crop of goldfish from a prolonged freeze. Other years we bring them inside and winter them over in the basement. The past two or three winters have been mild. We took a chance with the goldfish, this year, which may prove to be a mistake. They looked pretty good today, under the circumstances. Under the ice.

One good effect of a long, hard freeze is that the insect population is greatly reduced the following summer. This will mean fewer mosquitoes and manure flies, up at the river. Our old cat sleeps inside and doesn't mew to be let out at night, and hardly during the day. Amazing how strong his bladder and bowels have become. Usually he spends the night in our neighbor's garage, which he enters through a tiny opening in its side paneling, much as a rodent would. There—spotting his lair—I found him curled up on an old rug in the corner. Now it is too cold, thanks.

When I turned the gas heat on to warm up my study, intending to stay the day, he lay across the vent and blocked it with his body. I, busy writing, noticed the room was not getting warm. Cat and I had an argument about what was happening, and I hauled him away, protesting.

Siamese are articulate. I argued my case. He looked at me with genuine loathing; in a cat this is considerable. We have since made up. The new rule is that he must keep away from my heat vent, but he may sit by me or by the kitchen heat vent, which is only a third open, so that I get most of the heat in back.

There are two reasons for his banishment. One is that he takes all my warmth, and I come first. The other is that he gets so hot that it makes him sick and he upchucks his breakfast, usual into the grate. I have to clean it up, of course, for he won't. And his fur gets too hot to touch, when I must pick him up to move him. When the weather warms up, the rules will change. I will announce when.

In the meantime, we await the thaw.

183

The last day of the last month of the year. Mackerel clouds scud across the Southeast sky, approaching fast. They will bring an end to the cold snap. The change will probably arrive in the form of flurries of dry, drifting snow. Already the temperature has soared to 26 degrees, which is not exactly balmy but is an improvement from the low teens of last night.

Vegetable that I am, I am ensconced in wool and watching the Dallas-Atlanta football game, prior to the Super Bowl Game, a couple of weeks hence. The teams are tied, 20-20, in the third quarter, and the star quarterback for Dallas has been sacked and stunned. He's out for the remainder of the game.

The sky last night was bright with stars like Van Gogh's cornflowers. Each ordinary star became a planet in brightness. Today all remains frozen.

Tonight marks a half-year of daily effort on this book, "Country/City: A Year At The River." Each day I wrote my entry slowly in longhand, sometimes in ink, usually in pencil, hoping this method of composition would make me more deliberate and precise. Some future day I will begin to convert it to typescript. Then to a computer printout.

This afternoon I looked through Edward Weston's *Daybooks*. He is the photographer's photographer and his journals are deeply moving, the perfect counterpart to his photographs; the journals also help explain the photographs' content.

He attempted to destroy his daybooks and failed. How odd that he should have wanted to do this. Why? Do they say too much? Fortunately they survive. We would be poorer without them. They testify to the rigor of the creative process—its intensity and destructiveness, and how the artist often tears apart what he loves most. And the lives of those who love him.

Now Norma comes into the room to tell me my good friend, Captain Video, calls. Part three of Eugene O'Neill's *Mourning Becomes Electra* is on the air It is a play I recently read and fascinates me still. So we spend New Year's Eve viewing the tube, as most of America does, I presume. But the play is a quality production, an example of what TV can provide at its best.

A pause to welcome the new year in, with a kiss and a hug on the cold front porch. Here and there we hear a firecracker and the banging of a pot or pan. It is a tradition to let older children stay up this late, and greet the new year with a noise of their choosing.

Then it's on to whatever may follow. Let it be a happy new year. And then I think sadly of my father.

184

This is the day when hungover middle America watches its bowl games from deep within its easy chair, perhaps with a glass of hair-of-the-dog as accompaniment and antidote. And afterwards, there's the brown tree to be dismantled, the ornaments to be packed away in their boxes until another year. Why should it be any different in my household? A man is considered normal, healthy, to the extent he thinks and behaves like his peers. Hence the benefits of mediocrity.

185

I am reading another John D. MacDonald *Travis McGee Mystery*. This one is *The Turquoise Lament*. It is better than some of the others and has high literary merit.

Some vintage MacDonaldisms: "We drank until the buzz was exactly right, and then we ate the specialties of the house." (Page 44.) On Christmas, in a paragraph that is much longer: "Counter clerks radiate an exhausted patience leavened with icy flashes of total hate. The energy crisis is accelerated by five billion little colored light bulbs, winking off and on in celebration. Amateur thieves join the swollen ranks of the professionals in ripping off parked cars loaded with presents, in picking pockets, prying sliding doors open, shoplifting and mugging the ever-present drunks. Bored Santas jingle their beggar's bells and the old hymns blur loudly through the low fidelity speakers of department-store paging systems." (Page 92.)

And from page 15, this futuristic specimen: "In A.D. 3174, the busy, jolly nonsexicles on the planet Squanta III will sever our spinal cords, put us into our bright little eternity wombs, deftly attach the blood tube, move the eyelids quickly and painless, and, with little chirps of cheer, strokes and pats of friendship and fore-surrounded by a bright dimensional vista of desert, a smell of heat and sage, a sound of the oncoming hoofs on full gallop as, to the sound of a cavalry bugle, John Wayne comes riding, riding, riding. . . ."

Finally, this terrific commentary in allegorical form on casual sexual coupling from page 111: "The Great Magician has called us up from the audience. He had wanted a man and a woman. Marian and I had come from opposite sides of a packed theater, accepting the risk of volunteering, and had been locked together in the magic box by the Magician, feeling vibrant and short of breath. The trick has worked. We had disappeared completely and had materialized back in the real world, no better and no worse for the experience. We had fattened our memory banks with information which might be of use someday. And in a mortal world, in the midst of all the dying, we had once again proven we were desirable, trustworthy, and sexually competent."

186

According to Fish and Wildlife Department biologists, when the water temperature descends to 37 degrees F., the steelhead's heart beats once every 45 seconds. Though mine beats a little more

frequently, I have not gone fishing since Tuesday last, the 28th, when I encountered sufficient mushy ice flows and continual freezing of my guides to make the effort folly.

In town numerous waterpipes have frozen, broken, then flooded, leaving in their wake a vast sheet of ice. Otherwise, there is no snow or ice. Driving along residential streets, one suddenly encounters a great reach of ice, and is forced to be cautious, neither accelerating nor braking while any of the four wheels are touching it. Each day it is a bit warmer, with daytime temperatures in the mid-thirties, but it is not enough to produce a thaw, all is frozen so solidly. Meanwhile, the goldfish go about their minute business with total lethargy, only an occasional repositioning or tail movement to indicate they are not imbedded in the cake of ice.

Children and sometimes their parents, too, ice skate on nearby Green Lake, and the Seattle police attempt to chase them off, for it is unsafe, the ice thick in places, and thin as windowpane in others, above where springs lie. Ducks and geese walk flatfooted on what they formerly splashed in.

A thaw would be nice, if only to raise the steelhead's heartbeat and to persuade a few of us to venture out after him.

187

Yesterday I had the novel experience of working in a communal darkroom, which must be a bit like the public baths. Or worse—one of those clammy places designed for leisurely orgies among homosexuals, such as NYC's Plato's Retreat that I read about in *The Village Voice*.

It seemed very odd, men and women in the semi-dark together, each going about his or her shady business. I recall one couple in the amber twilight produced by the safelight, dipping their hands promiscuously in and out of each others fixer and de-hypo baths.

The counter clerk dries your prints for you on a huge drum-type print dryer. But before he or she will do this, you must bring in a sample of your wash water and have it tested for residual hypo. They don't want you to contaminate the dryer. My last batch failed, though the prints had been whirled about for more than fifteen minutes in the wash. I felt as though I had not passed my urine test, and was being sent away to try again, some other day.

188

"I'm selling the enlarger," said the voice on the telephone, "because I'm moving up to 4 X 5." His words had a snooty tone, as if he were moving up to a finer house in a better neighborhood, instead of simply to a big view camera, which necessitates a bigger enlarger. His price was too high, and the enlarger didn't come with a lens, so I told the elegant voice goodbye.

Photographers are snobs. They are always comparing cameras and lenses, often invidiously. When they start using larger formats, they become insufferable. The best of photography today is going off in an artistic, non-representational direction. At the Yuen Lui Gallery is an exhibition of Polaroid print manipulations by Rosamond Purcell that is arresting, thought-provoking, and beautiful. Her pictures look like artfully arranged still lives. This is what photography does so well today. It has taken over the imaginative area previously the domain of painting. And, in doing so, it has come into its own with a roar and a vengeance.

189

I have lost a lot of friends over the years through not staying in touch. This is a mistake. My father religiously sends out Christmas cards and thereby maintains relationships with people he has not seen in 20 or 30 years, and most likely will not see again in his lifetime. I think he has chosen the right course of action. Norma and I stopped sending out cards a number of years ago, in part because our list was comprised of so many people who had been business acquaintances of one or the other of us. Now I miss some of them and wonder what they have been up to. Many have moved out of town. They are lost to us, probably for good. As I grow older, this matters more to me.

I talked to my old college chum, Dave Norton, on the phone, the other night. He is in sad shape. Nobody can help him. He is alcoholic and psychopathic, by his own admission. He is going through a divorce and yet another nervous breakdown. I invited him to our house for a meal, but he didn't want to see anybody, just to talk to me for a few moments on the telephone.

He was living in a cheap hotel room in downtown Tacoma, watching TV and drinking heavily, all day long. Nobody can help him. He formerly worked as a parole officer in Santa Clara, California, and hated it, but then he hated everything. After more than ten years deliberation, he quit. Now he is making what I suspect are final contacts with old friends, people who matter to him but can be of no help. He is hopelessly lost. In fact, he may be on the brink of suicide. [Dave killed himself a few weeks later, and we only learned about it indirectly, a year later.]

I've lost others who are important to me, too. Bonnie and Julianna Holway were two sisters, whom I dated in turn in high school, then kept up contact with all through college; even while I was in the army we managed to see each other sometimes. Where are they? Probably married, with untraceable new names. And children, too, I shouldn't wonder. I hope so.

For a writer, his memories lie at the heart of what he is and what he does. He draws on them; he is their sum. Now those memories may be very different from the person who cohabits them. That is, they may remember different things. And that, for them, is their truth. This has to be recognized. And, as one ages, memories fade. Some of them can never be recalled. The loss is permanent and critical.

190

Unrequested, unwanted, yesterday's mail included a directory of members of my old college fraternity, the names and addresses of all who could be found. It was suggested that I read over my own listing, correct it if necessary, and return it with a check to show my gratitude for being sent the list. Fifteen dollars was the smallest amount they would like me to send. The names brought a twinge or two of nostalgia. It wasn't unpleasant. Perhaps I should send a check to them? Naw.

Most of the names I did not recognize. One spends four or five years at college, and there are legions behind him and in front of him, all strangers in time. We lived in the same house for a while and ate at the same table. We sang the same maudlin songs. We drank together—a lot. That was all. We were . . . classmates. What an odd and meaningless word that is.

Were we the Divorced Generation, or was that the generation after ours? Or just before? It's hard to remember, so long ago. An old friend, Jack Leahy, is listed as address unknown, though he's lived in Seattle his whole life. Hey, guys, didn't you think of looking in the telephone directory? That's what I do, whenever I have cause to call him, every decade or two.

So many ghostly names, attached to so many fading faces of yesterday's children. One thing sticks in the craw of memory. When we posed for our pictures in the college annual, *Tyee*, many of us wore the same white dress shirt and yellow wool tie, which we passed back and forth at the photographer's studio. It is one reason why we all look so much alike. The same haircuts, too. How cute we were, as boys. Now we are hoary men, aging fast.

191

The river gauge stood at 2.8 feet early this morning—about as low as I remember it in winter. Ice stretches solidly across the river, from Silvana to Arlington, and all the way upstream, but it is beginning to shrink in mass along its edges. All this the result of the two-week freeze.

Ice is cumulative. Though the daytime temperatures the past few days have been above freezing, the cold nights sustain the ice and cause the afternoon melt to refreeze and crystallize. This makes for pretty icicles along shore and crisp white bands of opaque ice reaching out from the water's edge. There is milk ice in the shallows, and solid deep sheets several inches thick in quiet backwaters, where the lapping of deeper water has caused it to build up in layers.

192

This afternoon I explored a stretch of the river I should know by now, but have never visited. It is the reach downstream from the Whitman Bridge and extends away from the highway to the cement open bridge a mile above Oso. It is the same stretch that Garth describes as fairly difficult, Type 3-plus water for a kayak or canoe rider, in the high water of spring. I can see why, for it is full of boulders and has a right-angle turn at the bottom. Now, with the river a good two vertical feet lower than usual, it is calm, benign. I crossed it easily on foot. But today's still-swift riffles that wend between gravel shoals show what the river must be like when it rises on a giant freshet.

That may soon happen, for it is raining hard here in town, even though the temperature is 40 degrees, or was when I last looked, which means that snow is falling at an altitude of a couple of thousand feet in the country.

It is difficult to appreciate a river this low. Yet I found two promising fishing reaches. The first lies downstream from the Whitman Bridge on the North side. A bit of barbed wire has to be negotiated at the start, but the walk is not too difficult, afterwards. A long wading bar forms just downstream. A natural cutbank lies along the far side. The current runs down the middle, then across. The river prescribes a gentle parabola, with a long tailout just below the bridge and swinging to the right.

Downstream farther, I found a great corner pool, which backs up at a clay cliff. It is sandy bottomed and vast, and quickly dies into slack water, soon after an impressive beginning. I walked a long ways, before turning back. Coming off the river by a dairy and a barn, I struck the railroad tracks within sight of the open bridge. The walk back was grueling.

I must return on higher water and see how it fishes. I hope to do this on the next rise.

193

When does the holiday end, anyway? I thought it was officially on New Year's Day; that was when I took down our tree, anyhow. But yesterday, driving around the Ravenna District of Seattle, I noticed a number of Christmas trees lurking behind living room windows. This is a cul-de-sac—a storybook section of town which calls itself Candy Cane Lane, and goes all out for the holidays, at considerable expense. The houses are mostly owned by well-off retired couples, often university professors, people who cling to the old values and cherish their traditions. They have a reluctance to take down the tree, which will signify the passage of yet another year, with one less left to go for them on the planet.

194

I am a man of no special talents. Wishing it were otherwise won't make it different. Star-gazing turtles do not achieve miraculous flight. Some men I've known from school days—Poets Richard Hugo and James Wright, for instance—are dead. They accomplished much more than I, yet they destroyed themselves in the process. For their art. But also by how they lived their lives. Other poets don't burn themselves up in the manner of tapers.

What are we to do with this precious life? The literary life, especially? Poets who die relatively young might be adjudged life's failures, in spite of the quality of their literary output. Or is the work worth it? Isn't the idea to live well and long? And, of course, to get one's work done.

Jim and Richard had little choice in the matter. They were driven men. They burned up their candles for poetry's sake. Was their art worth it? It is very good. Some would say yes, then. I'm not so sure I agree, not when I see the descent of another twilight on a bright beautiful river. Hugo would appreciate it. And so would Ray Carver, poor dead bastard. Another miserable, large-talented soul.

Many think they hear the siren song. They are mistaken. What they hear is their own heart beat, their ego speaking out. We live in joyous expectation of creating something good, perhaps enduring. How satisfying it is to write, and even more so on those days when you know you write well.

195

I have injured my back. Not seriously, I hope. How did I do it? Getting up too quickly out of a chair. In winter a man does not get enough exercise just fishing to keep in any sort of decent shape. Rivers flood too often, and you can't go out, or they are enduring a drought/freeze, like the one just ended, when there is not much point in going out, either.

My back woke me early this morning. I rose at seven to see if sitting upright on my couch would be any better. It was, and I promptly drifted back to sleep. The pain and the stiffness this morning were pretty bad, but after a couple of hours of slowly moving around my back began to loosen up and the pain to ease. Right now it is several times better than it was earlier.

My son thinks I am a whiner.

196

The Seattle Aquarium had a free day today. So Norma and I went to see it, along with most of the city. Garth begged off. I was impressed, she not so much. "Not so good as Vancouver's," she told me, "or even Tacoma's Point Defiance Park." She is the Connoisseur of Aquariums.

The aquarium makes use of contemporary Super Graphics. "The ocean is a soup," said one huge signboard. Next, they tell you that much in life is passive; for instance, fish wait for the current to bring food to them. It is a fine summary of how the good life works.

Parasitism is touched upon in a sign. I think it deserves further mention. Certain poisonous anemone are known to live harmoniously with a small, brightly banded fish of tropical origin. Anemone nervously wave their slender, thread-like arms and tendrils, as they lie on the bottom of the bay.

Many sea stars—which I've wrongly called "star fish," all my life—squat on the ocean's floor. They hunch right down on their hind quarters, like country crackers. Some sea stars are pretty. Mussels deposit those crumbly blue shards the tide leaves high on the beach; it means the mussel that lives inside is dead. Numerous bi-valves (which means two valves, Horatio), clams, and oysters are in evidence.

A great many exotic fishes from far away are on display, including electric eels. They live in only a small portion of their body; the rest is dedicated to electric generation. There are fish that exist in the dark and "see," or sense, things through their lateral line. Salmonids are among these. Of course they have eyes, too. Salmon have nostrils along their snouts which they use to "taste" water they "home" to.

I have noted nose holes on steelhead and wondered what purpose they serve. Now I have an inkling. Other fish have feelers or barbels—suckers, catfish, etc.—with which to grope along the bottom and feel things out. This is how they explore new areas and discover what is edible, what is not.

So many different kinds of fish live on this wet planet. Many seem to be—by their peculiar shape and rough configuration—throwbacks to prehistoric times. So ugly I wonder how people can go to the store and select them to bring home to prepare for dinner.

The climax was one grand room, round, with windows everywhere and brackish water sloshing about, full of fish that can tolerate a negative environment. Some species here surprised me. These included obese Donaldson broodstock rainbows, slender Chinook jack salmon, and some saltwater foraging species I didn't recognize. A skindiver with an airhose began to feed the fish dinner, and they schooled up and swarmed and churned the water hungrily for their fair share of fare of what was probably chopped up relatives.

The kids liked this part best. It is called the feeding frenzy.

Eventually we drifted away and found ourselves walking to the Pike Place Market, up a long flight of stairs and then an elevator ride to the top. At a stall Norma bought a cauliflower, half pound of mushrooms, and a small beefsteak tomato. We decided it would be prudent to shop here for a week's worth of vegetables every Saturday. We probably won't, however. Too far to travel.

197

I received a bulk mailer from a famous agent in NYC. He doesn't know me. His name is Scott Meredith. I associate him with Norman Mailer. He is Big Time. The flyer states that "Scott" is a workaholic and compulsive gambler who sometimes stakes "two hundred dollars on a single roll of the dice." He cannot sit still and is constantly seeking new challenges. He will read a short story, by the likes of me, for only $75. What a bargain. For a novel, he charges $300. [These are old figures, you understand; quadruple them for today.]

The irony is, if you are not selling and publishing your work, good old Scott will sock it to you at such prices, with no guarantee. But if you already are relatively famous, he'll work for 10 percent of what you get paid. How can he lose? Of course, if you are already selling, you shouldn't need him—though I suppose he can get you top price. Whatever that is.

Writers need a representative in NYC, where all the publishing action is. An agent is a middle man, an adjunct of modern marketing, a go-between, a wholesaler. He creates nothing himself. Much of today's economy is comprised of people providing nebulous services such as these. It does no good to dislike the system and long for simpler times. They are gone.

I am reading a book by one Donald MacCampbell, Literary Agent, on the perils of this writing business. Apparently there are many hucksters, fast-buck artists, and phonies in editorial work. The general idea is, don't trust anybody.

MacDonald's book will make him some money, which is why he wrote it. And it may keep novices from making certain errors in judgment and procedure. So the book is vaguely beneficial. MacDonald formerly edited and published *The Writer*. This puts him in the same ripoff business as people who run modeling schools. They prey on the ignorant and helpless. They make a living showing you how to make a living that they can't make themselves. This fits the classical definition of a teacher.

I suspect no writer benefits from paying reading fees, not even at the start of his career. Nevertheless, people like Meredith and MacCampbell find a lucrative niche. If they were good enough agents, they wouldn't have to develop money-making sidelines. Yet there are some benefits. MacCampbell says that most publishers don't know what they are doing–the remainder tables testify to the mistakes they've made. Publishers turn down work that might be good because they think it won't sell. But the stuff they buy doesn't sell, either. A few "lucky" books from each publisher make so much money that they subsidize the others, all the losers. Usually these are flukes, the exceptions to most publishing efforts.

Numerous publishing houses today have been bought up by conglomerates, and their publishing policies are determined by accountants and financiers hungry for money to pay off bond issues and create dividends for stockholders. There are writers with reputations for big sales, and their agents can auction off their work in a bidding war among publishers. Thus the sums paid these writers are astronomical. The rest of us live in a niggardly world.

Literary agents argue they can be useful in finding publishers who will bid against each other for potential best sellers. Unfortunately, the number of writers in America who can benefit from the process number about 40. MacDonald's book was not written for these people, only for the ones outside the fold.

198

Where do they sleep?
Where do who sleep?
Where do the herons sleep? The Cicero heron, for instance?
Heron sleep wherever nightfall catches them.
Do they sleep in nests, or rookeries?
They sleep in nests only when they're nesting—when they are incubating eggs or have pre-fledglings. Otherwise, see above.
Then herons have no home?
People have homes; herons, etc., have habitats. The Cicero heron's habitat includes the wide reach it patrols in search of daily heron gruel. This comprises a few miles of river and adjacent land.
How do you know all this?
Well, I don't, not for a fact. I merely surmise it. I infer it from heron behavior. It is how most naturalists start.
Where do I start?
It works like this. You go out of doors. You look around. You keep your eyes peeled. For instance, today I spotted the Cicero heron. Did I see it before it saw me? Probably not. One presumes all wild creatures see one first. The heron was on the other side of the river, standing on one skinny leg in the water. Then it moved a yard and was standing on two. It stood stock still, doing all it could to resemble a piece of driftwood turned battleship gray by the elements. The day was the self-same color.

When I entered the water upstream, it lumbered into flight. It flew low to a position 100 yards directly down the beach and landed on a strip of sand. It did this about as smoothly as a man setting up a lawnchair for the first time.

Often a heron so startled will loosen its bowels in flight, leaving behind a great, trailing arc of stuff that looks like liquid chalk. Perhaps it isn't fright so much as *flight* that does this. As I walked down the bar, the bird took wing again and flapped a second hundred yards down the beach, not shitting this time. I began fishing and forgot about the bird. But it did not forget about me.

As I moved along, rhythmically casting and retrieving line, my attention focused on the far side and I stopped being an amateur naturalist. I was a fisherman, pure and simple. After a bit I noticed an odd, slate-colored rock on the beach downstream from me. I didn't remember it from before. It was the heron. Though I hadn't been watching him, he had been aware of me. Our distance was about half of what it was. Was the heron getting used to me? That would be wonderful.

When I finished the pool with no strike, and waded ashore, the heron suddenly unfurled its great wings and beat them thunderously. "Hey, wait," I called out, but it was too late. I had committed the unpardonable: I had crowded him. The broad, finger-tipped wings pounded overhead. Gaining altitude slowly, the heron's shadow passed over me. For a moment, it was as if he had stolen the sun.

Upstream he landed at the riffle where Grant Creek spills into the river. Standing in the run, his legs more than shin-deep in the backwater, his long neck folded accordion fashion, the heron assumed a new and different silhouette. He looked like he was sleeping. Is that how herons sleep? Do they disguise themselves as deadfall snags and let their heads dip onto their chests, like readers dozing? Sleep must arrive differently from how it does with me. Does the heron's heartbeat slow, almost stop, at twilight? I have gained that impression.

So you believe that a heron sleeps along the edge of a river, disguised as a stick, standing in the shallows on legs too frail to support it, its head snuggled down, but always alert and quick to awaken, if its space is violated?

Yes, something like that. Or so it looked to me today.
Thanks a lot, brother.
Hey, no big deal. One last thing.
What's that?
Tomorrow will be different.

199

Yesterday I walked down the shingle at Blue Slough, intending to finish up the tagend of a roll of film. The sky exploded with birds. They included bald eagles, young and old, my friend the heron, and many crows. The crows resemble a flock of nuns, but are much noisier. They flew off to a bigleaf maple and began screaming at me for disturbing their vespers. One of the eagles was old and magnificent, with a crown that shone and tail feathers as bright as a mirror. The rest of him was so rich a brown that many would call it black. He and two younger eagles disappeared around a bend downstream and did not return while I was there.

One eagle flew off a short distance and took up a station on some rocks not far up the bar, where it glowered at me. I snarled back. I made my way towards it, for it stood near to where I wanted to fish. It nervously shifted its feet, retreated a few yards upstream, and finally was goaded into flight. It flapped two hundred yards upstream in the direction of the Stillaguamish Country Club, where many university faculty have summer cottages. The small houses resemble the mythic dwellings of gnomes.

It seemed late in the year for so many eagles. Then I realized that they had hungrily waited while the freeze held. They would not desert the carcasses, which were their sole winter food. They stood their ground (albeit, sometimes in a tree) and watched the dead fish, now hard as cement. Their beaks could not dent the surfaces, couldn't even scratch them.

Perhaps a dozen carcasses remained. They were commencing to thaw. Inside the skin they were pure mush. The birds ate them from the top down, turning the skin back, much like one removes a tight glove.

200

While driving up to the river, an idea struck me. Why not put the old parlor stove in my study in town? I nearly freeze to death, writing there. The stove will heat the room and enable me to burn up old newspapers and deadfalls brought back from the river. I will not only get rid of waste materials, I will save money. What a great idea.

The stove has been stored in the basement ever since we liberated it from the chicken coop at Norma's parents, where it lay for decades in sad neglect, half-buried in chicken shit. It was manufactured at the Everett Stoveworks during the Great Depression. A parlor stove has a flat top, with two removable cooking plates formed like a circle. It has two doors, one on the side designed to admit large pieces of firewood, and one on the front, with an isinglass window divided into tiny squares, which reveals a pretty orange flame when the fire is burning. The front door will open up so you can see your fire and allow you to toss in small chunks of wood.

Below the door is an adjustable grate, with a regulator that slides back and forth, admitting more or less air, as you wish. In the past, the stove smoked badly. Perhaps that was the fault of the chimney we had then, which did not draw well. Each winter our land produces windfall alder limbs that are just the right size and burn well. We gathered up many this fall. They require snapping off or sawing into stove lengths. Soon there will be more. Alders generate a constant, renewable supply of firewood, one stretching far into the future. Additionally they provide us with privacy, which was our original intention.

I could not wait to return home and start the project. Some immediate problems arose. The upper half of the window through which I would run the stovepipe was stuck tight. It had been painted over by the previous owner and we had never chiseled it free. It required much hammering and pushing before I could chip away enough paint to move it slightly, and by then I had a bad blister in the palm of my hand. Finally, I raised it a few inches by repeatedly tapping the frame and gingerly lifting the sash. Then I set up a ladder outdoors and worked on the outside seams of the window in the cold. Grudgingly, the window yawned wider.

I can envision the finished project. It excites me. The stove, tightly caulked, will sit on a heat-proof pad put there to protect the floor. A stove pipe will run up to the upper half of the window and turn an abrupt right-face to pass through a board I've cut for its escapement. Then the stove pipe chimney will rise until it is above the height of the roof, so it will draw better than in the past. A little Chinese hat will cap the pipe and keep it from filling with rainwater. Inside I will be snug and warm. The cat snugs up against me.

That is the idea, anyway. The reality will probably be different. The room fills with woodsmoke. Coughing, we must flee, or become asphyxiated, slamming the door behind us to protect the rest of the house. The neighbors call the fire department. They arrive too late. The house is a hopeless torch. We stand outside in our bathrobes, watching the house burn to the ground. There go my manuscripts and my prized photographic negatives. Not to mention Norma's things and all our lesser possessions. Clothes, furniture, appliances.

The next morning, I decide to do the job right. This entails a trip to the hardware store. (My favorite place.) The stove department is right next door to the electrical supplies; I had never noticed before. What a wealth of boots and bonnets and flat sections of pipe are there, waiting to be arm-wrenched into cylindrical form. It's a whole new world waiting to claim me. Or have I been here before?

201

I escape to the country, putting aside the stove problem for another day. The weather is fine. I spot five eagles perched in a tree a few yards off the Darrington highway. Does anybody stop to look at them up close but me? I hit the brakes, pulled onto the shoulder, turned off the engine, and climbed out slowly, so as not to spook them. No suitable camera and lens handy, I decided to use my eyes, instead.

The two eagles sat like . . . boles? I hunted for the best word. No, they were much bigger than that. I was about two hundred feet away. My eyes found another eagle, then two more. I couldn't believe it. There were five, all roosting like chickens. None was very far off the ground.

I ranged up and down the gravel, undecided. A "No hunting, no trespassing" sign stood in the field. Did this mean me? Surely not someone so innocent of purpose. Between the eagles and me stood a drainage ditch, with steep sides. A foot of water lay at the bottom. As I strode along the shoulder, trying to make up my mind, two eagles took flight, moving off low and lumberingly. This left three. It was a respectable number for viewing purposes. Should I climb down through the ditch and its water? As I pondered this, two more eagles departed. Only one was left. It seemed too few to comprise a closer occasion. I climbed back in the car and drove off.

I've always thought of eagles as loners, but must be wrong about this. Five seems an odd number. Two might be a pair, and four two pairs. But five? Was the odd bird a he or she? And what role did it play in the eagle community? Was it, as the gossip columnists say about movie stars in unusual, unexplained juxtaposition, "A close personal friend?"

One way or another, yes.

202

All this talk about installing a parlor stove was not idle chitchat. The stove is a fact. The fact sits on a thin insulated metal mat, under which I've placed an asbestos pad that measures 30 by 30 inches. Old and new stovepipe, the new deep blue in color, the old slightly rusted, runs up to an insulated thimble nine inches thick and passes out the top of the upper window, where I've inserted a three-quarter inch sheet of plywood, cut to fit.

Today I bought galvanized pipe for the outside portion of the chimney, plus a Chinese hat for the top, It will have to be assembled later, for I am tuckered out. Besides, darkness prevents further work. Thank goodness is all I can say about that. The image of a bright blaze sustains me. It won't be long now.

In the morning all is different. I find I have a mess on my hands. The pipe is galvanized, six-inch, 28-gauge, with two elbows outside and one inside. It is precariously hanging from ropes I've hastily erected along the edge of the roof. Somehow, a tremendous torque has been produced in the pipe, where the least amount of pressure will pull it apart at the fluted joints. The point where the pipe comes indoors through the thimble is the worst. And the chimney does not work. I mean, it will not draw. The room fills with smoke. The fire goes out.

203

Tomorrow will be different. This is my daily vow. And so it is. Different and better.

A fire is burning sweetly in the stove and the cat—with some urging—is lying in front of it on an old army blanket I put there, while the isinglass window is lit a golden orange from the flames inside. The weather cleared. Super Bowl Sunday proved to be a cool day, with flashes of bright afternoon sunshine. The Pittsburgh Steelers beat the Dallas Cowboys by eleven points, but that is insignificant.

While the game was playing, Norma and I fixed the stovepipe. It was mostly her know-how and effort that did the trick. I did a lot of run-up-and-down-the-ladder stuff, fetching things for her. We repositioned the pipe from yesterday and installed temporary rope hangers; when we had them in place, we held the pipe sections in place with piano wire.

I missed three quick first-half touchdowns, and the score stood at 14-14 half-time. We stopped work to watch the rest of the game. Well, I did. The stovepipe was firmly set up, wasn't it? Norma expertly caulked the stove and filled its many air holes with a special, fireproof cement I bought at the hardware store yesterday, anticipating the need.

How much better the world seems this evening, the fire crackling warmly behind the glass window, the cat snuggled up, all of us gathered round the blaze. This is how I had envisioned it earlier.

Some things come true, if you or your wife works hard enough at it.

204

Darrington reminds me of an Alaskan village, with its flat mud streets, every other store a bar or tavern, its fragile economy based on a single uncaring industry (timber this time, not a pulp mill) perched on the edge of town, where the road peters out and the indifferent wilderness begins. The frontier situation does not change with time or location. Some things are constant.

Darrington's streets are pocked and torn up from winter, dirty old snow piled up on each side, where the plows tossed it. Practically every other house has a for sale sign in its front yard. What a scruffy town it is at present, ill-kept and transient in its diminished population. In summer it swells with the newly employed. Now the workers retreat, as jobs disappear. Old Valdez was like this, back before the Alaskan earthquake. Its winter population shrunk to a hardcore several dozen. Perhaps the rebuilt Valdez is the same way.

Darrington's buildings are cheap and tawdry, as though facades set up for a movie long since departed. The children, all bundled up tightly against the cold, are playing in the thin sunlight in side yards. They wear a sullen, resentful, defeated look. Perhaps it is only the harsh weather that produces this, for the temperature remains in the forties and there is a wind. Darrington has the feel of a tent city, a hasty shelter set up for some single purpose, its people set to depart at a moment's notice.

Timber is brought in to the sprawling Summit Sawmill complex on the North end of town; lumber is carted away. The mill is what gives Darrington its raw, unfinished look. Too big to move away, as people can do, it may soon shut down and give its employees a layoff notice, and one final paycheck. It's happened before.

Everyone drives a pickup truck and, in season or out, there is apt to be a high-powered rifle hung in the rear window. The men dress in lumberjack outfits—jeans, boots, mackinaws—as if for the production of some campy musical, perhaps one starring a Nelson Eddy lookalike. No, that isn't fair. It is their daily costume and it is the people who make musicals who imitate them. It is important to recognize the real article, when you trip over it.

The women on the street wear K-Mart clothes and have hair coiled tightly on their heads. Often it is some strange color. This is a town where men look at women openly and women dress to be looked at. Some walk enticingly, in what you might call a hippy manner. At night you can go to one of half a dozen taverns and play eight-ball "tavern" pool on a foreshortened table. Last year, the favorite game was Foosball, before that a slick, reduced form of shuffleboard, played with sliding metal counters.

Again Darrington brings Alaska to mind, with its sawdust floors, games of stopdice played at the bar for drinks, country-Western juke blaring Hank Snow, and the call of "Timber" occasionally ringing out, which means that somebody "bought the house." You have a free drink coming. If you already are working on one, a clean, downturned glass is placed in front of you, signifying a fresh drink will be brought to you when you are ready for it. Only here nobody buys the house. People are too stingy.

Television has been recently brought to Darrington by cable. So now people have something to watch in the evenings besides rented videos. There is no movie theater, never has been one. It is the tavern in the evening, until it is time for bed. Bed comes early, for there is presently work in the mill and falling to be done in the low-altitude woods, where the snow remains scarce.

205

Bumps and dips comprise the Darrington-Arlington highway in winter, especially the stretch between Cicero and Oso, now that the freeze has ended. Ice has fairly exploded the road. Near Boulder Creek there is a sign which reads, "Bump." You had better believe it. You hit the brake gently and slow, anticipating it, and just when you begin to think it is a hoax, wham, it rises to greet you. If you aren't tied down by your seatbelt, your head will crash against the ceiling of your car.

I don't know what happens under the asphalt to produce this strange, rolling effect. The ground freezes: that is the key. And a short time later, after the thaw has arrived, everyone starts tooling around again at normal speed. The road takes on a wavy configuration. Then it starts to break apart in sections.

A load restriction is in effect, which means that logging trucks and other monsters are banned for the duration. Hooray. I think logging has finally stopped, and the mill is dependent upon what has already been cut and is in storage at the pole yard. Outgoing products from the mill are carried away by Burlington Northern. The railroad is impervious to snow and bad roads. It is the truck drivers who must wait for the road-repair crews to do their work, and the load restrictions to be lifted. The highway will eventually settle and have its dips and rises smoothed out with heavy equipment. Fresh asphalt will patch the holes and restore the grades. But it will not happen until after the last hard freeze.

Norma says the earth collects water during a freeze and its expansion causes the road to lift up and buckle. When the thaw comes, the water stored in the soil is released, all at once, and the receiving soil under the macadam, in her words, "turns to mush." Hence the rocking and rolling effect. Eventually the moisture "works its way out," the earth smoothes and levels itself, the asphalt returns to its original bed, and the huge cracks and craters appear because of the void. It is still driveable, if you are content to move along slowly, for the sake of your vehicle's shocks and springs. If the soft parts are merely rough, some oil and gravel may fix them.

A few eagles remain. Soon the great birds will move on. I've learned that they nest in the San Juan Islands. Exactly where, the wildlife biologists won't say. I asked one once, over the telephone, but he wouldn't answer me directly. I later learned where it was. The biologist said they didn't want the public to know because they might go to shoot the birds. What? It didn't seem likely. It's more likely it is because they don't want to share what they know. I think they like being superior and hoarding their small secret knowledge.

It gives them an importance they don't deserve.

206

Life, said Mark Twain, is just one damned thing after another. Doubtlessly he was speaking of home repairs. He might have added that problems come in bunches, like bananas. At home, in the city, the sewer line plugged the other day. I didn't mention it because certain boring things must go unreported here, if only to show self-restraint. But now the washing machine is out, and its companion dryer works only at medium heat. You have to coax it to get even a little warmth. We got all those things fixed, plus the slight smoking from the parlor stove.

Now it is the hot water heater.

A pressure valve is screwed into the top of hot water heaters and is set to blow out at 210 degrees. Ours blows whenever it feels like it. Often it is in the middle of the night. Water rapidly rushes out of the overflow valve and floods the basement. We are using a plastic bucket to catch the discharge, and when the water is really flowing, it will fill in about ten minutes. A friend advises me to bleed the valve a couple of times in order to assist the valve in closing. And, he suggests, I might lower each of the two thermostat settings inside the tank by twenty degrees.

I did both these things, but the relief was only temporary. As a matter of fact, the relief was misleading, since lowering the temperature didn't fix the valve and it continued to open up at odd intervals, mostly at night, and pour out large quantities of water now cool enough to hold my hand in. Today I am going to replace the valve with a new one from Sears. This will be my first venture into the field of plumbing. But I have no fear, having so quickly mastered electricity, and the installation of home stoves and chimneys. Besides, there is my wife's expert knowledge to fall back on, when I fail, as I expect to do.

First I must turn off all the electricity. Only then dare I remove the old valve. To loosen it requires a big wrench. I like the idea of climbing up on a chair, with a big pipe wrench in my hand. Theoretically at least I do. Muscle is the answer. And the prospect of a successful replacement is good.

207

It worked! At least I think it worked. The valve changing took about an hour, spent mostly up in the air, wrestling with a pipe wrench that must have weighed ten pounds. It is bright red and capable of dismantling anything in the stationary world. All joints but one yielded to easy leverage, and that one gave up the ghost with one good pull involving my shoulders.

Once I removed the pressure valve, I tested it manually, as a friend told me to do. It worked nice and smooth—which isn't how its supposed to behave. The one I bought to replace it is quite stiff. The temperature probe (see how much I've learned?) was thick with rust and had a break on its surface, which perhaps was the cause of the trouble. The probe is intrinsic to the valve and must be replaced along with it. The new probe is a bright, cheery blue—robin's egg blue, I'd call it. The color is wasted, for it goes inside the tank and can't be seen. I put the pipes connecting the tank back together with some soupy gray gunk that lubricates the joints, so in the future I should be able to take it apart more easily. But let's hope I don't have to.

The hot water heater lives on borrowed time. It came with the house, 15 years ago, and I've learned that most hot water heaters have to be replaced in less than a decade. We now have a plenitude of hot water, for I turned both thermostats up 15 to 20 degrees. And no rust comes out of the pipe. I'd gotten use to seeing it.

A success every now and then in home repairs is good for this old cowboy (me) and makes him easier to live with.

208

Where I go to fish is simply country. It's not the mountains or the deep woods. It is mostly fields and wide alder copses. The mountains are far off, but on a good day, they seem near. You want to reach right out and stroke their shaggy white crests.

I walked to the river at the mouth of Ryan Creek, near Cicero, through a field that was dense with cows. They had full udders, for it was toward dark and they hadn't been milked yet. They are the kind that shoo out of your way with one harsh word and the wave of your hand. All they want is to be relieved of their weighty load.

These are different from the eight Black Angus steers, each weighing over half a ton, that I encountered a few days earlier. They were cattle that wouldn't budge and looked—judging from their expressions—as though they were plotting a revolution in the form of a stampede. Shades of Pamplona. I had reason to fear them.

Though I have given up trying to comprehend human sexuality, in all its forms and vagaries, I thought the animal kingdom was pretty much unambiguous. Meet the Ryan Creek cows. Among them were three aging ladies, one a Holstein, one a Guernsey, and the third brindle colored, or spotted, with hues resembling one of Faulkner's painted horses. They were taking turns pursuing each other around the field, and when they caught up with one anther, a bit of fruitless humping took place. The one on top's huge udder swung wildly from side to side, as she banged away at her sister. Then she dismounted and wandered off to graze and await milking. Soon another cow approached her from behind and she was on the receiving end. And so it went, as the day drew down to a wintry close.

I returned to the city in time to eat a late dinner with Norma and race off to the University. We had tickets for the Philadelphia String Quartet, which is in residence. They performed two string pieces by Mozart, one a divertimento, the other with a guest horn added. It is the first concert in a series of three. Since the price is right, we plan to attend them all.

However, I must note a tendency to doze off in a warm theater seat, while the music is playing, following a day in the country.

209

Awakened yesterday to a thin snow lying on the lawn in town and across the tops of parked cars at the curb, all very pretty but unwanted. This has been a colder than usual winter, as some predicted, but a surprise because there has not been the snow one associates with the cold. Instead, a drought arrived and held. Aside from a short rainstorm over last weekend, after which the river fell back to its original low level, there has been no rain, and no rise in the river, since Christmas. That was a month ago.

I have been planning a trip to California in which there will be no fishing but I can do some photography. San Diego is my target. I am tempted to move up the trip because of the lack of fishing here. Fishing is my usual winter preoccupation—my respite from days of writing and correcting manuscript. I watch the morning paper for the daily high in San Diego. It is running about 61 degrees—not so warm as one might wish, though about 20 degrees higher each day than here. That's nothing to sneeze at.

210

The numbers of eagles on the Skagit are reported to be twice what they normally are. This has resulted from the refuge and sanctuary given them recently by law, plus the abundance of dog salmon. The bald eagle is a protected bird and the fine for killing one is $5000; successive kills bring $10,000 fines each.

It used to be considered clever in the country to pot yourself an eagle and bring back some souvenir feathers. It probably still happens among the bumpkin poachers, but they have to be more stealthy about it and the fine should scare them off. Most of them are poor and do not work winters. They have nothing better to do but pursue game out of season.

211

A day spent in the darkroom is a day lost, for all practical purposes. Many photographers dread it, for it removes them from the world of ordinary events. It is like venturing into the pit of death. Happily you reemerge, blinking, gorgeous prints in hand.

Darkroom work is grueling, the floor hard, the temperature cold, the chemicals strong and bad for your health. Yet the darkroom is where photographs are made; they do not simply "happen," or are given miraculous birth in the camera.

Photography thus has two parts, the first one with the camera in the real world of nature, people, cities, etc., the other one in the dark, with rank smells, the enlarger, powders to mix, wash-water running, manipulations to be made under enlarger light and in chemical tray, and much physical effort. The amateur takes his snaps and leaves the rest up to Kodak or Fotomat.

Darkroom craftsmanship lies at the heart of all good photography. It takes many years work to become proficient, and a fair amount of expense, which must turn many away. A lot of the cost is in printout paper expended, or wasted. The "easy-to-print" negative is rare; it is the one all photographers strive for, one that prints straight-forwardly, with a minimum of manipulation in the form of burning and dodging.

Today I have been printing tough negs, ones taken under extreme lighting conditions of snow and deep shadow. The problem is the tonal range exceeds that of, first, the film and, second, the paper's, capability. Small dark areas tend to go to black, with no details in the shadows; the bright, or highlight, areas block up and lose detail also, as is the case with snow. If one strives to burn in highlight areas with the enlarger light, the snow soon turns an unbelievable gray. So there are many tradeoffs in photography and for the most part they represent loses at both end of the spectrum. Yet few prints today required a second try under the enlarger light.

I discovered one useful trick in lightening a print that is too dark overall. It involves the use of potassium ferricyanide. In the past I have used the stuff selectively, in strong solution, to lighten or "open up" small areas on a print that did not lend themselves to dodging. Today I mixed up a weaker bath and dunked the whole print into it after the fixer stage. It lightened overall beautifully.

Good as it is to salvage a dark print, it has its drawbacks. The highlights tend to bleach out, giving the print the faded quality of old-fashioned photos whose fixer has failed. This technique may be used creatively in some instances, especially when toning is to follow.

I learned about the fading drawback the hard way. There was a lovely, snow-clad mountain on my negative that rose just downstream from a foreground snow scene, where the river disappeared in a rush of white water. The snow printed a dirty gray, so I bleached the print. Now the snow was fine, but the mountains had disappeared, along with every cloud in my favorite mackerel sky.

All this should be useful if I bring back some good negatives from San Diego.

212

What an extraordinary month this has been, from the standpoint of weather. I can remember one day of solid rain and another when it sprinkled. Every other day dawned bright and cold, but generally remained above freezing. At nightfall the frost descended, bringing with it a heavy condensation which soon froze.

Some early mornings a thin coat of ice covered the streets in town and a dense fog did not burn away until mid-morning.

This part of the country has a notoriously high suicide rate, not to mention alcoholism and drug-dependency. The rainy winter contributes greatly. Maybe this year the rates will drop because of the dryness and relatively bright skies.

A few natives use the rain and gloom of the Pacific Northwest winters to drive away people who might settle here. There is an organization calling itself "Lesser Seattle" that was formed in opposition to the booster group, "Greater Seattle." The opposition is dedicated to perpetrating tales of bad weather. Usually it is not an exaggeration. This year, who wouldn't be happy living here?

Yet I would trade all these fine dry days for some good fishing. If I can't have that, some warm California sunshine.

213

The San Diego trip is imminent. A letter from my father relates his and my mother's enthusiasm for a visit from their eldest son and his wife. They have rented a two-bedroom condo on a golfcourse for a month or more. I wonder if they aren't a little bored with each other, and hope we will to save them from each other? They drove down there just after Christmas, holing up in a Portland motel for a few days during a siege of freezing rain. He didn't want to drive through it, and I don't blame him any. But now the roads are dry and there is no threat of precipitation in any form.

In the letter are two large maps of the San Diego region. It is all new and mysterious to me. I pored over them for half an hour. Mexico—a foreign country—is not far away. And ocean beaches abound near there.

It is great fun to dream over a map. The new names are exciting, as one tries to trace out the capillary connections formed by roads leading to the arteries. One discovers named and unnamed throughways. After a while, it seems like you are studying a circulatory drawing of the human body. (With the patient lying on his back, the area I am perusing corresponds to his right leg. Thus, the trip starts at the groin, moves up to the knee at San Francisco, and proceeds to the ankle and foot at LA and San Diego.)

I find I am looking forward to this journey and some fresh horizons. If only the weather there would improve. It's been in the 56-61 degree range, in San Diego. Seventy-five is what I'm after.

214

Many small towns throughout this state, and others, fit the description of a hamlet. They have gasoline pumps off to the side of the road and, often, a general store, and maybe a post office that serves people living for miles on back roads that stretch in two or three different directions. The people are mostly small-scale farmers.

A post office brings federal money into the community in the form of a half-time job for some influential person, or (more often) his wife. It takes considerable political pull to land such a job and the competition is fierce.

Up at my river, George Anderson held this cushy job for decades. The post office was in the back of his general store. To get your mail, or to send away a letter, you had to walk the length of his store. The chance of finding something to buy was great. It was not unintentional. George's friend was Senator Henry Jackson. When it was rumored a number of small country post offices would close, including his, George gave the Senator a call. The tiny post office was reinstated. And so it goes.

Aside from the income generated by having it there, the town is dependent on people who live on the outskirts. Here everybody has a "hobby" farm, with a cow and maybe a horse or two. It means you can't make a living from your farm, and one of you must hold a job elsewhere, such as at the local lumber mill. You farm in your free time, for spare change.

Tomorrow is the start of February, and the sun is responding with a prolonged twilight. As the days lengthen out, there is more work to be had. Men who have already gone back to work find time after clocking out to fish for three-quarters of an hour before dark. If they are any good, it is time enough to catch a steelhead. Even in a poor season, there are a few fish around. This is the peak, most years.

215

For the past week I have been up to my ears in Mozart—all in all, not a bad place to be. The Philadelphia String Quartet has been in residence since 1966. Commencing a week ago Wednesday, they began a Mozart Festival, which continues this Friday and the following Wednesday evenings. The Quartet strives for as much variety as possible, but Mozart is Mozart, and the composer's cerebral, classical style precludes a full range of emotions. My mind (and heart) remain attuned to Beethoven, and so do, I suspect, the Quartet's.

The format given the three concerts is interesting. Each program consists of two quartets, one early and one late, at each end of the program, with various other chamber pieces inserted in the middle. The quartets are chronologically presented. Thus, three early quartets from 1772 are scheduled, plus three late ones from 1785, 1786, and 1790.

The first night they performed a divertimento for two horns, a string quartet, and a quintet for strings, featuring a single horn. The second night the program included the piano of Robert Merfield in the *Quartet for Piano and Strings in G Minor*, plus Stanley Richie and Alan Iglitzin performing the *Duo for Violin and Viola*. On the third evening we heard the *Concerto for Piano and String Quartet in A Major*, plus the *Sonata for Piano (forte) and Violin in B flat Major*, the latter a piece that can be compared favorably to any of Beethoven's nine sonatas for these two instruments.

I suspect there will be a summer series of strictly Beethoven. If it is structured as in the past, all 16 quartets will be performed in four long evenings. It will be interesting to see how the PSQ shapes the different programs. I expect it will be according to the composer's periods, with a chronological order within each period. This is a pleasing way to do it.

216

The weather in Southern Cal is astonishing. A newspaper clipping reads: "SNOW IN PALM SPRINGS—A TORNADO IN LA. A tenacious winter storm left Southern California wetted down and shaken up yesterday with flooding rain, deep snow—and a departing salvo of thunder, lightning and a tornado," etc.

This news was included in a letter from my father. The rest went on to state that San Diego had 2.65 inches of rain in one day, plus a high of 61 degrees. And in the mountains above Los Angeles to the North, there fell four inches of snow. None of which makes me eager to load up the car and head South on a lengthy drive.

I have been continuing my perusal of maps in an effort to familiarize myself with a part of the country I haven't seen. I've never been South of LA. A new map has always excited me, filled as it is with mysterious names and all those red and black threads winding across its face, which indicate roads headed for unknown destinations. What they primarily do is connect cities. If you choose a red thread, you will travel fast, for they are arterials and freeways. The blue and black threads are more interesting, though, but they'll take forever to get you anywhere. This is rudimentary knowledge: Map Reading 101. Maps have a charm, and provide the added benefit of making the unknown known, or rather less unfamiliar.

217

Raccoons again in town. They are growing more common. My son rushed in to tell us about it. This time it was spotted in the side yard. "It was huge," he said, "much bigger than a cat." Our cat, perhaps knowing this already, had prudently gone the other direction. He knows he isn't a fighter.

Raccoons are nocturnal, and may exist in fairly densely habituated areas, provided that there are clumps of trees in which for them to retire during the bright hours. Though I see many raccoon tracks up at the river, and occasionally their eyes at night as

I drive along the highway, I rarely come across one on foot. How odd. I think you have a much better chance of having a live raccoon encounter if you live in town. Or else I do. It must be because there are fewer trees in which for them to obscure themselves.

218

What are the birds of winter? Their names, please. Each of my answers is partial and incomplete. The truth is, I don't know my birds very well.

The other night, while fishing The Pipe Hole, down from the railroad bridge at Cicero, I heard a high-pitched, rattling sound. A woodpecker, I wondered? It was late in the day, toward dark.

No, it was an owl waking, getting ready for another exciting night of chasing down field mice and other small creatures of the darkness. At twilight, a whole new array of animals and birds comes to life. Thus the foodchain delivery system operates to sustain itself, even during this season of prolonged cold. It must have been the sun this afternoon that warmed the ground and woke the mice from hibernation. They are nocturnal, too. The owls respond, accordingly.

219

A definite break in the weather, at last, and I think the improvement is going to hold. I'm gambling on it. I've made a reservation in Medford for the night of February 6. Normal will fly down later, using up less of her vacation time away from work. Since I won't be arriving there until after six p.m., following a long drive, it will be necessary to stop along the way and pre-pay my lodging at some other Motel 6, or else I may lose my bed. I will do it in either Portland, Salem, or Eugene, for all have Motel 6s alongside the freeway.

Making Medford is critical. It is a good-sized city and lies on a high plateau, after several mountain passes have been achieved, including Grant's Pass, the highest. Medford is the jumping-off point for the Siskiyous and an even higher pass, which I've been dreading. This mountain range marks the border between Oregon and California.

The Motel 6 woman on the phone said the Oregon passes were clear and the only problems she had heard of were coming into LA. Most likely the weather will have changed by the time I arrive, two days hence. Of course I am a road worrier.

Strong winds are buffeting Seattle, coming in from the South, where I'm headed. The blast is giving my new stovepipe chimney a test of aerodynamic stability. Tonight I laid a small fire comprised of rolled up newspapers, and it is quietly and satisfactorily blazing away. This is to say, my room is not filling up with smoke—though the big door on the side tends to shoot a puff of woodsmoke into the room each time I load the firebox with newspaper rolls. And if I pile up the fuel too high inside, a backdraft is created, forcing smoke out through the top, where the two circles are for heating pots. Aside from these tiny imperfections, the stove is a joy and delight. I have a fire every day to take the chill off the room, then let it die out before I begin to write.

220

A small, woody tree—a shrub, really—grows outside my study window. Its roots are on the Johnstone side of the fence, which may explain why I never paid much attention to it before. Much of the year it lies hidden within a dogwood (*Cornus nuttallii*) and is overpowered by that tree's blooms and colorful foliage. In winter, when all the other trees and shrubs have dropped their leaves, it comes into its own. My tree-identification books don't list it, or else I'm too dumb to find it in their pages. I suspect it is an elderberry. I must look for a profusion of small, dense white flowers in the spring. That will be a clue.

It is presently covered with many berries, small and dark, almost black, with a purplish cast to their highlights. Its small branches are laden. The berries look a little like coffee beans. My attention is drawn to this obscure shrub as a result of a robin's peculiar behavior. It sat on the Johnstones's redwood fence, steadily defecating small hard dark pellets, which dropped a yard to the ground. Every so often it would take wing, then change its mind and sweep back to its perch on the fence. Not always could I see the single small berry lodged in its beak that it returned with. I could not see it because the bird often swallowed it quickly, *en route*.

The bird repeated its short flight many times and almost every time left pellets behind on the top of the broad fence or else on the ground below. The bird could gain little nourishment from the berries, they remained in its gullet such a short time. But there must be some benefit to the bird, for the robins and other species perform this ingesting ritual.

The bird's digestive system breaks down the shell containing the seed and hastens germination. The robin's surrounding dung provides the specific nutrients needed for the seed to sprout, two or three months hence. All bleak winter long, seed preparation activity of this type goes on. With each warm, wet interlude, the squirrels come out and whip around the yard, foraging, digging, planting, replanting what they buried in the fall.

All this compulsive genetic behavior is pointed toward some obscure goal. The land is being reborn, and the lengthening day strums such activity, while the sun awakens the sleeping soil. I wish I knew more about the minutiae of these processes. I must surmise a little from what I observe.

A Year At The River

The word from Medford is slush on the highway crossing the Siskiyous. But Southern California has providently turned warm and dry. I leave tomorrow morning.

221

In California, with no fishing to be had, I promise to run regularly. Who do I promise? Why, only myself. Accordingly, I've packed my special gear—my favorite Adidas running shoes, warm-up pants and jacket, jock strap, white shorts, light-weight wool socks.

Running (or jogging, for the less strenuously inclined) is not compatible with wading a stream, at least not for me. Perhaps it is because of my old knee injury, which still acts up. Wading puts tremendous lateral stress on the joint. I had never noticed it until recently. A healthy knee can take stress fine. Running uses the muscles above, below, and behind the knee, but causes no torquing. Torquing, I am convinced, is what is bad. Hamstrings, Achilles tendon, calf cramps, Charley horses—all come from running. Severe, they are usually brief. I've tried running and wading on consecutive days. It is terrible—the worst of both worlds.

Before I leave, I have some reading to do. I want to finish Doris Lessing's *Briefing For A Descent Into Hell*. Then I will run a bit. I miss running and the energetic feeling that follows, and the good sleep afterwards. It is probably these pleasant aspects that keep runners at their grim task, which is notoriously lonely and boring. It is also painful, at times, but a healthy, recoverable type of pain.

Running produces a dependency. If you don't run, you feel guilty. The guilt only goes away when you run again. Yes, it is a little like drug dependency. The running fix quiets the nerves, brightens the eye, and puts the soul at rest—however temporarily.

222

On my way, at last. The initial distance is to be about 450 miles, and is always grueling.

How many rivers are there between here and Medford, Oregon? Many people would notice nothing but the bridges across them. I am a river freak, who always looks below and recklessly endangers the drivers around him. I must check every river's height and condition. Is it rising or falling. And the color?

The rivers in Washington State are running high and full of mud. First to cross is the Green (where I cut my steelheading eyeteeth), even before I come to Tacoma, followed at a steady clip I pass over the Nisqually, Skookumchuck, Olympia Deschutes, Coweeman, Cowlitz, Toutle, Kalama, North Lewis (huge), East

Lewis (medium-sized). Finally there is tiny Salmon Creek and the mighty Columbia, which marks the entrance to Portland.

On the Oregon side are the Willamette (extremely high and light brown today), its middle fork nearly in flood, and the Santiam, which is over its banks near Albany. Many fields are heavily puddled, or completely under water from the spillover of numerous tiny creeks. The temperature is over 50 degrees, with intermittent rain all afternoon.

Arrived Medford at a little after 8 p.m. I have a reservation and a guaranteed room. It's an inside unit, to boot. It promises respite from the highway noise that keeps travelers awake half the night. As usual, I am directed to my unit from the reservation desk and get hopelessly lost, or turned round, before I find my door and turn in.

223

So this is California? Pretty weird. Forty or fifty miles into the state—well past Weed, Shasta City, etc.—I am funneled into a checkpoint and asked by uniformed officers, "Are you transporting any fresh fruit or plants?" I reply, "Just half a dozen Washington State apples, sir." "Pass."

And many hours later, I pull into a pleasant little city on Highway 680, basking under a sun splashing down on stucco houses with red slate roofs. A young male gasoline station attendant fills my tank with unleaded fuel, notes my license plate, and confides: "I hate California." "Why?" He doesn't know exactly. I ask, "Well, would you like it better some place else?" "Nevada" he says, "or maybe Oregon."

Always the booster, I ask, "Have you ever been to Washington?" "I've got an uncle who works there." "Works where?" "In the White House." Perhaps he means a burger bar with that name, or the discount store.

"What's that?"

"It's where the President lives."

Oh, yes—*him. That* Washington. I'd forgotten. My world is a small one.

At about 6 P.M., a gang of us are queued up at the reservation desk of Motel 6 in Monterey. There is no room at the inn, however. I find a bed in a place called Lone Oak. I see no oak in the vicinity. What can be lonelier than a lone oak, if there is none? What happened to it? The story must be a sad one. After something called a "Happy Steak," I prowl the darkened streets of Carmel-by-the-Sea, walking long distances to stretch my car-shrunk leg muscles and trying to get tired enough to sleep. I hike for what must be miles up and down the darkened streets of slumbering Carmel, finally stopping for a beer at The Watering Hole, a.k.a. Angus McFly. There I stare at the pretty untouchable California girls—clearly the property of somebody else, their young male counterparts, who are playing pool across the room. I finish my beer and leave. Tap Coors; as good as I remembered it. Something about it having to be constantly refrigerated, since it is not Pasteurized.

I drive on to the ugly town of Fremont and a huge cut-rate all-night drugstore, where I buy a six-pack of the same brew and return to my unit. On previous trips I used to buy Coors on tap at the same place (they don't remember me), and it constituted a special treat. Now available in bottles, in Washington State and the rest of America, the taste seems ordinary. I sip the not very cold stuff and feel cheated a little of an undefinable piece of my past.

224

The flora here never ceases to amaze me; it is so different from what I am used to. Monterey Bay is a whole new world, each time I come here, and I have to go through a major mental/visual readjustment. The drive out Highway One is beautiful. What scenery—the world's grandest. I turn around and head back at Bixby Creek Bridge, because of recurring acrophobia. It is an old problem. In Carmel I visit the Weston Gallery and the Friends of Photography Gallery and marvel at the prints by Edward Weston and Ansel Adams, who are practically household words today. Nobody did or will do better work. The Friends of Photography Gallery has been renamed the Wynn Bullock Gallery since my last visit.

Tonight I attempted some 15-second exposures at f16 with the Canon EF, which is superbly designed for measuring low light. The camera will make exposures up to 30 seconds, which ought to be long enough for anybody, and it can do multiple exposures, a world unknown to me and seemingly difficult to imagine ahead of time. I did not photograph Point Lobos, because of the bright sun. I had already shot it on a previous trip in sunlight. Perhaps tomorrow morning, before I shove off, we will have some clouds. The forecast is for a little early morning fog, then more sunshine. I would prefer clouds to fog, for photographic purposes. But isn't it the prospect of sun that drew me to California? Doesn't it with everybody? Yes, but it does play havoc with serious photography.

225

A few low clouds wafted in from the Pacific this morning, after breakfast, so I drove out Cabrillo—the King's Highway, also known as Highway One—but soon turned back because of my old queasy feeling, brought on by the steep cliffs on the oceanside of the highway. The drive is famous for its spectacular scenery. The land drops off the road's shoulder and meets the surf in a white ribbon at its base. My palms grew damp and tightened on the steeringwheel, until I could feel it compressing under my grip. I thought I might rip it off the post. It was time to turn back. But I stopped and took a few pictures, all the same. They promise to be short of what is theoretically possible. Often this is the case.

I decided to continue my journey South, and soon began to feel better. Blue California skies followed my route, as the miles stacked up behind me. It was in the mid-70s in LA, my radio told me. The traffic ahead was only moderately heavy, and I reached Santa Barbara by mid-afternoon, with much daylight ahead of me still. The traffic thickened as I pushed into LA. Fearlessly, I pressed straight on through, and soon found myself on the outskirts of the thick sprawl.

At Westminster I was met by fog. It grew eerie, preternaturally dark. I crept past Laguna and San Clemente, which were but distant lights, softened by mist in the air. As everyone must do, I thought about Richard Nixon and his folly—for about four seconds. Soon I reached the turnoff to Highway 78, which leads to Escondido and Rancho Bernardo.

I drove in circles around the stucco housing complexes that comprise Rancho Bernardo and confuse the uninitiated, passing the same Shell Station three times. Then I took a bold new turn. Soon I felt a little less lost. I spotted my father, standing by the curb. Who could he be waiting for except me? How long had he been standing there, in the cool of a long winter's eve? Quite a while, I suspect.

In a few minutes more my luggage and I were inside, where it was warm from the day. I kissed my mother hello. We had a drink and began to talk. I guess I started dozing off. One by one, we rose, stretched, yawned, and turned in. My mother—as always—was last to bed. And then it was morning.

226

Sunday: the day named after the sun, which is in plentiful evidence. I am not prepared for this sudden warmth. For one thing, I brought too many cold-weather clothes with me, or not enough warm-weather ones. We are inland 20 miles from San Diego and subject to a much warmer clime, 5-8 degrees daily, than the newspapers report for San Diego. I wish somebody had told me this. Well, already I've learned something, and I haven't had breakfast yet.

I am sitting on the edge of the fairway, up a little steep bank, watching the golfers. Below me is an asphalt track for golfcarts and where the players take their second shots on this hole, which is a long one. The track looks like something designed for running, and I may try it later, when they have all left the course.

How serious golfers are about their game, yet on the surface how jolly. The make light and joke about what is of dire importance to them. I have promised my father to play a round with him, though he seems to be a spectator, these days, and maybe we won't get around to it. He says he hasn't played in months. I wonder a little why they are here, then?

Perhaps when I grow old, I will hang out on a river, such as the North Fork at Oso, and not fish anymore but watch others do so. I will make snide comments on the style of the fishers and tell stories of my past feats, which by then will be legendary. I can imagine worse fates.

My mother is sedentary, smokes heavily, has a bad cough she can't shake, and says her "cold" produces voluminous phlegm, which keeps her from being more active. All of which is worrisome, but nothing new, only in degree. Her sister, Dorothy, died of emphysema, and the two of them were chimneys together. My mother has what is called chronic lung condition. It is irreversible. She also has osteoporosis.

This is beautiful country indeed. So describe it—you're a writer. Well, it is flattish, but the brown and green hills are not very far away. They are steep and barren. The houses there are built in clusters, called villas, and are concentrated in the valleys. All have red tile roofs. It must be required by the local chamber of commerce. Everyone went to the same architectural college.

The golf course is ringed with villas identical to ours. It would be easy to get lost, even in the daytime. The apartments rent for a modest $1600 per month for half a unit. The occupants keep to themselves and stay indoors, most of the day. The effect is a little spooky. You know there are people present, but you never see them. A drape moves in a window, you detect a car starting up, a door across the street slams softly. Rancho Bernardo contains all the makings of a good murder mystery.

It is going to be warm today, probably in the mid-70s. It is exactly what I ordered. My mother says my back is already pink, so I have begun to cover up by sections, exposing my face and arms, which will be burned a little by nightfall. As the golfers play by, my father studies their approach shots and comments to me; when somebody hooks one over into the iceplant below our terrace, he calls out to them their ball's location. Otherwise, the depth of that rubbery-limbed shrubbery would hide it and they would never find it.

Iceplant grows everywhere, like a weed, which perhaps it is, and people often make use of it as a convenient ground cover. It doesn't require mowing, nor does it turn brown from lack of watering. It forms a decorative barrier between house and street.

As the golfers walk over to the rubbery low jungle to claim their balls, my father insists on exchanging a few pleasantries with them, in that easy vernacular of people possessing the same value system. They are of the same generation and social standing. That reads money. It is an affirmation and a confirmation, both at once. It is jovial, communal. My generation has nothing like it, and we are the poorer. In time, I suppose, I will try to adopt it.

This would be better country, if only it had a few tall cedars. Cedars would make strangers like me feel more at home. Nearby is a murky excuse for a stream. It nearly goes dry, then refills when there is a sudden rain, which I understand is near nightly.

Tonight my parents and I are going to a nearby restaurant for prime rib. The place is a favorite of theirs and they want me to experience the food.

Tomorrow night Norma flies in. I find I miss her a lot.

227

Found my first golf ball today. This—in my father's eyes—is a rite of initiation at Rancho Bernardo. I am no longer a visitor but one of them. Well, sort of. I have some social status now. My father makes a great silly fuss over the golfball. I understand that he wants me to feel welcome. Well, I do, but this remains a foreign place.

Yesterday I wrote that my parents' villa is on a golf course, and players generally take their second shot right in front of us on a long par four hole. Across a tiny canal is the putting green of another hole with a higher number. Sometimes I hear shouts of glee from the green, as a player sinks a long putt and exclaims triumphant. Two younger men played through and seemed highly competitive. One yelled, "Son of a bitch," after making a poor approach shot, and his companion uttered a seldom-heard-here, "Fuck!" as he bobbled his. This serves as a reminder that the real world exists, even in Rancho Bernardo.

The golfcart track calls out to me. I must run it! Would anybody care? With a plan in mind, I rose at eight today and peeked out the window to behold my second splendid Southern California morning, and great-day-in-the-making.

Lo, I have spotted two brightly clad joggers making a circuit of the track. So it is not a secret. Good. If others run it, I won't be such an attraction. I wolfed down a Danish and quickly donned my electric blue warm-up suit. Then I put on my darling white *cum* blue and red side-striped Adidas running shoes. Away I flew, off on a jog of my own.

I ran only a short distance, following a week of inactivity. My knee began to pain me during my warm-up exercises. Having had a few bad experiences that started out this way, I was apprehensive about a long run and made it a short one, but three hours later there is no pain or swelling. Tomorrow I shall run again, a little farther, and if that goes well the following day attempt to double the distance.

Last night my father drove my mother and me to the Rancho Bernardo Inn, which is at the top of the golf course. It is next door to where people pay their green fees. The course is public, and

A Year At The River

there is nothing degrading about it not being private, for it remains expensive and exclusive, as though it had membership requirements. Rooms at the Inn rent for $120 per night. There are two restaurants here, a *grande* one that is reopening after extensive remodeling, and a *petite* one, which is downstairs and unpretentious. It has a dark cocktail lounge which I am urged to take Norma to, not that we are much drinkers. It might be a good escape from too much parenting.

All is spiffy, sparkling, neat. For a half hour before dinner, we rode around through silent neighborhoods of expensive homes, all in the Spanish idiom, with here and there a weird palm standing out in front, leaning at a tipsy angle. Most of the trees are sedate, weeping olives. There is another small, nondescript tree or shrub, with a profusion of slender, willow-like leaves. It may be a eucalyptus. Beneath the olive trees often is a little heap of ripe fruits that have fallen unheeded to the ground.

Early in the morning street cleaners and garbage men come to Rancho Bernardo and haul away the refuse. So it is never glimpsed. And there are neighborhood attendants who arrive at first light and move your garbage cans on Garbage day out to the street, so you won't have to do it. I tried to talk to a man who does this and other things today. He was a young Chicano, who spoke no English. We soon gave up, with helpless grins and shrugs of our shoulders. His job is to turn on your lawn sprinklers each morning. He drove me out of my sunning chair—where I write—just long enough to wet down the blades, but not to soak them. The sun is blistering them dry. Soon they will be the color of toast.

I have just been driven on by a man with a wicked slice who failed to shout "Fore" to the people playing the fairway in front of him. They were safe enough, for he drove short and crookedly. The ball ricocheted off the corner of my parents' villa and came to rest on the lawn just behind me. Unless asked pointedly, I am not about to point out its location and shall claim it, after they've played by. I am very different from my father, in this regard. I am not a fellow golfer.

The ball came so close to hitting me I was annoyed. Most balls landing here are reshot from the fairway, with the golfer taking a one-stroke penalty. I'm positive this man won't stop to look for his ball, which costs $1.50 or $2.00 to replace. He'll drive another ball, instead. I'm right: He walks on by, without looking in my direction.

When his three-some has reached the green, I dash out and claim the ball. Proudly I carry it inside and place it alongside the one from earlier this morning. Now I have two. They lie companionably side by side on the mantle. At a little desk, my father is writing a letter to his sister, my Aunt Ruth.

"Chicken just laid another egg," I tell him. He marvels at how I can find so many balls, when I've only been here a couple of days. It's good to have one marketable skill.

228

Norma arrived last night, almost an hour late on United Flight 407 from Seattle, which was kept circling an additional fifteen minutes and then made to sit on the apron for half hour on account of crowding, for LA. was socked in for the fifth consecutive day. One thousand unfortunate displaced souls were flown to San Diego, instead, and transported to LA by every available vehicle, including chartered school bus. As we left, they sat in long sad rows out in front of the depot, baggage stacked alongside them, waiting for Godot, or whoever brings them a ride.

The United Airlines desk was a complete jumbles; nobody knew when a flight would be permitted to land, or when a gate would be made available for debarkation. But at last a mid-range jet rolled up on the concourse, a man with a foreign accent (Dutch?) confided to me in authoritarian tones that it was Flight 407 from Seattle, indeed. A few minutes later Norma departed, about a third of the way down the line of passengers. We found her baggage quickly and would have been home to Rancho Bernardo in half an hour, except Dad's big Olds missed a key turn, and we ended up poking through a dark industrial district of San Diego, as he tried to find his way back to an on-ramp. For the price of a full tank, a gas-station attendant put us on target.

Today, Norma and I have spent a pleasant morning shopping at Von's, a short walk down the street from the villa It is a great variety and grocery store, the first we've ever seen of its kind, and practically everything a body might want can be bought there. Why shop elsewhere? Then we stretched out parallel to the golf course and started to sun our pale bodies.

Earlier, before anybody was awake, I got in a good, hard run, covering twice the distance as yesterday. I had to stop to walk only twice. Knee feels pretty good.

229

A half-inch of rain fell overnight, while we slept, or tried to. On a tile roof, the rain sounds like the cavalry. Southern California rain is something special. The roar and whoosh of so much water being caught and carried away in troughs and gutters makes a different sound, much like the passage of a freight train. It is nothing like a raging river. Norma and I lay awake and listened in wonder to the din. Sleep was impossible.

By morning it was all past, the storm's legacy remaining in the form of sodden lawns, fairways, and greens, the sky busily whisking away the storm's last clouds over the rocky rim of the horizon. Blue skies and sun are the agenda.

My rain-volume data comes courtesy of Ernie, resident major domo of Caminito Compana, Rancho Bernardo, who collected that much in his little measuring glass. He is retired Army, obviously a high-ranking officer, full colonel, at the least. E-4 Arnold recognizes the type.

Old Ernie has style and *mucho* knowledge. Additionally, he is famous for finding more golfballs than anybody else. I take beating him as a personal challenge. I guess I did, my first day, but since then have found no more balls, while he continues to come up with the odd one. He likes me, for some reason—perhaps because I will stop and listen. He has lived all over the world and is at home anywhere. He keeps finding himself in charge. He cheerfully issues orders and reprimands. Maybe that is why some people avoid him. Me, I like him back. It must be an old military hangover, which doesn't bother me, now that I don't have to obey him or anybody else.

He is practically a nonstop talker, who amazes me with his vast storehouse of special knowledge. He knows everything that is going on in Rancho Bernardo. For our clutch of villas, he is Area Representative. He cheerfully outlines for me his duties. There is actually a representative government here. It is necessary to reach agreement on housekeeping issues of common concern. But I, a guest, do not need to hear more about the nuances of how it operates. I steer Ernie onto another subject.

Later, I take Norma on a long, circular drive. Half the time I don't exactly know where we are. I get lost easily, but found again almost as rapidly. Here, as best I can recall, are some of the day's place names:

Escondido, Vista, Oceanside; then over to U.S. Highway 5 North to enormous, sprawling Camp Pendleton, home of many Marine Corps atrocities. Here we turn around and follow Highway Five South past the UCSD three campus entrances and the turnoff to LaJolla, until we come into San Diego proper and its fascinating but somewhat sleazy Mission Beach area, where we eat a picnic lunch on a streetside bench beneath a hot sun blasted by side winds launched from off the ocean. They seldom abate.

Many tightly jammed apartments and cabins clot this populous beach area of SD, and many young people are on the prowl in an ambiance of beer, dope, and sex. The usual condiments. Mission Beach stands out as a needed contrast to Rancho Bernardo, where nothing eventful happens, except a death every few days.

Here you can rent rubber-wheeled skates by the hour and whiz along the boardwalk, among the comical bicycles of all sizes and shapes. We see beer and taco fast-food joints, disco halls, all facades comprised of weathered paint, and bright lights, which are charming—if you don't stay too long or look too closely. Otherwise, the scene is instant sleaze.

Rancho Bernardo is far away, unreal. In fact, it rises fantastically in my mind. I decide to rename it facetiously. It becomes Rancho-Rancho. They loved the town so much they named it twice; the second time is for effect. How's that for irony? We must be the only people young enough to screw occasionally. Here we seem old, in contrast to the vibrant youth. We check things out, walking fast to dodge the skaters, who are oblivious to anybody else and will blithely run you over. Prices for two bedrooms, two baths, and a fire place are quoted at $800 a month—it seems tolerable. That's half of what Dad is paying. The beach is yards away, with booming surf. Half the beach is reserved for hardy swimmers. The remainder is dedicated to surfers, and ordinary swimmers must keep away.

Then on to Balboa Park, with time left in the day only enough to take in the museum and row of art galleries. We glimpse the botanical gardens and the Putnam Gallery, a closely guarded mausoleum for art, with one/each Rembrandt, Brueghel, Rubens, El Greco, Cezanne, Titian, and much 18th Century Russian Orthodox iconography, replete with gold leaf. It is beautiful. They have a nice representative American 18th-19th Century collection, again with one painting by each artist and no repeats, mostly landscapes.

On we drive, past Penasquitos, Escondido, and Lawrence Welk's Country and Golf Club, which I badly wanted Norma to glimpse, for it is yet another world, highly unbelievable. Well, maybe not that, but culturally peculiar and unique. This is probably what drew my parents here, year after year. They love him and he knows them by name.

230

I run. I run for the sheer joy of feeling myself sweat and grow short of breath, which is vaguely beneficial. I run for the fifth time this week. I run because I am bored. And I run to prove to myself that I am not old before my time, trapped eternally in Rancho-Rancho, never to affect my escape. (All this running may be preparatory to actual flight.)

When you run for the relatively short distances that I do—two miles daily, now approaching three—it does the body no harm, I think, to do it each day. The hardest part is putting on your running shoes, which signifies there is no getting away from what comes next.

Shoes have the greatest importance to the runner. Usually they are Adidas or Nike. Adidas have three stripes and are widely imitated; Nikes have a "swoosh" stripe, a kind of stylized comet on their sides. Both designs are familiar to people between the ages of 4 and 55. Old folks are oblivious to comets or stripes, and what they stand for.

A runner sees much less than there is to see, when he runs. If he were out walking, he might behold a rich parade. I begin my day's run at a loose jog, feeling my muscles tighten, on the outlook for pain in the right-knee joint. If there isn't any, I will lengthen out my stride manfully. The strictly vertical stress of jogging probably does no harm; it is any sideways, twisting action that does the real damage. Everything feeling fine, I run easily past the porches and sundecks of the villas strung like rosary beads along the edge of the golf course. Running is my benediction, this morning.

Most villas are dark, seemingly unoccupied, at just past eight o'clock. Rarely do I see anybody. Once Herb—the grain-farmer/accountant from the panhandle of Texas—hailed me and a couple of times Doc from Iowa, a big, burly huge-bellied, hard-drinking physician friend of my dad's—who is a prime candidate for a heart-attack, I'd say—called out to me. Occasionally I see some couples out for a walk. There is a solitary golfer who goes out by himself early, the fairway shrouded in mist, awaiting the burnaway sun. He will often hail me with a friendly word or two. Later in the day, people aren't so gregarious. The golfers don't speak to non-golfers, and hardly to each other. Yet off the course people are friendly enough. An oldster will tell you, "A stranger is somebody I haven't met yet."

I reach the end of the villas and cross the wooden footbridge leading to the tee for the fourth hole and the grade increases perceptibly, so I shorten my stride. Slap, slap, slap, go my feet. I find people putting on the Thirteenth Green, in a tense situation, and see the players hunched over their flat-faced clubs, studying the roll of the terrain. I put my feet down as quietly as possible.

Soon I must slow for my first short walk, checking again for muscle cramping or the start of any pronounced tightness that may lead to it. So far okay. Now begins the first hard run, and I expect it to accomplish some distance. I must go a half mile without a stop. It is a vow I made to myself. The course is slightly downhill, which helps considerably.

After a bit, the asphalt turns to packed dirt, and frequently—because of recent sprinkling or nightly showers—I find it puddled. I veer left to circle the gardener's shed, then round a corner, cross a little gully, and gently climb up the slope on the far side. The grade is telling. Now I come to the villas where I began. I have made nearly one full circuit. I slow to a walk, shaking out my arms and shoulders, like a marionette, flexing my knees to see how they are holding up. They are fine.

I walk back to my parents' villa, but remain on the track. Then I begin to run again, because walking is boring to a runner, even an amateur one like me. I am lightly sweated and hardly out of breath, feeling fine. This type of running is called aerobic exercise. It isn't meant to exhaust you. I understand only a few of the principles at work. I want to work my lungs to near-capacity and fill my bloodstream with fresh oxygen; break into a hearty sweat and get my heart-rate up. I occasionally find that I can run on and on, without getting any more tired than I presently am. The distances unravel.

Today I repeat the run and leave out the third walk at the Fourteenth Tee. To do this, I must maintain a short and regular stride. My shoes thud softly beneath me. I like their sound. I yawn widely, and feel a pop in my ears. I study the passing trees and try to identify them, their species. I guess at the ones I don't know for a fact.

Coming home, into the backstretch, I round the dirt path and trot onto asphalt again, feeling good, believing there is no possibility I will falter and have to stop. It is tempting to sprint the last hundred yards, but that would be tempting fate and I might fall on my face, exhausted. Besides, as soon as I cool down, I am going to eat a big breakfast. The idea of breakfast is what sustains a morning runner. Ahead I see my starting point, there among the iceplant, where the dirt path from the villa descends to the track at a steep slant.

I'm done for the day. After my cooling down, I will eat, drink coffee, and shower. Another day stretches ahead. I am prepared for it.

231

Yesterday, after my morning run and breakfast, the four of us headed for the San Diego Zoo. It is world-famous, and justly so. For a fee, there is a guided-tour bus, which Norma and I declined, though my parents eagerly boarded it and disappeared from sight, waving spiritedly.

We bought a four-color program for the same price as the bus tour. It included a complex map of the area, without which a person could never find his way to all the animal grottoes and aviaries. Instead, he'd keep disappearing into the ravines and getting lost amid the towering greenery.

We saw all manner of beast and bird, but not the reptiles and hippos. The day was not long enough. We virtually walked our rubbery legs off. When we were done with the zoo, we headed for the San Diego Public Library, which Norma wanted to see, out of professional curiosity. What a sad specimen. They have had huge budget cuts and a crisis in administration which have crippled it. It is housed in an ancient building, replete with decaying varnish and crumbling plaster, much like a school. It conforms to the stereotype of what a library is, and should not be.

The effect of visiting the zoo was positive, in spite of my reluctance to see wild beasts incarcerated. Without zoos, people would never see real animals. In the future—because of today—I shall vote in favor of zoo bonding issues, simply because they provide more tolerable living quarters for the animals. It seems the humane solution to a prison situation. But better yet would be to rely solely on photographs, especially movies made of animals in their natural habitats.

232

They come to fashionable places like Rancho-Rancho to wait out the days until they die. If fortunate, death will be fast. Most are in their seventies, in apparent good health. The ones you see seem vital. Inside the villas it may be a different matter.

Everybody is tan. The sun rays give the impression of robust health to everyone. The lean predominate. It is a fact that they live longer. But there are some men with a proud paunch, the ancient badge of the squire class and a worldwide symbol of affluence. Rarely—seen through a window or while entering or exiting a discrete porch—one gets a glimpse of somebody in a wheelchair or using a walker. Someone pale. One medical group here advertises that it takes no prisoners—I mean, no new patients. They are full-up with oldsters. They will not treat some ailing person, even in an emergency. Their ads means, Don't come here, whatever you do. They will refer him to the medical center across Highway 15, which brags that it has 78 physicians, most of them specialists. The specialties represent various sectors of geriatrics.

I've also come across a place that calls itself a "Dental Arts Center." One's imagination evokes what goes on there. The nearest hospital is eight miles away in Escondido. Equally close is Miramar Mesa, to the South, which includes an extended-care facility. It will charge you $50 just to walk in the front door, they warn you. If they decide to treat you, it costs more.

The real-estate business is terrific, because Rancho-Rancho is deemed a desirable place to live, young or old. But you must have money. It is the elderly who have the most. New developments are going up fast. All are pre-subscribed. People are lined up to pay $170,000 to $225,000 for a villa. Demand is such that there may be an auction; I'm sure it has entered the minds of the developers. There is fairly rapid turnover of housing units among the elderly. That is a way of saying that old folks die, and their villas are recycled back onto the market. It is simple, actuarial economics at work.

There are encouraging perks. You can own a condominium, for instance, and live in it but two weeks out of the year, and it can be written off in a few years and, in the meantime, you get to depreciate it and deduct the interest from your income taxes. You can also deduct expenses related to renting it out.

The physician next door is in his mid-fifties and is living here for a year because his own doctor ordered him to stop working for that long. He bought the villa as an investment, intending to stay here only the two weeks required by law. People talk freely about money and investments. My parents rent their villa on a time-share for two months. The owners live elsewhere, but I hear in the area. They benefit greatly from the arrangement. Most other units are lived in by people other than their owners.

This arrangement has created a high-income transient population able to pay $1500-2500 per month for a place where the weather is warm. The temporary aspect is appealing and practical, because they know a disabling illness is likely, at their age. It is best not to get too tied down to property and a long series of future payments.

The elderly have a chilling, superior quality. Perhaps it is from desperation. They greet each other with pumped-up good cheer, and each morning peruse the home-town newspapers flown in specially for them. They turn to the obituary section, in search of the names of friends and acquaintances. Each one they discover brings a little smile of triumph at having outlived a peer.

233

The gas station attendant I chat with at Shell is in his twenties and loves the idea of the Pacific Northwest. He visits his uncle in Portland, Oregon, and gets excited when he tells me about the lushness of the country I just left. Me, I love California. How contrary we are. He wants to sell me on where I'm from—how close the skiing is and the mountains. Yes, I counter, but here you have these wonderful beaches. It is a regular rite of ours, and we enjoy it, as I gas up for the coming day.

Norma and I are going back to LaJolla. It is beautiful. We skirt the Southernmost edge of the University of California at San Diego campus and discover a tall steel-reinforced structure rising dramatically on a bluff high above the ocean. A huge building complex is underway. The UC is undergoing an extensive expansion program. I noticed the same thing at Santa Barbara and Santa Cruz, as I passed through them.

From the bluff is a breath-taking vista. Below we can make out a long crescent of beige beach, with white surf nibbling at its edges. Clotted specks signify groups of people on the sand and some must be playing volleyball, judging by the alignment of the dots. A thin haze softens the world. The view is gorgeous and stirring. I find it exhilarating here. LaJolla must be a wonderful place to live. I'd never stop studying the ocean.

The Shore Drive does not follow the shoreline, as we were led to believe. Instead, it quickly pulls inland. You must travel Cabrillo de Oro, instead, if you want to keep the water in sight, and you have to leave the unsigned boulevard to search for it. It lies about four blocks further West; the space in between is filled with attractive homes, all in pastel colors, with white dominating. Just before you come to the public beach and huge unmetered parkinglot is a large private beach club with tennis courts. Next comes the posh Ocean Lodge Hotel, with restaurant, outdoor tables with sun umbrellas, and various bars. We didn't investigate these.

A Year At The River 187

The hotel is AAA-rated and costs $110 per day, double occupancy. I wouldn't mind staying there for a night, but I can't afford it.

The wind off the beach today is strong and chill, too cold for sunbathing except for the young and hardy. We are not among their number. After a few minutes in the sun, shivering, we retreat behind a screen of bushes to a grassy park encircled by trees, where we discover many cowards like ourselves. Here are some picnic tables upon which we can eat our sack lunches.

Two large groups of people seated in circles on the grass are conspicuous by their attire. They are scuba divers. They are listening to their instructors explaining the intricacies of diving procedures, safety measures, and how their equipment functions. All wear bathing suit bottoms but have black neoprene tops. They wear double tanks and have their face masks pushed up on the tops of their heads, like fashionable sunglasses. Their instructor has a professional two bands of red on his neoprene top and thus resembles a blackbird. Suddenly, one group gets to its feet and heads for the water in a quick file. A few minutes later, the second group repeats the vanishing act. It is time for all non-swimmers to get out of the pool. We are left behind, seated on our grass-stained pants on the lawn.

We read in the thin sun, toast our backs, then decide to go out upon the boardwalk. Back home it is raining, we inform each other, with grins. We stroll along the retaining wall that protects the park from the wind and waves. One of our groups of scuba divers is intently roaming up and down the surfline, flippers flopping, all engaged in deep conversation. Why aren't they out swimming? It is not until evening, while listening to the 11 o'clock news, back in Rancho-Rancho, that we learn a diver may have drowned. We see the scene where we were a few hours earlier, in chilling detail. All comes rushing back. There is the tiny, grassy park where we ate our picnic lunch. We watch the boy's instructor talking to the camera. He is distraught. We recognize him as one of the blackbirds. We see the other divers wander up and down the beach, looking forlorn.

The next day on the tube, we learn the body has been washed ashore by the tide. The boy was wearing two tanks. One was empty, the other full. Apparently he didn't know how to switch them over. He panicked and swallowed water. Norma and I feel as concerned as if we knew him previously, though our only link is that for a minute we sat on the same lawn.

234

Our visit here is due to end. We must soon return to the Pacific Northwest and our attendant responsibilities.

It is interesting to experience a world you are unfamiliar with— the one of wealthy oldsters. Their uniform is unvarying. It is as specific and prescribed as at an American high school, yet the players are elderly and some of them feeble.

Nobody departs from the dress code. To do so would make him conspicuous. He would grow nervous and self-conscious. The novelty would make his peers uncomfortable, as well. So everybody obeys and draws strength from the conformity obligation.

My father has a dozen carefully coordinated costumes. Most are pastel—like the stucco houses. In our ten days here, I haven't seen him wear the same outfit twice. He always tastefully varies his wash-and-wear slacks, golf shirt, and cardigan. The colors are impeccably chosen and "go together." (Perhaps my mother advises.)

Double-knits are the order of the day for both sexes. Usually the garments are made out of polyester. The women wear pantsuits, with blouses. Sometimes they wear golfing skirts, full of pleats for easy motion. Norma says they have one deep pleat, fore and aft. On a cool evening, they don cashmere cardigans, which they drape over their shoulders and button only the top button, leaving the bottom of the sweater to flare at the waist. When they play golf, the women wear fitted slacks. They are never seen in jeans, except for gardening. Gardening over, they change back immediately, for fear of being discovered out of costume, I guess.

Men wear doubleknit pants. Ones with checks or tightly laid-out plaids show up more than half the time. It seems odd to me that conservative men would wear "loud" pants. I, a comparative radical (more or less), wear only solidly colored blue jeans. But I admit to a secret craving for the bright plaid pants. Where would I ever wear them, though?

With the colorful trousers are worn color-coordinated knit socks in solid colors and a leisure shoe of soft, sueded leather, such as Hush Puppies. Tops are always golf shirts, with little dickey collars. Such shirts used to be called polo, but we play little polo in America, and a lot of golf. Shirts carry emblems on the pocket, appropriately at the heart, such as tiny alligators or raised umbrellas. These are class symbols. It is how we recognize each other and fit in. Over the shirt, along towards evening, is worn an alpaca cardigan, in a keyed color. Those made by Lord Jeff are popular. They are double knit and sell for around $90. In such an ensemble, you are accepted everywhere, even, I suspect, at a funeral.

Keep your hair cut short, Jack. It helps to gain acceptance if your sideburns are whacked off, too. A cocoa tan is coveted. A little billed golf cap will do nicely when the wind comes up on the fairway. It should sport a pair of tiny crossed woods or greens flags. A jaunty straw is permissible, but probably should be reserved for evenings. It is important to blend in, at the same time you want to stand out a little. These goals can be achieved only if you are an acrobat.

There is a general dislike of young people, who are known to use drugs and make noise. I see no blacks here, except ones working in restaurants. There are many Hispanics. They have a monopoly on the menial jobs, generally ones nobody else will perform. The Jews in Rancho-Rancho tend to stick to themselves and live elsewhere, perhaps in wealthy ghettoes. It is a good thing, for they are known to be pushy, and pushiness will never do. Not here.

There you have it, Rancho-Rancho, in a nutshell. Nothing much happens here, and the inhabitants want it this way. The long days go on and on, in desperate harmony. Tomorrow Norma and I will depart this double-knit burg for points more miserable and varied.

235

Tonight finds me back in Utilitarian Motel 6, in Woodland, CA, after a grueling five- or six-hundred mile drive out of San Diego. I feel peculiarly at home here, among such Spartan surroundings. Norma flew back a day earlier.

I enjoyed my visit to Rancho-Rancho. It is a world I'm glad I experienced. In contrast, this motel unit is plebeian, its spurious Danish-modern furniture cranked out with a cookie cutter's precision and cheapness. The bed is a rock, but won't break down for a hundred years, which is what they were after. The TV is black and white, and costs extra. I pay the fee for the oblivion the set provides, and watch crap until my eyes close.

I am driving the white Mustang. It is not a great road car. A half-inch of rain fell, this afternoon, which made the highway slippery and dangerous. Deep puddles stand along the shoulders. Now strong sidewinds are buffeting the motel windows. It is 50 degrees outside.

236

Wake to thunderous hard rain falling hard on the tile roof. The roar makes it impossible to get back to sleep. I rise early, for there is a long drive ahead, and I want to make it all the way home in a single day. I will have to average fifty miles per hour.

There are three major mountain passes between the Mexican border and Canada, on Interstate 5. All lie in California—unless the Siskiyous Pass is shared with Oregon, which seems only fair. You might say it is a border-line case.

The first lies between Los Angeles and Bakersfield. It marks the summit of the Tehachapi Mountains and includes the settlement of Gorman. It is not a town, just a collection of gasoline stations. The elevation is 4,014 feet and it is shiveringly cold, as I step out of the car. The woman behind the cash box at the Chevron station says the rain will turn to snow by afternoon. I take a drink from a refrigerated tap and am reminded of Washington's pure cold water;

in San Diego, what we had was warm and so hard they sold salt in the stores with which to soften it. Nobody drank out of the tap.

This water is so good that I ask the woman if she'd mind if I filled my water jug.

"Go right ahead," she says. "Isn't water free?"

I was never sure that it was.

The second summit is in the winding Shasta Lake region, near Dunsmuir. Its height is posted as 3,940 feet, but there is light snow on the ground and some heavy-duty stuff hanging in the trees. It is beginning to fall from the pines because of its weight. There is no sun, and a little light rain descends, with the odd wet flake mixed in. Snowplows drift by like ghosts, purposeless, for they are done with their work by noon and are returning to wherever it is snowplows go, until called out of their lairs into service again. They have left a wide swath on the shoulder for trucks to use on the long upgrade, so passenger cars can pass them easily and safely.

Trucks inch along the ponderous grade, then come roaring up behind you on the descent, which is posted as six percent. For the trucks, there is a brake-testing area, and two miles ahead is an escape route, if their brakes fail—an actual road that goes nowhere but will slow them down over a long rise before they crash. It works like the arresting gear on an aircraft carrier.

The third summit is the Siskiyous. It is 4,300 feet and Mt. Ashland is close by, with skiing. Old snow lies on the ground in dirty patches, and overhead I glimpse an intense blue sky, as formations of cloud and fog scud by. Some cars are pulled off on the shoulder and have spilled out kids who are having a great time throwing wicked chunks of road ice at each other and trying to erect hasty snowmen with shards of snow left by the plows before their parents say it is time to pile back in the car.

Grant's Pass is not much over 2000 feet and hardly counts, though the car notices it. And there are minute crests to accomplish before I slide into the flats of Eugene. When I enter Washington, there are no passes to encounter along I-5; Washington passes aren't found unless you head East. And only skiers do that in winter.

It is good to be home again, in this land of flat light that lends itself so well to black-and-white photography. A beer, and my familiar bed calls out. Norma was wise to fly, but then she only got to see the interior of the plane's cabin, while I have my succession of five mountain passes to recall.

237

Yesterday I fished the Flat Water for the first time in a month. I hooked three fish. The first was a small, fresh steelhead that came off the hook seconds after the strike. I saw it plane to the surface when I struck, and I hauled it across the top of the water, for the fish lacked the weight to set the hook. The action took place at the bottom of the run, out from Phil O'Lone's place.

The second fish was hooked above the culvert, and proved to be a spawned-out male of only six pounds, a badly wasted and weak fish that had badly injured its eye and appeared to have lost the sight in it. A blind steelhead or, rather, a half-blind one. I released the fish carefully, but suspect it will die. Still it was hardy enough to have endured for so long.

The third fish was a bright little jack, very strong for its size, just over 20 inches. It fought and fought, never stopping until it was on the beach. I killed it for the table, having not brought one home in a long time. I left it high on the beach and continued fishing. When it was time to go home, I found the fish gone. I saw the track where it had been dragged away by an animal. I traced its route across the sand and through some flattened sedges. The trail disappeared by Phil's front door to where there is some gravel that leaves no traces. No more signs of my fish.

I knocked on his door, suspecting a practical joke.

No, he told me, he had not appropriated my fish. Maybe one of his cats had. They were practically wild and fended for themselves. Look on the *back* porch, he said, and closed the door. Sure enough, there was my fish. Phil's orange and white tabby looked at me suspiciously, over his shoulder. The little steelhead was practically untouched.

"Give me that fish," I told the cat angrily, striding forward and snatching it up.

The cat stalked away, indignant. Poor cat, it was only doing what a cat does best, trying to feed itself.

Four days left in the season. I probably shan't be back before it closes.

238

A pale gray morning, with no mountains or sun in evidence, and a soft rain falling. Only, at a quarter to eight in the morning, the light begins to fail. The day is but an hour or two old, and already the sky is moving towards dark. House lights snap back on, all over the neighborhood. You'd have to be a hermit not to know what is happening, for the papers and TV have been full of the news for weeks.

The moon is passing directly in front of the sun; it will occupy that position for 44 seconds. In Goldendale, Yakima County, and in Portland, Oregon, the eclipse is total. In cloudy Seattle, it may go unobserved because of clouds. Here, the cover is 99 percent. Anybody less than a perfectionist ought to be satisfied with it. But the cloud cover is absolute.

I listen for signs of confusion from the birds, for it is said that the bird and animal kingdom grows confused in an eclipse, but I detect no consternation. I've turned the TV on and the volume up high, for TV is the only way I am going to be able to observe the eclipse "first hand"—though of course it isn't first-hand at all. "Near live," might be more like it. If I don't watch it this way, I will have to wait for pictures in the evening newspaper, and that is way too far away.

I wait in heavy anticipation. The sky remains overcast, but darkens. Our old cat comes mewing in through the front door. Does he knows something is amiss? No, he's simply demanding his morning snack. I give him some kibble. My own empty stomach growls empathetically, as he bends to eat it.

It grows darker. A storm cloud might be passing overhead, that's all. Sometimes the sky turns this dark just before the first big drops begin to fall. Today the rain is slight and diffused, however; more of a mist. I can hear the TV description. The report comes from Goldendale, where Annie Dillard has gone with some guy to watch the event. So have hundreds of others, who drove there in the night. I envy them, but not much.

The sky perceptibly lightens. It lightens by degrees. The orb is emerging from its artificial night. Only a bit of sun is still obscured, according to TV. I snap off the set and begin to assemble my breakfast.

The eclipse belongs to history. The next full one will be in 38 years. I doubt if I will be around to experience it.

239

We are creatures of habit. Well, I am—the only one I am authorized to speak for. Having spent 10 days with my parents in Rancho-Rancho, their daily routines became obvious to me. They are not allowed to vary. My own are just as bad.

My father rises at 8. He makes a pot of coffee and fills a thermos (which he preheats) for my mother. Then he pours out a fixed quantity of juice in two glasses; it is about four ounces each, and comes from a can. Usually it is a grapefruit/pineapple combination.

He drinks his, while my mother's slowly warms to ambient temperature, for she is still abed. She doesn't mind drinking it warm. My father opens a pill jar and lays out a white (250 mg ascorbic acid, or Vitamin C) and a red (a multivitamin, probably One-a-Day) for each of them. He washes his down with the last of his juice.

My mother's empty coffee cup, thermos, juice glass, and two tablets go on a tray, which he delivers to their bedroom like a mouse, afterwards softly closing the door behind him. She will rise about eleven. Sometimes he has to call her. Then she is grumpy. The tray delivered, he relaxes visibly. It is time to eat his breakfast.

Because of his cancer of the prostate, I want to urge him to double or triple his Vitamin C dose, but do not, because it would constitute juvenile meddling. Linus Pauling, whom I believe in as some people believe in Jesus Christ, says you cannot take too much Vitamin C, for your body will excrete what it doesn't need. If you have cancer, you need a lot, just to hang in there.

I will eat with him, as I did when a boy. The main bulk of my father's breakfast is either Corn Flakes or Rice Krispies. He alternates. This is the fodder I was raised on and from which I have not far departed. My own pair of cereals is Cheerios and Rice Chex—on a given day I will eat his choice, and happily regress. Invariably, half a banana is sliced on top of his cereal. When I eat with him, he slices the first half on mine. He does it precisely, with care. I enjoy watching him do it. It takes me back to a simpler time. And I like the efficiency of helping to use up my father's unexercised banana. I even like the taste.

That out of the way, my father goes for a walk. Every day he buys *The Los Angeles Times*, which he says is a superior paper. I agree. But I think he likes it because it is so big and thick, and constitutes a good buy—a lot of paper for the money. A boy has offered to deliver it to the door, but Dad says, No thanks. He tells the boy they will be here only another couple of weeks. The truth is, he loves his morning stroll along the cool streets of Rancho-Rancho, his legitimate time away from my mother. Both need time by themselves, but seldom get it.

In the evening, the process is reversed. My mother stays up late and enjoys her period of aloneness. My father is in his pajamas, slippers, and robe by 10:30. He has showered and washed his thin hair about fifteen minutes earlier. Eleven is the time he retired, all his working life. He now stretches that out to 11:30, and feels deliciously guilty (I suspect) about the advanced hour. And though he saw the news at 6 P.M., a fully hour's worth, he now watches the shorter version, and stays alert, in case he missed an event, or something of importance has occurred since the dinner hour. Often it has, at least in the world of sports.

Before he goes to bed, he mixes my mother a highball and carries it to her chair, where he sets it down on a napkin on the side table. (Who needs servants, when you are married?) Now he can retire in peace. He will sleep straight through the night, he tells me.

My mother quickly downs her drink and mixes a stronger one. The "Tonight Show" flickers on. She lights up her fiftieth cigaret of the day. She is more alert than at any other time. She is restless and critical. If a guest she likes is scheduled, but doesn't come on until later—an old trick of Johnny's—she will turn the sound down with the remote and watch the screen silently, as a form of protest. Her eyes are bright. She'll put on the sound, from time to time, to catch the gist of what is happening, but not enough to get caught up in the action. It's a form of outrage and self-denial.

Often, while waiting, unknown to her, she dozes. If nobody "good" is on, she'll snap off the set and turn on her pocket radio. She listens through a headphone jack with a single earplug. Normally, it's TV, though. When Johnny is over, it is late. She'll sample Tom Snyder. The same soundless technique is employed until a favorite arrives. Finally, she rises and goes to brush her teeth—her own, though she is eighty—and joins my father in paired-up singled beds, with a common coverlet. She frequently has trouble sleeping, she reports. She'll lie awake, worrying about the mistakes of the past, until swallowed by a sleep that drugs her deep into the morning.

Sons and daughters judge their parents severely. In turn, in time, they are judged harshly, if they are parents. It is their mirror image they behold, given a little time.

240

I am obsessed with the role TV plays in our lives. I watch too much myself, judged by my own standard. TV obliterates thought and eats up your leisure. When you walk around the neighborhood at twilight, the corner of everybody's livingroom window glows pale blue. People are seated like humps on a log, their faces drained of expression. They might be statues by George Segal.

Many families have more than one set. My parents have three for the two of them. We have three for the three of us. Let me explain.... No, there is no good excuse, not even if I add that one of the monsters is defective and another is rarely turned on. The third we bought for Garth. The idea was, if he has his own, maybe our own livingroom would be quiet in the evening and we can read.

Down in his room, the fool thing plays all the time. It sits on a little stool, only a few inches from his face. I suspect it is on, even when he sleeps. You see, we don't go into his room, as a matter of principle. TV is his sole companion. Does he really watch it? I suspect it is for background noise, most of the time. And background goes unheeded. It is much like radio used to be.

In Rancho-Rancho, my parents turned on the set each morning upon arising. If one didn't, the other would. I think the silence bothered them. Silence "made too much noise." It ate at their nerves. They explained to me, "It's just to see what's going on." But I noticed they left it on for the rest of the day. Somehow it comforted them.

Once, alone in the livingroom, I dared to turn it off. A heavenly quiet enveloped me. My mother entered the room. She knew at once something was wrong. She snapped the set back on. All was right in the world again.

My son, in spite of the omnipresent TV set, does well in school. This surprised me, for I expected him to do poorly, and then I would say, "I told you so," and ban the set. When I was young, my parents used to caution me against having the radio on, all the time. They worried about my studies. Now I see them as TV addicts. What did they know then? What do I know now?

Television is stupid, where radio was intelligent. But many of those radio programs were dumb, too. It is much easier to ignore TV than radio. Radio is persistent and demanding. It rattles your cage. I woolgather a lot to TV. And this is harmful, for often I miss important things. Then I say, "Eh?" to my wife.

Except in sports, there is no instant replay. As in life, you must catch it the first time, or else it is gone for good, and you only have somebody else's word for what took place. I suppose that is why the man invented video tape. It can be quickly backed up to show what we've missed. So there are second chances in life, only they are for the things that really don't matter.

241

We all make mistakes, don't we? I mean, pencils come with erasers. If we didn't make errors in thought or writing, we could sharpen each end, and write twice as much, or twice as long.

Similarly we have accidents. Once I was driving North in a pickup truck and came to a stop on a road that ran alongside the freeway at an exit. It was an unexpected stop and I was not the only one who was surprised by the sign at a minor intersection. A car piled into the back of me. It bunged up my rear bumper, but did me no real damage; I mean, I was able to drive on. The car behind me, however, had its radiator pushed into the engine. Rusty water streamed everywhere. A young woman was driving the car. A state trooper just happened by, headed the other direction, at the exact moment of impact. He whirled around and came up behind us, parked, and was soon directing traffic around us. It was minor, the traffic, that is; the damage to her car was major. It was totaled.

She did not know this and neither of us wanted to tell her. It was an old car and belonged to her boyfriend. She was distraught; in fact, she was in tears. I felt bad for her and so did the trooper.

"I didn't mean to hit him," she said, between sobs.

He had more experience at this than I.

"We know you didn't," he said, with ultimate kindness. "That's why they call them accidents. It isn't intentional. Nobody does it on purpose."

The words calmed her. In a moment he told me I could drive on and I did.

242

I am reading a novel by Kingsley Amis, an English novelist who has been around for a while, and whose first novel, *Lucky Jim*, was a blockbuster back in the '50s. This novel, *Ending Up*, is about a bunch of old people and the ways—contrary and compassionate, helpful and antagonistic—in which they relate to each other.

The book has made me think—that in itself is a good thing—about the aging process, abetted no doubt by my recent stay with my parents on the outskirts of San Diego. Old folks have a negligible role in society. Nobody has any use for them, anymore. Their world grows narrower and narrower, as they are ignored by young people and, in turn, look inward of their own volition. "If you don't want me, I don't want you," is their feeling. I sympathize.

Our society says you must be young to be worthy of attention. This is excruciating in the case of women. The role of ingenue is the only acceptable one. And a woman must always be agreeable, regardless of how she feels. If she isn't, she isn't feminine, and God help her. As she ages, she substitutes other qualities for the ones of her youth—maturity, wisdom, grace, style, pleasantness—but learns none will do. Men look right through her. The key to her self-esteem is her ability to attract men, to have men find her attractive. And they—fools that we are—seek only youth and beauty, probably in that order.

An older man—one who is middle-aged or even older—proves his virility by seducing a younger woman. He wears her on his arm like a merit badge. It is not difficult to do. (Don't ask me how I know this.) It is a bit like trading in the old car for a new one. New models are out there, every year. A man wants a bright red convertible, or the female equivalent. The car is . . . a virgin. I won't belabor this comparison, but most new cars I've seen have a few miles on the odometer.

When a woman stops being able to attract men, woe is she. To be found attractive is different for men. Men, as they age, often become dignified, affluent, powerful, even if they are no longer athletic, handsome, virile, sexy; that is, everything that smacks of youth. A woman must not show her desperation, or go out on the prowl, the way a man can. It is another masculine privilege. As she ages, she spends more money on cosmetics, only half-believing in the advertising claims, but not being able to afford to pass up the hope they offer. And many women submit to plastic surgery, with its pain and expense, in hopes that it will add another few years of power to their lives—the power of attracting men.

Yet the time comes when, male or female, you can no longer pretend you are young. You must accept what life has dealt you. The old are past pretension, really. When the childbearing years are over, women believe they have lost their purpose in life. They literally dry up and become wrinkled. There are hormonal reasons for this. They panic, when they see it happening, and become foolish. They paint and they paint, hoping to cover over the reality. But it is there for the reading. The face is a terrible book.

Men at the climacteric become vain, which is their way of expressing fear. They join a gym and start working out frantically, striving for the flat stomach they haven't had in decades. They devote useless hours to acquiring a tan. They dye their hair (and beard), appalled at the sight of their father (or grandfather) looming again in the morning mirror. Often they divorce their wife of the years, the mother of their children, and take up with younger women. They usually marry them. The young woman doesn't want yet another bad love affair; she wants the money and comfort an older man provides. A recent lover pains her still, and she may already have a child or two to support. Her biological urgency is sliding behind, and she faces the majority of her years ahead. She hopes to find solace in the gentle appreciation of a man who puts only domestic demands on her. Simple kindness counts for a lot, when you've been through the mill. And if he has money—as he often will have—so much the better, for money eases the burden and relieves the tedium.

The older man is elated that a young woman finds him attractive. In a way, divorced yet or not, he is in competition with his wife and the accumulation of years. If she has lost her attractiveness, and he has not, it's her tough luck. Of course, this is cruel and unfair. But it is how life goes.

The vainglorious man becomes foolishly confused, divorcing the wife he loves to marry the young woman he doesn't for her clear skin and firm body. An older man finds he can simply *look* at a young woman and be content with what he sees. Though sex matters, it matters less. He takes for granted that all young women today are skilled at sex. Of course they aren't; it is often acquired with time and practice.

Women past their first flush like to believe they can attract younger men. It requires a lot of effort and is not without attendant grief. It helps if they have something to offer that most pretty young women do not. This can be money or a certain kind of sex. A woman as she ages has no line to draw anymore, not when it comes to sex. She must serve up whatever is on his menu. It is how she competes with youth. And . . . she doesn't really mind doing *those* things.

243

Apropos to the above: My friend Roberta has a live-in lover who is ten years her junior. So has my friend Sally, though hers is only four or five years younger; it is just enough that she is keenly aware of the age difference. Together the two women bracket 35. It is the age of decision; it used to mark the start of middle age. Reaching that milestone today makes people anxious. Life is all downhill and the mirror tells you what you don't want to know.

Though my two female friends have taken up with younger men, they *like* older men. Maybe they just like men. At 35, a woman may still bear children, but they fear their child-bearing years are slipping away. Their options are disappearing. This is called "hearing the alarm on your biological clock." Sally has two kids, one from an earlier marriage and one from the crazy period following her divorce. She says she can have no more—biologically speaking. In a way, this is an advertisement for herself. She announces her sexual availability. On the other hand, Roberta *will* not have children. She doesn't want the responsibility and, she states, she has trouble conceiving—which is another way a woman may advertise herself and her availability. But in Roberta's case, it is a blessing. She'd make a terrible mother.

Many women by the age of 35 have had one or more abortions. It is a surprise to learn how many some women have had, and still have their health and fertility intact. But a few have paid the price. They are infertile.

As for the men involved with these two friends of mine, I can't speak for their feelings. Men do not become friends with other men, not where women are concerned, even if there is no direct sexual competition. These two men may be looking for Mama, as we used to say, during our collective intellectual infatuation with Freud. But that is too pat, too simplistic, an explanation. Older women have their attractions. Invulnerability is not one of them, however. Both these men can and do wound their lovers by flirting with younger women in public. Knowing how successfully it works, and the anger and jealousy it provokes, they are wont to do it often. The women justly fear the threat posed by a younger woman. It is not fair, of course, for the men to play upon these insecurities. But lovers are deft in finding the weakest spot and driving home a telling blow.

244

I seem to be much concerned about the role of old persons in society. After all, I will be there one day myself. It is not so far off, either.

Old people have quit playing sexual games based on performance; instead, they exercise other pseudo-sexual forms of leverage, such as guilt and intimidation. The older people that I know seem reconciled to their role of relics without utility or social value. That is, none is fighting hard against it. Instead, they accept the slot allocated them. They shun the company of people younger than they are, even the middle-aged ones. And the commotion of children makes them nervous. They allow infrequent guests in their tidy homes, and wish them to be discreet and unchallenging.

Amis's *Ending Up* is about the interdependence of septuagenarians and how they accommodate each other's idiosyncrasies. It is a warm book, quite funny in places. Anthony Burgess says of Amis that he is one of the few living novelists who never bores him. Quite a compliment.

245

Archie Satterfield writes in "The World of Books" section of *The Seattle Post-Intelligencer* about the current state of publishing in America and how the big bucks of the industrial conglomerates are swallowing up the individual publishing houses, one by one. One such instance is the takeover of McGraw Hill by American Express. (Random House and Knopf are owned by RCA, of course, and there are numerous other cases.)

What results is a literary carelessness and lowering of editorial standards, leaving the business in a jungle. Satterfield quotes from a editorial put-on formulated by Jerzi Kozinski and a cohort. They submitted a typescript of a novel by K., which won a 1959 Pulitzer Prize, to numerous publishers and agents. All rejected it, even the house that originally published it. One agent lost it.

Jack Olsen, a Bainbridge Island writer, relates the tale of how another writer submitted the first chapter of Faulkner's *The Reivers* under his own name to a dozen publishers, all of whom turned it down. Only one editor recognized it for what it was and wrote back amusingly that the book "had already been written."

What is indicated by these events is horrifying. Publishers today seem to want books that come "pre-sold," because of the writer fame or notoriety, or else they seek books which will easily convert into a TV series. Satterfield believes that this will lead to the publication of only books which "appeal to base emotions and desires." About American Express he says they have "screwed up" and lost force in the credit-card business, and are now eager to move into an entirely new field and screw it up, too: Publishing.

Perhaps, perhaps. Or do I find these ideas consoling because they cast my own relative lack of success in a more favorable light? At any rate, it seems hard, if not impossible, to get agents and publishers to read original works by unknown writers, let alone publish and promote them with confidence.

246

Wilfred Sheed, also quoted in this Sunday's *Seattle Post-Intelligencer's* "World of Books," speaks ironically and affectionately of the writer's life. If asked to choose between writing fiction and what passes for fact, he will take fiction "all the way."

"You feel so good after you've done fiction," he says. "I would rather be a third-rate novelist than a first-rate essayist—and there are those who say I have had my wish."

Sheed is exactly my age and a thoroughly literary man, with quite a bit of success in the past several years. He adds, "The minute you find you can do it"—write, that is—"you find you can't do anything else. It makes you instantly unemployable." How true.

On the same page, in an interview with Jacqueline Briskin, William Arnold reports her saying, "When I'm in a book, I write all day. That's seven days a week. I work all day and research at night. I generally don't talk about the book while I'm working on it and I may do ten or twelve drafts.... The whole process may take three years." She says it is difficult to withdraw afterwards. "It is very hard, very painful. It's like a death. You see, I live in that world and I love my characters. It's what's real to me."

She has just completed *Paloverde*, a long book, a saga about Los Angeles. The book is published by McGraw Hill—the very company just taken over by crass and unfeeling American Express, according to Archie Satterfield. Is something wrong here?

247

My father is seventy-five years old today. Happy birthday, Pop. (I never call him that, but the word seems to fit the occasion.)

248

The North Fork reads 10.1 feet on the river gauge, following a rise of six true vertical feet in one day. How awesome. It is a record, no doubt.

This spells "flood" to me, though the papers mention nothing about the prospect for one. It is probably a short-lived great "crest" of water. We have had three such events since November, but this is by far the worst. Such a torrent will alter the river bar in front of my property, either adding to or taking away from it. I will have to wait to find out which. Either way, the event is not good.

I fear for my tall leaning alder, which will go one of these days, taking a chunk of the bank along with it; I've promised myself, and the tree, that if we both survive the floods this year, I will limb it, even if I have to climb it myself. More likely I will persuade my son to do it, but first we will reduce the tree's weight some by cutting off some lower boughs with the chainsaw. It will have to be done after mid-August, when the river is entering its seasonal low flow and the current won't sweep away the big limbs, the moment they've fallen into the shallows, and I can salvage them for firewood.

I have hopes the river will continue to build up the bar out from the path on the original property. This will gain us more beach, which would be nice, and also scour out the tiny run against the far bank, so that in the future it might hold a fish or two. It is too swift and shallow now to give them the cover they seek. How nice it would be to have a fishing hole, right out from my beach. And have nobody else know about it.

The radio announces, "Many Western Washington rivers are running bank-full, but no major flooding is expected." This is from the weather bureau. That crest I've recorded is more than a day old. Is the weather bureau trying to protect their reputation by withholding the true nature of what is going on? Let's call it by its true name—a flood.

I won't return to the property, or be able to assess the damage, until the river has receded a great deal, which will take a week of no rain. My hope is that the leaning alder down by the beach will be still there. And perhaps my sandy beach will have increased some.

249

Back in town, waiting for the mail. If there is going to be a day on which the mail isn't going to arrive, it will be a Tuesday. I don't know the reason, only that it happens, time after time. Occasionally there is a piece or two, but never much. Usually none, which is untrue to the facts, for we always have something, albeit junk mail.

Our route is used to train new hires, and they hate it, because of all the steps leading up to the towering front porches. What we don't need is a mailman with a chip on his shoulder. We are always getting mail addressed to our street *number*, but the wrong street. It is intended for NE 65th Street, not NE 60th. And they get ours.

An old lady lives there. She is forgetful, so it is sometimes a long wait until our misdirected mail gets returned to us by the carrier. It must be easy for a mailman to mistake a zero for a five, when he's had so many pieces to sort through each day. But it never used to happen. Well, rarely.

After several years of having the same mailman—a tall, slender, bearded guy of invariably good cheer, who always brought the mail by 10:30 a.m., even in a blizzard—we now have a progression of stealthy, slovenly rejects from other lines of work. They are invariably late. Late, later, latest. Perhaps today the post office marks the lower end of the employment ladder.

Am I being too unkind, or not kind enough? They are well paid, due to a recent big raise their union got them. They make more than most college graduates. It is, admittedly, physically taxing, the bag heavy, the weather often rigorous. But then there are no worries that come from intense interaction with other people. They are on their own, each day. It is just the mailman facing the elements, which makes it basically primordial. I can think of worse jobs and more stressful ones.

As I sit here writing, I hear the postman sneak up the front steps and deposit my mail in the box. It's 2:30 P.M.—why so early? What, only two letters? Oh, yes, it's a Tuesday.

Three or four minutes later I hear footsteps again. The trainee has found the rest of our mail. Again there is nothing of consequence. Most of the fistful of stuff is for our son, who has developed the hobby of clipping coupons.

250

Susan Sontag's book, *I, Etc.*, has a charming Zen Buddhist anecdote, which is not inappropriate here, after my raving of yesterday against the postal service. It goes like this:

The Master is adjudicating a dispute between two angry women. His disciple listens silently. After hearing the first woman air her many grievances, the Master pauses and tells her, "You are perfectly right." She departs with a smile.

Enter the second woman. She commences her recitation. She has fully as many complaints and delineates them at length. When she is done, the Master tells her, "You know, you are right." She departs, smiling.

Angrily the disciple exclaims, "But, Master, you told both women they are right. Surely that can't be true. You've made a mistake."

"Yes," agreed the Master, "you are right."

Love it.

251

The skin on my forearms is peeling hideously, coming away in chunks. This is the result of the San Diego sun, which seems so long ago and far away. It was less than four weeks, however. My skin has a slightly jaundiced look, and soon my tan will be gone, wasted. Still, it is more than the sun-starved people of the Pacific Northwest sport. I am so proud of my bit of color that, at every opportunity, I turn my face and arms to the thin March sun, and shiver bravely in the breeze, trying to enhance it.

Norma and I faced the dentist today. We were scheduled for exactly the same time, due to a diabolical mishap. Her new gold crown was due for delivery last night, but it hadn't come by closing time, so the dentist called and rescheduled her for 11:30 this morning. It was the same time I was due for a cleaning by his hygienist. But by 11:30 the crown still hadn't come.

I was being scaled in one chair, while Norma waited out with the magazines. A boy ran in with a box containing the crown. The hygienist soon finished me up. (My own ceramic crown is due in exactly a week, and I wear a temporary.) I scrambled out of my chair, just as she was settling down into hers, in the room next door. I went in to kibitz.

I liked the idea of her being helplessly, supine, while I was newly free to rove. I peered into her mouth, which was wedged open with tools. "Tell me, is it true," I asked Dr. Eric Ranta, our dentist, "that a man loses all romantic interest in a woman, once he sees the inside of her mouth?"

"Better not be," he said, "because my wife was just in for a filling."

252

Spring is coming, albeit slowly. Crocuses have shot up—purple, gold, and pale blue—in our neighbors' yards, but not ours. Our crocuses got destroyed, every last one, in a freeze several years ago. But two daffodils have bloomed in the side yard that faces East.

Up at the river, the thermometer read 71 degrees. Norma, Garth, and I spent the day gathering up deadfalls. We used the little electric chainsaw they gave me for my birthday, back in November, to cut it up for firewood. Garth was reluctant to try it, but after I showed his mother how it worked, and she timidly gave it a turn, he took it from her and soon proved proficient. Don't say I lack subtlety and indirection.

We have two large projects looming, involving use of the saw: one, a large dead alder or cottonwood is breaking apart in sections during storms and is dropping rotten limbs, a few at a time; second, there is the leaning alder down by the river. The last near-flood did not claim it, as I feared. Is it my imagination, or is it now leaning lower? There was talk today about Garth climbing the leaning tree, with a rope attached to his waist with which to haul up the chainsaw, like the pros do. This would be in August, when the river is low and there is lots of beach. He will bring a second rope with him to tie on to the limb he cuts off, so we can guide it gently to the ground where we want it, not on top of some favorite plant or shrub. He seemed to harken to the project.

Farmers are burning their fields. A couple of unattended fires at dusk worried us, but nobody at the Oso General Store where we reported them seemed much concerned. So why should we be? With consciences clear, we put our worries out of mind. There is no fire department until the alarm sounds and volunteers come scrambling from all directions in their pickup trucks, like spokes converging on a hub.

The earth and its assorted grasses are packed flat from accumulated rains, snow, and ice. The river willows are starting to unclench their leave buds, but nothing else is stirring. The river is running very high from the flood of a week ago—that ten-foot crest.

We ended the day by going to the Bluebird Cafe in Arlington and eating six-ounce sirloin steaks. Garth had never been there before. For dessert we had their specialty, bread pudding, which they say they are famous for. Maybe they are only famous around the block, but the food is good, and we shall be back.

253

Once I bought a photograph from a man. It didn't cost much and it was pretty. A picture on the wall ought to look nice. It is a color shot of a storm breaking over some mountains—probably the

Pyrenees—and there is a slightly out of focus poplar tree in the foreground. It is monochromatic, an over-all golden brown. It was taken by Professor Christofides, chairman of the Department of Romance Languages at the UW. The print came already matted, with a beveled window cut into the mat. He sold it to me for the cost Kodak charged him for printing it. It was a bargain.

A year ago I found a walnut frame for it at a used-furniture store, and the print now hangs in Norma's room over her sewing machine, though it is mine and I am the one who likes it most. It is in her room because she has space on her wall. Mine are full up with prints and paintings.

Anyway, a green lacewing insect came to rest on the glass, right by the inside edge of the mat, last summer. It was the insect's "appointed time," you might say. A lacewing doesn't "turn into" anything, like a moth or a butterfly. It simply dies in due course—*in situ*, as we scientists say. This particular lacewing crawled behind the glass and rests eternally there. *In vitro.* In a way, it is part of the picture.

The back of the picture is not sealed. The air gets in, and when a breeze through a window stirs the room, in a certain manner, the lacewing's antenna and wing tips quiver. You don't have to be particularly observant to notice it. The lacewing has been dead over two years.

What am I to make of this?

254

A rainy day, and I am having a delightful time. It is the first really wet day in a long while. Remaining in pajamas and bathrobe, I read late into the morning and listen to tapes of Beethoven. Don't tell anybody!

I am reading Erica Jong's *How To Save Your Own Life*, which gets pretty lyrically obscene, towards the end, and makes me think that a Jong wouldn't be possible if a Henry Miller hadn't broken the sexual ground for her. Miller actually appears in the book—which is partly a *roman a clef*, thinly disguised and highly recognizable. He is lovingly presented, as he ought to be, and it is poetically appropriate.

Jong writes well—clearly and understandably, if those are still virtues—but the extreme biographical content of her book becomes quickly tedious and boring. I suspect it is so, even to her, and this is why she writes so many sex scenes. She is famous for them. In another time, it would be called pornography. Today it is merely "permissive."

Cat and I are listening to more Beethoven. Does he hear and appreciate music—a dumb cat? Who cares? I have a maxim for this day:

A cat in your lap helps you face the world.

The mail arrives, nearly on time. It is comprised mostly of periodicals, but includes a letter from my Aunt Ruth in Florida, thanking me for the photographs of my parents and wife and me, taken while in San Diego. It was at her request, but I find I am glad to have some, too.

255

In *Time Magazine* I come across a startling photograph of six men, clumsily blindfolded, awaiting execution in Iran for the crime of homosexual rape. The picture is chilling because, when it was taken, the men were alive. Now they are dead, legally murdered. It gives one pause, at least one like me.

We comfortable, insulated Americans, leafing through the magazine, come across this atrocity-about-to-happen on page 40. It catapults us into another dimension. We are submerged in a far different world. Its values are impossible for us to comprehend.

Strange, repressive, and punitive measures are being taken in the name of God in a country that does not put much value on human life. Six men dead for raping another? It is a terrible thing, admitted, but is it so horrible that they should die ignominiously?

In Tehran recently, four men were put to death for raping an 18-year-old male university student. The *victim* was then given 13 lashes. Why? What happened to him was a sin against God. A man and a woman were convicted of adultery. She was married. He was given 80 lashes, she 40. It makes no sense, not by our values.

The photograph of the men about to die powerfully symbolizes the continual upheaval that faces an emerging nation. What is so chilling about it is the knowledge we bring to it of impending death. We know the men—regardless of their crime—now lie in the cold ground. Do we feel more alive, because they are dead? Do we . . . exalt in our knowledge, secretly? Do the dead know something we do not, some ultimate truth? Yes, but that truth may only be the knowledge of what death is.

To know death, one must die. Then you take that knowledge and experience with you. It lies buried in the earth, or else goes up in smoke, depending on the ultimate disposal of your solid waste. Whatever you've learned, it is not communicable.

The dead have the most accumulated knowledge, but it does them no good. Nor us. They cannot tell us or we benefit from it. Death is shrouded in great mystery and fear. Each of us will gain his own terrible knowledge of it, in time.

But those poor, sad, dead men in Iran. It came to them too early, and without good cause.

256

My old friend Julianna Pickrell has an acre of land on which grows many tall old trees, some of them dogwoods. They are of the *nuttallii* variety, which I seek. They grow there like a weed. Each year new ones sprout. I have found a source of small dogwoods, at last.

The proliferation of dogwoods is the result of birds feeding on the seeds and scarifying them by passing them through their digestive systems. This prepares the seed for planting. The birds' excretion is full of nutrients, which help the seed get off to a strong start. Try as he might, a person will not be able to sprout a dogwood from seeds that he gathers. For a bird it is easy. The dogwood is a handsome tree which flowers whitely and quite prettily.

Julianna has offered us our choice of several small and middling-sized dogwoods. In the past, she has cut them all down, but dislikes this aspect of horticulture because she recognizes them as splendid. She simply has many more than she can use. She says she would like to see her seedlings "go to good homes." It is the nurturing instinct. I assure her that our land up at the river is just such a place. We love our trees. Julianna and Norma seem to have hit if off passably well, but you really can't tell, women gush and smile so. Off we go off to dig up six *Cornus nuttallii* of different sizes and year classes, and bind up their tiny root masses in burlap sacking Julianna thoughtfully provides. We try to keep as much dirt clinging as we can. We also take a sample of salal, a leathery leafed ground cover we are lacking and ought to go well under our alders and among the new dogwoods.

Julianna tells us she would like some ferns, in return—something other than the bracken type, which grow freely in her area. Up at the river we have many sword ferns and some licorice ferns growing in deep shade on the trunks of alders. We will bring her some on our next trip. It will be a good exchange, making use of each other's surplus. It is how community began, and the art of barter.

257

Today we planted the dogwoods up at the river. It is the second mild day in a row. A good time. Garth declined to participate. Well, he is a teenager and some reluctance to join in family events is to be expected. We don't want a surly boy around, when there is a lot of work to do in so short a period of time as we have now. Friends assure us this is normal behavior.

The placement of each tree on our half-acre lot requires much discussion between husband and wife. This is an intimate, not unpleasant thing to do. Finally we agree. Each tree becomes rooted in the world's best place for it. The salal Julianna gave us as a bonus is stuck in the ground.

And then, because I promised to do so, and know that Julianna is a bit of a nag and will ask me about it later, I lug river water up the steep path and puddle each tree thoroughly, even though the ground seems plenty wet without it. When some of the trees die, as surely trees will, I have to answer to her for it, and I want to make sure I have done nothing blamable or negligent.

Norma and I end the day by raking up alder leaves from last fall, thousands of them, a very tedious job. We retrieve more deadfalls, which always keep arriving. I pull up some blackberries by the roots, all that I can, and whack away at those roots I can't with my dull Army-surplus machete. Later I turn the machete on the tall salmonberry canes. Work of this kind has to be accomplished anew every spring. Miss one season and you are buried in greenery the next.

There is time for a quick burn. We pile high a mixture of green cuttings and dry tinder from the woodshed in a glorious bonfire that reaches high, high, into the air, showering sparks at the top. We have to stand far back from it and can only draw near when the flames die down. We cap off the day with burgers-in-a-basket at Rotten Ralph's, a drive-in restaurant in Arlington. It sounds like the worst place in the world, but produces burgers famous at least to the far edge of Snohomish County.

258

With true spring only a couple of days off, this is a good time to perform the annual inventory of flora, as though we were a small business specializing in the production of nature's products. Spring arrives sooner in the city because it is warmer. In the country, only the willows have burst out yet, while the alders are dormant, but show great promise.

Spring cannot be denied. The most one can do is see it retarded a little. Unreasonable cold, such as we've had, will do the job as well as anything I can think of. But it's a losing cause. If you look away for just a moment, the greenery pushes forward.. Soon it smothers you. It requires immediate attention. As Peter De Vries says, "Horticulture is nine-tenths destruction."

Around the yard we go, on a walking tour. Better put on some shoes appropriate for mud. Ready? Hyacinth, white, blue, and pink; single daffadown-dilly. We had more, along with iris, narcissus and crocuses, but the schoolchildren wantonly whacked them off. Across the lattice fence I think I see verbena, or else some other yellow plant, which reminds me of Scotch broom; a lonely trillium, out in the backyard; wallflower, of course; chives beginning anew from roots left over.

Across the Johnstones's fence the dogwood we share as good neighbors is unfurling its first leaves; about fifty percent of the boughs contain the green seed pods which will soon be surrounded by faceted blossoms of the same lime color. The blossoms—favorites of mine—fade slowly, turning paler and paler, until they become the brilliant shade of white everyone associates with dogwoods. But I remember best their green.

Previews of coming attractions just making their presence felt: red tulips under the three birches, the latter with no signs of life; pink camellia by the front porch steps, budded; lilac leafing but with no signs of exploding, as they always do; the purple will be burst first, the white soon to follow. (Or is it the other way round?) Other things found leafing around the yard include raspberry, quince, rose. Slower to show, but spectacular when they do, are azaleas and rhododendrons, generally in that order, though often they come on close.

In the backyard, the goldfish have wintered over successfully. The Big Guy is surrounded by his four colleagues, all themselves of the same size, a third of his. They relate keenly to each other and comprise a group, perhaps a family. The sixth goldfish always requires searching out. At last I find him, off by himself, "doing his thing," which is hovering near the edge of the pool. He remains the loner.

What makes a goldfish—or a person, for that matter—a solitary creature? Why does he shun his peers? What sets him off from the others, and why? Was it some early trauma?

They do not take turns at being shy—the shy one. It is always the same goldfish that is standoffish. He looks just like the other small ones, but behaves much differently. Off alone, all the time, what is he doing—writing the Great American Goldfish Novel?

259

Those tulips I spoke of only yesterday as still being deep in the bud sprung into crimson blooms overnight. What a surprise and delight. Nature does not conform to my schedule, but follows its own. It is a better one.

Tonight, while fishing the Flat Water, I watched a beaver swim across the river, heading upstream. Phil O'Lone was standing out on his dike, chatting with me. At first I thought it was a river otter, which I see fairly often. Then I looked again. Beaver, I decided. I had the point driven home when the creature slapped its tail down—like a board meeting the pavement. The beaver submerged and never appeared again, though I watched for him into the deep twilight.

260

I run. I run nearly daily, which goes unrecorded here, because it is so boring an activity. I do it for the sake of my general health. I am suspicious of group activities that involve exercising in public, especially out of doors, but this one feels right. And it feels even better when I stop.

If Walt Whitman were alive today, he would write, "I hear America running." That thunderous clop-clop-clop coming up from behind is a pair of feet clad in Nikes or Adidas. At first, I used to turn quickly and assume a defensive position. Now, I just smile and draw off a little to one side of the path, so that the runner can pass me. Nearly everybody passes me, even when I run.

I suspect that the elderly hear runners behind them so often they are no longer cautious, which may be a big mistake. Were I a mugger, or a snatch-and-run thief, I would dress as a runner and conduct my business in that disguise. After I'd robbed my victim, I'd run off with the rest of the nation's joggers and mix right in with them. Nobody could identify me. Green Lake would be the perfect place. It probably happens often. To catch these crooks, we need cops in running shoes. It would be a virtual Keystone Comedy chase.

261

My dentist is a big guy in his late twenties and athletic. He believes me to be a fellow athlete. What could I have said to give this erroneous impression? After filling two enormous cavities and having the rubber dam ripped from my mouth, he tells me he thought he saw me playing basketball. Was it at a neighborhood playfield, he asks?

Possibly. My son and I have shot a few there.

"Have you tried the court at the UW Intramural Building?" he asks, excitedly.

Well, yes I had, but it was long ago. I had worked for the University.

Could I have ever played in a make-up game with him?

Not in a pig's ass, I wanted to reply, but only said, "No, I don't think so." He is six-feet four or five and believes in giving no quarter—in sports or in the dentist's chair. I'm too old for rigorous make-up games, even half-court ones. I've avoided these for two decades now.

He looked at me out of one cocked eye, disbelieving what I said. He is certain we played together. Am I being coy? I wondered—if he believes this nonsense—how many other untrue things he subscribes to, and whether any of them involve dentistry? I think of my sore mouth.

I am tempted to ask him what kind of player I was—fair, good, excellent? I would like to be thought excellent in this fictional account. It might help my game—such as it is—to know how I appear to others on the court, especially to somebody I never played with. Call it vanity. I have the feeling he thinks I am pretty good. Perhaps I should let the matter rest there, while I am briefly ahead.

One thing is for certain: He will never see me so much as shoot a free-throw. I perform best in the basketball court of the imagination, where nobody else is able to see me, and there is no score.

262

Today we salute Henry Field, of Shenandoah, Iowa. He runs a mail-order nursery business. Each year he sends me his comprehensive four-color garden catalog, all prices post-paid. As sure as crocuses, each spring Mr. Field's catalog will arrive. You might say it is a perennial.

I have long confused the Henry Field catalog with the Burpee one. Everyone is acquainted with Burpee. It is mainly a seed catalog, whereas Henry Field's contains seeds and small plants. Both are colorful wonders of modern Webb Press publishing and are to be admired. It is possible to learn a lot from catalogs, and each year I read them avidly, trying to file away obscure bits of gardening wisdom that I fear I will never utilize. Writers should know the names of all the flowers, for you never know when you will want to throw one into a piece of writing for effect.

Flowers, fruits, and vegetables beckon seductively from the cover, each urging, "Buy me. No, buy *me*." Inside, the vegetables come first, the tomato displaying itself in splendid variety and array. A few come already sliced, so you can glimpse their luscious insides. There are more kinds of tomatoes here than anybody will ever need or want.

Next comes beans. Their world is complex and varied. There are so many shapes and sizes and colors of beans that I soon grow confused. Which do I want? The yellow wax beans leap out and demand attention. I want some; I want them *now*. I can practical taste such a bean on my tongue. A selection of pea pods appears, some broken open and smiling with rows of green teeth, while others loll wantonly, their innards hidden behind zippers.

Peas are seeds, of course. You can plant them or eat them. Field's peas are lush and hardy. (Note: this isn't the same thing as "field peas.") Corn is a seed, too, but grows in rows on a thing called a cob, Horatio. You can buy the kernels dried and detached, ready for planting. And there is Indian corn, pretty to look at but you wouldn't want to eat any. It looks like the jaw of the hundred-year-old man.

Turn rapidly past melons and apples until you come to the world of berries. In this department I think of myself as an expert, having tasted so many tiny fruits in the past year and written about them. Raspberries come in colors other than red, I discover. There are purple, black, and fall gold. And there are dewberries, which make me think of dewworms, which is what Canadians call nightcrawlers. Hence, I would never knowingly eat a dewberry, for fear it is really a worm.

Grapes, nut trees, cherries run the spectrum, from gold to black. Peaches, apricots, and—in all their range and extravagance—apples. Who doesn't love an apple? How many apples can I recognize and name, evoking their taste on the back of my tongue?

Jonathan, yes; yellow delicious, assuredly; red delicious, of course; Grimes' golden, I think not; McIntosh, yes; chieftain, no; anoka, no; haralson, no; red winesap, yes, probably my favorite; lode, no; Whitney crop, no, never. And where is the yellow winesap I think I remember, a luscious apple prone to spotting and worms? Sorry—not available here.

Plums. Never my favorite fruit and preferred in the form of prunes, though I am not troubled by constipation, which gives the plum a bad name. Pears. Dwarf species of fruit trees. And lastly trees that bloom furiously but don't produce any fruit. They are strictly ornamental.

The rest of the catalog is assigned to flowers, each species shown as though you could reach right out and pluck it. America most loves the rose. It comes in florabundas and grandifloral forms. These translate into "a lot of little blooms" and "a few huge blooms." And there is the tearose, for the minimalists.

The last pages are dedicated to (1) bulbs, (2) hardy perennials, (3) sturdy annuals, and (4) shrubs. Henry Field would like you to purchase species by the threes, fours, and fives, for they are easier to ship in bulk—better for him and for you. He offers special savings when you buy in volume. All items are shipped postpaid, and if any fail to live they will be replaced, postage-free for the second time.

I am planning to buy a number of items, and mark my order blank accordingly. But I always forget to mail it in, until it is way too late to plant them.

263

I have just finished reading John Updike's novel, *The Coup*, which takes place in a mythical African nation newly emerged and headed by a "president," a man named Ellelon, who is actually a dictator and has deposed and personally beheaded the king, a blind man who loved him much. E. was educated in America, at a college in Wisconsin, where he found the girl destined to be his first wife, Candy, a rather representative black-loving upper-middle class college girl. Since then he has married a variety of black women, all unique and quite distinct, and purportedly has had many children, though all were sired by others. Impotence is one of his problems.

He is deposed, in turn, and goes into hiding in the modern city ironically named after him. (Ellelon means freedom, in dialect.) His namesake city is the product of an oil-rich economy and incorporates all the worst features found in America, a country he despises. Eventually he is pensioned off to Paris, with his most middle-class wife, to live a dull bourgeois life filled with modern conveniences and to write his memoirs.

It struck me this novel would provide an interesting contrast (remember "compare and contrast," from college exams?) with Saul Bellow's *Henderson The Rain King*, published many years earlier, when small African nations had not yet "emerged" and were still ruled—many still are, of course—by despots, some of them benevolent, others not.

The two novels are most interesting when examining an American intellectual's perception of African nationalism, especially as seen through eyes most thoroughly American. Telling perspectives of America and American life are revealed, as a result of this unique juxtaposition.

264

This month is winding down. They all seem to do this, given enough time.

The Johnstones's dogwoods are really mine and I think of them paternally. Today they are multiple green explosions along the bough. Because the day is cloudy, and they think it is night, I guess, our emperor tulips remain closed, like a few stores still do, for it is Sunday. My parents are on their return journey from Rancho-Rancho. Last sighted in Carmel, the recent bad weather of California is following them North. They will arrive Wednesday or Thursday. The cold hard rains are one day behind them.

I am reading Mary Welch Hemingway's biography of herself and Ernest, which is full of much that is pretentious. How she loves to drop names. I would hate to be in her path, for the number comprise a virtual bombardment. (Who says words can't hurt you? I would not finish the book, except for my commitment to finish every one I start. Often this is a conspicuous waste of time.)

But funny. On page 93 she removes her suit jacket because of the heat, revealing the tight sweater beneath. She says: "Ever since I was twelve or thirteen years old and my mother tried to harness me into a brassiere, I had never owned one. 'God bless the machine that knit that sweater,' said [Irwin] Shaw, who was present and whose name required dropping.

"'Haven't you ever been inside a museum?'

"'A matter of texture,' said Shaw. 'Paint is not skin.'

"Two or three friends paused on their way downstairs to mumble, 'Nice sweater. . . .' 'The warmth does bring things out, doesn't it?'

"'Mary, I'd like to see more of you.' Mr. Hemingway stopped hesitantly and said, 'Introduce me to your friend, Shaw,' and shyly invited me to lunch the next day." And more of the same drivel follows.

"Shyly" and "hesitantly"? I would have rewritten this to read, "And Mr. Hemingway, staring, said he would like to meet both of us."

265

I am fascinated by the response of the emperor tulips to the sunlight. During bright days, as they came out of the bud, they opened fully; they came out so wide that I thought they were done blooming, that is, were all bloomed out. But comes a cloudy day and they shut right up, and resemble buds again. It is an intense physical accomplishment. Yesterday they remained resolutely slammed shut, all day, just as they do before nightfall, when the available candlepower begins to drop off.

Now today, with more sunlight trickling through the clouds, they timorously open their petals again. If the process continues, they will be wantonly yawning wide, right at twilight. Then they will close up shop again.

The response to light intensification is strong and quick, though I am not sure how fast. Doubtless, these conditions could be recreated in the laboratory, or in a greenhouse, and probably have been. All this data must have been measured, charted, analyzed, and published. I wonder where it can be found? Probably is some library, in a book with foxed, brown pages.

There is a direct ratio of tulip response to light, perhaps best expressed in exponential terms, since it happens so rapidly. I do not wish to know the details, in purely scientific terms. It is enough for me to observe the behavior and experience the annual beauty of the living tulips. It is, as Keats said about beauty, truth: "all you need to know."

266

Spring inventory up at the river:

Yesterday I checked on the dogwoods we transplanted in winter. I reviewed the troops, you might say, one by one. They stood tall as soldiers on parade. They are continuing to open their tiny leaf buds, though slowly. Meanwhile, the alders are unfurling leaves about a centimeter long, each perfectly formed and delicately veined. These trees will grow and provide us with a screen between us and the road and the white house to the East.

What surprised me most was the sudden growth of the salmonberry. The tan canes are pushing green furls out along their boughs. Purple blossoms are everywhere, like small bright moths.

Each blossom will be a juicy berry, when the river opens to steelhead flyfishing late in May.

The canes are becoming dense, and soon passage among them will be impossible. I want to thin them, and have sharpened the machete accordingly with a file. But I hesitate. Each year I must cut them down, or else be burdened by canes for the rest of the year. Last year, I waited to cut them back until after they had stopped bearing. Too late. It was my year for eating salmonberries, and I was overly respectful. Now I don't feel so responsible for them, and view them as a barrier to free passage.

We have lost one small alder. The PUD ran over it with their utility truck when they drove in to hook up my power pole. They hit it again on the way out, for good measure. It is the same tree they struck when they brought the pole in and stuck it in the ground. It seems a matter of extremely poor luck for this particular tree.

The first time, Norma carefully righted the tree and staked it until it stood vertical again. This second time it was traumatized past the point of recovery, or so I fear. But she says the root mass may be intact, though the tree *looks* dead. We should wait a full year before we remove it, she tells me. A good tree is worth waiting for.

The river willows are fully unfurled and bright emerald. Someone once likened them to cardinals' hats. The choke cherries are rapidly extending their slender, saw-toothed leaves, for we have left them standing as convenient ground cover.

Two of last year's fir seedlings look poorly and may be dying, though they are still carrying enough green needles to rekindle hope. But I wouldn't be a bit surprised to see them turn rusty-brown, as the sun strengthens. Everything else looks pretty good, and should make it into summer at least.

267

In the mail comes a small catalog whose florid cover proclaims, "At Last!" I might not agree. "At last another catalog," I wonder? But it is only a teaser for the comprehensive J.C. Penney catalog. They want me to return a postcard if I want to receive it. In retail stores of any size are catalog departments. Sears is a good example. They have done a great catalog business for years. Now it is Penney's turn.

A sexist bias is built into almost every catalog I have seen. This one is no exception: "258 pages of women's apparel," it advertises, "90 pages of men's wear."

Men, then, require a third fewer articles of clothing than women. Why? Have we both not two arms, legs, feet, hands; a trunk, a head? Should not the number of pages dedicated to our clothing be . . . similar, if not the same? I think so. The retailers do not.

They argue that women purchase two to three times as much clothing as men. The statistic holds true, year after year, location after location. It is how the world is. Not to mention shoes, where the percentage of women's purchases is much higher.

Retailers are not about to devote more pages, and a greater area of their stores, to men, in hopes of changing the world and its buying patterns. They like the world as it is, and will hold up a mirror to its trends and fashions, for it is how they make their money. Why change a good thing, or even try?

My father, who spent his working life in the retail business, says J. C. Penney does not manufacture goods in its own facilities; instead, it contracts for whatever it needs in huge purchase orders to manufacturers around the world, not just in the U.S. For example, the "plain pocket" jeans, which looks just like a Levi, except that the red tag on the edge of the rear right pocket is missing, and a certain gull-winged gold-thread stitching is gone from the back pockets, sell for $20 regularly, but is now on sale for $16, competes directly with Levi at about half the price. Levi has been known to market cheaper goods under another label.

My father explains that J. C. Penney's order would be so large and profitable that Levi couldn't afford not to bid on it, putting the company in direct competition with itself. I do not pretend to comprehend the complexity of modern business, and where and how profits are made. But it seems to me odd.

The idea of direct imitation of a product, but at a lower price, goes back to pre-war Japan, perhaps farther. Today this practice is blithely being conducted in many areas. A popular golfshirt features a tiny alligator on the left breast. The company is Izod, and it is foreign. Penney has designed a fox emblem, which looks very much like an alligator from a near distance. The two shirts are almost identical and contain the same percentages of polyester and cotton. The JCP one sells for $5 less. It will fool some, but not those who care about such status symbols. They want the "real thing" (not a Coke substitute).

Penney sells color coordinated trousers to go with the golfshirts. These are imitations of Haggard, Farrar, and Daks. They are machine washable, like the original, and will "tumble dry." If I wore these, I would be tempted to buy the cheaper brand. That way, you can have twice the number of whatever you like to wear.

A writer does not need fashionable clothing. Comfort is his chief concern, and he needs pants that don't wear out in the seat, sweaters with elbows of steel.

268

My great love of Beethoven continues and now extends itself to smaller chamber pieces, including those for piano and violin, or piano and cello. And my appreciation of Bach grows, along with listening to transcriptions of his music from harpsichord to piano, especially when it is played by Glenn Gould—that is, once I learned to overlook his infernal humming.

I love much other music, including rock, that expressive music unique to our time. At its best, it combines the bardic and courtly love traditions of France and Britain with the blues and rhythm indigenous to America. At its worst it is compounded noise.

269

Is your left foot longer than your right? Mine is. A shoe salesman pointed out this out to me yesterday, when I was buying a pair of Nike waffle-trainer running shoes at Warshals. Most people have left feet longer than their right, he said. So I am not a freak, even though the toe on my left running shoe hits the end of the nylon and suede toe cap. The salesman says not to worry, the shoe will stretch to accommodate the extra length.

However, the news of my deformity astounds me, and keeps coming back to annoy me mildly, all day. It is a little like heartburn. *Why* is my left foot longer? How did this come about? And, if it so prevalent, why don't shoe manufacturers take it into consideration and manufacture their shoes, accordingly? Perhaps they do, and nobody has noticed.

This is the pair of shoes I promised myself, if should ever run all the way around Green Lake without a recovery walk mixed in. Well, I did it, but the advertised shoes went off sale before I could get downtown. Warshals advertised Adidas TRX for $19.95 (regularly $32.95, or more), so I went down to try them on and look them over. The salesman said Nikes were cooler (and, I already knew, lighter in weight), so I bought them, even if they cost more.

Nikes don't last as long, though, the salesman added, which is borne out by Garth's wearing the tread smooth on his Nikes after only a few weeks. But he is more active than I and I don't wear out such shoes, even when running. I recognize this as a sign of middle age. Even when running, I don't run fast or hard enough to lose my tread.

Monday I ran two miles to break in the new shoes. No blisters, but my knee aches again. Recently, I read about an athlete who injured his knee, jumping out of bed. It's close to how I hurt mine. I jumped out of a simple car. Immediately I felt a bond with this man. His injury was to the meniscus cartilage, too.

270

You go off to the woods and they are wet, for it has been raining for days. You put on your oldest, grubbiest clothes and go to work. You saw and you chop and you haul deadfalls. You pull, then break up, brush such as salmonberries. You get progressively wetter. When your feet begin to feel clammy, you change over to waterproof boots. The bottoms of your trousers are soaked. Your hat and the hair on the back of your neck is wet. Then your hat begins to leak. Your hands are wet and caked with mud and grit. Your palms are slippery. You perspire within your rain jacket and it grows wet inside from trapped sweat. It is the worst kind. You rest for a few breaths. You remove a sweater to try to adjust your body to the day's temperature and the amount of exertion. Too wet, you put on dry clothes. Pretty soon the new dry clothes are as wet as the ones you took off. You resign yourself to wearing them. On a break, you go inside your travel trailer. It turns steamy and you can't see out the windows. You turn on the electric fire to get rid of the chill you encounter. You change into the last dry clothes you have, with a sinking feeling. You write in your journal (this) and read more of Mary Welch Hemingway's atrocious biography of herself and Ernie. You decide you would rather be working in the rain. You take up the bucksaw and start to apply it to the old downed log that is in the way of the camp you intend to build next summer.

At first the sawing goes quickly, because you are going through the rotten part first. Then the sawing begins to slow, as you comes to the good wood. You grow sweated and weary. The saw begins to bind. You find a heavy log and attempt to use as a lever arm to take the pressure off the cut, which is what is causing the saw to bind. The log snaps, and you go reeling. This log is also rotten. You search the woods for other substantial limbs that will do as a prybar. You find that all are rotten and break, as you try them in turn. Everything that is not growing and deeply rooted is decaying. You work on, alone. The rain descends at a clip called steady. Finally, you finish making your cut cleanly and push away the far section of the log, which measures about 20 inches in diameter. It is only a third rotten, you discover. Great. Much of it will be worth salvaging for stovewood with the speedy chainsaw. But you do not use the electric chainsaw when you are alone because of the risk of serious injury, when another would be needed to apply the tourniquet and drive the rescue vehicle, etc. Besides, in the rain, you might electrocute yourself. (Perhaps this is being foolishly cautious.)

When you are thoroughly soaked, solace arrives in form of the knowledge that there is no more of you to get wet. You relax—your shoulders first, then as much as will follow suite.

Dark is approaching, so you stop bucksawing. You write for a while, for daily writing is what you do. Suddenly you discover an enormous appetite. It takes over your being by quick stages. You remember the Noodles Romanoff, w/*bœuf*, in the wide-mouthed thermos you brought from home. You bend to the task. Ummmm, delicious.

271

One is gratefully a part of one's times; therefore I run. I join the rest of foot-thumping America—a herd creature. I pride myself on my sense of difference, but I wonder if I'm not . . . ordinary, my life mundane? Running is clearly a fad that belongs with dancing the Mambo, twirling the hoolahoop, getting the barber to cut your hair flat on top, or else snugged off neatly at the shoulders. But there are benefits to lockstep social behavior, including the act of running. It is good for you.

Often I see other runners and wonder what is going through their minds, for running is deadly boring. Do they have great difficulty getting started, each time out? I do. I do not run against time, even my own time. I run against a set distance. It is presently in the 2-3 mile range, and I try to complete the course without stopping. Some days I can, some I can't. Today I had to stop twice, but only to retie the laces on my new shoes. Laces seem to have a will of their own and resist all known knots. But the shoe is highly satisfactory, with a large heel surface to strike the ground and absorb the shock, plus a strong supportive arch.

The stopping today tired me more than if I had kept on running, and I had to fight to get my breath all over again.

272

The emperor tulips caved in, a couple of days ago. Their flattened leaves resembled the ears of a six-month-old German shepherd dog. The blossoms have turned inside out and the petals are convex. The stamen and pistils are decomposing. The tulips are on their last legs, you might say.

The dogwood blooms are paling prettily, retaining much of the apple-green that makes them distinct as flowers. The lilacs are nubbed but not yet exploding into clusters of blossoms. The white come first, each year, with the purples a week or so behind them. I had it wrong, earlier.

Garth and I played basketball for the first time in two years. He said it was that long. He is about six inches taller than last time we played, which aids him greatly in his close-in or "garbage" shots. He and I are the only people left in the world who shoot two-handed set shots. I think it is disallowed in the NBA today. I can remember, though, when everybody had to have such a shot. It has a quick release.

I can shoot a push shot about equally well, or equally poorly, with either hand. Oddly, my left is a tad stronger than my right, and the right fails first to be able to continue shooting from any distance. I missed a lot, and felt my wrists turn weak from disuse. Sunk four consecutive free-throws, however.

273

A short but productive day up at the river, with my family in attendance, all of us working hard against the dying of the light, for we got a late start. Garth is a fiend with saw or ax. Today it was the small electric chainsaw and, later, the splitting wedge. We—he mostly—cut up the old downed fir, the rest of which was pretty rotten and full of water. It measured about 18 inches in diameter. First, he cut it into four-foot sections, then went back and cut those in half and split them. It is the kind of work which he enjoys, for it is somewhat analogous to lifting weights, which he has taken up.

We found one old log which turned out to be cedar, so we saved it, since cedar is slow to rot and remains useful. Parts of it we will use for a walkway through the muck, where the second trail down to the river passes under an old, twisted hemlock. The rest will be put in storage for kindling and used to replace sections of the walkway when they fail through prolonged wetness.

I cut a great deal of salmonberry and wild rose, but none below the high-water mark, where it helps hold in the bank and resist the ravages from flooding. We used downed woody debris to reinforce the natural bulkhead formed by trees above the beach, forming a groin or jetty to protect the bank of my neighbors downstream. (They don't understand how this works, and would be at a loss to comprehend how or why their land got taken away from them by the river.)

Norma pulled up all the young nettles she could find and discarded them in a pile where they will soon turn to mush, with all the rain. I urged her to cook some for dinner, for when they first emerge they are said to be tasty, very much like but better than spinach. They are to be served with butter or vinegar. No, thanks, she said. Ours will rot, instead.

Later, we climbed the hill leading to The Outback, and dug up some sword fern and polypody belatedly for Juliana, as we had promised her. We brought back the ferns in wooden flats which fruit had come in, lining the bottoms first with plastic so they wouldn't leak, and then covering the plastic with old newspapers.

Now a soft spring rain is falling.

274

I sit in what can only be called a "loft," high above the showrooms of the William O. McKay Ford, Lincoln, and Mercury Dealership, wondering about the future of America. A sign across from me reads, "Labor fee is $80 per hour." There are several such signs in prominent locations, for Mr. McKay doesn't want you to be too shocked and angry when you get the bill.

I am here to replace the Mustang's radio antenna. Some vandals broke it off Saturday night, while Norma and I were having a beer in a University Way tavern, on a busy street. Cars fore and aft of ours kept their antennas. Did somebody single us out? If so, why? Is this a cause for paranoia? Are Mustangs a favorite target of vandals?

Allstate Insurance said it would cost about $50 to replace the slender rod: $20 for the rod and $30 for the labor, at $60 per hour for the body shop, which is less than a mechanic costs. They were wrong. After a two-hour wait in the loft, the bill came to $86.70. The difference in estimates for the work produced a second trip to the Allstate claims window in Northgate. Blithely, blandly, the adjuster tore up the old check and handed me a new one. The whole affair took about four hours. It could have been worse.

The loft at the dealership was dimly lit, the furniture cast-off filthy stuff, chrome and plastic, whose holes had been patched and repatched with silver gaffers tape. While I waited, various McKay staff trickled in to eat their lunches and smoke. The place doubles as a staff room. Also, the entry to the women's john is at the far end of the room. This produced a steady parade.

A man sat on the sofa reading the *Post-Intelligencer* funnies, chuckling to himself, while another was seated in an oak desk chair opposite, gazing out the window at the cars streaming by the busy street. Was he looking to see how many were Fords or Mercuries? Both were employees on their break. I could see the sales manager at his desk in an outer office through a crack in the door. He was probably Japanese. I could get no clear reading from his expression about how he felt about life. I had to guess wildly. The world was a serious place in which levity played no role. He seemed anxious that nobody mistake him for a frivolous person. No danger there.

Waiting, I had lots of time to think and reflect. People today seem to me sly, covert, secretive, protective of themselves and what they have achieved, if anything. Nobody could afford an innocent smile. Everybody is full up to the eyes with self-importance, even the salesman reading the funnies and the other guy, busy studying the street. There is no joy in their lives.

A young woman and a man occupied the loft, when I arrived and took a seat. They talked about cars and about how boring their weekends had been. In fact, they vied to see whose weekend had been the worst. It was a draw, I'd say. Mileage became the topic of discussion. None of the Ford cars measured up their expectations. They were a choosy pair. A car needed to be fast but economical. An accident had taken place recently near where the girl lived and a person was killed. Later, there was a blood spot in the street. It was icky. Rain wouldn't wash it away, she said.

They discussed directions to find a specific road in the Maltby area. You should turn *here*, she said; no, the turn was further on, he replied. They named the cars they wished they owned. Neither wanted a Lincoln towncar. I listened, remembering what was said, for a writer stores up such things for a rainy day of the imagination. Their half-hour lunch break over, they rose and filed out of the room. He went back to the shop, while she turned into an office.

Another woman promptly entered the room. She was young. She wore blue jeans. She behaved as though she were on a stage and was responding to theatrical directions none of the rest of us could hear. Her complexion was badly broken out and her mouth small and pouty, her body without any female definition, though slender and small-boned. She smiled at the space over my head and looked away before I could return her smile and have it registered.

The service writer who logged in my car now entered, carrying his lunch in a brown sack. He ate it slowly, solemnly, as though he would never eat again. His dessert was a banana. He ate it as though he had never seen one before and was trying to figure out how to approach it. "Take off its skin," he decided, "and see what it looks like." He decided the naked banana was okay and began to munch away. Next, he brought out a thick paperback, which he was close to finishing; only a few pages remained to be turned. I was curious to see what a service writer might read, in his spare time. I leaned forward and squinted to focus across the distance. The book was Mary Welch Hemingway's *The Way It Was*—the same book I had just finished reading. What a strange coincidence and how small a world! I wanted to talk to him about the book, yet I didn't. A book shared hardly makes us brothers.

The girl with the ravaged face spoke to the service writer about her marriage and impending divorce. She was going to spend a lot of money for a car and get a stereo first, she said. Why not, since her husband would be responsible for half the bills. Further, she wanted to buy a house, so that when she told him about the divorce she would get it as part of the settlement. Wasn't that smart of her, she asked the service writer?

He was a prim, precise person. He was twenty years older than she and the careful type. He picked over his words. She wasn't being fair to her husband. She laughed nervously at the suggestion and shrugged her shoulders, as if to say, "What has fairness got to do with it?"

"How old are you?" he asked. I was curious, too. It seemed a follow-on question to his statement about unfairness. He appeared disturbed by her sense of inevitability over the failure of her marriage. Didn't she want to save it? Why not?

"Me?" she asked, pointing at her chest with her thumb, as though there might be some doubt as to whom he was addressing. "Oh, I'm twenty." She laughed. "Going on fifty."

Another young woman entered the room and waved my bill at me. The car was done, the antenna replaced. I rose to go pay it. Next time I will try another dealership. It can hardly be worse.

275

Has anybody ever written about the joy of being dirty and wet—all gritty and grubby from working off in the woods; hair wet and oily, scalp itchy—and then gone on to praise the glory of a long hot shower, climaxed by a shampoo? No?

Afterwards, you climb into clean *everything*. Most inviting are jeans that haven't been ironed and a flannel shirt that has been. You dry your hair with a blower, and it gives you a warm, airy feeling. It is a little like being born again.

276

Rivers become strange when property owners post their property, then patrol their borders to enforce the new ban on fishing. The area soon resembles a war zone. Owners erect signs, and then more signs, when the first ones fail to deter fishermen, and then they erect insurmountable barriers, usually of barbed wire or expensive cyclone fencing. Ex-infantrymen such as myself are expert at crawling under bottom stands of barbed wire and do it without a second thought. If a man wants to fish and is determined enough, he will figure out a way to get in anywhere. The only thing that will stop him is a guard dog, and I would try to negotiate passage with one of those. Up to a point, that is.

Yesterday on the East Lewis was horrible. I'd made a quick drive down I-5 to try to find some rivers that were open still or not running mud. It was not my first visit here, but might be my last. I've had medium good luck in the past.

One trip found the river too high to cross to reach a favorite pool. So I tried to gain access from the opposite side, stopping at homes and asking permission to trespass. At house after house I was turned away. They uniformly told me that if they let me in, they would have to let everybody else in. It does not follow logically, but seems to be what they had all agreed on. Yesterday I ignored a No Trespassing sign posted by a gravel company and had an ugly encounter with a watchman, who patrolled the other side in a pickup truck. He ordered me to leave. A few minutes later he circled back, to see if I had. He shook his fist angrily at me, when he learned I had not. I was not to cross the river—did I understand? Mournfully I nodded. I left and fished there no more.

It does not seem fair, only mean. I suspect the employees were fishermen who wanted the water for themselves, after work. They don't want anybody else catching what they believe to be "their" fish. It is not a company policy, only the expression of some workers. Fishermen are innocents. What would we do—fill our pockets with gravel? Steal a backhoe? Private property reigns supreme in America, and the local sheriff will act to protect the owner's right to halt trespassers. This is wrong.

I drove on to Lucia (pronounced Loosh-a) Falls. It is a section of the East Lewis which turned out to be privately owned. Fishermen are barred from several entire miles of water by homeowners perched on the edges of 50-foot lots, jammed into narrow shelves on both sides of a turbulent river. At the Lucia Cafe, you can pay a toll to enter a tiny park and fish there. The river is characterized by a big roaring pool, where the hatchery fish gang up, for the falls is impassable. My old friend Bill Stinson lives somewhere nearby. No doubt he has acquired special landowner rights of access.

I drove on. It is discouraging and depressing, after having driven so far to fish a new river, to be turned away repeatedly. Somebody ought to write an article about the most inhospitable streams of the West, and rank them, accordingly. Maybe *I* should do it. It would be a public service.

We expect to encounter private water along famous streams in the East, in Britain, and in Norway, where a wealthy few get to do all the fishing on, say, a quarter-mile of a great river. But this is the American West, where it is unheard of. Or unheard of until recently, I mean. And now it is becoming commonplace.

277

My own river is not immune to this posting and fencing problem. I am thinking of the Boulder Creek reach, where a man recently bought 10 acres from Dick Bowman, including the trail along which we used to have a pleasant walk through the woods to reach the river. Quickly the new owner posted it. He was alarmed by the sight of fishers regularly walking across the edge of his property—big as it was. When the first signs were ignored or, worse, torn down, he became furious. He became more determined to keep us out. It was all he could think of. It became his mission. What a thoroughly miserable time he is having with his new property, when he should have been enjoying it fully.

The land is mostly floodplain and is inundated annually whenever the river overflows its banks. He cannot build there—legally or illegally. The best he can do is put in a travel trailer for the summer, when it is safe. In fall, he must tow it away or lose it. The county will allow him no more; they want to protect him from his own bad judgment. If they didn't, he'd immediately build a home in the flood zone. When it got washed away, he'd cry and ask for financial aid.

He belongs on the East Lewis, I think, next door to the gravel company or, perhaps, at Lucia Falls. He'd be at home with the other misanthropes. He doesn't belong on my sweet river, where such behavior is rare. People such as he are new on the scene and don't understand the long tradition of granting responsible access. They proclaim the doctrine of private property, forgetting about the public right to reach a river nobody owns, or can own. Their punishment is making themselves sick with worry and anger. And they alienate forever nice people like myself, who only want an hour or two's quiet fishing at the end of the day.

278

I drive on, seeking a river that will happily admit me and offer me free access. Dream on.

The Washougal is one of the least hospitable rivers in the state, judging by what I saw of it, in the two hours before dark. It enters the Columbia a little East of Vancouver, after flowing parallel to it for several miles near Camas. The small town of Washougal lies but two miles away and merges with it to form one thin city stretched along Highways 500 and 14—the former a state road, the latter an interstate.

The lower Washougal is largely urban, with year-round homes on its banks and the river running closely through adjacent pools and rapids, with easy gravel wading bars along the shallow side; it resembles the lower East Fork of the Lewis. But upstream the river becomes typical summer steelhead water, with canyons and boulders in the middle of each reach and steep walls of rock on both sides. This makes it pretty but difficult to fish, unless one is an expert boater or is content to perch himself on a large rock and cast lures or bait from a single location into a cauldron.

For the angler who loves to wade and cast a fly, the going is tough, if not impossible. And yet this river—in the six miles of it that I saw, before dark—is more sociable than the East Lewis or Kalama, which I'd describe as hostile. Their configuration and distinct ownership boundaries do not invite people to stop and fish a while or long.

The Washougal is only 16 miles from Portland, via I-5 and heavy traffic. It has numerous pull-offs along the river road, with short steep paths dropping down to the water. And it is a splendid looking river, with big, brawling riffles and a few long, slick pools scattered between them. It would fish well with spoons cast from shore by an agile angler who doesn't mind scampering among the rocks. My knee would prevent me from doing this, even if it were my sort of thing, which it's not.

The river is good producer of steelhead and worth getting to know, though it is a long ways off from Seattle. The distance is about 200 miles. This requires an overnight stay. Motels aren't far away. But today I hasten home in the dark, disgusted with the general situation.

279

In the mail today comes a catalog of remaindered books from a place calling itself Publishers Central Bureau. Its pages are crammed with thousands of books, most of which interest me not an iota. Do they appeal to anybody? How on earth did they all get published, in the first place?

The fault may be mine. I may not be interested in what others are. Or else nobody is interested in much of anything, anymore. Nothing calls out for special attention. All is a jumbles of competing concerns. Watching TV or a movie is easier, since naught is worthwhile. Most books lack general or specific appeal.

Are publishers out of touch with what is laughingly called the real world? Or is it the real world that is out of touch with itself? Do publishers wildly have books printed out of some terminal desperation? I hear that many more books are being published today than in any other time in history. And more are being bought. Of course there are more people around to buy them, but that isn't the whole story.

I suspect that many books are bought because people *hope* to read them. They will never get around to it, however. Something always gets in the way. It may only be the dirty dishes. Good intentions is how book clubs survive. What lies inside a book does not matter, if it isn't going to be read. It only matters how the book *looks*—its dust jacket, its shape, its size. The guts might as well be blank. In fact, blank books are being manufactured so you can insert your own contents. Not a bad idea. Perhaps I will write one.

But if nothing is being read, nothing will be written; at least nothing of substance or value.

280

In the mail arrives a large, flat envelope addressed to Mr. and Mrs. Bob Arnold. Now, nobody addresses us this way. I picked it up with annoyance, and opened it with curiosity mixed with pique. It must be from my wife's relatives. We never hear from them, except for a Christmas card. Sure enough, the return address is Mt. Vernon.

Since it had my name on it, I opened it. Inside the first big envelope was a smaller one, forming the start of a kind of Chinese puzzle. How many envelopes will there be? On the second one is written, with admirable concision: "Bob, Norma." I liked the comma. It was personal, economical.

It did not look like much could be inside the second envelope, it was so thin. First to be extracted was a piece of flimsy—that deckle-edged white tissue stuff, with many fine horizontal fibers running visibly through the paper. Behind it was an embossed invitation, with white raised roses on a pale blue field. Dark blue ink in script announced that Norma's cousin, Duane, was marrying his daughter, Karen Louise Bretvick to one John Michael Hernandez (*Hernandez?*) in the Immaculate Conception Catholic (*Catholic?*) Church in Mt. Vernon. Reception to follow at the Swinomish Yacht Club. This is in LaConner.

All of this festivity will take place in two weeks, at seven o'clock in the evening. Isn't this a peculiar time to get married—over the dinner hour? One will have to eat early, say, at mid-afternoon, or else wait until after the wedding, when it has grown late, and one's stomach is devouring its lining. Either way sounds plenty awful.

I don't remember the girl. Norma barely does. The family is Lutheran, Norwegians. Married . . . in the Church of Rome? Isn't this what Martin Luther fought against? I thought he was successful and had formed his own church? Is Karen pregnant by young Hernandez, as so often happens in the country? And in the city? Will it show? Will she dare to wear white? Of course she will; to wear anything else is to give away the show.

I will have to wait to get my answers from Norma, for she will be attending, not I. I won't be missed. I can picture the caravan of Maupin women, all jammed together in one car, headed North, nattering away. How rarely do they get such a chance to chat. They will forego a meal and snack copiously on canapés at the reception. Or else they will head for McDonalds afterwards. Or both.

We will buy these strangers, Karen and Johnny, a suitable gift. Or rather Norma will, for it is her family, the gift selection her department. I suspect she will spend an amount that will surprise and anger me. Best not look at the incoming bills for a month.

281

Last night was the final concert for the year of the Roosevelt High School Orchestra, Chorus, and Band. A cheer for us all who have been attending. The concert marks a milestone in the life of the musicians, and in our own, for we have followed the orchestra, band, and chorus from the sixth grade on. This is a span of seven years. Our son plays the trumpet. He sits among the second trumpets.

In that time, I have not noticed a great deal of improvement in the orchestra. They sound pretty much as they did when we started out together. The strings remain watery and uncertain; the horns come in as individuals and build to a roar, as if to make up in volume what they lack in timing and tone. Crotchety, middle-aged music lover that I am, I have found pleasure in these concerts, all the same. What I shall miss most about them is the Sousa marches, as conducted by Mr. Wilfred King, their teacher and leader.

The marches are executed with fierceness and gusto. Mr. King shows a lot of style and enthusiasm. He bobs and he bounces, with no economy of motion, but with unmistakable élan. The band responds and behaves as if the goal is to bring down the walls and reduce the school to ruins. Not a bad idea. They almost succeeded, several times, tonight. It is the first time I have ever heard 100 decibels exceeded by something other than a jet aircraft or a rock band.

Mr. King raises the brasses and percussion instruments with his outstretched hands in a joyous crescendo, then hushes them right back down, apparently to regroup for the next musical assault on our sensibilities. Each concert ends with a blast of affirmation. The students believe in what they do, their concerted noise tells us. And we forget the dreariness and dissonance that precedes such enthusiasm.

First in the program is the orchestra, which is comprised mostly of young women who have been provided with violin lessons for years by dutiful parents who did not want their daughters to grow up without a cultural heritage. The more players there are in the string section, the better chance there is for some errant individual to get absorbed in the amassed sound. Yet that sound remains mushy from so many of them studiously sawing away at once. A few are quite good and can be singled out above the general din.

I, the middle-aged spectator, with jaded tastes, study the females for nubility. This is not easy, for the boys and girls in both the band and orchestra wear a unisex costume of heavy wine-colored mohair. It is thick and shapeless. The girls who do not play in the band, too, wear white tops and dark bottoms. Others wear gowns. Gowns belong solely to the chorus. Since some individuals perform in band, orchestra, and chorus, they undergo speedy costume changes between numbers, which gives the production an aspect of burlesque.

These multi-talented individuals doff mohair jackets and quickly put them aside. Underneath, they wear white. They weave and wend and form new groups, new combinations, while others, in their original dark garb, flee the stage. There is a moment of great confusion. Now we are looking at the orchestra. They hold their instruments poised, waiting for Mr. King's downstroke. The baton does this, and they are nearly all together on the first note. The slight discord is to be ignored.

I review the orchestra for female pulchritude. The girls for the most part have long shiny hair, legs in short skirts that go whisk in their nylons, pert noses, bright red lips, and shining eyes. Perhaps it is the effect of the lights that makes everything so brilliant. My eyes seek curve of bosom and thigh. There is plenty of it. Then the lights dim and I see nothing but the tops of heads, boys and girls indistinguishable. The music swells. A long interval of music follows, for this is a symphony. I think it belongs to Tchaikovsky.

Always I find a few girls who bear further study. I don't exactly fantasize about them, but I keep my eyes alert for any special movements. When the house lights come up, I stare wantonly because of the great distance. I don't mentally undress these girls; my prurient imagination doesn't work this way. I mean, I can't do it. My imagination ... fails.

More music and darkness follow. The orchestra reaches its climax and desists. The lights go up. Another quick costume change and the chorus files on stage, compactly, slightly militarily. They arrange themselves (by height? by sex? by both, for there are a few boys?) and Mr. King raises his hand, as if to admonish them. Instead, pursing his lips, he bids them sing in the manner he indicates. They do so with gusto. The pitch is good. But the voices are shrill. The music is heavily syncopated, which is the kind Mr. King likes best, I gather.

The chorus being female predominantly, I review it closely, and find just enough beauties to please me. There are three "maybes," but the conditions would have to be just right. What are these? A bus might break down, or there might be a storm and a car in trouble, or we might find ourselves at a strange hotel, surrounded by snow. An encounter might follow, the nylon stockings whispering, perfume rising from a young, heated body, mild, murmured protests, a sudden thrusting on my part....

But the chorus depresses me. They are always performing *lieder* by Schubert. It is antiaphrodisiac. I can't wait for the dirge to be over. It goes on and on. And then they are done, the group transforming itself into—*voila!*—the Roosevelt High School *Band*.

The Band is best. It is best because it is loud. Where it is not good it is loud. Where it is not precise it is loud. Where it is not together it is loud. Where it is not in pitch it is loud. Is it anything else but loud? Yes, sometimes, at moments.

Often it is joyous, triumphant, a victory of strength over finesse. It is what a band ought to be. It is the Life Force at work, when Sousa plays, and I Am An American. We are ALL Americans. America is Great and Good. So, let's hear it, Everybody. America under God is formidable. And so is the Roosevelt High School Band.

I listen for my son's horn, but cannot detect it among the multitude and the noise. The cacophony is considerable. Mr. King leads the band to a great crescendo, a veritable explosion of brass notes. Then the concert is over—for the night, the year, forever. Mr. King bows deeply to show his appreciation for our support. We respond by applauding like wild persons. He smiles and bends and nods again, beaming.

Our son will graduate. We will not be back for more. A collective tear forms. Long may you wave, Roosevelt High.

282

We are in the midst of a "three-day blow." It has lasted nearly a week. That makes it something else.

Without having to go out to look, I can state unequivocally that all the rivers are running thick with mud. The worst of the storm lasted only half an hour and deposited less than 2/10 of an inch of rain, but caused minor flooding in town in basements and left water standing in highway depressions that caused a rash of accidents.

And the wind has continued, with powerful shocking gusts that surely exceed gale force. Our poor cat avoids going out because the wind will blow him off his course. He doesn't like this one bit, and when the showers hit, he gets drenched. All the while spring advances. The trees are lightly budded and their branches have turned a hopeful shade of green.

Trees are optimists.

283

In a day of mixed sun and rain, I erect my summer camp. It is provisional and I may have to move it. Like the trees, I may be unduly optimistic about the season, and it will prove to be too early. Last year's camp was so satisfactory, so satisfying, that I strive to retain its best features and not depart much from them. Thus, I use the same 9X12-foot woven nylon tarp—medium orange, though I would prefer sedge green, which isn't available—and this time I construct the frame of green alders, lashed together with rope, remembering how the deadfall limbs broke, one after another.

Garth cut the standing deadfalls with the little electric chainsaw, lengthened out to its maximum 100-foot range on the extension cord. Then we matched lengths and diameters of straight green alders to find five good poles: two forward ones to reach a six-foot apex, when lashed together; two slender ones to place in the rear to lift the tarp three feet off the ground; and a long ridge pole. We put the shelter together on a section of high beach we cleared last weekend. It is above the winter high-water mark, which means we won't have to move it in the fall. This will allow me to sleep outdoors longer—surely through October.

After we got the shelter up—a relatively simple matter, though we argued about how to do it, all the while—Norma, Garth, and I went off to resume bucking the huge fir log he has been working on, the past several outings. After a while Norma and I drove off in the stationwagon to "appropriate" some discarded railroad crossties from Burlington Northern. They are heavily creosoted and should last forever. We plan to use them for a walkway down to the beach and my camp. This is so we won't continue to get wet feet.

By summer, the muck along the trail will be dried up. But summer is such an impossible distance away. Pacific Northwest summers are long and wet. We carried in the heavy ties and dropped them into position, and Norma started shoving them around by herself in the mud to find solid places for each to fit. With everybody busy on personal projects, I put up the tarp cover and jockeyed it around until it was straight and tight, so it would drain well, and then lashed it down. I placed the opening so it would face away from the prevailing wind, which is upstream. This means I won't be facing the river, while I sleep, but then I won't get the rain or sun in my eyes, either. This is the tradeoff.

I am 85 percent satisfied with my camp. But it can easily be altered, if it doesn't work out as planned. The big danger is having a strong wind reach under the edge of the tarp and carry the whole thing away.

284

When the wind dies down, the sun comes out, and flying insects resume their lives. They don't seem to be able to fly in a strong wind. There is a fly season, and a mosquito season, and the two overlap to make life miserable. When the sun is shining, the flies dominate. Cloudy, we have hordes of mosquitoes to face—and face is the right word. They aim for the ear. Since the weather is doing either one or the other, there is no peace.

Because of the month-long freeze in January, the problem of insects should be less than in past years, which were milder. But the bugs are bad, every year. Already the little rascals are up and about, lighting on us and biting, every time the wind makes pause. I find myself batting at the air with whatever hand is free, and brushing at my cheeks and forehead with the backs of my arms. In previous years, about the time I break up my camp down by the river, they disappear. Overnight, they are gone, and I gain a pleasant glimpse of what summer would be like without them.

The river is flowing on a high note. It has rained every day I think, for the entire month, so now we can say the drought is over. With its characteristic spring green reflected on the surface, the river looks clearer than it is, and definitely fishable. It is not. The river remains closed for another month and a half. It seems an eternity.

The purpose of closing the river is to protect the smolt migration, but I think simple flyfishers are not much threat to it. Many rivers to the Southwest remain open at this time of the year, with no damage to the young fish, if bait is not allowed. To be able to fish and cause no harm is an important part of my lifestyle, and that of my friends.

285

It is Easter Sunday, the time when the Giant Rabbit is reborn out of the Marshlands and Prairie, making his annual visit to little boys and girls, some of them good, some of them bad, most of them neither but in between. He gives out hard-boiled eggs and chocolates to all three classes. Then there's the race through the meadows—still wet from rain—to hunt for the eggs. How can a rabbit lay eggs? There is a basic biological mix-up here, and the kids know it.

We worship Spring. The search for hidden eggs is just an excuse to run around in the woods, investigating things—the great new abundance. We plant seeds and submerge our hands in the rank soil. Easter is the time of Jesus, too. How convenient that Jesus was born at the start of the Winter Solstice and died at the beginning of the Spring Equinox, when the days are lengthening out nicely. Both are signs of hope. I simply note the green advance and rejoice. I like it best when it doesn't promise too much too fast. This year, the skies are clouded, and a soft rain is falling.

What is Easter, without rain?

286

I run, after a 10-day hiatus, mainly due to laziness, but with other alibis to excuse myself to myself. If I wait any longer, I will be badly out of shape. So I force myself to suit up. My body responds unwillingly.

The first half-mile is slightly uphill, against a mild northerly headwind. It is hard to run; it is always hard. And since it is uphill, I go slowly, like an old man "on his last legs." My pace is not much more than a jog. But at the three-quarters-of-a mile point I am nicely sweated, the sore knee and mild hip cramps gone, and I am breathing well. I'm feeling good. (Sometimes it is hard to tell.)

Garth says there are two types of legs: the breadstick ones, like mine, and the drumstick ones he claims to have. He got them from his mother. The former can't go uphill very well, while the latter are poor on the flats. Maybe so. This would explain why Norma climbs hills so well. Garth, after a few sweaty tries, said running was not for him. But he runs too hard. It's probably because he's ashamed at being seen running at anything less than full out. He's at the age where appearance—even in the eyes of strangers—is of the utmost importance. It is no longer for me, thank goodness.

Today I run but a mile and a half. I find myself badly overheated early on, on this fifty-degree day. I'm breathing hard, but not really "winded," as people get from overexertion. I'm simply tired from not having run lately. Two days hence will be better.

My plan is to run three days a week, working up to covering three miles on the third day. If I could find a flat running surface, or a track, I would try to lengthen out my distance sooner. Must look around, say, up at a school.

287

The Oregon grape is in bloom. I have never seen it, at this stage. It is handsome, with many bright yellow blossoms, quite small, which resemble, except for their color, lilies of the valley. I do not find this plant growing abundantly in my area and think of it as exotic, consequently. I've located it in the mountains underneath a medium-sized fir or springing up at the foot of a giant cedar. But one day on a run in town, I discover a huge clump of the stuff growing in somebody's yard and—encouraged domestically—it has done well.

Elsewhere, many flowering cherries are blossoming, both white and pink. They are finishing up their season. If not indigenous to the Pacific Northwest, they have been here so long that—like the rest of us—they claim to be natives. Nobody dares dispute them.

The dogwood outside my study window in town has green blooms, which makes me glad, for I don't want to see them fade to white. It will mean spring has advanced, and I want it to last longer. When the bracts turn the color of dirty snow, then fall off, the tree becomes ordinary, indistinguishable from all the others. A few of the dogwoods flower again in the fall, but not many.

None of my dogwoods from Julianna will bloom this year. It is expecting too much for them to do any more than survive. I'll settle for a few leaves on every limb. Seeing them gives me a special kind of faith, but don't ask me to describe it, for I can't. To recognize it as faith is enough.

288

I am spending the night in Motel 6, Kelso, in order to fish the Kalama tomorrow. Just South of Longview on I-5 is a billboard that annoys me. It is read by all motorists headed North and South. It goes, "The wages of sin is death." It is the grammar and usage that bother me. Hang the religious message, which otherwise I'd ignore. I've never been worried about sin, or its wages.

Perhaps the use of the singular verb is justified as a collective, but it doesn't sound right to me. The ear knows what's right and what's wrong. Now for "wages": "They paid him his wages" is singular, though the final s fools the eye and ear. Nobody would say, "They paid him his wage," at least not in an informal context, though they might write it down, if they thought it was meant to pay him "his due." Still, it bothers me.

On the back of the billboard is another message. The billboard is placed so that either side can be read, headed both directions. This makes it doubly deadly. The second message is: "Believe on the Lord, Jesus Christ."

Definitely grating on the ear, isn't it? It's the "on" that is painful to me. Now, I've been told to "think on" something, by people who want me to think *about* it. It is country-Western parlance, and I hear it a lot lately, at least in song. I would never use the locution, except jokingly or ironically.

To believe "on" something must be psychobabble. A minister tells you he wants to "share" something with you. It means he's got something to profess. You might want to run for the door, when you hear this word. Often, when somebody has something to "share," it means he wants to tell you something for your own good. Beware.

Don't people believe "in" something, anymore? Not even the religious zealots who put up billboard messages? Do they have to believe "on" it, instead? And, what's the difference? I have a feeling that to believe "on" something is sinister. It's just a hunch of mine. To believe "in" something is bad enough.

Note: the fishing was nothing to speak of, so I won't.

289

A day with the afternoon temperature hovering around 65 degree F., and plenty of sunshine, though most of it is sifted through thin gray clouds. A shower arrives, but the sun continues to shine. It's a strange, mixed-up kind of day.

My terrible handwriting [this was originally written by hand, and I could hardly decipher it later] is the result of four solid hours of ditch digging. Norma and I decided to put in a waterline, while the sale of the Mines/Lennox property down the road is in escrow. It is a nether time, one on which we hope to capitalize. Water is all.

My hands are sore from the hard use of a five-foot spade again. Hands remember the underground cable and electric service ditch. In fact, tenderness and blisters start to form in exactly the same places. Norma and Garth undergo a similar trial. We dug, in four-hours time, a ditch 24-inches deep and some 60 feet long. It is not exactly arrow-straight, though that was our goal and would be the most efficient way to do it. Alder roots slowed us and altered our course slightly. Roots are constant. My hands retain the shape of the shovel's grip from its tip meeting roots and catching on them.

One hundred feet of ditch is what's needed, plus another fifteen feet so we can install a blow-back valve. This will enable us to shut off the water and drain the forward part of the line, come winter. The reason the line is two feet underground is to keep it from freezing, of course. I kept this in mind, every time I was tempted to come up short. In some places, where there was sand, our line is closer to 30 inches deep. It is easy to keep going, once you hit sand.

And so we dug, and dug, and dug. There is another good half-day's work ahead for the three of us, and the going will be slower, tougher, because we are in the heart of alder country, and the roots are shallow and wind everywhere.

Hands too crabbed from day's effort to write more tonight. Going to sleep by the river's edge and return to the city tomorrow morning late.

290

Bernard Malamud writes, in *Dubin's Lives*, "The wild begins where you least expect it, one step off your daily course. A foot past the road and you're fighting with death." (Page 149) It is a fine novel, very gripping. There is a lot of Thoreau in the book. It is intentional. Dubin is a biographer, and his subject is Thoreau. Malamud won a national award for the book.

Yet he seems not very much at home in the woods. Aside from learning how to identify a few trees and wildflowers and birds, nature is a terror for him—and we are talking about only the rural and pastoral scene, not the fierce mountains and rugged valleys. The relationship between man and nature (they used to capitalize Nature—for a good reason: it is holy) is important in world literature. One idea is that nature is indifferent and harsh, offering no consolation or sympathy to human endeavor. This can be disputed, though not easily. Nature can be seen as less than cruel, more than indifferent. It offers many rewards, if approached right. Approached wrong, it will destroy you. But—I agree—it provides not a modicum of sympathy.

Man is fascinated by nature, obsessed by it—dependent on it, spiritually as well as physically. I sure am. Disaster lurks just an inch behind the seductive greenery. Yesterday, while working on the property, I stepped on a nail. A nail is man-made, not part of the natural universe. None the less, I found it in the shallow woods. I was poking around in some scrub. It was breakfast time, and I had a can of fruit juice in my hand, admiring the work we had done yesterday and how nicely spring was coming on. My foot went down on a board, and I felt a sting on the sole of my foot.

Quickly I stripped off my shoe and sock, and assessed the damage. The pain wasn't much, but my fear was of lockjaw; dying tongue-tied would rob me of my chance to complain loudly about my fate. I detected a tiny puncture wound. Was it enough to kill me? I didn't want to wait to find out. I squeezed the wound hard enough to bring a drop of clear liquid to the surface. It was followed by one of blood. Red, it was mine.

I wondered: With lockjaw, would a writer be doomed not to write another word, because he vocalizes first? Often I form the words on the tip of my tongue. Is my foot connected to my mouth? Or is it just when I unintentionally put my foot in it?

It was no joking matter. I headed back to town to get a tetanus shot, taking my place in line at Group Health Emergency on Capitol Hill. *Dubin's Lives* made my wait pass faster. Finally I was admitted to the examining room that lay beyond a pair of swinging steel doors. I was shown to an open area, where two metal tables stood ready to receive patients. I was given a large sheet of paper and told to lie down on it. Instead I sat.

Soon I was joined by a pleasant-looking Oriental youth, clutching a bright red cloth in one hand. The bright red was from blood, his. He had been slicing a watermelon, he told me, embarrassed by attracting my or anyone's attention, in a restaurant where he worked, when—gotcha—the weapon turned on him. He seemed apologetic. It was a bad cut and he got first attention. I watched, while a team prepared him for sutures. In a moment, a Medex examined me and asked me how long it had been since I'd had a tetanus booster.

I couldn't remember. Perhaps twenty-five years?

Several interested medical personnel gathered round me, disbelieving. What? So long? Unheard of. Don't you ever *do* anything? Guess not. They went away. A nurse came in and gave me a jab in the shoulder. This morning it is sore. But there are no signs of festering from my tiny wound.

291

Warm sun and soft breezes, followed by an hour spent in the late-morning chair, reading and writing. Late coffee and orange juice were my companions—not bad. All in all, a good life. What more can a man ask for than leisure to do what he wants? "Naught else is worth the having," says Ezra Pound, long-time dead, and quite rightly phrased. The simple joys count for so much.

The old cat lengthens out on the warm wooden stoop and stretches luxuriously. Nothing quite like a cat stretch—he fairly doubles his curled length. He does even less real work than I, the bum.

A Siamese is articulate, if nothing else. He mews to come back in the house, then tells me what he wants next. It is a supplementary feeding of dry gruel. Funny looking stuff, it greatly resembles in shape and color my Cheerios. For a moment I can't get over the illusion that I am eating . . . cat food. Could they possibly be made out of the same ingredients? By the same people? He eats his, while I eat mine. Then he asks to be put outside again, so he may lie in the sun and bake. A cat is primarily a heat-seeking missile.

This year the purple lilacs lag only a few days behind the whites. The warmth of this morning will bring out the lavender buds in minutes, judging by their ripeness. The bud is purple, but the bloom is lavender. They grow pale with time, and fade. Most flowers do. (Name me one that doesn't. Can't.)

I am a latent gardener. I plan a lot, but don't accomplish much. Gardening is Norma's realm and she preempts me. Rousseau writes that the aging man wishes only to cultivate his garden. A shame. I cultivate my wife's. Yesterday I spaded the compost (i.e., decayed garbage) into her vegetable garden, then added 150 pounds of steer manure, raking the mixture together repeatedly until it became almost level. Level was my goal, anyway. She came after me, picking out the largest flotsam that I had missed, raked it again, and planted beets (for greens) and leaf lettuce. You could say she nitpicked me. This is just the start. She is barely warmed up to this year's gardening.

Not to be outdone, I planted four roses, three in the front-yard rose bed and a climber on the Northwest corner of the house, where I expect it to grow wildly. These are the first roses I have ever owned, and I have high hopes and fears just as great. I suspect a case of brown thumb. One has to wait for results in gardening. Gardening repeats the other forms of life, and death.

One cannot expect too much from free roses. They were given me by my neighbor, Marshall Johnstone, and were left over from a Parker Paint promotion; his wife had first pick, opting for the whites, her favorite color. Have you ever heard of somebody whose favorite color was white? Karen's is.

If anything positive comes from the roses, I will be surprised and take all the credit. If they fail, it is because they were give-away roses from a paint company. How can I lose? My deck is stacked.

292

The Saga of The Waterpipe, continued.

I am aware that this saga bears a curious resemblance to my account of connecting up the electrical-service, but bear with me. There are similarities, but there are differences, too. Life has an uncanny way of repeating itself in slightly different forms, often to completely different conclusions.

Unloosening the threaded nut in the 3/4-inch stepdown tee of the waterpipe required a pipewrench and frequent bailing out of muddy groundwater that kept seeping into the hole at the two-foot level. And when the plug was out, clean water gushed forth from the long open pipe, filling the hole back up and requiring more bailing on my part. There was an awful lot of water, even though it was not under pressure, for I had remembered to turn it off at the main valve. When the waterline was clear, and the water level in the ditch rose again, the water began to run back into the waterpipe. This was greatly to be avoided. I had to work fast.

I quickly threaded my plastic joint into the tee and tightened the connection first by hand and lastly with the aid of a crescent wrench. Luckily I threaded it right on the first try. The hardest part came next: forcing the 3/4-inch pipe (mine) into the tee (theirs). And while I had tried to heat the plastic waterpipe first with water from my teakettle to make it softer, more malleable, the cold water absorbed the heat instantly, cooled the pipe, and the barbed nipple wouldn't ease on.

Meanwhile, more brown water kept gurgling into the community pipe. (I could picture it coming out into various people's sinks, but nobody was at home, thankfully.) Finally I stepped into the mucky ditch with both feet, poured the last of the hot water over the end of the smaller pipe, grabbed it in both hands, and shoved it on as hard as I could. I hadn't known I was so strong. The pipe slid on beautifully. I tightened the clamp down with my screwdriver and straightened up with a creak of my back to inspect my work. If the junction was faulty, I would be at a loss to know what to do next, for it was impossible to unthread the coupling, for the lugs were torn up from my wrench and the wrench would no longer grip them. But it looked okay.

The other end of the 100-foot waterpipe was much easier to work with. I softened the end with more scalding water and, working above ground, this time, slipped on another barbed nipple, a twin of the first. It went on, slick as butter. The clamp was easy, too. The Teflon tape clung to the threaded portion much better above ground, that is, out of water.

Next, I fastened the threaded part of the connector at the other end of my 100 feet of pipe to my all-metal gate valve, placing the blow-back bleeder valve toward me, where I could easily reach it in the hole when I needed to. I tightened down the clamp with my screwdriver. When all was secure, I hurried down to the white house and turned the main valve on. I could hear the roar as the water burst into the big, two-inch communal pipe; the pressure must have been enormous. Then I ran back home to check my main connection.

It looked good and tight. I studied the tee and connection, now under puddled water, and looked for air bubbles, which would mean water leaking. I saw a slight disturbance and panicked momentarily, but it was from two water bugs that had fallen into the hole and were trying to mate or fight or something. Tight. I walked the 100-feet of buried pipe until I came to my gate valve. There was a small leak, but it turned out only to be from my not having screwed down the tiny bleeder valve hard enough. I did so now. Metal gripping metal, the leak stopped.

It was time to test the gate valve, which released the community water into my trailer. Gently I opened it up. The pent-up water began its own roar and slowly issued forth. I had no use for it now, so I turned it off. The water, I saw, ran clear. I turned it back on and filled the pail with which I normally carry water up from the river. I took a little sip. Delicious. The rest I used to wash off my mud-caked face and hands. Finally, I buried the last six feet of pipe in the ditch by the road and covered over the short section coming in to my gate valve.

At sunset, I sat by the water's edge, and listened to my portable radio and tape player, feeling satisfied and happy, too. The tape was Beethoven's *Archduke Trio*. Out over the water the beautiful notes soared. I leaned back on my favorite boulder at the shoreline and smiled. It had been a good day.

293

Today Burger Bryson delivered the load of crushed rock we had talked about, oh, eight months ago. It is for our drive. The other night, I reminded him of his promise, and he said, Yes, he'd better license his truck, this year. I guess he finally did. Part of the load he laid out smoothly, but when he came to the big depression in the road he was forced to halt and dump the remainder, in two tall humps.

This means, blisters or not, I had better get my shovel again and smooth out the road, if I want to drive on it. And I do. I spread the soft fill around with my shovel and tried to level the holes just enough so I could drive over them. It was back-breaking work. Plain dirt is heavy stuff. Two hours passed in agony. Finally, done, I straightened up—it was like trying to open a rusty jackknife. At last I stood tall. I started up the stationwagon and drove it repeatedly back and forth over the dirt, flattening it down a little more each time. It remained soft stuff, and rain would turn it to mud for a few days. Backed down over the summer, I would have a superior road, one that would hold up through next winter. Or so is my weary hope.

294

About four P.M. yesterday I went into a discount record store called Tower to buy the Beethoven sonatas for violin and piano; recording them all off the air proved impossible. The artist is Aaron Szigeti (never heard of him), and the recording is in mono, which is not a disease but means it was done with one mike, probably in one take, and the result is less than a quality recording. But the price was right.

My ear is not attuned to the stereo effect and will not miss it much, with only two instruments performing. The store had only two or three customers, but soon cars began pulling up in front and disgorging teenagers. They were dedicated rock-and-rollers. They swarmed into the storefront. Suddenly I was surrounded by scores of young black men, short-haired punk rockers, girls in heavy makeup and the four-inch high heels the hip wear now. All the while in the background, heavy rock music blared forth its welcome to them. It was played at an ear-crushing volume. I made my purchase in a hurry and found a hole in the crowd through which to depart.

My friend Sally Fichet says this is a daily occurrence. Among the high school set, it is popular to flood record schools in late afternoon, in order to see and be seen. She says I should have known better. She was laughing at how unworldly I am.

295

Awoke this morning to raucous clamor of jays outside my bedroom window. My watch said that it was five, straight up. It was light already; tomorrow it will be dark at this hour, for Daylight Savings Time goes into effect. The jays were so angry, and so close, that it was impossible to go back to sleep, with all that racket, so I lay abed, wondering what all the fuss was about. The birds are Stellar's jays, dark blue-black in color and handsome, with cardinals's crests and perky tail feathers that rise straightaway whenever the bird dips his beak.

I suspect the jays are nested and squirrels are after their eggs. Or perhaps they have fledglings and the parents are protective and use their voices to chase off intruders, namely the squirrels again. They are not past stealing an egg or two, just to be mean. They are the kind that would drop it from a tree, just to see it go plop.

We have many crows in the city. They are worse than the jays and nearly as bad as the pernicious squirrels. Maybe the crows are after the eggs or the young of the jays, the squirrels but innocent bystanders. That may be the situation. I can't picture a squirrel eating an egg. But I can a crow.

Crows are street-wise birds, who mix natural food with side dishes of garbage. Any tidbit will do. They are vital to the disposal of roadside kills. They are notorious nest-robbers, thieves, bullies, etc. Yet the jays's annoyance may have another source. Something is bothering them, something new and different. The source lies close to our house. Could it be a raccoon? A bird's egg would be a treat to a raccoon.

After fifteen minutes of continuous scolding from the jays, I lifted myself on an elbow, raised the shade from the window, and peered out. Not much was visible. Then I looked up. On the edge of the roof, near where a long limb from the *deodora* brushed the shingles, sat a raccoon. He looked at me fearlessly. He didn't bat a bandit eye. We were about twelve feet apart and—as they say in foreign affairs—eyeball to eyeball.

What a handsome creature—alert, intelligent-looking, large, unperturbed, with a neat robber's face. After a moment, I dropped my head back on the pillow. This was their world, not mine. The screaming continued. I kept listening (how could I not?), but think I must have slept, for the next thing I knew the sun was high and all was quiet again.

Did I dream it? No.

296

I've cut the grass and now I sit in the side yard, drunk with the lotus smell of lilacs. Both purple and white are blooming overhead. I've always thought the purple ones smelled more—the stronger, the sweeter—but now I'm not sure. It may simply be that we have more purple ones and so they dominate. Purple is the classical sign of passion, white of chastity. It is an unholy combination, and has nothing to do with the realm of the lilac, except perhaps to describe its perfume, where minor liberties are permitted.

Poet Richard Hugo, whose book, *The Triggering Town: Lectures and Essays on Poetry and Writing*, I am reading, detests the semi-colon and won't use it. He says the "halfstop" is never needed. He finds the mere appearance of it on the page offensive. (I wanted to put one between the last two sentences, but he frightened me off.) I shall strive to avoid them for a while. I have a hunch, though, it won't be for long; I rather like them.

Hugo's book is witty, but at the same time serious as can be. The two elements can occur together without disharmony. I didn't know this before, and wouldn't have guessed it. It is probably the best book on writing I've read, from the standpoint of understanding the creative process. The idea of the writer's use of what Hugo calls "the triggering" place or incident is a remarkable concept. It is what springs the writer free and bids him go out and create. The poem says what it is going to say, Hugo adds, and is no way expository. It grows on the page, full of surprises, both for the writer and the reader.

297

It is the time of the lilac, its dominance. Purple and white, in the breeze the colors merge, forming a brilliant spangled effect. They wave, they weave, they burst forth—a mawkish banner waving in the sky. Reddish blue is its color.

Meanwhile, the dogwood has faded to a ghostly white. Soon the bracts will fall off and the tree will hold only leaves, making it like every other tree in the neighborhood. The azaleas are coming on, the long flowering season of the rhododendrons about half over.

Up at the river I admire Turk's big red rhododendron. He died this winter. It goes on, though he does not. How wonderful. Is this sad or joyous? Can't say, for a fact. But the rhododendron remains, big as a two-car garage, as red as anything can be. In the gray light, it is brighter than fire.

298

The waterline is in. Long live the waterline. It is fully buried, the valve protected by a concrete tile eight inches in diameter and two feet deep, set flush with the ground. From it rises two faucets that rush its water and do not leak. I run it a bit, to make sure the line is flushed out, and draw myself a drink. Cool and sweet, but without the flavor of chlorine and fluoride, as in town. A faint aftertaste of plastic—after all, it's a plastic waterpipe. I reckon that will disappear, with time and use.

299

I run along the Burke-Gilman Trail for the first time. It is an old railroad bed in the city that connects the University District with points North, including the Sand Point area. Of course, I've known about it, and walked along it, for years. But now I've found a new use for it.

What could be more fun than running a new track? The air is heavy with the scents from wildflowers blooming in nearby yards. I run into invisible walls of different sweet smells, then run out of them. There is Scotch broom, for instance—a weed and ground cover planted along freeways to retain the bank and protect it from wind and water erosion; in California, where broom doesn't grow, they use a nameless shrub with tiny red rose-like flowers. It stretches for miles and miles along the nearly deserted flatland, where the wind whips without interruption. Here, besides broom, we have little purple flowers growing along the shoulder, perhaps phlox or fireweed.

The trail was built for bicycles along an abandoned railroad grade not much used in recent years. Its rails grew rusty and tufts of grass and daisies rose from between the crossties. Finally, Burlington-Northern deeded it over to the county, the tracks and ties were removed (the ties were scrounged for firewood and retaining walls and fence posts, since they were creosoted), and the county paved the swath with asphalt. Today it is mainly used by cyclists, though runners and joggers contend. And fine weather brings out older couples for their morning and evening constitutionals along its pleasant winding route.

I run in my new knee socks and old white gym shorts, a cool combination for warming weather. I run against my wristwatch, too, not knowing any other way of measuring distance except with time. My start is annoyingly slow. (To anybody watching, it must seem as though I am lame or halt.) After ten minutes, I have gained speed and am approaching Albertson's grocery on 40th Avenue Northeast; I forge into unknown territory until the pathway splits. Here I have a Frostian choice. Instead of making it, I reverse my course and retrace my route, leaving that decision for another day. Headed back, I begin to cool rapidly. Then, bored with mere walking, I run again. The return journey proceeds at a good clip, and I end up by running hard—in a nearly vertical "sprint" position. This brings me back to my starting point. Ahead I see the old stationwagon parked on the gravel siding, awaiting its driver, me.

I am hot and blowing, and it takes me nearly ten minutes to cool down enough to enter my warm car and drive it home. It's great to feel my lungs working hard, my oxygen-deprivation state rapidly being overcome. By the time I cover the six blocks to home, I'm breathing normally and have that feeling of elation which is the main benefit of a good hard run. It will carry me through the rest of the day.

300

The Japanese maple outside my study window is in full foliage, the fragile-looking leaves going from green to russet and presently bearing a pretty mix of the two colors, producing a kind of artificial orange in places. All this happened while my attention was fixed elsewhere. The other trees in the neighborhood are fully leafed and mint green.

301

I notice an item in the personal column of *The Nickel News*, a free tabloid featuring hundreds of classified ads. It is from the "People" section, though it might as well have appeared in the one called, "Personal." It reads: "AEROSPACE ENGINEER, 47, 5 1/2 feet, wishes to meet youthful communicative woman to share interests in backpacking, camping, climbing, marriage, music, sailing, skiing. P.O. Box 81071, Seattle, Washington 98108."

Note that the activities he wants to share are listed alphabetically, not necessarily in the order of importance. What *is* the order of importance, Mr. Engineer? Does "marriage," which appears in the middle of the pack, really deserve to come higher? Lower? It is, of course, up to the "sharee" to find out.

Can a lonely engineer achieve happiness through a personal column? Who knows, or cares? Well, the engineer does. And he will have to wait to find out if this is the route to true happiness. Or even to the inferior kind.

302

This verb, "to share," has developed a specialized use, which troubles me. A simple enough word on the surface, it has deep associations not immediately apparent.

We "share" a soda (but no more, since they've stopped making them) or a milkshake, with straws one or two, depending on how much of ourselves and our spit we want to exchange. We share a room, a bed, a similar attitude. We divide the land or the pie into "shares." Common enough applications.

Out of popular psychology—transactional analysis, in particular—comes a wealth of terms called psychobabble by the cynical. The term itself, of course, is psychobabble. Sharing seems to relate specifically to a group-therapeutic process in which a circle of practitioners (i.e., patients, subscribers, victims, participants) goes round the room (clockwise, or does it make any difference?), uncovering old hostilities and as many repressions as can be rooted out before an audience, in one's allotted time.

This is called "sharing," though it seems to me to be less than gratuitous and probably gets boring and burdensome fast. So sharing also means revealing and saying. It can mean telling you what you need to know for your own good. In this sense, there is a strong hint of the moral, spiritual, or intellectual superiority of the one who does the sharing: He is telling you "how it is," the truth of the matter. Often he believes it to be "God's Own Truth." You are expected to agree and behave accordingly; that is, obey.

If there is a "sharer," I muse, there must be a "sharee," or several of them. "The Sharees" sound like a Motown singing group. (I don't believe I'll buy their record.)

The above comprises just a few of the ideas I would like to "share" with you. (But please resist it—strenuously, if need be.)

303

At eight o'clock in the evening comes the sounds of children playing in the street. Summer is headed our way. This isn't exactly a warm summer evening, but it is a novelty that comes close. The days are lengthening out in a becoming fashion. Whenever the sun breaks out from behind its cloud cover, the day turns hot in a jiffy. It becomes cool again, whenever one of those gray, puffy jobs returns and conceals the sun.

Whenever I run now, I encounter a severe heating problem. At the start, I find the weather coolly invigorating. I pray the sun stays hidden. But it pops out and I am enveloped at once in a liquid blanket of heat, which soon becomes intolerable if I am headed uphill, as I am about half the time. It is the heat accumulation, more than the oxygen debt, that debilitates me, though the two seem to go hand-in-hand. Heat build-up may stop me from running in hot weather. Soon it will be encountered every day. But then we are coming into the summer fishing season, and I hope to get lots of exercise. Last year I was injured about this time. I'm not completely healed, but I'm much better. I ought to be able to wade without excessive discomfort, if I'm careful. It is easier in so many ways than running—easier on the knee, as well.

I'll miss my daily trot. The Burke-Gilman trail is a pleasant place to go. Most of the runners speak or at least smile in passing. Of course: We are brothers and sisters in torment.

304

When I run, I often recall the man from the Holy Water section of the Kalama. He is not a holy man, I mean, only an extraordinary runner I came across there. When I called out to him affectionately and asked how far he had come, he told me I wouldn't believe him. I pressed and he said it was sixteen miles. All, or surely most of it, was uphill, I immediately realized.

Rivers flow downhill. He had gone in the steep opposite direction. He'd begun where the river road left the interstate. I remember the route well. It is torturous, unforgiving. And it is long.

His feat remains with me, as I run my puny short distance. Sixteen miles: Then he would turn around, I suppose, and run the distance back. It would be all downhill, or mostly downhill. There are a few short level stretches in the middle reach. But it would be sixteen miles again. You don't have to be good at math, or at running, to add those figures together and come up with an impressive total. The Boston Marathon is less far and grueling.

305

I have not been up to the river for twelve days and must guess at what the landscape looks like. I can. The buttercups are knee-deep, resplendent with so many tiny yellow blooms, a sea of them, swaying and glittering in large golden patches that in the breeze swim before the eyes. The grass will be high and badly in need of an initial cutting—scytheing first, for if the blades are too long, they'll snarl the wheels of my handmower and it refuses to cut until I rip them free.

The new road will be packed down by light showers from last weekend, and it will be wearing puddles in its dips. The azaleas will be bloomed out—white and peach and pink and scarlet. The rhodies will be starting to blossom, all reds and purples (the ordinary ones), with a few that are pale yellow and one, rare, that is orange. And salmonberries will have ended their blossoming, and there will be burgundy and orange-gold fruits forming at the bloom's core, along the canes.

This piece of land is so much me, so much mine, and I its, that I can see it with terrifying exactitude in each hastening season without actually being there. True, I miss it, but I have it with me recently in my mind. I could be a thousand miles away (and was) and it would be no less with me, no less mine.

Twelve days is long enough away. No, it is too long.

306

A man's history might be written from the standpoint of all the watches he has owned. Or all the cars. Or all the women he has known. This is not just an idle thought.

There is bad news again from the watch front. The gold number I bought back in September consistently gains a minute a day, which I'm told is within Timex's tolerances. It oughtn't be, for it is way too much to be acceptable. A week ago, mine jumped ahead and began gaining two minutes per day; in a week that totals nearly fifteen minutes. It is intolerable. It is bad to be early to your appointments. At first it seems to people to be a pleasant surprise. Then it becomes an annoyance. "What, you here already?" And a glance at their own watch to confirm that the mistake is not theirs.

So I contacted the Timex repair station for the Seattle area. There are two of them. They are able to make in-house adjustments the wearer cannot. Both are at Sears stores. They are at opposite ends of town. I chose the Southern one because—though a bit farther away—it has the nearest the freeway exit. It is how we travel today. Time is distance.

The woman behind the counter expertly snapped the back off my watch, using a special small tool that appeared to be a butter spreader. She picked up a second instrument, a pointy little number much like a dentist uses to probe the soul of your decay, and made a deft movement in the guts of the watch. She handed me back my watch with a smile. The repair had taken about twelve seconds.

She told me that—if this didn't take care of my problem—the watch would have to be replaced. It would have to be sent back to the Timex factory in New Jersey, which is about as far away as you can get from here and still remain in the contiguous USA.

I wore the watch home confidently on my wrist, checking it frequently. Had she set it wrong, or was it already gaining? At the end of the first short day, it was five minutes ahead of all the clocks in the house. Perhaps, I told myself, this was the result of the woman winding it too tightly, before she handed it back to me. Its innards got disturbed and needed to settle back down. I had never wound it; it was the kind of watch that winds itself from normal activity.

"Hey," I had told her. "What are you winding it for? It's a self-winding watch."

"Oh, I wind them all."

"Yeah, but it's not good for them."

"Whoever told you that?"

I don't know; who *had* told me that? I couldn't remember where I had picked it up. She ought to know best, for she worked for Timex. I decided to give the watch the benefit of another day's performance. Maybe time would improve it before I had to make an ultimate judgment on the watch's dependability. But I was already suspicious.

On the second day after her repairs, I set my watch by telephone time, paying sixty cents for the privilege. Eight hours later, I checked it again with the telephone. It was right on the button. I relaxed and began to feel optimistic. Half an hour later, the watch quit. Neither shaking it softly nor shaking it hard persuaded it to start again.

This morning—a Saturday—Norma and I drove back to Sears. The route was familiar and we made excellent time. The woman who fixed my watch before—the boss, I learned—was not in today. Saturday was her day off. Of course: Bosses don't work on Saturday, not unless there is an emergency. (Watches don't have true emergencies.)

The underling fussed with my watch for a few minutes, but did not pry open the back. The watch started and ticked heartily. She handed it back to me with a cold smile. I asked if they would keep it for a few days to see if it continued to run. The woman looked at me as if I were mad. She went off to confer with a colleague, a man. He said they wanted to keep their eyes on it, too. If it stopped again, they would put a new unit in it. A new unit? I didn't know it could be done. But . . . ten days? Yes, it would take ten days. If they had to replace the unit, there would be a service charge of $1.50. It seemed reasonable, especially if I got what constituted a new watch out of the deal. All right, I said.

I decided to press my luck and ask for a "loaner" watch, since I had already made two special trips to Sears. The man studied me for a moment—checking my reliability visually, I guess—and nodded. I knew the store had "returnee" watches, ones that had been left for repairs and never picked up because of the cost to the owner. I could see how that well might be. The man said to go "next door" and they would loan me one. This meant to the adjacent counter. So I did. This entailed another wait, but it was short.

It was the counter where they sold new watches. I had to explain my plight over again. This man looked at me as though my request was insane. Then he dipped into a box under the counter and fished out three watches that looked identical. They were Pulsar 1000, digitals. I remembered that Pulsar was a trade name of Sears. Any of the three would be acceptable, I said. The problem was, I have a small wrist, and all the bands were big and sloppy. Gratefully I picked the one that came closest to tight and left.

My wrist now swims in the borrowed watch band. The watch on it is heavy. Usually I carry it in my pocket. (It has become a pocket watch.) Or, if I'm wearing a sweater, I put it on over my shirt cuff and sweater sleeve. This effectively narrows the band's width, and the watch fits snugly.

A digital is a nice watch to have. It opens up a whole new realm of possibilities for contemplating time. Time no longer must run round the merry-go-round, forming a continuous circle that never ends; time is a string of numbers—hours, minutes, and seconds—each separated from the other by a nifty colon. (Are colons all right, Richard Hugo?) And when you go to set it, the colon *blinks* to tell you where you are, in serial time. It is wonderful.

To read this concealed data I must first push a button or two that is located on one side of the watch or the other. Often I must push two or more buttons together, or in a sequence. It gets confusing, all the combinations of pushes and what they all mean.

There are four buttons, two on each side of the watch. Of course, I am always forgetting the button combinations that tell the watch what to do—which function to activate at a given time. Then the watch does unexpected things and locks in on them. It is reluctant to budge.

One button provides a continuous readout. A blinking colon (not a disease) not only tells me what mode I am in, but whether the battery is any good. If I look at the blinking colon for very long, it makes me nervous and I have to glance away. Fortunately I know the button combination to terminate the blinking colon. The colon now returns to steadystate. But often I am locked into Army/Navy time, in which there are twenty-four consecutively numbered hours.

The watch and I get along fine. I understand how to work only a fraction of its functions. That is probably for the best.

307

I sit reading in the sun, after a good run, a haircut from Norma, a shower, and a shampoo. I comb out my wet beard and let it dry in the warm air. How much time does a man save, once he decides to stop shaving? In an adult lifetime, it must add up to days or weeks. Perhaps months of minutes.

The Big Guy plops in the pool behind me, with a great slurping sound, like a feeding cannibal brown trout. Of course I've never heard one feed. Every fisherman houses in his imagination such a sound, waiting for the day it will arrive and he will know it for what it is. His knowledge of course comes from reading.

My experience is mostly with rainbow trout, and they sup. Usually, when I am around, they make no sound at all. They go off their feed. Perhaps they are busy sleeping.

I am reading Tucker's biography of Beethoven. It is stilted and badly dated, consisting mostly of Beethoven's letters. Beethoven is better known for his music than his letter writing. I am concurrently reading Nick Lyons's *The Seasonable Angler* and Anthony Burgess' *1985*, which carries that title, he says, to avoid charges of plagiarism with George Orwell's book. The remark is meant to be a joke. Also, today, I am perusing the two Sunday papers. All in all, a pleasant day's work is cut out for me.

This is Mother's Day. Ding-a-ling. The sky is high with a cloud canopy, through which breaks the afternoon sun, at last, bringing the temperature up to 75 degrees in a wink. Norma and I are going to pay due respect to a pair of Moms this afternoon. This means buying them flowers. We give flowers in pots, not cut flowers, for the two of them are gardeners. Half the thrill is in planting them after they've stopped blooming.

308

Larkspur found blooming along the East Lewis reportedly is a cultivated flower. Don't tell the larkspur it is not wild. You may break its heart. Evidently some domestic blooms produced seeds that got blown over a vast landscape and the plant now is found broadly.

Deep in the shade along the riverbank, the blossoms spot the greenery with an intense blue—almost the same shade of royal blue as my running pants. The Stellar jay has the same color below his dark crest. The single stalk of larkspur I brought home not quite two weeks ago still has some blossoms clinging to it. But the three lower spurs have withered and died back. They have left scars along the stem. The upper spurs have opened up, one by one, and are much more pale. Norma predicted this.

Why so? Some valuable nutrients are lacking in water that they find in soil evidently, and we have deprived it of its food. The water does the flower no good except to create the illusion it is still connected to the ground. We hope to get some bloomed-out blossoms for seed. But I think there is small chance.

Deep gold of the Scotch broom extends for miles in a solid swath along the highway. On my way home from the river I saw several people in passing car windows vigorously sneezing. The stuff affects me, too. My head tightens up, as though in a vice, but sneezing a few times relieves the pressure and soon causes my nose to empty copiously, and I begin to feel better.

All the world enjoys a good sneeze. Isn't that why people used to take snuff?

309

Lilacs are from the dooryard gone and the dogwood is a scraggly reminder of what used to be, a few bracts still clinging to a bough the color of fire-charred paper. But the small double-white lilac is holding its own. It was a gift from my mother, a sprout taken from her big one a year before they sold their house and moved into an apartment. It is important to her that we prolong its life. We are doing our best, and the lilac is responding.

A light rain last night shattered what was left of the purple lilac blooms and caused them to explode. Now they litter the lawn with tiny brown shards. They look very much like the stuff at the bottom of a popcorn sack.

Under my bedroom window the late rhododendrons are budded voluptuously, red as sin. Others are in the early-flowering stage, with a peek inside revealing flame and an intense pink. D.H. Lawrence would have a field day with these, especially the scarlet ones trying to turn themselves inside out.

310

A shadow races across the earth. I flinch instinctively. Is it my doom arriving? No, it is a bird—only a bird. My response is primitive and irrational. Birds regularly pass between me and the sun, but I don't duck. It takes a really big bird—a heron or an eagle—to trigger my response. It must be a bird big enough to cast a huge moving shadow. Then it is a tribute to a bird to be able to flinch me so. It is the great blue heron.

Today three more are parked downstream from where I fish. One of them came in low to join the others. He created the momentary pall. But now he is poised sedately, standing in dignified repose with the others, each perched on one foot. The other foot is drawn up to the extent as to appear missing. Poor, crippled heron—three of them, all ruined so! Of course, it is only a trick of the eyes.

311

Up at the river tonight, with clear skies overhead and a temperature rapidly descending from a high of 70. Time only to make a quick journal entry, after a day of hard fruitless fishing. I hear the crunch of tires in the drive. Norma has driven up to spend the night. Wonderful. I knew there was a chance, but it seemed small. I help her unload. She has ice-cold beer in the cooler and fresh meat.

Now a sharp noise from outside, as I write this. It is a dry branch being broken. She is building up a blaze for our fireside. Enough of the unreality of writing. It is not life. I rush out and join her, a beer in each hand.

312

The volume of green growth in the past two weeks is incredible. I thought I was prepared for abundance, but this surpasses my expectation. When I drove away from the river last, it was from woods just being released from the fist of winter. I return to find almost tropical growth. Whose woods are these? Why, they're mine.

The grass stands a foot tall; it will be a nightmare to cut. But being fresh and tender, the blades of the mower will gnaw right through the grass and press flat what won't be cut. The salmonberry canes reach eight or ten feet, and are bloomed out, except for a few laggards, the green berries well started out from the base of the flower. A couple of porcine bumblebees with dirty feet fumble at the last magenta petals and add to their suitcases of pollen.

Little manure flies buzz everywhere, but would be worse without the steady breeze that thwarts their flight. No mosquitoes yet this year. An immaculate blue sky darkens toward night, bringing on an evening in which the mercury stands at 44 degrees by bedtime. During the night Norma is cold in the trailer, while I, down by the river, have to pull the old Army blanket over my sleeping bag, rising chilled in the night to do so. We do not rise until after nine, the next morning, and spend a lazy day beneath a steady sun that nudges again into the low 70s. Perfect weather, the easy life.

On a distant hill a chainsaw growls like a disturbed beast. The neighbors are cutting their lawns with power mowers at opposite ends of our enclave. The country is nothing more than the city with big borders. Tomorrow, after church, Schlotman will arrive and mow his lawn with a power cutter, too. It is what people do at Stillaguamish Meadows, if they don't fish. And I seem to be the only fisher among the ownership.

After mowing, people invariably have a cookout. It serves as a climax to the day's work party. How people love hard work; they are lost, unhappy, when there is none to do. I suspect that one reason is because most jobs don't permit it, only some inferior activity that brings small reward. Hence all this weekend effort. Physical work purges the blood, clears the lungs, and cleanses the soul. After a week in the market place, the soul is badly in need of ritual purification.

313

It is impossible to lie perfectly still, with your eyes closed, and have ideas "come to you"—especially ideas for stories. Instead, your thoughts go hopping around like Mexican jumping beans. Perhaps there is a little worm trapped inside one's head, or in each thought, and the creature wants out. It is fighting hard to be born. I think it is only the person without ideas, without conflicts, without a nervous worm trapped in his brain, who is truly happy today, in this disjointed world. The intellectual always remains miserable. Think of the great Russian writers. I often do.

The writer is the most tormented of people, always wondering where his next idea is coming from, and whether it will be any good. His chronic unhappiness is the irritation from which he will build his pearl—the pearl of meaning, or whatever else he comes up with. Usually it is only a cultured pearl. Or paste.

In order to get ideas for stories, one must keep moving. Let no grass grow underfoot. Do not remain idle, but be in a receptive state. Ideas happen to he who does something other than advertise his availability to them. They evolve, like the frog from the slime. One must be open to all things new and obscure. A life of indolence helps prepare the way. The ability to make one's mind a near-blank is hard for some, but invaluable. Me, I find it easy. (I jest.)

Poets often drink and eat to excess, in order to encourage inspiration. They believe it is the price they must pay for the ideas that come to them. Bloated with food and drink, they are at their best when they are at their worst. They know this. It is when their best ideas come visiting. They want to be hospitable to them, their visitors. Thus, the artist leads a life of a wastrel—often total debasement. It is how art happens. Artists would like to be more like ordinary people. They try to acquire the usual vacant stare, with the lips slightly ajar. The idiot's look is just right.

The artist throws away a great deal of time. It is for a good reason. He believes—often falsely—that waste is necessary for inspiration, when only indolence is. Everything is worth the price of being struck by an idea, or by a story prospect. You can watch TV or go to a movie. Mind and emotions remain in a state of readiness. They await the zap of art. But the zap isn't the whole point. It isn't creation. It is merely the starting place. Art is created by the hard work that takes place daily at the loom or easel or keyboard, be it musical or computer.

A zap may occur many times in a day, or not at all. When and if it comes, you will know it, for it is like a controlled nuclear explosion, the kind that generates electricity in the core of a reactor.

314

A subject for a book that keeps nudging me hard—with a lewd wink and a sly giggle—is about the comic strips. Write a book about the comics—what they truly say and mean. It is unexplored territory. But the field is fraught with land mines.

Never call the comics "the funnies," for as soon as you do, you will find that they are serious as all get out. They push frontiers into unknown regions, and soon you are being tossed about on uncharted seas. And a cartoon doesn't die, when its creator does. It continues to push into a long future. The syndicate (or the heirs) hire a new cartoonist. The profits must go on. The quality usually goes down a little.

Millions read the comics each day and get something from them besides a chuckle. Comics influence our lifestyles and values in many subtle ways. Take Blondie and Dagwood. Most men would love to have Blondie around to bang. She is presented as a brainless sexpot. Yet she is shrewd, domineering. She has curves on top of curves. Does Dagwood ever look at her with a lecherous eye? No, he is a sexless jerk. So what does Blondie see in him? Without his pants on, is he something special? That must be the case, for at work all he does is get humiliated by Mr. Dithers. At home he eats sandwiches that nobody else can get his mouth around, but does little more. Usually he is asleep on the couch. He dreads going to work, getting up in the morning, riding in the dreaded carpool—that leftover from World War II gas rationing.

Perhaps the price in America of having a Blondie, plus two children and Daisy, the dog, is to have a boss like Julius Dithers. He has his own comeuppance in the form of a battle-ax wife, Cora.

There is more to this life of implicit violence. It is not so simple as it may seem on the surface. Dagwood and Herb Woodley lend each other tools, but don't return them until one beats the other bloody first. It is just like Sarge and Beetle Bailey. Yet they remain the best of friends. They often have cookouts together. Oh, the American cookout. This pair is the quintessential American family, times two.

Do the comics provide us with daily fantasies about a richer life? It doesn't seem so. But why, then, do we read the damn things? What is the great appeal that keeps drawing us to the comic section? This is not a personal obsession on my part. I mean, they don't publish them just for me. To write a book about the comics, I would have to observe them much more closely than I'd like to do. I would have to rip them apart with my eyes and dissect the multiple complex relationships within each strip.

To look solely at Blondie is revealing enough. Why does Cora beat Mr. Dithers so hard, so often, when all he does is make a snide remark when she spends so much money? If he really means it, why doesn't he cut up her credit cards? Why doesn't he find himself a young cookie? He easily could, with all his money.

What about sex in the comics? What do Dagwood and Blondie *do* in bed—I mean, aside from listening for burglars? I can only guess. I've read my Freud; also Masters and Johnson and Kraft-Ebbing. Blondie and Dagwood haven't, apparently. Does Blondie (as we say today) go down on Dagwood? Does she take it from behind? Heaven forbid. But it's only because Dagwood has never thought of it, either, or so is the inference. He's got his mind on what's inside the refrigerator.

"No, thanks," I keep saying to the idea of a book on the comics. But the urge won't go away for long. It keeps circling back, sniffing at my heels like a dog that wants me to think it won't bite. Then, snap, it nails you on the hamstring.

The only way you can be rid of some ideas is to write the story and see where it leads you. The act of writing gives some relief.

315

A warm, muggy day, the temperature in the mid-70s at noon, but with strong southerly winds gliding in, which usually portend a change. There may be thundershowers by evening. Yet other times these masses whiz on by, with nothing to show for the threat except scudding cloud that shed no moisture.

Once we get within a week of the official opening of the fishing season for local rivers, I relax and my nerves calm. It's all downhill now. A wait of a few days more is tolerable—actually a joy. The open season represents freedom to me, the opportunity to go out and fish whenever I like. It is about as important as anything I can think of. It is the *idea* that matters most to me. Freedom lives in the head. The lion in its carrying container in 'Born Free" believed it was free, and adapted to its tiny environment, accepting it as "home," the broad world It was content. If I am free in my head, it is unimportant where my body may be, or what is happening around me. But to be missing an inch or two of freedom is maddening. It signifies I am the prisoner of something or somebody.

The three-day Memorial Day holiday traditionally marks the start of the summer here. The long weekend contains elements of folk ritual, which guarantees a large turnout. Because I don't like crowds, I will wait until the weekend is over to fish. Or so I always say. But I may tiptoe out anyway, if there is a break in the crowd succession. I have had too many good Memorial Day fishing excursions not to try for another.

The season is officially here. Sing, Hurrah! That's what the bards used to say. What is important is that Memorial Day has arrived. Now all things are possible.

316

We have entered that period when it is not necessary for the sun to shine for the early afternoon temperature to climb well past 70 degrees. Anticipated storms fail to materialize, or else turn out to be showers of no consequence. I heard a sprinkle on the roof early this morning, but when I arose there were no signs that rain had fallen.

In town my first rose—a Tropicana—has bloomed. It is a pretty, red-orange color and special to me. It is quite distinct, and readily recognizable from the pack. I keep my eye out for new species of flora whenever I am out running. Along the Burke-Gilman Trail, every fifty feet or so, some twenty Norwegian maples have been planted by the city. They stretch gracefully upward, tall and straight. The bark is silvery dun. Their leaves are newly unfurled and a delicate pale green—except for one tree near the entrance to 40th Avenue NE. It is olive and russet, a bit like the Japanese maple outside my study window. But there is a big difference. The Norwegian maple is dying. That accounts for its different look and might explain its special ephemeral beauty. Each day when I run, it becomes browner and less beautiful.

Yesterday I spent two hours with my old boss at the UW, Howard Miller. He is director of publications. We had coffee together on campus and our chat lengthened out. He was a runner long before it became fashionable. At 52, he is locally famous for it, and when last sighted was disappearing over a hill. He is looking forward to entering a marathon for men over fifty. He believes he can win it. I do, too.

When I worked for him, I remember him running every noon. And he would run to work and home again, a distance of about fifteen miles each way. This puts him in the same classification as the man from the Holy Water on the Kalama.

Modestly—because I have much to be modest about—I told him I ran "a little" now. His eyes brightened. He was glad to hear it, he said. He had tried to get me started years ago. We talked about running, and mostly I listened. I quickly began to revise my ideas based on what he said. For instance, it is better to run for a full 30 minutes, even if I have to walk in the middle of my run, than to run for only 20 minutes. This makes sense. He says I shouldn't hesitate to stop and walk when I grow tired, after which I ought to be able to do another mile.

"Another mile?" I asked, groaning.

He smiled.

"Anything that works," is a popular slogan, applicable to many things, and, in my case, might be interpreted to mean, "Anything that increases stamina and builds up one's general conditioning is good." Walk, when you need to. Run when you want to, or when you feel the need. It is important to listen to messages from your body and to obey them. This is only good sense. Someone my age ought not to be competitive in his running, when his goal is strictly physical conditioning.

Yet the example of Howard Miller proves that we remain competitive, whatever our ages, whether we choose to admit it or not. I suppose I am that way, too, though I try to suppress it.

317

The man who lives in the tulles often has a need to escape to the city. He may not recognize what he does or why he does it. He goes to the department stores or the malls as much to see the people as to buy things. So much density and diversity thrills him. He seeks one kind of crowd to avoid another, for the weekend throngs are headed for the country. He hates them, and this is his escape. Yet he finds the city worse.

It is one world. American culture is homogenized, whether we like it or not. There are three major TV networks, several minor ones, plus all the cable stations, and each is distressingly like the others. It matters little which one you watch for news and events. Different faces say nearly the same things, at about the same time of day.

Competition makes us more alike, oddly. Quickly, what is the difference between a Chevy and a Ford? If you say, "the grill," you didn't hear my question correctly. Country, city? In the country are more trees—unless they've cut them all down for lumber or pasture.

Some city parks have taken on a wilderness aspect because the people demand it. It is beautiful from a distance, but it is where most of the muggings and rapes take place.

What is a writer to make of all this? Is his job to point things out, then move on? Is it to say something new, whatever the cost? Or is he to say old things in a new and startling manner? For instance, I need words to describe the color of a rose. It is my job. I must define the Tropicana, let's say, in such a way that it is unmistakable from any other rose. But it is impossible to do. A rose is a rose, etc.

My rose is neither red nor pink, but a shade or color in between. Sorry, man—not good enough. It is a luminous pale tomato, the color of an October sunset over the Olympic Mountains. Better, but still not close enough. I must nail down the color so the reader encountering a Tropicana will say, "That is the rose he was talking about. It can be no other."

When I have achieved that goal, I can put the pencil down for good. There will be no more to say.

318

I killed a cat today. I didn't mean to. Driving into Fortson to fish, I saw a small white shape spring out from the tall grass, pause, and—as I started to brake sharply, then lessened the pressure—dart straight into the path of my small stationwagon. I felt a soft bump and knew it was all over for the cat. Ahead two boys were playing with a BB-gun by a culvert. I stopped the car on the shoulder. I called over, asking them if either had a white cat. One boy's head nodded.

"I just killed your cat," I told him. "I'm sorry. It dashed right out in front of the car. I couldn't stop."

"That's okay," he told me, looking aside.

I doubt if he realized what had happened yet. But perhaps he did, and I didn't, for cats are always being killed in the country, one way or another. In my rear-vision mirror I could see a pale form crumpled by the edge of the road. The boy started walking home, in the direction of the dead cat. I parked and followed him on foot. His mother and father came out on the stoop.

I repeated my short story.

"It's all right," said the man. Yes, he was the father. "It wasn't your fault. Thanks for stopping by."

But it *was* my fault. I was driving the car. Just the same, I was glad to see the father, for it meant I wouldn't have to go back and pick up the dead cat and dispose of it in some awful way I hadn't yet figured out. Now I could drive on and go fishing, which was my original intention. How cowardly.

As I drove away, I saw the boy down by the culvert again. His friend was gone. His bike was flung on its side. He was lying on the grass, clutching his BB gun. And he was sobbing.

319

Hard rains. Garth, Norma, and I are ensconced in the travel trailer, listening to music crackling on the radio. Lightning flashes, followed by thunder, rip across the near sky.

"Two miles away," sighs Norma, from over her Iris Murdock novel. She is counting seconds, presuming a normal temperature, in order to judge the distance. And I, who have to hold my hand lightly over the back of the radio to ground it and bring in any station at all, feel safe with my music playing for another few minutes.

Rain clatters on the aluminum roof. Each of us is wrapped in a coat and blanket against the pervasive coolness. If the rain doesn't stop soon, we will probably pack up and return home, for the river is high and getting higher. Plans for building the woodshed (in preparation for this, I brought up a load of 2X4s) are put on hold.

In fact, all the people who've came to the country for the three-day weekend are packing up and heading back to the city. The lesson of the rain and thunder is, this storm will last for days. Through the gap in the trees, across the river and up on the hill, I see cars pass by increasingly often, headed West. Soon there will be an exodus. Many of our long anticipated weekends end this way.

320

Every so often, a three-day storm rolls in, with winds so strong they turn the trees inside out and cause them to lean, as Poet David Wagoner says, "in a palisade." May is as good month as any to encounter such a storm. I passed three horses standing in a field. The wind canted their tails at the same forty-five degree angle. They all wisely leaned into the gale. Their manes flew.

Then came rain. A spring shower is no less wetting than a winter one. I went to Fortson. The water remained clear. I hooked a magnificent steelhead on a small no-name fly. I fought the fish for twenty minutes. A hatchery fish, the season's first, I killed it. It weighed just under 18 pounds. Marc Bale, who was standing on the other side, said it was the biggest steelhead he'd ever seen. I modestly agreed that it was pretty large.

The fish rests in the refrigerator, awaiting butchering and distribution to many friends. There is much to share, this exceptional day.

321

Spring has burst, and the river is running high but clear. The trees are full and the undergrowth is lush. Salmonberry and blackberry thickets have laced their canes impenetrably. It is impossible to pass through them in any spot.

Caddis creepers are one-quarter inch long, practically in the seed stage, while two weeks ago in the Lewis they were a full one-half inch in length. The streams to the Southwest are warmer, year round, and are lush with insect life, consequently. Basaltic soil contributes to their richness.

In front of the Oso cabin blooms a deep blue double-larkspur, which I picked for Norma, since it was nearly gone, and I wanted her to see it. From other unopened blooms there ought to be seeds produced which we can gather later in the year and plant elsewhere. Never knew it was there.

322

It is as natural to write as it is to talk, to drink beer, to eat beef, or to make love. It is a perfectly normal activity, not one to be set off from ordinary life so much as incorporated into it—an inseparable element, one not very special. If writing is "creative," it is so in an ordinary way. What is called creation is part of the warp and woof of daily life.

Everyone is creative to some degree. Each year I have this fact driven home to me by the University District Street Fair, the queen of local fairs. It comes just after the opening of the boating season. The number of artisans showing their wares is impressive. In fact, there are so many of them that each year a number are turned away.

The sponsors have developed a complex selection process in which not just the earliest applicants are chosen. They fill the open slots by category and also utilize a lottery system. Sales are unpredictable. The artisans who did well a year ago will probably do well again—but not necessarily. Life is a gamble. Many prepare stocks of wares over the previous winter. Often the items don't sell. They can be carried over as inventory to next year's fair. A host of new shoppers will see the goods for the first time.

Or the old ones will have forgotten them.

323

I am being visited by a fly. Greetings. A horse fly we call any fly larger than a given size. We may well be wrong, we generalists. The fly may have another name. So be it.

This one is on a harassment mission, and will not light and let itself be killed by my flat palm. It keeps buzzing off to a safe distance, say, about five feet away, mocking me, its wings abuzz. I can't find the fly at all, as a matter of fact, only detect his presence from the noise he makes. His evasiveness is annoying. Then I am struck by a feeling of empathy. It is a frantic world in which we both live, so I can understand how he is driven to buzz and dodge so. Given his situation, I would, too.

Perhaps he is attracted and repulsed by me, the two at once. Ambivalence I can understand, even in a fly. This fly doesn't want to bite me, only come near. It is lonely, perhaps. It is content to bump me lightly, then veer off. So why won't I tolerate this? Well, I won't. The fly glances off my arm, returns, buzzes, veers off again. It is maddening. Why can't I see it? Then its buzz . . . disappears. Where did you go, fly—to the city? Does the city need flies badly enough to import them? Come back, fly. I miss you.

It hears me. It returns, as from a great distance. It returns with a vengeance. A bite is what it is really after. Fly I rescind our truce. I set a trap, waiting poised and cocked to strike with open hand. I wait, breathing heavily. Finally the fly alights. It is not so big as I had imagined. It doesn't have big green goggley eyes, for one thing. It is just a common, garden-variety manure fly. I strike with all my amassed strength and swiftness. I miss, of course. My arm sting from where I hit myself. I retreat to my writing. Once warned, the fly seems twice shy of another blow.

I recognize this as a maneuver, another tactic. The fly is tempting me into a state of unpreparedness. It understands that I know what it is about, so sets a counter trap. I respond in kind, though I am stiller than before. Inside my skin I am tightly coiled. Fleetingly, the fly lands on my notebook page. Instantly it darts off again, leaving me with a cocked wrist. I am getting next to no writing done.

It cannot stay away from me, though. It finds me oddly attractive, perhaps because I am clad only in bathing suit and sandals. So much available skin. It draws near, and I try another swing and slap. Finally I slam closed my notebook and go inside. I bang the screen door behind me before he can follow me in.

Safe!

324

Earlier I noted that human excrement smells worse than animal. If the animal is carnivorous, its shit smells more like ours. This should make us examine our eating habits. Surely vegetarians don't produce such evil-smelling stuff? To verify this would require a whole new field of science. It is not for me.

My roses continue to bloom their little hearts out. What folly. Why do roses make beautiful blooms with which to enrich our lives? Haven't they something better to do? If there is a higher reason, nobody is saying. Certainly not the rose.

A Year At The River

A rose blooms like crazy because that is what it is programmed to do. It contains a rose "chip," you might say. It is no worse off for extending its effort to produce blooms. In fact, it thrives on doing so. It puts out new shoots and leaves and blossoms until the first hard freeze, and sometimes later. But each bloom has a relatively short lifespan. If you don't pick it, it lasts longer. And roses require manure, which is the subject of this entry. It is why my nose burns and I am fixed on the subject of shit. My nose is full of the smell of steer manure. This stuff is a concentrate and must be diluted, or else it will burn the rose's roots and the rose will die. This is not my goal. I want my roses to grow splendidly. So I must cut the manure with soil, or any other inert material I can find lying around, such as mulched leaves.

A rose plant is a manufacturing device, producing many blooms in a season. It requires spraying on a still day so that multifarious insects won't eat up its foliage and buds. A rose bit in the bud is no longer a lovely thing, but a basket case.

I said a day or two ago that my first rose of the season has bloomed. Now dozens more are out, in a vast competition of colors. "Look at me," one is saying. "No," says another, "look at *me*."

I do, gratefully. I study all of them (however briefly). I wander among my roses and snip off a few, being careful to nip the stalk above a five-pronged leaf, so the plant will split and engender more branches and leaves and roses. I want all the roses in the world for myself. A rose blooming in the deep woods, in a place where no person visits, is a lost rose. A rose is meant to be seen. Its beauty is all. It has no other purpose.

325

As I am writing this, a boy comes up our city street with a companion—he on foot, his friend on a bicycle. I hear them before I see them, and, listening, become anxious to see their faces—cherubic or otherwise. Otherwise, I suspect.

The one doing all the talking comes into view, brown-haired, in one of those bowl cuts, with spectacles, wearing a blue down coat that makes him look fat. He calls his companion "a fucking idiot." He looks to be about nine, and is probably twelve, the age at which boys join the Scouts; I am a poor judge of a boy's age, because I am so greatly removed from him by time. His bicycling companion hoves into view, then vanishes across my field of vision. He is tall, slender, with ash-blond hair that sweeps across his face.

The boy in blue crosses the street and begins to sing an updated version of, "Row, row, row your boat," only it goes, "Roll, roll, roll that joint,/Gently take a toke,/Merrily, merrily, merrily , merrily,/Try to hold the smoke."

I call out to him, from my sunning station, "You don't really mean that, do you?"

"No," he shortly replies, and turns his face back to the street.

Hurrying no more than before, he too passes out of eye shot. Since I represent the adult world, I can hardly believe anything he deigns to tell me. Perhaps he is only a pretend doper.

326

June arrives with a vengeance. On the first, in the city, it is 88 degrees F. by 2:30 in the afternoon, according to a radio station I pick up in my little trailer. It's hot in the country, too. This is the first time I've turned on the radio in three days; I've been listening to tapes, instead, because the reception is so poor when the weather is good. In fact, when stormy weather rolls in, the radio reception improves fantastically. It is when we sorely need it to be good. Now the few stations that come in have a terrible crackle and hum.

It is tolerable here in the morning, and in the heat of a long afternoon I can take a dip in the river, that is, if I can stand water so cold. The promise of high temperatures in the city may keep me here longer, I suspect.

327

I am reading Joseph Heller's fiercely satiric novel, *Good As Gold*, and have mixed feelings about it. In places the satiric elements are so grotesque, so unreal, that the book becomes burlesque; but perhaps this has always been Heller's method, and I am only just noticing it and letting it get to me. In his mid-seventies, he feels a strong identification and competition with his peer, Norman Mailer, but has not produced a comparable output. However, *Catch*-22 has become a household word.

Heller offers us a Jewish family headed by a remarried (widowed) patriarch so vicious and intentionally cruel that he cannot be liked or even taken seriously. The *goyim* in Washington D.C., where the novel takes place, are presented even less lovingly, that is, even more grotesquely. They fail to achieve even caricature status. Yet the book is very funny and compelling, if only on the level of buffoonery.

A question of esthetics arises. If the artist (that is, the novelist) does not take his material seriously, and make it even halfway realistic, then why should we bother with it? How *can* we? Burlesque is pure slapstick entertainment, with little or no significant content. It is best enjoyed on a superficial level, quickly, and then erased from the mind without a second thought, for it has no staying power, and no direct illumination comes from it.

328

There is practically no snowpack again this year. This became apparent early, when April proved to be a gentle month and little snow fell in the Cascades. April is the month—oddly—when the snowpack either materializes or doesn't, and the long winter season preceding it forms the snowpack's base, with alternative periods of snowfall, thaw, and rain to make it solid. The April snows fall on the early pack and insulate it from the sun. This makes it last into the hot days of summer.

When the April snows do not materialize—as they have failed to do, in something like the past three out of four years—the warm days of May and early June bring down the unprotected snow, all in a rush, and there is no more left to feed the rivers, when they really need it.

Now, early June, with cool conditions up until recently, the river is running at a level we normally wouldn't encounter until well into July. The river is more than a month ahead of its season. The low water may be an omen of worse things to come. Seems to me this promises the second drought year in a row. This will be bad for fish production.

329

Driving up to the river last night for several hours fishing on a long June evening, I was met by hard showers which developed into a steady, thunderous rain lasting all night. I quit fishing early and returned to the trailer for dinner. I didn't bother taking off my waders first.

A moment later I was startled by a voice. It was that of my new neighbor, Tom Crabtree. He said he had wrapped on the door, but I must not have heard him, over the roar of the rising river. So he spoke. I nearly jumped out of my boots, for I believed myself to be alone in the woods. Then I saw him through the cracked glass window. He was tall, bearded, slightly ominous, but proved to have a big disarming smile and easy manner. He had seen my car lights returning, he said, and came down to make my acquaintance, calling out several times to avoid startling me. Recovering my poise, we exchanged names and shook hands.

His purpose was not entirely social. He had a piano to move into the white house at the end of the road, and only two women to assist him in getting it out of the U-Haul van. Would I give him a hand? How could I say no? Still in my waders, I hurried on down, hard on his heels.

He had a huge horizontal freezer to move, additionally. Oh my aching back. Sweating inside my waders, I grabbed one end of, first, the piano, then the freezer. The women stood watching, smiling, as we shuffled along a makeshift gangplank leading from the back of the truck to the front door. A fall by either of us would have been disastrous.

The piano was old, dilapidated, an upright, made of mahogany or some other dark wood that is dense and heavy. It had many middle keys missing their original ivory. Crabtree's wife was a gaunt country-looking woman, quite pretty; she had charge of three children, all under three years of age. Her name was Karen. The other woman was a friend. I found the friend gorgeous, with fine hands and . . . hips, well call them, plus a great smile. She knew her attributes and wore them well. I gathered she was related to one or the other of them—a sister of the husband or the wife. The latter, perhaps, for the women had a similar appearance. But maybe it was only their youth. All were in their mid-twenties.

Crabtree confided that he had paid $62,000 for the house and property, which comprises more than an acre. It fronts on the river. The house is run down, with only two small bedrooms, and is constructed of cement blocks, which will make it damp and cold, year-round.

Eighteen months ago the property went through receivership, Norma and I bid $22,000 for the house and land at an auction, but that was too little to be considered seriously by the court. (I guess we were trying to finesse it.) A man named Lennox bought it later through a real estate agent. He paid $42,000. In just over a year, he sold it, making a nice profit. It's probably what I intended to do.

Crabtree is likable, enthusiastic, boyish, and does (whether he knows it or not) a medium-good George Carlin imitation, which he may not be conscious of, when he is trying for a laugh. This is often. He and his wife intend to raise flowers, he said. What? He says he will be home most of the time, and has a job that requires he be gone only one and a half days a week. I can't imagine what kind of job that might be. Obviously people from the city—California, I think. It will be interesting to see how they take to life in the country, especially when a long winter's rains arrive, and the land turns sodden for many months.

Perhaps they will like it better than most. It may be that the frontier spirit is alive and well in them. Crabtree has promised that I can continue to draw water under pressure from their well, which eases my backache from moving the freezer and piano. It's great to know my privilege isn't threatened and I won't have to go to court to fight for my right to draw my minimal drinking water.

330

To reach the river from Bryson's public access above Boulder Creek takes precisely five minutes of fast walking over a pretty little trail that winds through some old alders. They drop their deadfall branches across the path and they merrily go *crunch* underfoot. The

A Year At The River

alders rise in stands from the salmonberry and blackberry thickets, with here and there a sprawling big-leaf maple thrown in.

The five-minute walking part is critical when the light is failing and there is less than an hour left to fish before dark. Then every moment counts. Like so many runs in the upper river, the pool looks great when the river is running high and fast, but when the river drops, as it is now doing, the pool shrinks rapidly and proves a disappointment. It is shallow and sandy in many places, with only a boulder here and there to afford the fish resting places, and a back eddy soon forms at the heart of the pool. This is not conducive to good fishing.

Last night was the first time I've fished the pool, though once, years ago, Norma and Garth and I hiked into it. The time was April, I think, and the river was closed to fishing. The greenery was fresh and bright. Norma loved the setting, but I was not impressed with the water and its short sandy pools, and I never went back. Last night was the first time.

As expected I didn't touch a fish. No fish have been reported in the past few days. Perhaps they have not ascended the river so far. I've heard that the Indian nets are back in the river. This would explain the absence of fish at this key point in the season.

331

A big white full moon over Eby Hill, as I fished the Grant Creek Drift yesterday. It looked like a great China saucer stuck up in the sky—the effect due to magnification from the atmosphere. So low, I could easily see all the pocked-marked features that contribute to the Man-in-the-Moon theory. But now that Neil Armstrong has walked on that inhospitable surface, we think of it differently. The moon is bleak, nothing but rock and sand and sub-zero temperatures. It is no longer romantic, and the Man-In-The-Moon theory is absurd. (Then why can't I forget it?)

As it rose, it grew paler, smaller. This is an optical effect. It increased the margin between itself and the hemlocks and cedars standing along the river bank, out-reaching their crests by a fraction of an inch at first, then by a larger amount, while all the while a rosy sunset glow hung in the sky. Gradually the glow faded, and the light cast by the moon took over the heavens.

The moon becomes ordinary, as it rises. Ho-hum. It loses its size and color and brilliance. After a while, it might be mistaken for a streetlight, back in the city. But for a while tonight it lit up the sky beautifully. I found I could fish until an hour or two after dark, and afterwards walk out under a sky lit as if by a torch.

332

Across the front of the house in town, the roses are blooming as though there is no tomorrow. (Let's hope they are wrong.) They put out large single blooms or many smaller ones, ones with weak stems that won't support such heavy heads. The heads start to nod, as soon as you pick them. You put them in a vase and come back an hour later to find them drooping at the guillotine. The colors stay true and intense, however.

Most of the roses belong to Norma. They are her pets. Mine are almost an after-thought. Of the four "freebies" given me by my neighbor Marshall, two are dead. I think they were dead when he got them and didn't know it. Some terrible history preceded them. Perhaps they froze in a warehouse. Convinced they were dead, I pulled them up today—they left the ground much more easily than I expected. I saw they had established no roots; the tap root was the same length as when I'd planted it, and no tiny fibrous roots shot off from it. A couple of tentative leaves had pushed out from the stem, but had withered in the leaf bud. They turned a powdery brown. I never knew what still-born meant until I saw those roses.

But two survived, though only about 50 percent of each. That is, half of their shoots died. They had a late start; there were many handicaps for them to overcome. I am waiting for my first rosebud from them. It will be a long wait.

The roses require work. I cut away the old blooms and the long spidery runners Norma said were suckers and detrimental to the plant, for they won't produce blooms and take nourishment away from the stems that will bear. The plan is to develop a well-shaped rosebush that stays in its place, not one that creeps toward the street like a blackberry. The huge white rose is the one with a tendency to creep. Each year, no matter how much I cut it back, and shape it, encouraging it to grow tall, it remains unwieldy. It follows the path of the sun and aims for the street.

The red rambler by the corner of the porch has grown and each year smothers us in blooms. They are wonderful—small, bright blood-red, and provide beautiful bouquets, though the blooms don't last very long. They endure about four times longer, if you leave them on the bush. That is a excellent place for them, for they amass bright clusters and cover over one end of the porch, like a spangled umbrella.

Up at the river, the wild roses are all bloomed out. How sad. What is left is pale pink pedals flaking away from the open center, which will turn into a boll. The stems have a wicked thorn that curls back like the beak of a bird of prey, anxious to rip your flesh. It is best to give the wild rose a wide berth.

333

Caddis are about an inch long, some with shaggy cases built out of twigs, bits of driftwood, sand, and the tiniest of pebbles. Often the heads of the insect are visible, while they go about their buggy life under water; along with the head can often be seen the fore-pincers. These they use to pull themselves along the bottom and haul their cases up the faces of rocks. Sometimes they get a hankering to travel. Then they relax their grip and let the river carry them away. The journey is ever downstream.

When you reach under water and pick up a caddis, it draws in its head like a turtle. They build their houses, as they go along. They secrete a sticky substance that acts as a mortar and binds together the sticks and stones. Every caddis "house" is an original design, though they testify to having the same architect.

When we were new to the river, I used to spend hours happily studying life under water. Much of what I saw was caddis. I also discovered many kinds of fry swimming around in the shallows, for it was August and they were abundant. The salmonids occupied the same kind of water as adult fish, but on a micro-scale. Each tiny rill and rivulet was a channel to them, and they held their stations boldly, without fear, challenging each other for the best locations. Always they maintained a watch upstream for food swept along by the current.

What I remember most is how caddis would inch—no, inch is too fast a word to describe their movement—across the flat face of a rock; their creeping pace would make a turtle look like a racehorse. A person could grow old, watching them. There are worse fates, I suppose. As I studied them, suddenly one would relinquish its moorings and simply float away in its case. Why? To what purpose? What was wrong with my property Did it lack something beneficial, or was I watching them too closely?

The caddis didn't know or care what I thought. They were simply moving on, in a hurry. The caddis is the nomad of the river.

334

Recently I have been writing for two magazines in Seattle. They are tabloids, not slicks. I was distressed to learn how few people read them. Read *me*, I mean. Mostly those who do are other writers and editors, people in the publishing business. They cannot afford not to know what their counterparts are saying. The ordinary, workaday people who subscribe run their eyes over the pages, but rarely settle down in a chair with an article and see it through to the end. In fact, according to my personal survey, few of them ever even scan the article. Perhaps they are too busy.

When I first started writing for *The Argus*, I was astonished to learn that its publisher, Phil Bailey, didn't read my stuff. He was editor/publisher, after all, but there was also a managing editor.

That should have been a clue. The ME told me that the publisher wasn't interested in the arts, only in business. And in politics. Those articles he read carefully and wanted to see before they were published. Often he held a story over or killed it outright.

The other paper, *The Weekly*, also reports on Seattle's political-business-economic activity because its publisher (also its editor), David Brewster, is interested in these matters. Birds of a feather. He isn't as different from the publisher of *The Argus* as he thinks he is; in fact, he used to work for him. If either publisher was interested in tennis, horses, golf, or flyfishing, the magazine would reflect those subjects, but its appeal would grow narrower and fewer people would buy it than even now.

There are probably about 200 people in Seattle interested in what these publishers are offering. You could put them in one large room and they would probably already know each other. Small town.

So what do the vast majority of subscribers read? The ads? The calendar of events? The movie reviews? Yes, and this is probably all. Frankly, I don't read much of them, either. *The Argus* is free to me. If I wasn't writing for it, I wouldn't bother to look it over. I certainly wouldn't buy it. It is a terrible situation to be writing for a magazine you wouldn't even read.

There is another magazine I write for, this one a slick called *View Northwest*. It is full of ads for goods too expensive for me to purchase, and even if I had enough money I wouldn't. It strives to appeal to a monied professional class. Its subject matter is strictly local. Its contents are about shopping, traveling, and eating out. It is even less interesting than the regional political and business scene. Again, I wonder who buys and reads it. Perhaps its issues perish on the newsstands.

My interests are esoteric. They involve literature, music, and nature. Nature often takes the form of flyfishing. I am about as regional as a person can get. Or am I? Maybe not.

A writer must feed his head. It is good advice Grace Slick gave us. All of us must nourish our heads, or risk starving to death, spiritually. The writer takes his food wherever he finds it. And the search for intellectual nourishment consumes much of his productive time.

335

Another two weeks and I shall have completed this journal. One full year is enough for most good things. Or else it is just right. I shall put it down with a sigh of relief. It will be a little bit like the air being let out of a giant balloon. Or delivering myself of a baby.

But I will miss it, too. The daily travail and trauma of having to write helped sustain me. The obligation of finding something new and worthwhile to say was a challenge. It is also a burden. City and country complement each other. When I am done with this journal, there will be a big gap in my life. Right now it seems impossible. But I recognize it as being true.

336

Somewhere—without a doubt—may be found a university professor who has given his whole life over to the study of the earth's ugliest, slimiest, and most repellent creature, the common garden slug. It is a subject not spoken of, in polite society. Everyone despises slugs. Many of the women I know (mother and wife, for instance) get weird satisfaction out of jabbing them with garden shears. These are normally peaceable women, you understand.

Slugs do great damage to a vegetable garden. Leaf lettuce they systematically destroy, and over the years we have given up hundreds of tomatoes and strawberries to the slug's savage appetite. It would seem they do no good, no good at all.

Slugs love rain and dew. Up at the river, they seemingly multiply overnight, whenever the earth gets wet. To turn on the water valve at Crabtree's house, each visit, I have to stick my hand down a narrow cement tile which is always lined with fat brown slugs. They go there for the moisture, clinging to the walls. There is no avoiding them on my hand's slimy plunge to the bottom. The hand valve always holds one or more tightly curled brown slugs. You have to brush them, if you want water. It is the price.

Consequently, I announce a policy of leaving the water valve turned on for the remainder of the summer. Schlotman won't like this, and always insists that the valve be turned off by each of us, after our visit. It is his flair for German precision and routine. I intend to stand up for my rights, if I have any. We'll work it out, some way.

Slugs abound in town, too. Their gleaming brown bodies drag clear trails of slime after them, producing a winding course. As they move along, their tiny antenna grope to the sides, feeling the air of the course ahead of them. They are much like the horns on cattle, only flexible, always probing. Behind them their trail is like the stuff that comes out of your nose with a bad cold. It glistens and glows obscenely. They would be icky without it, but they are ickier because of it.

Up at the river we are always stepping on slugs in the dark. It is best to have a shoe on. You start to go sliding, as if on ice. Afterwards, you must clean off your shoe on some clean grass. Otherwise, you come traipsing inside with some slug slime on your shoe, into which some blades of grass and fir needles are pressed. It dries like Epoxy, some on the floor.

When you sit by the fire, outside, and the fire dies low, and you reach for another stick to throw on, you invariably grab the part with the slug on it. "Yuck," shouts Norma, and I know exactly what she means. Time to go wash your hands. You need soap and hot water, or the slug icky won't come off. Nobody ever died from slug slime, or was even hospitalized. The injury is mainly to one's pride. "To have sunk this low...," is what one says to himself.

A final thought. Have you ever noticed how a slug looks like a miniature sea lion? The sea lion doesn't have those horns, admittedly. And the sea lion is much bigger. Nor does a slug swim—not that anybody cares. Allowing for these small differences, they have the same slow, heavy body, the same shape, the same profile, even the same coloring.

337

We are rained in, just Norma and I. Our son, the paper boy, is still in town to do his route. He is old enough to stay alone and get his own meals. It is a Sunday. A romantic situation, eh? Not exactly.

Drops started falling about two-thirty in the morning. To both of us, far apart in our separate beds, the first drops sounded like leaves scudding across a hard surface. She was in the trailer, with its "tin" roof, while I slept down by the river, under my taut nylon tarp. Both produce a similar, noisy sound. And when it rains harder, the noise both places becomes a din. It is as if somebody is up there, practicing his drumming.

It is necessary to absorb the sound into one's nighttime frame-of-reference before sleep will resume. Sometimes it is hard to do, and sleep holds off. I laid there awake for what seemed like hours, but was probably only minutes. Then I fell back into a light sleep. Over breakfast, we discussed the storm and our lack of true sleep. I maintained that, if you stayed in bed, you got as rested as though you were asleep, all the while. Norma thinks this is specious. She is all in favor of a deep sleep. I argued that, when you sleep like a tomb, you often feel drugged the next day, not rested.

It was my first night under the tarp in a hard rain. One reason I remained awake so long was that I was anticipating leaks. If the roof leaked, I wanted to be ready for a quick evacuation. It was as though some other person, not me, had to be convinced the camp would remain dry, before he could go back to sleep. And this act of persuasion took time. If this doesn't make good sense, remember, I didn't sleep very well last night.

Today, under continuing light rains, Norma and I are confined to the trailer, much as an Alaskan is holed up because of deep snow. Each of us occupies one side of the small dining table that converts (reluctantly) into an extra bed. What we do is read. Emerson said that books were for the scholar's (read: thinking man's) idle moments. Well, what is more idle than being rained in?

She is finishing Heller's *Good As Gold*, while I am beginning Jay Martin's 500-page unauthorized biography of Henry Miller, *Always Merry and Bright*. An insipid title, the book reveals it was the motto of Henry's gang of young *bon vivants*, the Xerxes Society, in NYC, about 1910.

We read, and occasionally blankly lift our eyes to each other or exchange a word or two. Mostly it is at my instigation. She can go a long distance in pure silence. Sipping cold coffee, we listen to the rain falling softly now on the roof and eventually make uncomfortable love on the hard, narrow couch of our daybed. Beethoven's *Pathetique* is playing appropriately on the tape deck. We hope the sky will clear so we can do some outdoor work.

One must be an optimist in a Pacific Northwest spring, for it will generally be raining. A lot of outdoor works waits to be done. Well, it will have to stand in line.

338

A chilling experience, yesterday. I paid a visit to an old friend, a girl I dated back in high school and, later, when she was at Stanford. I even saw her when I was in the Army at Fort Ord. I came across her phone number almost by accident and decided to give her a call. Boy, was she surprised. Reluctantly she agreed to meet me. She invited me over to her apartment in Tacoma. It was the city where I was headed, anyway. I had this in mind. So our meeting took place after I'd run an errand to the Tacoma Art Museum, where I am one of many in a state-wide juried photography show.

She later told me she was hesitant because she feared the meeting would bring on one of her anxiety attacks. She is evidently in bad shape and has had many breakdowns. She's been under a psychiatrist's care for years. Her apartment was located on the edge of the city's industrial area, a not very pretty or pleasant part of town. When she opened the door I saw the apartment was squalid, filthy.

What shall I say about Bunnie, who I hadn't seen in 28 years? I was appalled. All of us children of the '50s—those of us who came of age in the early part of the decade, during that period of McCarthyism, war, and personal repression that marked what Kerouac called the silent or subterranean generation—are lucky; we are the survivors. Many are dead. We have endured. But some of us are life's victims. We have lived on, true, but are the products of our own private terrors and what might be called bad luck.

My friend Dave Norton killed himself in a bleak hotel room in Tacoma—this selfsame city—after trying to drink himself stupid for years, and failing. He was too smart for any simple solution. One afternoon, in front of the TV, terribly isolated from the rest of suffering humanity, and no longer believing himself an essential part of it, he put a revolver in his mouth and kissed the world goodbye.

It is industrial Tacoma that reminds me of Dave, as I take a long hard look at Bunnie; it is where he was from. She too is an alcoholic, but that is just the start of her problems, or perhaps only one of its symptoms. What bugs her specifically I will ever know. Life acted on Dave and Bunnie in a manner that was intolerable. Each had numerous breakdowns that required long psychiatric care. And finally Dave couldn't stand it any longer and ended it.

It is hard for those of us who haven't been shattered to understand the problems of those who have. Bunnie has had drug therapy and electroshock treatments. The latter terrify me. Imagine having your brain . . . fried. Her sister speaks bitterly about this type of psychiatry. I don't blame her. Bunnie admitted to having between 200-300 electroshocks. Think of it. She must have been shocked daily, during some of her bad periods. It is a wonder she survived with any mind left. I can see the damage. A Stanford graduate, she was not stupid to start with, but the electricity was applied with the intention of inducing a state of mindlessness. Perhaps only smart people have stupid problems, or rather problems in having to be made to be stupid. Maybe only the dumb survive intact. If your problems draw attention to you, or disturb others, the forces of society will converge to render you helpless. Or—like Bunnie—agree to be shocked in hopes of ending the psychic pain.

Bunnie's memory is gone. She barely remembered me, and I tried repeatedly to remind her of our old good times. We had few bad ones. She can't remember either. Back then she often seemed a little nervous and uncertain at times, but didn't we all? Vagueness and nervousness were traits not found unattractive in a young woman. In a woman pressing fifty, they are not pretty. Prodded to remember, she dredges up a few scenes involving me; there were hundreds. And maybe she is only acknowledging those to be polite. For instance, she doesn't recall taking me to her senior prom in high school. She thinks she went with somebody else, but can't recall his name or face. Me—memory's fool—rushes to tell her how we stood in the doorway to the terrace, that cool night, smoking, but she wanted to hurry back to the dance floor because she was worried that her hair "might come down." All that damp coolness. Ludicrous, wasn't it? To her it never happened. Another blank in a life of blanks. Sweet Jesus!

My memories are plainly *my* memories. As a writer, they are the stuff I build my caddis house of sticks and stones out of. They are my baggage, surplus sometimes, burdensome always, but available whenever called upon. I can haul such stuff out of the attic at will. Memory is all important. My heart cringes when I discover that the doctors—in the name of sanity—have burned away her mind, and left her without a past. I am a stranger.

She is fifty or more pounds overweight (a pound a year, is it?), with a plump face into whose folds I must search to find vestiges of the girl I want to recognize and cannot, quite. Her pretty blonde hair is cut short, and is streaked with dark at the roots. It is ill-kept and greasy. She looks—forgive me here—like a woman who seeks the sexual company of other women. And this is the sweet girl I once gave my mouth to by the hour.

She tells me about AA, how it saved her life, but she lapsed a week ago and got stinkingly (her word) drunk. She sounds half-proud of it. She chainsmokes, all the while she tells me this. She offers me a cup of instant coffee, which I dare not refuse, and I learn that a mentally disabled person can't make a passable cup of coffee, even out of powder and hot water.

The cup is filthy and the water not hot enough and she spoons in twice as much coffee distillate as is needed. When I put my cup down on the coffeetable, and leave it there, she asks me if I don't like my coffee and I smile and lie; I pick my cup up again and touch my lips to it and put it back down. I'm sorry, Bunnie.

In fact, I'm sorry about everything I hear and am anxious for it to end. But a weird fascination keeps me here. She tells me she has been drug-dependent for years. I think I heard as much. She uses some kind of stuff that sounds like Mildrum, when she says it, and is of the Thorazine family. That is pretty heavy stuff. She gets it from a pharmacy and it costs about $125 per month. The state pays for it because she is on welfare. It makes her "normal," she says.

By normal I gather that she means she gets no high from it. It keeps her functioning, which is what she means by "normal." If she doesn't get her medicine, her demons regain the upper hand. A minor demon is the anxiety attacks she mentioned on the phone today. She tells me about various social situations which leave her twitchy, and how she is visited by hallucinations or "visual distortions," and attacks of "fears." These are her words—a mix of private terms and clinical vocabulary she's picked up. The fears which attack her remain unspecified, and I don't want to learn any more about them. She says booze helps vanquish her fears, but brings on new ones, ones that it originates, for which she needs other drugs. She has had both booze and drug treatment as an outpatient.

The shock treatments were for acute depression. She is in a relatively cheerful state, she tells me. Shock was also used in Dave's case, too, I remember. Both suffered from what is called clinical depression. Now, a person like myself often gets "down in the dumps," but has no real understanding of the nature of acute, chronic depression. It is vast, overwhelming.

Electricity may or may not blast you out of your pit and the well of deep sadness. Instead, it may induce a near-catatonic state, which is the tradeoff and may be worse. Institutions don't mind, for such patients are little trouble. They don't range up and down the hallways, screaming and destroying property. Shock destroys the brain cells. The general idea is, you have too many to start with and they are the source of your torment. Burn some away, and you may get rid of the bad ones and the patient will become happier. At least he will be quieter. (Are they the same thing?)

This theory goes: Madness stems from too much personality. Destroy the self, burn away the brain cells that cause an excess, and the patient becomes normal, or closer to it. It is the mental profession's modern version of bloodletting. They electroshock and they drug, alternating the two therapies, until you are cured. Cured means docile. You are crippled mentally. What you end up with is someone like Bunnie. A sad case.

Her friends are alcoholics, she tells me, all on welfare, and many are prostitutes or ex-prostitutes. She has a boyfriend, a man of 62, who comes to her apartment and stretches out on the sofa with a book and won't talk to her. Bunnie was married once, long ago. Her husband wouldn't talk with her, either. (Am I the only man in her life who would listen to her and talk? I don't ask this, for what's the point? She won't remember whether I was. And, so what?)

Her husband came from a millionaire family. He was a petroleum engineer and they were married for 16 years. I wonder what those years were really like? He "stole" all of her money, before he departed, she says. Here it comes, I think; the paranoid version, unmistakable. The millionaire engineer . . . *stole* her money? What need would he have for it? She is unaware of any contradictions in her narrative and rapidly proceeds to matters that interest her more. After her mother's death, she and her sister inherited about $90,000 each. Hers was invested for her and grew to about $150,000. While she was married and exempt from California state community property laws governing inheritances, the husband absconded with half the full amount. Why half? Why not all? She fought him in court and the "shyster" lawyer took the other half of her inheritance. Something about this makes me queasy. I feel that important facts are being left out that might help me see matters more clearly.

The lawyer was a friend of her sister. Her sister worked closely with him on the case. It resulted in the sister becoming the court-appointed trustee for what's left of the estate. I thought it was all gone, stolen? Well, not quite, Bunnie tells me. Between the tiny amount that is left, and the dole from the state, she survives. She draws $600 monthly from the estate, the most the state will allow and still contribute its share. With the combined sums, she pays the rent on the apartment and buys food from the Safeway down the street. Also whatever drugs and liquor she needs.

She insists that I acknowledge that she lives frugally. All right, I do. In spite of her carefulness in expenditures, the estate is rapidly vanishing. Soon it will be gone; this is her big fear. For her "help" in administering the estate and paying Bunnie's bills and income tax, her sister collects a fee as trustee. It is the same as her hourly rate as free-lance nurse: $40 per hour. It seems a lot to me, for writing out checks to help a disabled sister, but I do not know the particulars and shouldn't judge.

We talk for a moment about her sister, who I know well and who I have talked with lately. In fact it was she who gave me Bunnie's phone number, under duress. Bunnie is up-to-date on everything that has happened involving her. The sister does this. (Does she charge for this, too?) The situation is distressing, messy, and likely to get worse. For some problems there are no solutions. I am anxious to be gone from here. Maybe it was a mistake to come here. The past shouldn't be looked at closely, I'm beginning to believe. I am grateful my memories (such as they are) are intact. I see no hope here, for this sad woman, formerly my friend. Not now, not in the unforeseeable future.

I can see that she is anxious to have me gone, too. That's right, my visit might have brought on an anxiety attack, and probably has. It's not what I would want to give her as a parting gift. Who would want to add to another person's anxiety? Not I. So I affect my departure.

I shan't be back.

339

Nothing is too trivial for this daybook. For instance: Some mosquitoes have slipped into the trailer through a failed seam in the screen in the aluminum front door and have become trapped side with us. Angry at being restrained, they whine in our ears and try to bite us. We are determined that they won't. It is better than a standoff. The confined quarters are greatly to our advantage. But the mosquitoes are clever and have excellent diversionary skills.

Whenever it is cloudy, hoards of mosquitoes descend; when it is sunny and warm, we are besieged with manure flies. I don't know which is worse.

Right now the mosquitoes plague us. Norma and I snatch the air as individuals fly by, with a piercing whine, but we seldom catch any. They must think it a game. They enjoy it because they believe there is little danger. They may be right. When we do manage to nail one, we must make a fist first and squeeze it so tightly that Mr. Mosquito will get crushed flat, for if we don't ball up our fist really hard, painfully tight, he will fly away as soon as we open it up for inspection. And the tight fist hurts, if you do it right.

Better yet is to kill mosquitoes with applause. A good swift clap of the hands will catch one and smash it, if you are fast enough. As a method, it is superior to the squeeze. I think the clap works best because a clenched fist, or a single flat hand slap on an arm or forehead, forces a column of air ahead of the blow, which sends the lucky skeeter away on a compressed column of air. Two hands coming together, though, sandwiches the little whiner and he is doomed. He becomes flattened beyond recognition, his little legs and feelers all mixed up in a jumbles. It's what I like to see.

As I read two skeeters glide by with minimal warning, that is, no sound. The first lands on the window glass and I expertly flatten him against the pane with a sidearm swat, which is my best shot. I see bright red blood all over the pane. Alas, it is mine. The blood is bright, I know, because it has just been withdrawn via a mosquito's hypodermic needle from my forearm and has not been exposed to air. This my memory of biology informs me. But I may misremember. I do a lot of things.

I kill a second mosquito a few minutes later; it also is bright with blood. I hope it is Norma's. Why am I so slow? Is it because the book is good and I am preoccupied with it? Or am I just bad at this, as with many other things? A third mosquito that I murder much later, using the reliable clap method, proves to be providently dry.

I will not need a blood transfusion tonight.

340

Addendum to slug memo of several days ago: Slugs come in several colors. There is the common rich black variety. And there is one that is dark brown. The infamous "banana" slug is not bright yellow, as you might expect, but sort of a pale diarrhetic brown or deep gold.

Often a banana slug will have tiger marks along its flank, or spine, or whatever you call its long shiny side. (If it was a vertebrate, you would call it its ribcage.) These marks are generally black, but do not give it the fierce look of a tiger. Nor does it look anything like a tiny sea lion. It is, plainly, a garden slug.

I awoke this morning down by the river in my tarp camp to see that a slug had made its way painstakingly up one of the ridge poles, some ten or twelve feet high above me, and now hung upside down, right over my face. It posed a direct threat, since it might fall at any time. And often I sleep on my back, with my mouth open. Yuck!

It was a black slug, of average size. There was nothing exceptional about it, except for the difficulty of its journey. If it erred in its ability to cling there, it might land in my face or my mouth. I rose earlier than usual and made my exit.

Why did the slug travel so far up the alder pole? What was it seeking? Was it on a spiritual journey, like the snow leopard in Hemingway's story about Mt. Kilimanjaro? If so, it was a spiritual or mystic-type slug. I didn't know there were any. We live and learn. This must be the Edmund Hillary of all slugs.

341

The clay has disappeared from Boulder Creek, just as mysteriously as it arrived, and the river is running clear, both upstream and down. What a delight. This I discover on a quick overnight trip to the river. My purpose is to fish.

I caught a hatchery fish and kept it, intending to give it to our new neighbors up at the river, the Crabtrees, as a housewarming present, but everybody was gone, even their two dogs. I stayed overnight and in the morning found them still missing. So I returned to the city in the morning with my fish. It is just the right size to feed three.

342

June 21. I am but a few days away from the end of this book. I may have complained, from time to time, but make no mistake I have greatly enjoyed the labor of writing it. (Not so much the work involved in paring it down and revising it, which came later and took years.)

The year could be almost any year on the river, for they differ only in their particulars. They are strangely alike—or not so strangely, then. I suppose the years in the city are highly similar, too. Time is a great river, and it is passage constitutes a river's flow. This book is about the passage of days. They combine themselves into months, seasons, and ultimately years. They flow. Unlike a river they will end.

Each summer on the river I greet old faces, new friends. This year will be no exception. Soon I will meet fellow fishers and add them to my human data base. But it is especially good to encounter old friends each spring and learn from them the news. Who has weathered through, who has not. Some are too sick or feeble to make the annual roll call of fishers. This I learn from those who are present and accounted for. How sad!

It is a pleasant time, all in all, with the foliage fresh and green, signifying renewal, my own included. I am seeking a certain elusive word for how I feel about things. Is mellow it? Then mellow it is!

343

What does it all mean—a story like this one? What does it add up to? What does it state? Why, that a man lived. This is what he saw and felt and thought hard about, for a time. What other reason is there to write than to try to capture in word's one's life experience? I want you to know what it was like to live my life and to be me. If that is too egocentric, I'm sorry. It's all that I happen to know about. And I know it well.

My life is an ordinary one, quite mundane. I sometimes wish it had a broader scope, or that my subjects were more exciting. Would you rather that I made up a tale? Heightened the facts in an artificial manner? Well, I can't, I won't. You'd like it even less, I'm sure.

Time is a long arm with a short reach. I find I do not remember as much as I'd like to. Much has fled from my clasp. The sense of loss would roar in my ears, if I'd let it. So I stopper them up. There are moments when this life of mine bogs me down. It becomes too heavy. Yet it's all I've got. It's what I must love first, if I am to love anything else.

We are the sum of our experiences. They must sustain us in hard times. What have I learned from this year? A lot. I am a cityman, first of all, proud of it, but one who loves going to the country, every chance he gets. It is my mental second home; it nourishes and revives me. It gives me strength.

I live in and love the city for its richness and diversity. I wouldn't trade it for anything except, perhaps, a future life in the country. I think that is what I ultimately seek.

344

The best cities of the American West are those perched on the edge of the sea, the broad Pacific, and have a university attached, generally running along one perimeter. A number of such cities come quickly to mind. Most are in California—Santa Barbara, Santa Cruz, Berkeley, San Francisco, Los Angeles, San Diego. You might call them the Santa cities. I have spent various amounts of time in each of them, but I find Seattle most dear. It has been my home for years. I would much rather live there, than in one of those sainted warmer climes. But there are moments when I have my doubts.

For one thing, none has a great river near by. The people there are poorer for it. If a river wasn't close, I probably wouldn't bother driving to the country. Fishing is my main reason, but rivers are fascinating on their own account.

I respond to their call with joy, if they're not in muddy flood. Then it pains my eyes to look at them and the destruction they can cause, though I know that floods are part of the natural course of a river and enrich the land. They perform a certain amount of hose-cleaning, as well. What a river does cannot generally be said to be bad. I can hardly tear myself away.

345

Is there a new sound in my voice? Can you hear it? Listen closely. It is lyrical, joyful. It is the sound a river makes when it is tight in its banks, flowing, approaching its summer low.

That cello you hear in the woods belongs to Pablo Casals. No matter that he is dead, he lives on in the form of recorded music. I am playing him down by the river today. He is performing as only he can Bach's sonatas and suites for unaccompanied cello. They are simply magnificent. If there is a better word to describe it, please, tell me and I'll write it in. No?

Presently Sonata No.2 is playing at unaccustomed high volume, for nobody else is in residence today in the cabins at Stillaguamish Meadows. I feel and behave just like a teenager with his favorite rock artist. Stay away, if you don't love Bach and the cello. The sound soars out over the water and mixes sweetly with what the current says. There is no competition between them. They are one.

The river purls gently between its banks, happily confined. The banks are ringed with dappled light coming through the cedars and alders. The sun speckles the foreground with molten butter. Then the pattern shifts, as a breeze rustles the leaves, creating bright kaleidoscopic patterns. The sky is so blue I can detect a red wash behind it. Eighty-some degrees, it is too hot to fish. I must wait for the coolness of evening. So I simply sit, listening to the river and the music. Nice.

It has been summer for less than a week. Thus, the days have been getting longer since a few days before Christmas. They will soon start getting shorter, but not noticeably for some time. In fact, they are about as long now as they will ever get. That is cause for celebration.

The sun falls hard on the page as I write. I think of my father and his illness. I love him—does this come through in my writing, or have I failed again? We talk on the phone regularly. Often there isn't much to say. He is interested in my work, though he understands little about the act of writing anything other than letters to friends, but knows it is the only way you can communicate, aside from the spoken word, which lacks permanence. Writing is the product of what a writer does. You can weigh it in your hand, like bricks. In fact, laying words down on a page is very much like laying bricks.

His cancer *seems* restricted to his prostate gland. But who knows? I've read the statistics. Fully 80 percent of the people over 70 have cancer lurking in their bodies. (Or is it 70 percent of the people over 80?) Anyway, my father's cancer may have spread to other parts of his body and be resident there, undetected. This is often the case.

Soon my father will die—of cancer or of other causes. It may come as a heart attack or stroke. This is the way with cancer patients. Then I will become "The Father." My son will assume the role I presently play. ("Play" is not a good word for it, but I can't come up with a better one, off the top of my head, or working on it longer.) Some day not too far off I will die, too. Life may seem long, but it really is short, I know. Then my son will be "The Father," even if he has no son of his own to badger. And so it goes. Life is absorbed into the continuum.

346

Across the river I hear the rumble of logging trucks climbing Skagland Hill. They rattle when empty, when carrying their piggyback trailers; fully loaded, they have a different sound. They chug more slowly, plodding their course, with much up and down gearing. The note of their diesel exhaust is heavier, deeper. I need not look up to know which way they're headed, or if they are carrying logs.

Birdsong sprinkles the air. It is sweet. The screech of a merganser comes from a distance—rattling his gourd. Or is it the belted kingfisher? And what difference does it make? Well, to know them apart has some small importance, but does not matter much in the grand scheme of things, I'll admit.

It is a perfect morning, and a full day stretches ahead. It is mine to do with what I will. Tonight my son goes graduates from high school. The ceremonies will be held in Seattle's Kingdome. I must leave the river early, return to town, clean myself up some, dress with a necktie, collect my wife, drive downtown, and find a parking place on a crowded street. Perhaps I'll put the car in a lot. We can't afford to be late to our only son's graduation.

What does the future hold for any of us? There is no way to know except by taking life head on and seeing what will happen next. I find I am eager for it. In the world of fishing, we call this suiting up. We also refer to it as getting our feet wet in the river.